The American Recovery and Reinvestment Act

T0292919

The American Recovery and Reinvestment Act

The Role of Workforce Programs

Burt S. Barnow
Richard A. Hobbie
Editors

2013

W.E. Upjohn Institute for Employment Research
Kalamazoo, Michigan

Library of Congress Cataloging-in-Publication Data

The American Recovery and Reinvestment Act : the role of workforce programs / Burt S. Barnow, Richard A. Hobbie, editors.
    pages cm
    Includes bibliographical references and index.
    ISBN 978-0-88099-471-2 (pbk. : alk. paper) — ISBN 0-88099-471-1 (pbk. : alk. paper) — ISBN 978-0-88099-473-6 (hardcover : alk. paper) — ISBN 0-88099-473-8 (hardcover : alk. paper)
    1. Manpower policy—United States. 2. Labor policy—United States. 3. United States—Economic policy—2009- 4. Economic development projects—United States. 5. Economic stabilization—United States. 6. Recessions—United States. 7. United States. American Recovery and Reinvestment Act of 2009. I. Barnow, Burt S. II. Hobbie, Richard, 1945-
    HD5724.A58145 2013
    331.12'0420973—dc23
                            2013041953

Cover design by Alcorn Publication Design.
Index prepared by Diane Worden.
Printed in the United States of America.
Printed on recycled paper.

Contents

Acknowledgments

This report was prepared for a grant awarded to the National Association of State Workforce Agencies (NASWA) by the Employment and Training Administration of the U.S. Department of Labor (USDOL). The success of this project depended on the efforts of many. The most notable contributions were made by the more than 200 state and local workforce development and Unemployment Insurance (UI) officials who, in the midst of the Great Recession and tremendous workloads, provided their insights, experiences, and data to the research team, thereby ensuring documentation of the workforce system's response to this major economic event in our country's history.

We received valuable input and guidance from Wayne Gordon of the Employment and Training Administration, USDOL, who not only served as project officer but also initiated the study when the Recovery Act provisions became law. Wayne ensured we could tap into the knowledge and valuable work of other USDOL staff members who deserve thanks and acknowledgment, including Scott Gibbons, Anita Harvey, Russell Saltz, Jonathan Simonetta, Ryan Sutter, and Susan Worden.

A team of researchers was involved in gathering qualitative information from states and localities for the report, by conducting workforce program site visits or UI teleconference interviews. Researchers who conducted site visits include the following: Burt S. Barnow (George Washington University), Lauren Eyster (Urban Institute), Martha A. Holleman (Capital Research Corporation), Joyce Kaiser (Capital Research Corporation), Christopher T. King (Ray Marshall Center, LBJ School of Public Affairs, University of Texas at Austin), Fredrica Kramer (Capital Research Corporation), Erin McDonald (Urban Institute), Dan O'Shea (Ray Marshall Center), Juan Pedroza (Urban Institute), Tara C. Smith (Ray Marshall Center), and John Trutko (Capital Research Corporation). Yvette Chocolaad (NASWA), Richard A. Hobbie (NASWA), and Wayne Vroman (Urban Institute) conducted the UI teleconference interviews.

Randall Eberts (W. E. Upjohn Institute for Employment Research), Stephen A. Wandner (Urban Institute and Upjohn Institute), and Jing Cai (Upjohn Institute) used administrative data from the USDOL's reporting system to create the Public Workforce System Dataset, which is the basis for the quantitative analysis and discussion presented in Chapter 9.

Primary authors by chapter include the following: Chapters 1 and 2—Burt Barnow; Chapter 3—John Trutko, with Burt Barnow; Chapter 4—Joyce Kaiser; Chapter 5—Tara Smith; Chapter 6—Stephen Wandner; Chapter 7—Joyce Kaiser; Chapter 8—Yvette Chocolaad and Wayne Vroman, with Richard

Hobbie; Chapter 9—Randall Eberts and Stephen Wandner; Chapter 10—John Trutko and Burt Barnow; Appendix A—Joyce Kaiser; Appendix B—Jing Cai, Randall Eberts, and Stephen Wandner.

Several NASWA staff assistants supported the project, including John Quichocho, Benjamin Fendler, Gina Turrini, and Mariann Huggins. Ben Jones (W.E. Upjohn Institute) edited the manuscript, and Erika Jackson did the typesetting.

Common Acronyms and Abbreviations

ARRA: American Recovery and Reinvestment Act, or simply Recovery Act

DW: Dislocated Worker Program

ES: Employment Service

ETA: Employment and Training Administration, USDOL

FTE: full-time equivalent

LWIA: local workforce investment area

NASWA: National Association of State Workforce Agencies

TANF: Temporary Assistance for Needy Families program

UI: unemployment insurance

USDOL: U.S. Department of Labor

WIA: Workforce Investment Act

WIB: workforce investment board

W-P: Wagner-Peyser Act

1
Background, Purpose, and Methodology

Burt S. Barnow
George Washington University

BACKGROUND AND PURPOSE

The American Recovery and Reinvestment Act of 2009 (Recovery Act, or ARRA) was a response to the Great Recession, which began in December 2007. The legislation, signed into law in early 2009, was an economic stimulus measure designed to "save and create jobs immediately" (whitehouse.gov 2009).[1] Other objectives were to provide aid to individuals affected by the recession and to invest in improving schools, updating infrastructure, modernizing health care, and promoting clean energy. State workforce agencies faced important and serious policy challenges in response to the severe economic recession, and while the provisions in the Recovery Act offered opportunities for relief, implementing some of the programmatic provisions presented challenges to states and local areas in expanding eligibility and services, adding staff to meet the increased demands, and making appropriate program modifications expeditiously and efficaciously. Additionally, before the Recovery Act was enacted, governors and state workforce agencies began taking actions to adjust their Unemployment Insurance (UI) systems to meet economic needs.

This book is intended to provide useful information about the nature of the workforce development and UI policy decisions made nationwide in response to the recession, state and local administrators' perspectives on the policy developments and economic challenges, and implementation of key Recovery Act provisions.[2] The majority of the book's chapters, as well as Appendix A, focus on workforce development initiatives in the Recovery Act, and Chapter 8 focuses on the Recovery Act's UI provisions.

At the time of its passage in February 2009, the cost of the Recovery Act was estimated by the Congressional Budget Office (CBO) to be $787 billion over the period 2009–2019, through a combination of tax and spending provisions. By February 2012, the CBO had revised the estimate to $831 billion. That month, it reported that "close to half of that impact occurred in fiscal year 2010, and more than 90 percent . . . was realized by the end of December 2011" (CBO 2012). Table 1.1 is a list of agencies receiving the majority of the Recovery Act funding. Only two agencies received more funding than the United States Department of Labor (USDOL). The Employment and Training Administration (ETA) at the Department of Labor was the primary recipient of the USDOL funds.

Table 1.2 summarizes the formula allocations for the major USDOL workforce development programs in Program Year 2009 (July 1, 2009, through June 30, 2010), and the additional funds provided for these programs through the Recovery Act.[3] States had two years—through June 30, 2011—to spend the Recovery Act allocations. Among these programs, the Workforce Investment Act (WIA) Dislocated Worker Program received the largest increase in funding through the Recovery Act, both in relative and absolute terms, with over $1 billion in additional funding. The unrestricted Wagner-Peyser Act (W-P) funds were

Table 1.1 Agencies with the Most Recovery Act Funds ($ billions)

Agency	Amount
1. Department of Health and Human Services	122.9
2. Department of Education	90.9
3. Department of Labor	66.0
4. Department of Agriculture	39.4
5. Department of Transportation	36.3
6. Department of Energy	26.8
7. Department of the Treasury	18.9
8. Social Security Administration	13.8
9. Department of Housing and Urban Development	12.7
10. Environmental Protection Agency	6.8
Total	434.7

NOTE: Categories do not sum correctly because of rounding.
SOURCE: http://www.Recovery.gov, updated 07/27/2012.

Table 1.2 Summary of Baseline and Recovery Act Allocations for Adult Workforce Programs ($ millions)

Program and time period	Allocation
WIA Adult	
PY 2009	859.4
Recovery Act	493.8
Total	1,353.1
WIA Dislocated Worker	
PY 2009	1,183.8
Recovery Act	1,237.5
Total	2,421.3
Wagner-Peyser (unrestricted)	
PY 2009	701.9
Recovery Act	148.1
Total	850.0
Wagner-Peyser Reemployment Services	
PY 2009	0.0
Recovery Act	246.9
Total	246.9
Total, WIA and Wagner-Peyser	
PY 2009	2,745.1
Recovery Act	2,126.3
Grand total	4,871.4

NOTE: States had two years (from July 1, 2009, through June 30, 2011) to spend Recovery Act allocations.
SOURCE: USDOL (2013b).

increased by the smallest amount, $148 million, but an additional $247 million in Recovery Act funds were included for Reemployment Services (RES), which had received no funding since 2005.

By far, the UI provisions of the Recovery Act account for most of the Department of Labor's Recovery Act stimulus expenditures. The Recovery Act included several major UI program tax and spending provisions, which at the time of passage were estimated to result in federal outlays totaling approximately $45 billion over 10 years, with most outlays occurring in fiscal years 2009 and 2010 (see Table 1.3). Note that the estimates in this table were made in the early months of 2009, well before the depth and duration of the Great Recession were widely

Table 1.3 Estimated Budget Effects of the UI Provisions of the Recovery Act

Recovery Act provision	Explanation of provision	Estimated budget effects, FY 2009–2019 ($ billions)
Interest-free loans	Temporarily waived interest payments and the accrual of interest on federal loans to states through December 31, 2010.	1.1
Administrative funding	Transferred $500 million to the states for administration of their unemployment programs and staff-assisted reemployment services for claimants.	2.6
UI modernization	Provided up to a total of $7 billion as incentive payments for states to "modernize" state UC benefit provisions. Payments were available through September 30, 2011, and states could use them for UI benefits or UI or ES administration.	
Benefit extensions	Extended the Emergency Unemployment Compensation program for new claims from March 31, 2009, to December 31, 2009 (subsequently extended through the end of 2012). Provided 100% federal financing of the Extended Benefits (EB) program for weeks of unemployment beginning before January 1, 2010 (subsequently extended through the end of 2012).	27.0
Benefit increase	Provided a temporary $25 per week supplemental unemployment benefit, known as the Federal Additional Compensation (FAC) program, for weeks of unemployment ending before January 1, 2010 (subsequently extended through beginning of June 2010); prohibited states from reducing average weekly benefit amount for regular compensation below level of December 31, 2008.	8.8
Suspension of federal income tax	Temporarily suspended federal income tax on the first $2,400 of unemployment benefits (per recipient) received in 2009.	4.7
Total		44.7

NOTE: Figures do not sum to total because of rounding.
SOURCE: U.S. Joint Committee on Taxation (2009); votesmart.org (2009).

understood, and substantially underestimate actual costs. The estimates also do not include later benefit extensions related to the Great Recession. Estimates of all benefit extensions subsequently totaled more than $200 billion for the 2008–2012 time period.

Many other spending provisions in the Recovery Act also relate to workforce investments and were designed to provide investments in areas in great need to improve infrastructure, accelerate the development of a range of energy-efficient "green" sectors, and increase the supply of trained and skilled workers needed in high-growth sectors such as clean energy and health care.

Also, there are three Recovery Act provisions that involve state or local workforce agencies and One-Stop Career Centers but are not the primary focus of this report: 1) use or expansion of tax credits for hiring particular workers such as veterans or disadvantaged youth, 2) WIA Youth programs, and 3) designing or implementing major parts of subsidized employment programs that could be funded with the Temporary Assistance for Needy Families (TANF) Emergency Fund, although Chapter 7 briefly describes some of the states' involvement with the TANF Emergency Fund. The role of the workforce investment system in the TANF-subsidized employment initiative is in addition to the roles states and local workforce agencies may already have for the work program components of TANF (i.e., in many states, the TANF agency contracts with the workforce agency to operate the TANF employment program or parts of it). Other grant programs included in the Recovery Act also fund job training. Most notable are these three: 1) the Trade Adjustment Assistance for Communities Grant Program ($56.25 million, administered by the Department of Commerce), 2) the Community College and Career Training Program ($90 million, administered by the ETA), and 3) the Sector Partnership Grants Program ($90 million, administered by the ETA).

In sum, the Recovery Act provided the workforce system with a large increase in resources to improve its structure, increase capacity, and provide additional economic support and services. ETA stated that spending under the Recovery Act should be guided by four principles, described in Training and Employment Guidance Letter (TEGL) 14-08 (USDOL 2009):

1) Transparency and accountability in the use of Recovery Act funding

2) Timely spending of the funds and implementation of the activities

3) Increasing workforce system capacity and service levels

4) Using data and workforce information to guide strategic planning and service delivery

The purpose of this project is to measure progress and challenges in implementing the workforce and UI provisions of the Recovery Act, to highlight new and promising practices, and to provide guidance to the ETA, the states, and local workforce investment areas. The ETA received monthly reports from the states on their expenditures and activities, but it did not receive systematic in-depth information about the implementation of the workforce components of the Recovery Act. This project is intended to help fill this gap by providing feedback to the ETA based on document review, on-line surveys, and in-depth field visits to and teleconferences with officials in selected states and sub-state areas.

COMPONENTS OF THE PROJECT

Several approaches were used to monitor Recovery Act implementation. First, the National Association of State Workforce Agencies (NASWA) independently financed and conducted five surveys of all states (many through the Internet), related to their experience with the Recovery Act. NASWA staff analyzed the data from the surveys on workforce and UI programs and produced reports on the findings (NASWA 2010).

The second major component of the project included two rounds of site visits to 20 state workforce development agencies, as well as teleconference discussions with UI officials in the same 20 states. The site visits included meetings not only with state agency officials but also officials of two local areas in each state, and one round of visits was conducted in each year of the project. Because the research plan for the UI portion of the project differed in approach and timing, it was decided that the UI provisions of the Recovery Act would be best studied centrally, and so teleconference interviews instead of site visits were held. The site visits and teleconference interviews were conducted by researchers from the Trachtenberg School of Public Policy and Public Administration at George Washington University, Capital Research Corporation, the Ray Marshall Center at the University of Texas, the Urban Institute, and NASWA.[4] During the site visits and teleconference interviews, researchers probed in-depth into topics such as how states used stimulus funds, how spending and policy decisions were made, and challenges and accomplishments of the Recovery Act activities. Note that although the WIA Youth Program was an important component of the stimulus program, this report does not cover the WIA Youth Program to a substantial degree because the ETA had another research organization document its Recovery Act experience.

DESCRIPTION OF THE 20-STATE SURVEY

This section describes how the 20 states were selected, lists the 20 states, and shows how the states in the sample vary on key characteristics. States for the site visits and UI teleconference interviews were chosen from the 50 states and the District of Columbia. The states were selected purposively, to create a sample balanced on several key attributes. To expedite the site visits, three of the 20 states, New York, Texas, and Wisconsin, were visited first; their good working relationship with NASWA allowed for quick traveling arrangements to obtain feedback on the survey instrument. The 20 states were selected to achieve the desired distribution based on the following characteristics:

- **Population.** It was decided to emphasize more populous states so that a larger proportion of the total U.S. population would be covered by the site visits. The sample included 12 of the 17 most populous states, four of the next most populous 17 states, and four of the least populous states.

- **Co-Location of Employment Service offices.** The presence of the Employment Service (ES) in One-Stop Career Centers varies significantly among states. Because some Recovery Act activities might take different forms when the ES is more isolated from the One-Stop system, a mix of relationships between the ES and One-Stops was obtained. We used the taxonomy developed by the Government Accountability Office to classify these relationships and selected states roughly in proportion to their prevalence (USGAO 2007).

- **Total unemployment rate.** States with relatively high unemployment rates are of more interest, so a disproportionate share of states with high rates of unemployment were selected. The sample of 20 includes nine states in the upper third in terms of the unemployment rate, seven in the middle third, and four in the bottom third, based on the unemployment rate at the time of state selection.

- **Reserve ratio multiple (RRM).** The RRM is a measure of UI trust fund solvency, with a higher multiple indicating a greater ability to avoid borrowing during a severe economic downturn.[5] We wanted to oversample states with insolvency problems to better observe how states under stress dealt with the UI reforms and other Recovery Act provisions. States were arrayed according to their RRM, and we selected five states from the upper third, six states from the middle third, and nine states from the bottom third.

- **Region.** We wanted to achieve rough geographic balance among the four broad census regions. The sample included four states from the Northeast, six from the Midwest, six from the South, and four from the West.

- **UI recipiency rate.** This variable measures the proportion of the unemployed that are receiving UI. We wanted to achieve a balanced sample on this variable. The sample included seven states in the upper third, seven states in the middle third, and six states in the bottom third.

Overall, the sample of states selected appears to do a good job of meeting the criteria we identified. Figure 1.1 shows a map of the 20 selected states. Three of the originally selected states declined to participate—California, Connecticut, and Kentucky. They were replaced with Colorado, Montana, and Rhode Island. Adding Montana provided a second single-WIB state (in addition to North Dakota). Colorado added a second state (in addition to Michigan) that was permitted to

Figure 1.1 Map of States Selected for Recovery Act Study

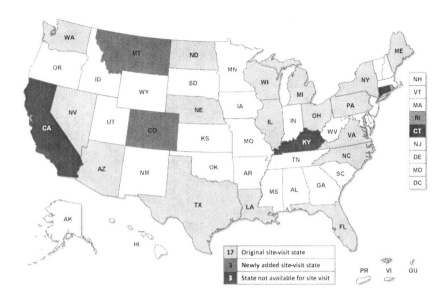

17	Original site-visit state
3	Newly added site-visit state
3	State not available for site visit

SOURCE: Authors of the NASWA (2013) study.

provide Wagner-Peyser services through local merit staff rather than through state merit staff employees. Table 1.4 contains a listing of the codes used to categorize states by key characteristics and the number of sample states in each category. Table 1.5 shows the states selected (shaded) and the other states, and includes data on their characteristics. When the interim report was prepared, 19 state site visits had been completed, but four of the states (Rhode Island, North Carolina, Maine, and Nebraska) had been visited too recently for their findings to be reflected in the report. This later report, here published in book form, reflects findings from both rounds of site visits to all 20 states, as well as the UI teleconference interviews, which were conducted after the interim report was prepared.

As mentioned, for each state in the sample, visits to workforce development programs were conducted at the state level and at two local sites.[6] Local sites were selected to provide variation in the types of areas visited and, to a lesser extent, geographic convenience. Meetings

Table 1.4 Listing for the Coding of States According to Key Characteristics, and Distribution of 20 Visited States

Region		Number
1	Northeast	4
2	Midwest	6
3	South	6
4	West	4
Population		
1	High third (from TN at 6,214,888 to CA at 36,756,666)	12
2	Middle third (from UT at 2,736,424 to MO at 5,911,605)	4
3	Low third (from WY at 532,668 to NV at 2,600,167)	4
ES/One-Stop relationship (USGAO 2007)		
1	Category A	3
2	Category B	3
3	Category C	1
4	Category D	13
Total unemployment rate (at the time of site selection)		
1	High third (from WA at 9.3% to MI at 15.2%) (9)	9
2	Middle third (from TX at 7.5% to MO at 9.3%) (7)	7
3	Low third (from ND at 4.2% to MD at 7.3%) (4)	4
Reserve ratio multiple		
1	High third (from VT at 0.71 to NM at 1.60)	5
2	Middle third (from TN at 0.30 to IA at 0.68)	6
3	Low third (from MI at −0.02 to MA at 0.28)	9
UI recipiency rate		
1	High third (from HI at 0.359 to CT at 0.553)	7
2	Middle third (from NE at 0.278 to MN at 0.358)	7
3	Low third (from SD at 0.153 to SC at 0.277)	6

SOURCE: Authors of the NASWA (2013) study.

were held at the state and local levels with key officials responsible for workforce programs affected by the Recovery Act—WIA Adult, WIA Dislocated Worker, Wagner-Peyser funded activities, Trade Adjustment Assistance, and the agency responsible for Reemployment Services. Each state and local site visit required approximately one day, for a total of three days per state in each round. The site visits were conducted using semistructured guides for the state and local levels. The guides

Table 1.5 Characteristics of Selected and Unselected States

State	Region	Population size	ES/One-Stop relationship	Unemployment rate	Reserve ratio multiple	UI recipiency rate
Connecticut	1	2	1	2	3	1
Maine	1	3	4	2	1	2
Massachusetts	1	1	4	2	3	1
New Hampshire	1	3	4	3	2	3
New Jersey	1	1	4	2	3	1
New York	1	1	4	2	3	2
Pennsylvania	1	1	4	2	3	1
Rhode Island	1	3	4	1	3	1
Vermont	1	3	4	3	1	1
Illinois	2	1	2	1	2	2
Indiana	2	1	4	1	3	2
Iowa	2	2	1	3	2	1
Kansas	2	2	3	3	1	2
Michigan	2	1	4	1	3	1
Minnesota	2	2	4	2	2	2
Missouri	2	2	4	2	3	2
Nebraska	2	3	4	3	1	2
North Dakota	2	3	4	3	1	2
Ohio	2	1	4	1	3	3
South Dakota	2	3	4	3	3	3
Wisconsin	2	2	4	2	3	1
Alaska	4	3	4	2	1	1
California	4	1	2	1	3	1
Hawaii	4	3	1	3	1	1
Oregon	4	2	4	1	1	1
Washington	4	1	4	1	1	1
Alabama	3	2	4	1	2	2
Arkansas	3	2	2	3	3	2
Delaware	3	3	2	2	2	1
District of Columbia	3	3	4	1	1	2
Florida	3	1	4	1	2	3
Georgia	3	1	4	1	2	3
Kentucky	3	2	1	1	3	2
Louisiana	3	2	4	3	1	3
Maryland	3	2	4	3	2	3
Mississippi	3	2	4	2	1	3

(continued)

Table 1.5 (continued)

State	Region	Population size	ES/One-Stop relationship	Unemployment rate	Reserve ratio multiple	UI recipiency rate
North Carolina	3	1	2	1	3	2
Oklahoma	3	2	1	3	1	3
South Carolina	3	2	3	1	3	3
Tennessee	3	1	2	1	2	2
Texas	3	1	4	2	2	3
Virginia	3	1	1	3	2	3
West Virginia	3	3	1	2	2	2
Arizona	4	1	3	2	2	3
Colorado	4	2	4	2	2	3
Idaho	4	3	4	2	2	1
Montana	4	3	1	3	1	2
Nevada	4	3	4	1	2	1
New Mexico	4	3	1	3	1	3
Utah	4	2	4	3	1	3
Wyoming	4	3	4	3	1	3

NOTE: Shaded states are those selected for site visits. See Table 1.4 for codes.
SOURCE: Author's compilation.

were tested in the first three states, Wisconsin, Texas, and New York, and then revised for the later site visits. Prior to each site visit, the site visit team obtained key documents from Internet sites and from the state and local staff.

COMPARISON OF SAMPLE STATES TO THE NATION

The 20 states in our sample can be compared with each other as well as with the country as a whole. In this section, the sample states are compared on the basis of their unemployment situation in recent years prior to the Recovery Act and their funding levels. Table 1.6 shows the seasonally adjusted unemployment rates for the 20 states in the sample and the United States as a whole for May 2008, May 2009, and May 2010. For the nation as a whole, the unemployment rate surged between

Table 1.6 Seasonally Adjusted Unemployment Rates for the United States and Sample States for May 2008, May 2009, and May 2010

State	May 2008	May 2009	May 2010
Arizona	5.2	9.7	10.6
Colorado	4.5	8.4	8.9
Florida	5.7	10.2	11.2
Illinois	6.1	9.9	10.7
Louisiana	4.0	6.8	7.3
Maine	4.9	8.2	8.0
Michigan	7.6	13.6	13.0
Montana	4.3	5.9	6.8
Nebraska	3.2	4.7	4.7
Nevada	6.4	11.3	13.7
New York	5.0	8.3	8.7
North Carolina	5.8	10.5	11.0
North Dakota	3.0	4.2	3.8
Ohio	6.2	10.3	10.1
Pennsylvania	5.0	7.9	8.6
Rhode Island	7.3	10.6	11.7
Texas	4.6	7.4	8.2
Virginia	3.7	7.0	7.0
Washington	5.0	9.4	9.9
Wisconsin	4.4	9.0	8.6
United States	5.4	9.4	9.6

SOURCE: BLS (2013); USDOL (2013a).

May 2008 and May 2009, rising from 5.4 percent to 9.4 percent. In the subsequent 12 months, the national rate increased slightly to 9.6 percent.

Tables 1.7, 1.8, and 1.9 show formula and Recovery Act funding for the WIA Adult, WIA Dislocated Worker, and Wagner-Peyser/RES programs for the 20 site-visit states and the entire country for Program Years (PY) 2008, 2009, and 2010. The tables provide some important context for the general observations that follow:

- Overall formula funding for all three programs was flat for PY 2008, 2009, and 2010. The changes for the 20 sample states in total were small (under 5 percent).

Table 1.7 WIA Adult Formula and Recovery Act Allocations for Sample States, PY 2008, 2009, and 2010

State	PY 2008	PY 2009	Recovery Act	PY 2010
Arizona	14,729,041	13,256,136	7,616,346	15,202,194
Colorado	9,267,816	8,341,034	4,792,362	10,012,034
Florida	26,037,659	33,848,953	19,448,002	43,930,907
Illinois	38,269,186	44,888,169	25,790,612	40,332,578
Louisiana	16,831,051	15,147,944	8,703,290	13,610,616
Maine	3,100,278	3,146,947	1,808,086	3,270,719
Michigan	54,246,181	53,707,324	30,857,680	48,256,699
Montana	2,148,466	2,148,465	1,234,406	2,277,572
Nebraska	2,148,466	2,148,465	1,234,406	2,144,914
Nevada	4,541,567	5,904,037	3,392,179	7,662,562
New York	53,779,185	54,853,314	31,516,111	51,212,616
North Carolina	17,815,089	17,991,679	10,337,165	23,350,524
North Dakota	2,148,466	2,148,465	1,234,406	2,144,914
Ohio	45,226,257	40,703,627	23,386,373	36,572,714
Pennsylvania	29,938,257	28,797,617	16,545,744	28,986,240
Rhode Island	2,820,312	3,666,405	2,106,542	3,913,058
Texas	66,418,400	59,776,554	34,344,771	53,709,977
Virginia	8,520,288	9,098,617	5,227,634	11,808,652
Washington	18,747,476	16,872,727	9,694,268	16,535,738
Wisconsin	10,024,911	9,022,419	5,183,854	11,709,758
Study states	426,758,352	425,468,898	244,454,237	426,667,520
All states	859,386,233	859,386,233	493,762,500	857,965,710

NOTE: Program Year 2010 figures include the impact of a rescission enacted as part of Fiscal Year 2011 appropriations legislation.
SOURCE: USDOL (2013b).

- Although the overall formula funding was flat over the three years, there were substantial changes in individual states. For example, Florida's WIA Adult formula funding increased by 30 percent between 2008 and 2009 and by an additional 30 percent between 2009 and 2010. Texas, however, lost 10 percent of its WIA Adult funding each year, while Rhode Island and Nebraska remained virtually unchanged for all three years.

- Year-to-year changes for individual states were small for the Wagner-Peyser formula allocations. Changes from one year to

Table 1.8 WIA Dislocated Worker Formula and Recovery Act
Allocations for Sample States, PY 2008, 2009, and 2010

State	PY 2008	PY 2009	Recovery Act	PY 2010
Arizona	11,442,222	16,648,405	17,403,029	22,761,022
Colorado	11,038,608	13,837,694	14,464,916	14,493,167
Florida	31,390,061	77,059,075	80,551,937	82,926,540
Illinois	46,802,246	65,561,923	68,533,653	54,617,380
Louisiana	9,714,609	8,857,065	9,258,530	9,801,581
Maine	3,640,936	4,373,817	4,572,069	4,573,454
Michigan	130,811,617	75,050,239	78,452,046	64,477,068
Montana	1,584,735	1,679,893	1,756,038	2,172,390
Nebraska	3,186,136	2,478,758	2,591,113	2,425,657
Nevada	5,820,504	13,691,153	14,311,733	14,109,081
New York	50,790,224	63,490,356	66,368,188	65,461,775
North Carolina	33,828,640	42,493,181	44,419,273	43,990,709
North Dakota	1,171,809	876,713	916,452	689,396
Ohio	79,971,002	55,974,110	58,511,252	51,555,231
Pennsylvania	32,959,310	40,639,918	42,482,006	39,519,031
Rhode Island	4,600,258	7,601,362	7,945,909	6,090,031
Texas	57,630,386	51,436,825	53,768,305	61,307,760
Virginia	12,727,010	13,503,287	14,115,351	18,450,205
Washington	22,166,920	21,181,897	22,142,010	24,243,473
Wisconsin	25,748,373	15,363,236	16,059,607	19,910,847
Study states	577,025,606	591,798,907	618,623,417	603,575,798
All states	1,183,839,562	1,183,840,000	1,237,500,000	1,182,120,000

NOTE: Program Year 2010 figures include the impact of a rescission enacted as part of
Fiscal Year 2011 appropriations legislation.
SOURCE: USDOL (2013b).

the next rarely exceeded 3 percent, with the exception of Florida, whose formula allocation saw the largest increase—7.85 percent—from PY 2008 to PY 2009.

- The WIA Dislocated Worker formula allocations were the most volatile. Florida and Nevada, which were hit particularly hard by the recession, had increases in their WIA Dislocated Worker formula funds between PY 2008 and PY 2009 of 145 percent and 135 percent, respectively. Michigan, which has had the highest or nearly the highest unemployment rate in the nation in recent years, had a decrease of nearly 43 percent in its WIA

Table 1.9 Wagner-Peyser Formula and Recovery Act Allocations and Reemployment Services Recovery Act Allocation for Sample States, PY 2008, 2009, and 2010

State	PY 2008	PY 2009	PY 2010	RES	Recovery Act; other W-P
Arizona	12,160,434	12,477,755	12,822,660	4,389,354	2,633,613
Colorado	10,962,418	11,037,674	10,944,825	3,882,771	2,329,663
Florida	36,484,397	39,347,985	40,350,319	13,841,612	8,304,967
Illinois	29,255,214	29,435,140	29,258,315	10,354,527	6,212,717
Louisiana	9,697,828	9,223,752	9,018,836	3,244,680	1,946,808
Maine	3,788,482	3,789,556	3,789,556	1,333,069	799,841
Michigan	25,087,225	24,621,640	24,475,871	8,661,262	5,196,757
Montana	5,206,014	5,207,490	5,207,490	1,831,862	1,099,117
Nebraska	6,256,606	6,258,380	6258380	2,201,537	1,320,923
Nevada	5,753,058	6,167,234	6,370,598	2,169,475	1,301,685
New York	41,433,656	40,607,026	40,405,589	14,284,511	8,570,706
North Carolina	19,216,352	19,706,162	20,093,605	6,932,122	4,159,274
North Dakota	5,301,280	5,302,783	5,302,783	1,865,383	1,119,230
Ohio	26,981,411	26,681,937	26,537,471	9,386,022	5,631,613
Pennsylvania	27,184,396	26,826,020	26,651,245	9,436,706	5,662,024
Rhode Island	2,550,164	2,661,374	2,652,902	936,203	561,722
Texas	49,518,743	48,305,269	48,080,415	16,992,555	10,195,533
Virginia	15,191,777	15,659,584	15,795,653	5,508,640	3,305,184
Washington	14,814,472	14,623,623	14,688,343	5,144,216	3,086,529
Wisconsin	13,355,215	12,954,947	12,881,393	4,557,218	2,734,331
Study states	360,199,142	360,895,331	361,586,249	126,953,725	76,172,237
All states	701,661,936	701,860,926	701,860,926	246,896,681	148,138,009

NOTE: Program Year 2010 figures include the impact of a rescission enacted as part of Fiscal Year 2011 appropriations legislation.
SOURCE: USDOL (2013b).

Dislocated Worker funds from PY 2008 to PY 2009 and a further decline of 14 percent the following year.[7]

- The Recovery Act funds represented a sizable increase for the states. As a percentage of PY 2008 formula funds, Recovery Act funds were 57 percent, 105 percent, and 56 percent for the WIA Adult, WIA Dislocated Worker, and Wagner-Peyser (including RES funds) programs. The Recovery Act funds could be spent in PY 2008, 2009, and 2010.

The widely varying experiences in economic conditions and funding allocations play an important role in the experiences of the sample states. For example, a few states in the sample are small and have low unemployment rates—Montana, Nebraska, and North Dakota. These three states received the minimum allocation for the WIA Adult Program in at least one program year. Thus, these states are likely to have more resources per eligible person than the other states. For the WIA Dislocated Worker Program, the Recovery Act added more funding than the states received in aggregate for each fiscal year, but the experiences of individual states varied significantly. For example, Wisconsin's WIA Dislocated Worker formula allocation dropped by 40 percent between PY 2008 and 2009, from $25.7 million to $15.4 million, and the Recovery Act WIA Dislocated Worker funds of $16.1 million largely served to replace the drop in formula funds.

OUTLINE OF THE REMAINDER OF THE BOOK

Chapter 2 of this book describes the general approach states have taken to administering the Recovery Act workforce development provisions. Chapter 3 describes how WIA Adult and Dislocated Worker Recovery Act funds were administered and used. Chapter 4 discusses the Wagner-Peyser Act's provisions. Chapter 5 provides an explanation of how the funds allocated for Reemployment Services for UI claimants were used. This is followed by a discussion in Chapter 6 of the Trade Adjustment Assistance program. Chapter 7 outlines state initiatives in other areas of interest, such as green jobs initiatives, labor market information, and TANF-financed jobs for low-income individuals. Chapter 8 provides analysis of the Unemployment Insurance system under the Recovery Act. Chapter 9 provides analysis of administrative data, showing how enrollments and expenditures were affected by the infusion of Recovery Act funds. Finally, Chapter 10 summarizes states' views on their most significant challenges and greatest achievements in implementing the Recovery Act's workforce development and UI provisions. Appendix A catalogues interesting or innovative changes and initiatives that were identified during the site visits and were fostered by Recovery Act funding.

Notes

1. Public Law 111-5 was signed by President Obama on February 17, 2009.
2. A version of this book was previously published as the National Association of State Workforce Agencies report *Implementation of the American Recovery and Reinvestment Act: Workforce Development and Unemployment Insurance Provisions* (NASWA 2013).
3. These data do not include amounts allocated to outlying areas, nor do they include National Emergency Grants from the WIA Dislocated Worker Program.
4. In the first year of the project, the Institute for Policy Studies at Johns Hopkins University also participated.
5. The reserve ratio multiple is an actuarial construct that incorporates the trust fund balance, the size of the state's economy, and the benefit payout rate. The denominator in the RRM is the highest-costing benefit payout period in the state's history, measured as total benefit payouts over a 12-month period and expressed as a percentage of covered wages for that period. The numerator of the RRM, termed the reserve ratio, is the year-end trust fund balance divided by covered wages for the year and expressed as a percentage. As the ratio of these two ratios, the reserve ratio multiple is thus a measure whose numerator incorporates information on the UI trust fund balance and on the scale of a state's economy (as approximated by covered wages), while the denominator is a measure of risk (the highest previous 12-month payout rate).
6. Information on the research plan for the UI teleconference interviews is presented in Chapter 8.
7. The large swings in funds to particular states are caused by the allocation formulas, which are based on the relative shares of people with characteristics used in the formulas, such as unemployment and low income. Thus, a state with high but steady unemployment will see its funding decrease if overall funding is flat and unemployment rises in other states. Also, the WIA Dislocated Worker formula does not have a "hold harmless" provision, making large swings in funding much more likely for that program.

References

Bureau of Labor Statistics (BLS). 2013. *Databases, Tables, and Calculators by Subject.* Washington, DC: U.S. Department of Labor, Bureau of Labor Statistics. http://data.bls.gov/timeseries/LNS14000000 (accessed March 5, 2013).

Congressional Budget Office (CBO). 2012. *Estimated Impact of the American Recovery and Reinvestment Act on Employment and Economic Output from October 2011 through December 2011.* Washington, DC: Congressional Budget Office. http://www.cbo.gov/sites/default/files/cbofiles/attachments/02-22-ARRA.pdf (accessed March 5, 2013).

National Association of State Workforce Agencies (NASWA). 2010. *Results of a Survey of State Workforce Administrators on Early Implementation of the Workforce Provisions of the Recovery Act.* Washington, DC: National Association of State Workforce Agencies, Center for Employment Security Education and Research (CESER). http://www.workforceatm.org/assets/utilities/serve.cfm?path=/sections/pdf/2010/NASWAFinalWorkforceSurveyResults.pdf (accessed March 5, 2013).

———. 2013. *Implementation of the American Recovery and Reinvestment Act: Workforce Development and Unemployment Insurance Provisions.* Washington, DC: National Association of State Workforce Agencies, Center for Employment Security Education and Research (CESER). wdr.doleta.gov/research/FullText_Documents/ETAOP_2013_23.pdf (accessed October 10, 2013).

U.S. Department of Labor (USDOL). 2009. *ETA Advisories: Training and Employment Guidance Letter (TEGL) No. 14-08 (March 18, 2009).* Washington, DC: U.S. Department of Labor, Employment and Training Administration. http://wdr.doleta.gov/directives/attach/TEGL/TEGL14-08.pdf (accessed March 6, 2013).

———. 2013a. *Local Area Unemployment Statistics.* Washington, DC: U.S. Department of Labor. http://www.bls.gov/lau/ (accessed March 5, 2013).

———. 2013b. *State Statutory Formula Funding.* Washington, DC: U.S. Department of Labor, Employment and Training Administration. http://www.doleta.gov/budget/statfund.cfm (accessed October 10, 2013).

U.S. Government Accountability Office (USGAO). 2007. *One-Stop System Infrastructure Continues to Evolve, but Labor Should Take Action to Require That All Employment Service Offices Are Part of the System.* Washington, DC: U.S. Government Accountability Office. http://www.gao.gov/products/GAO-07-1096 (accessed March 5, 2013).

U.S. Joint Committee on Taxation. 2009. *Estimated Budget Effects of the Revenue Provisions Contained in the Conference Agreement for H.R. 1, the "American Recovery and Reinvestment Act of 2009."* Washington, DC: U.S. Joint Committee on Taxation. http://www.jct.gov/x-19-09.pdf (accessed March 5, 2013).

votesmart.org. 2009. "Baucus Hails Senate Passage of Bill Creating Jobs, Cutting Taxes for America's Working Families and Small Businesses." Press release, February 10. Philipsburg, MT: votesmart.org. http://votesmart.org/public-statement/407786/baucus-hails-senate-passage-of-bill-creating-jobs-cutting-taxes-for-americas-working-families-and-small-businesses (accessed March 5, 2013).

whitehouse.gov. 2009. *About the Recovery Act.* Washington, DC: White House. http://www.whitehouse.gov/recovery/about (accessed March 5, 2013).

2

State Approaches to the Recovery Act's Workforce Development Provisions

Burt S. Barnow
George Washington University

This chapter examines the general approach that states and local workforce agencies took in planning and initiating workforce investment activities with Recovery Act funding. As will be discussed in the chapter, states and localities were strongly encouraged by the USDOL to begin spending Recovery Act funding quickly after they were notified of their allocation—and to make certain that expenditures adhered to Recovery Act requirements and provided long-term benefits to worker and employer customers of the public workforce system (i.e., through the WIA, Wagner-Peyser/ES, and TAA programs). The chapter describes early planning and start-up of Recovery Act–funded activities, organizational and staffing responses to the availability of Recovery Act funding, training approaches and technical assistance activities involved in initiating Recovery Act–funded employment and training activities, early patterns of states' expenditures of Recovery Act funds, and changes made while the Recovery Act funds were being spent.

EARLY PLANNING AND START-UP

All state and local workforce agencies mentioned that the time they had to plan and initiate Recovery Act–funded activities, from the time the president signed the Recovery Act into law in February 2009 until they first began spending Recovery Act resources on employment and training services (as early as April 2009), was very short. States had to move quickly to begin spending Recovery Act funding within a matter of weeks after being notified of their Recovery Act funding allocation in March 2009. There was strong pressure on states and local workforce agencies to spend Recovery Act funding rapidly (if possible, front-loading expenditures into the first year of the two years available) and, at the same time, to spend the resources wisely. In particular, states and local areas indicated that they were under intense pressure to plan and implement WIA Summer Youth Programs, which in many localities either had not been operational or served small numbers of youth because of a lack of program funding. These programs had to ramp up and be fully operational (and capable of serving thousands of youth in some urban areas) within a few months (by no later than June 2009). For many states and localities, this meant recruiting large numbers of organizations (government agencies, nonprofit organizations, and for-profit firms) willing to hire youth temporarily for the summer, as well as reaching out to youth and certifying their eligibility to participate in the programs. As is discussed later, when asked about their greatest early accomplishments with Recovery Act funding, many state and local officials pointed to their rapid start-up of the WIA Summer Youth Program and their ability to place hundreds or thousands of youth in summer jobs so quickly.

While states and local workforce agencies were pushing quickly to initiate or expand their WIA Summer Youth Programs, they were also digesting the rules and regulations for spending Recovery Act funds in other programs (e.g., the WIA Adult and Dislocated Worker programs, the Wagner-Peyser Employment Service Program, Reemployment Services [for UI claimants], Trade Adjustment Assistance, and the UI Program). For example, workforce programs were exploring ways to do five things: 1) increase the number of customers receiving training, 2) offer new and innovative training options in high-demand occupations, 3) expand services available to unemployed and underemployed customers, 4) respond to a surging volume of customers in One-Stop centers, and 5) improve data systems to track Recovery Act expenditures and produce better reports on program results. Table 2.1 provides several accounts from states of their quick responses to the sudden availability of Recovery Act funding. However, as noted later, some states expressed concern that in a few instances guidance from the ETA was slower than they would have liked.

One reason states were able to respond quickly is that they had heard that Recovery Act funding might become available in early 2009, and governors and state workforce agency staff proactively began planning how to react if funding did become available. Second, as soon as the legislation was enacted, state workforce agencies immediately identified agencies and staff (generally, existing administrators) to be involved in planning the state's response, and they formed steering committees to help with planning and overseeing Recovery Act implementation. As discussed later in this chapter, states also relied upon and sought out training and technical assistance provided by the ETA national and regional offices, as well as guidance provided by national workforce associations.

State and local workforce agencies felt a great deal of pressure to plan carefully their responses to the Recovery Act. The pressure built for three reasons. The first stemmed from the magnitude of the Recovery Act funding received. For example, WIA Adult and Dislocated Worker funding under the Recovery Act often nearly matched the formula funds that agencies received for an entire year. Adding to the pressure was a second reason—the agencies' awareness of the scrutiny that this funding was likely to receive. And third, the speed with which Recovery Act funding was to be spent meant that the agencies felt pressure to hit the ground running, despite the need for careful planning.

ORGANIZATIONAL AND STAFFING RESPONSE

All of the visited states indicated that they worked within their existing organizational structure to plan and implement Recovery Act activities. As noted above, states did not have the time to develop new or elaborate organizational structures in response to Recovery Act funding. And because Recovery Act funding was temporary, states were reluctant to change their organizational structures, add new units or permanent staff, or build new infrastructure (except for modernizing information systems), all of which would have required funding when Recovery Act support was no longer available. In addition, states already had the substantive experience within existing organizational units and programs to plan and implement Recovery Act–funded employment

24

Table 2.1 Examples of Start-Up and Planning Efforts Undertaken by States in Response to Recovery Act Funding

State	Overview of state start-up and planning response
Arizona	Arizona began planning for Recovery Act funds before the signing of the law. Arizona Department of Economic Security (DES) officials maintain good relationships with USDOL officials at the national and regional levels. In addition, the then-head of Arizona's Employment Administration served on a number of advisory committees and was active in NASWA. These connections helped the state to stay on top of Recovery Act legislation and to begin planning in advance. Officials noted that since the funding flowed through the governor's office rather than directly to DES, there was some delay in receiving the funds while the governor completed strategic planning processes and prepared a Web site to track the funds. Arizona officials participated in a number of informational and technical assistance forums, including webinars and conference calls. There were statewide meetings with local boards to discuss plan modifications and other requirements.
Colorado	The start-up time was very short for the state with regard to learning about and beginning to spend Recovery Act funds. The agency learned about funding under the Recovery Act in TEGL 1-08 (issued by USDOL in late February 2009). Recovery Act WIA and W-P funds were allocated and made available to the workforce regions within the state on March 6, 2009, and, with the exception of RES funds, were targeted for total expenditure by June 30, 2010. Recovery Act–funded Summer Youth Employment Programs were launched between May 1 and July 1, with 70 percent of WIA Youth funds targeted for use by September 30, 2009. Local workforce areas were encouraged to spend their youth funds during the first summer in which Recovery Act funds were available.
Florida	As soon as discussion began about the federal stimulus effort, Florida officials knew that the key was to move quickly and to get the local WIBs involved. The day following receipt of the funds from USDOL in March 2009, the funds were distributed to the local WIBs. State staff also attended many meetings in Washington, with NASWA and with the USDOL, and communicated everything they learned to the local WIBs. The state agency held regional meetings with the local WIBs, quickly set up a Web site and posted Q&As on the site, and set up a separate Web site for the "Florida Back to Work" program. They established several teams (e.g., for RES, Summer Youth, Workforce Florida, and agency and regional workforce boards) to make sure the information got out and to convey the urgency to spend funds wisely. Through conference calls and lots of communication, the local WIBs knew everything the state knew. Out of this process, the state developed extensive plans, program guidance, and training. State officials had an experienced workforce investment system that was prepared to deliver services, and they had no need for additional training. They pushed the local WIBs to

spend as much money in the first year as possible and required all local WIBs to submit their plans for implementing the Recovery Act by late August. They also required all local WIBs to submit a plan modification for the Recovery Act, just as the USDOL required of the state. The state distributed funds in March 2009.

Louisiana   State officials heard about the Recovery Act as soon as the president signed the bill. Within a few days, state officials were informed of their funding amounts by USDOL regional office (RO) officials. These regional officials inquired about Louisiana's plan, and the state officials started planning immediately, before the funds were in fact awarded. Similarly, the state officials initiated conversations with the local WIBs in order to get their planning started. The state in turn provided some training to the LWIBs; this consisted of one major meeting and weekly conference calls, principally focused on the WIA Summer Youth Program. For example, state staff helped one LWIB develop its recruitment approach.

Wisconsin   The start-up time was very short for the state with regard to learning about and beginning to spend Recovery Act funds. The timeline was as follows:

2/09—The Recovery Act passes.

3/09—The USDOL informs states about funding, rules, and regulations for the Recovery Act.

4/09—Wisconsin plans for and begins to expend Recovery Act funds.

6/09—The state makes substantial expenditures of Recovery Act funds on the WIA Summer Youth Program. Prior to the Recovery Act enactment, the governor pulled together his cabinet to initiate planning for activities and rapid start-up (and expenditure) of stimulus funds; a statewide committee was also formed, the Office of Recovery and Reinvestment (ORR), which met beginning in December 2008 to plan Recovery Act activities and spending so the state could hit the ground running. Two state staff persons were assigned to work full-time to help plan and coordinate Recovery Act activities. The Department of Workforce Development established a cross-divisional steering committee with various internal work groups, which planned activities and aimed at both maximizing funding and getting funds out the door as quickly as possible.

SOURCE: Table is based on site visits conducted in states between December 2009 and June 2010.

and training activities. A further impetus to maintaining organizational structure was that the Recovery Act did not create any new programs, so funding flowed directly to existing programs.

Despite making no discernible changes to the organizational structures of their workforce systems, all states—and to varying degrees local workforce agencies—used Recovery Act funding to add new staff to respond to the legislation's mandate to provide additional or enhanced services (e.g., expansion or creation of Reemployment Services) or to meet the rapidly rising tide of newly unemployed and underemployed workers flooding One-Stop Career Centers. Because Recovery Act funding was temporary in nature, the main staffing strategy implemented by states and local agencies was to bring on temporary staff to fill new positions. Hiring occurred at both the state and local levels. For example, states distributed much of the WIA Recovery Act funds by formula to local workforce investment areas, where hiring did occur—much of it by LWIBs or contractors (e.g., to staff resource rooms in One-Stops or to provide intensive/training services). The number of staff hired at the local level—particularly those hired by contractors—could generally not be estimated by state workforce agencies. Some hiring of new, usually temporary, staff also occurred at the state level. Often this staff was hired to augment state staff involved in administering Wagner-Peyser/ES activities, Reemployment Services, and Trade Adjustment Assistance (TAA). Much of these temporary, Recovery Act–funded state Wagner-Peyser/TAA staff operated out of One-Stop Career Centers, providing direct customer services—staffing resource rooms, conducting a wide variety of workshops (e.g., orientations, job readiness workshops, RES sessions, job clubs, etc.), and providing staff-assisted (case-managed) services.

Several state and local workforce agencies indicated they experienced some difficulties or delays in bringing on new staff (even temporary staff hired with federal funding) because of state or local hiring freezes, which sometimes occurred despite ETA requests to exempt from hiring freezes the positions funded with federal Recovery Act dollars.

Also, in some states, as hiring was occurring using Recovery Act funding, regular staff may have been experiencing furloughs or layoffs. State and local workforce officials were in agreement that given the very sizable increase in the volume of One-Stop customers, the availability and use of Recovery Act funding to hire additional staff to meet escalating demand for services at all levels (i.e., unassisted, staff-assisted, intensive, and training services) was critical. In some local areas, workforce agencies indicated they needed even more staff than Recovery Act funding would permit to meet the surging number of customers. Additionally, some state and local workforce agencies indicated that mandates to spend WIA Recovery Act funding primarily on training limited their flexibility to add staff to work in the resource room and provide assessment and other intensive services required before individuals could enter training. Table 2.2 provides estimates (at the time when site visits occurred) of staff added by the states with Recovery Act funding. Table 2.3 provides detail to illustrate the approaches that states and local agencies took toward staffing with added Recovery Act resources.

TECHNICAL ASSISTANCE AND TRAINING IN RESPONSE TO THE RECOVERY ACT

With states and local workforce agencies under tight time constraints and intense pressure to plan responses and begin spending Recovery Act funds, they sought help in understanding Recovery Act requirements and in planning Recovery Act–funded activities from a variety of sources. In particular, states looked to the ETA—both its national and its regional offices—for guidance and technical assistance. In planning for Recovery Act implementation, states carefully reviewed the ETA's Training and Employment Guidance Letters (TEGLs) and Training and Employment Information Notices (TEINs, now called Training and Employment Notices, or TENs) as they were released. States also participated in a series of ETA-sponsored webinars that provided technical assistance on the Recovery Act guidelines (e.g., they were tied to the issuance of a TEGL). Of particular interest early on were the guidance and technical assistance provided on implementation of the Recovery Act–funded Summer Youth Employment Program. Some states reported that it was difficult to get clear guidance on countable activities as well as guidance on how to assign customers and activities to Recovery Act or formula funding.

Table 2.2 Estimates of State-Level Hiring with Recovery Act Funds

State	Estimates of state full-time-equivalent staff added because of the Recovery Act (including WIA-Adult, WIA-DW, WIA-Youth, and W-P)
Arizona	ES/RES temporary and seasonal staff positions peaked at 160 under ARRA; 60 permanent positions have been retained.
Colorado	1 FTE (full-time green jobs coordinator).
Florida	9 FTE (full time/temporary).
Illinois	53 FTE—RES/ES (full-time/intermittent/temporary).
Louisiana	11 FTE (for Youth, RES, WIA) + 60 FTE (RES for Career Centers), all temporary. (Note: state hiring freeze includes federally funded positions.)
Maine	1.5 for coordination, leadership; 18 FTE (RES).
Michigan	2 FTE (full-time green jobs specialist and Summer Youth coordinator).
Montana	23 FTE—W-P/ES.
Nebraska	10 WIA; 32 ES/RES—permanent FTE.
Nevada	RES 16.5 and 10 unknown; WIA staffing 21.5—no breakdown by program available.
New York	194 FTE (new staff for RES and rapid response activities).
North Carolina	Employment Security Commission (ESC) hired about 450 temporary FTEs for UI and ES activities; there were 2–3 permanent hires for its labor market information (LMI) office.
North Dakota	Added temporary staff: 5 RES, 8.7 ES, and 4.6 WIA staff.
Ohio	W-P—300–400 temporary.
Pennsylvania	153 FTE (permanent hires in state's planning, monitoring, fiscal, rapid-response, grants, and performance-management units). 50 FTE (permanent hires for RES using UI Recovery Act funds).

Rhode Island	30–35 temporary staff (10 W-P, 2 WIA, ~6 RES, + TANF).
Texas	Added 325 ES staff.
Virginia	18 FTE (state-level ES/UI temporary, some rehires may be made permanent); 75–80 FTE (local ES/UI).
Washington	36 FTEs were hired, primarily for reemployment services and business services activities.
Wisconsin	50 FTE (W-P/RES; temporary) and 21 FTE (TAA).

NOTE: In Colorado and Michigan, the hiring of ES staff was at the local level. The figures in the table are estimates provided during interviews and may not be precise.

SOURCE: Table is based on site visits conducted in states between December 2009 and August 2010.

Table 2.3 Examples of State Approaches to Hiring with Recovery Act Funds

State	State approaches to staffing using Recovery Act funding
Arizona	Before the Recovery Act, Arizona had adequate workforce development funds. State-level budget issues, however, restricted hiring, and the Department of Economic Security (DES) was not able to fill many permanent positions, particularly in the ES. The department was able to get UI positions exempted in order to handle the increased claims, but it had to request critical needs waivers from the state's Department of Administration to spend Recovery Act funds on other staffing. The waiver process added about one month to the hiring process. The DES was able to fill 20 seasonal ES positions that had been vacant. The department also added 25 temporary RES staff members for the reemployment centers; these workers were funded by formula ES funds when the Recovery Act expired. In addition, the department added seven trade counselors to the staff of five in order to handle the expected 35 percent increase in TAA activities. In all, the DES increased its staff by approximately 25 percent. The WIA program still had vacancies to fill but has not yet received a hiring freeze waiver.
Colorado	The state workforce agency did not add staff for Recovery Act planning and implementation; rather, the state used existing state staff members (who were required to work overtime in some cases). The one exception was that the state hired a green jobs coordinator with Recovery Act funds to oversee the many green jobs initiatives in the state. Staff members were overloaded at the state office for a while through planning and early implementation of the Recovery Act. Existing staff members charged part of their time to Recovery Act administrative funding, allowing more non–Recovery Act funding to be released to workforce centers. The state had several other new grants to absorb some additional staff costs. Most staff members with additional work demands were exempt from required overtime pay. Limited overtime was granted to nonexempt staff. The state (and some local areas) were involved in implementing the Recovery Act, but at the same time the state was cautious about making new hires and was furloughing workers. Recovery Act funding was dispensed to local workforce areas in the form of staffing grants. Local areas were encouraged to hire additional temporary staff to meet increased demand for services in the One-Stop centers.

Illinois	At the state level, the Department of Commerce and Economic Opportunity added one new staff member to coordinate state-level planning for and disbursement of WIA discretionary funds. LWIBs made staffing decisions, though they were encouraged not to increase permanent hires given the one-time nature of the funds. In the Illinois Department of Employment Security, 52 additional staff members were hired to help administer and carry out Reemployment Services. These staff members were hired in an "intermittent" category—a job classification that limits hours to 1,500 under an initial contract, with the possibility to move into a permanent position. Intermittent employees also can be rehired in a subsequent year for another 1,500 hours. RES hires were cross-trained to be able to provide ES services. No new ES, UI, or TAA staff members were hired.
Louisiana	The state was able to use some of the Recovery Act funds to hire additional staff members back who had been let go because of FY 2008 WIA budget rescissions. The state used Recovery Act funds to hire 11 staff members (for Youth Services, RES, and WIA programs). In addition, the state hired 60 new temporary staff members with Recovery Act funds to handle RES in the career centers. The governor instituted a freeze in hiring. Because of the previous year's reductions in WIA and W-P funds, Recovery Act funding permitted officials to postpone further reductions in staff or program funding.
Ohio	Most WIA Recovery Act funds were distributed by formula to local workforce areas. Local areas were encouraged to use funding to support training rather than building infrastructure or hiring new staff. Many local areas faced hiring freezes that limited their ability to hire new staff. The Recovery Act's Wagner-Peyser funding was used to hire 100 intermittent (temporary) ES/Wagner-Peyser staff members, who were deployed throughout the state at One-Stops to handle the increased volume of customers and to conduct Reemployment Services orientations. Some additional temporary staff members were hired by local areas to administer and staff the Summer Youth Program.
Wisconsin	Approximately 50 new full-time workers were hired for the state's Wagner-Peyser program to provide RES. A total of 21 new state ES workers were hired to provide TAA case management services. The state's approach to meeting staffing needs with Recovery Act funding was to hire temporary full-time staff and authorize overtime (especially for UI). The main challenge with regard to staffing was to get new staff members trained to perform on the job. After exhausting Recovery Act funding, the state expected few layoffs within the Department of Workforce Development. Finally, the state imposed furloughs for all state staff—eight days a year, which amounted to about a 3 percent annual work and pay cut.

SOURCE: Table is based on site visits conducted in states between December 2009 and August 2010.

Several state agency officials noted that ETA guidance related to reporting came out late in some instances, but they understood that the USDOL had very little time to produce this guidance given the short time frame between when the Recovery Act was enacted and when states and localities were to begin spending Recovery Act funding. State agencies also indicated that the guidance provided in TEGLs, TENs, "Questions and Answers" postings, and webinars was helpful. In addition, the ETA regional office staff was available (both in person and by telephone) to answer questions and provide additional guidance, and state workforce agencies, to varying degrees, relied upon these offices for help. State workforce agencies indicated that they had received useful guidance from national workforce associations (including the National Governors Association and NASWA) and, in some instances, from talking with other state workforce agencies. Overall, most states—particularly in light of the tight time constraints that the ETA (as well as the states) faced—believed that the provided training and technical assistance were useful for implementing the Recovery Act requirements. Nevertheless, some states mentioned technical assistance as one of the overall challenges in implementing the Recovery Act. Some states indicated they would have appreciated more timely guidance on fiscal reporting requirements.

Once state workforce agencies had received ETA guidance and attended training workshops, they provided guidance to local workforce areas. State workforce agencies passed along ETA guidance (e.g., TEGLs and TENs) and made certain that local workforce agencies were aware of their existence and content. States also generally conducted webinars of their own for local workforce agencies, and they issued state policy guidance letters to local workforce areas on fiscal reporting, the WIA Summer Youth Employment Program, and other related Recovery Act issues of importance. States also conducted technical assistance sessions with the One-Stop directors and operations managers, financial managers, and management information system (MIS) coordinators, as well as the youth program coordinators. Finally, like the ETA, state workforce agency officials were available at any time for technical assistance.

PLANS FOR SPENDING RECOVERY ACT FUNDS AND EARLY EXPENDITURES OF THOSE FUNDS

During site visits, states discussed their plans for spending Recovery Act funds and provided assessments of expenditure patterns. As noted previously, the initial site visits were spread over a fairly long time span—December 2009 through July 2010—which was relatively early in the Recovery Act period. Almost one-half of the states interviewed, nine of 20 states, experienced some delay in spending Recovery Act funds. Delays resulted from a variety of factors, including hiring freezes put in place at the state level (as in Arizona) or at the local level (as in Colorado), delays by the legislature in approving spending of Recovery Act funds (as in Illinois and Montana), civil-service hiring processes (as in Colorado, Illinois, and North Dakota), and changes in ETA implementation of waiver authority, which states had previously used to transfer funds from the WIA Dislocated Worker Program to the WIA Adult Program (as in Colorado and Florida).[1] During the site visits, state and local agencies were generally optimistic about their ability to spend the Recovery Act funds rapidly once they overcame the barriers mentioned above. In tracking spending of the Recovery Act funds, the Department of Labor found that 18 of the 20 states in the research sample were projected to achieve federal outlays of 70 percent or more of their WIA Adult funds by September 30, 2010, and that 14 of the states were projected to have outlays of 70 percent or more of their Dislocated Worker funds by September 30, 2010.

Note

1. ETA staff indicated that waivers to transfer WIA funds from the Dislocated Worker Program to the Adult Program were subject to greater scrutiny because of congressional intent for the funds, the severe economic climate, and the large increase in dislocated workers.

3

Workforce Investment Act (WIA) Adult and Dislocated Worker Programs

John Trutko
Capital Research Corporation

Burt S. Barnow
George Washington University

The Adult and Dislocated Worker programs under Title I of the Workforce Investment Act of 1998 are designed to provide employment and training services to help eligible individuals find and qualify for meaningful employment, and to help employers find the skilled workers they need to compete and succeed in business (USDOL 2010). Among the key goals of the WIA program are the following:

- To increase employment, as measured by entry into unsubsidized employment

- To increase retention in unsubsidized employment

- To increase earnings received in unsubsidized employment for dislocated workers

Services under the WIA Adult and Dislocated Worker programs are usually provided through One-Stop Career Centers. There are three levels of service: 1) core services—which include outreach, job search and placement assistance, and labor market information, and are available to all job seekers; 2) intensive services—which include more comprehensive assessments, development of Individual Employment Plans (IEPs), and counseling and career planning; and 3) training services—where customers learn skills for job opportunities in their communities, through both occupational training and basic skills training. In most cases, customers are provided a voucher-like instrument called an Individual Training Account (ITA) to select an appropriate training program from a qualified training provider. Supportive services, such as transportation, child care, housing, and needs-related payments, are provided under certain circumstances to allow an individual to participate in the program. "Rapid response" services at the employment site are also available, both for employers expected to close or have major layoffs and for workers who are expected to lose their jobs as a result of company closings and mass layoffs.

States are responsible for program management and oversight, and operations are delivered through local workforce investment areas (LWIAs). Under the WIA Adult Program, all adults 18 years and older are eligible for core services. When funds are limited, priority for intensive and training services must be given to recipients of public assistance and other low-income individuals. In addition to unemployed adults, employed adults can also receive services to obtain or retain employment that will allow them to be self-sufficient. States and LWIAs are responsible for establishing procedures for applying the priority and self-sufficiency requirements.

Under the WIA Dislocated Worker Program, a "dislocated worker" is an individual who meets the following criteria:

- Has been terminated or laid off, or has received a notice of termination or layoff from employment

- Is eligible for or has exhausted UI

- Has demonstrated an appropriate attachment to the workforce, but is not eligible for UI and is unlikely to return to a previous industry or occupation

- Has been terminated or laid off or received notification of termination or layoff from employment as a result of a permanent closure or substantial layoff

- Is employed at a facility where the employer has made the general announcement that the facility will close within 180 days

- Was self-employed (including employment as a farmer, a rancher, or a fisherman) but is unemployed as a result of general economic conditions in the community or because of a natural disaster

- Is a displaced homemaker who is no longer supported by another family member

The Recovery Act supplied additional funding to support employment and training activities provided by states and LWIAs under WIA. The act included funding aimed at helping states and local areas respond to increased numbers of unemployed and underemployed customers entering the One-Stop system, as well as some specific provisions (discussed in greater detail later in this chapter) that were intended to enhance services provided under WIA. The sections below synthesize findings from an on-line NASWA survey conducted in all states in the summer and fall of 2009 and two rounds of site visits conducted in 20 states with respect to how key Recovery Act provisions have been implemented and have affected WIA Adult and Dislocated Worker program services and operations. The two rounds of site visits to the states, held at two local workforce areas in each state, were conducted approximately one year apart, with the earliest of the Round 1 visits being conducted in December 2009 and the last of the Round 2 visits being conducted in April 2012.[1] The following eight areas under the Recovery Act provisions focusing on the WIA Adult and Dislocated Worker programs are covered in the next eight sections of this chapter: 1) assessment and counseling, 2) changes in training requirements and policy, 3) links to apprenticeships, 4) Pell Grant usage and issues, 5) relationships with institutions of higher education, 6) targeting of low-income individuals, 7) supportive services and needs-related payments, and 8) challenges, including expectations when Recovery Act funding is exhausted.

ASSESSMENT AND COUNSELING

Under the Recovery Act, the workforce system was to place more emphasis on long-term training, on reemployment, and on linking workers to regional opportunities in high-growth sectors. To this end, TEGL 14-08 advised states to consider how assessment and data-driven career counseling could be integrated into their service strategies to support WIA participants in successful training and job search activities aligned with areas of anticipated economic and job growth. The NASWA survey of all state workforce administrators on early implementation of the workforce provisions of the Recovery Act found that the Recovery Act had some early effects on assessment and career counseling services provided by states and local workforce programs:

- Survey results suggested that the percentage of WIA and Wagner-Peyser Act customers receiving assessment and career counseling services had increased in the majority of states: about three-quarters of states reported increases for the WIA Adult and WIA Dislocated Worker programs.

- The majority of states indicated they had made moderate or substantial enhancements to assessment and career counseling services provided to WIA and Wagner-Peyser Act customers—for example, nearly three-quarters of the responding states indicated they had enhanced their triage processes and tools; their skills assessment processes and tools; staff training in areas of triage, customer assessment, and skills transferability analysis; and the availability and use of labor market information.

As discussed below, a slightly different and perhaps more nuanced picture emerges from the two rounds of site visits conducted under this study. As with the survey, a majority of states visited indicated that they had seen an increase in the number of individuals receiving assessment and career counseling. This increase, though, was only partially attributable to Recovery Act funding. Much of the increase in customers receiving assessment and counseling services was a function of the large increase in the number of unemployed and underemployed workers coming into the One-Stop system in search of job leads and training to enhance skill levels. Thus, the Recovery Act funds enabled the states and local workforce areas to respond to the increased demand for services.

In addition, the Recovery Act provided additional funding that states were encouraged to use to expand the number of individuals receiving both short- and long-term training (see the next section for details). In order to receive training, all states required WIA Adult and Dislocated Worker customers to first be assessed and to go through intensive services; hence, with the elevated number of customers coming into the One-Stops and the greater number of WIA Adult and Dislocated

Worker customers entering training, it is not surprising a majority of states indicated that they had experienced an increase in WIA customers receiving assessment and career counseling. However, when asked whether they had experienced a change in the percentage of WIA Adult and Dislocated Worker customers who received assessment and career counseling services, states generally indicated (during our visits) that there had been no change. In fact, several states indicated that because the system had been so deluged by unemployed and underemployed customers as a result of the recession, they believed that the percentage receiving counseling and assessment may have declined slightly (though not because of the Recovery Act or a desire on the part of the workforce agency to decrease assessment and counseling activity).

During site visits, state workforce agency officials were asked, "Since enactment of the Recovery Act, has your state issued new policies or requirements on assessment and career counseling under the WIA Program?" Nearly all states indicated that they had not issued new policies or requirements on assessment or career counseling under WIA since receipt of Recovery Act funding. The states that had issued new policies said that such policies were not a result of the Recovery Act, but rather the product of recent or ongoing efforts to enhance assessment and career counseling. Several states indicated that in the year or two prior to the Recovery Act, they had initiated statewide efforts aimed at improving assessment services, usually centered on improving the testing methods used by local workforce agencies.

Table 3.1 provides examples of several states that initiated changes in assessment and counseling procedures, though in most states such changes had been started before receipt of Recovery Act funds. State workforce agencies indicated that while the state workforce agency typically set the tone with regard to assessment policies or procedures and provided guidance as to possible assessment tests and procedures that could be used within the state, local workforce areas had considerable discretion in choosing the specific tests used. A key observation of several state workforce agency officials was that the Recovery Act provided additional resources that helped to continue and even expand or accelerate the use of new assessment procedures within their states. For example, several of the 20 states visited—including Colorado, Louisiana, Michigan, Ohio, Pennsylvania, Washington, and Wisconsin—were at the time of receipt of Recovery Act funding already in the process of

Table 3.1 Examples of Assessment Policies and Procedures in States Visited

State	Assessment policies and procedures
Colorado	The state issued no new policies or requirements on assessment and career counseling under WIA in response to the Recovery Act. Under WIA, the state (and LWIAs) had always placed strong emphasis on assessment, and WIA participants had to be carefully assessed to qualify for WIA training. Because of the emphasis in Colorado on local control or autonomy, there is flexibility with regard to how and when assessment is used by local workforce areas. Prior to the Recovery Act, the state had launched a statewide initiative to emphasize use of the CareerReady Colorado Certificate (CRCC), which is currently based on the National Career Readiness Certificate (NCRC). Recovery Act funding (state discretionary funds) supported the expanded use of the CRCC—as of May 2011, more than 10,000 workers had received certificates. Overall, the Recovery Act did not bring about changes in assessment policies, procedures, or the overall percentage of individuals receiving assessment.
Michigan	Prior to the ARRA, the state and local workforce areas had adopted the Career Pathways model, with an emphasis on WIA intensive/training participants completing the NCRC certification process (covering four areas). ARRA funding provided a resource base that allowed the state and the Michigan Works! agencies (MWAs) to expand the use of the NCRC. Although NCRC testing was initiated before receipt of ARRA funding, ARRA funding facilitated the expanded use of the NCRC by paying for the NCRC testing for WIA and other customers of the MWAs. ARRA funding also provided needed resources for marketing NCRCs to employers, so that employers would increasingly recognize the NCRC during the hiring process. State policy required all WIA, Wagner-Peyser, and TAA participants receiving staff-assisted services to take the NCRC (though participants could opt out of taking the test). ARRA funding was used to pay for thousands of NCRC tests (with a cost averaging about $60 per participant).
Nebraska	Since enactment of the Recovery Act, Nebraska has not issued new policies or requirements on assessment and career counseling under the WIA Adult or Dislocated Worker programs. However, it has increased the role of the Employment Service's provision of these services and emphasized self-directed, on-line assessments. In most offices, the first point of contact is with Employment Services/RES staff. An initial, up-front assessment is a (core or staff-assisted) function of the One-Stop client flow process and the state services model. The initial assessment (using Kuder assessments and additional on-line tools) is available at all points of the system through NEworks. NEworks also allows the state to track the use of self-assessment tools accessed through the One-Stops; this method is under consideration as a performance measure. The movement toward on-line assessment is a practice associated with ARRA resources and increased demand for services.

New York | In October 2009, the state issued revised policies relating to assessment and counseling. The state's policy is that all One-Stop customers are to receive an initial assessment. The only exceptions are customers using self-help or informational services only and UI claimants who are "work-search exempt" (e.g., those who are part of a union with union hiring arrangements or those temporarily laid off or on seasonal layoff). The new policies were not issued as a result of the Recovery Act—the state's position is that assessments should be conducted for all customers as a first step to determining which services should be offered.

Ohio | The state issued no new policies or requirements on assessment and career counseling under the WIA program in response to the Recovery Act. Local workforce areas determine the specific assessment tests used and the policies or procedures. As a result of ARRA, there were no changes in assessment, assessment tools used, or customer flow. Two local areas visited indicated that they wanted to keep the process the same because ARRA funding was temporary. Under WIA, prior to the Recovery Act, the state (and local workforce areas) placed emphasis on assessment, and WIA participants had to be assessed to qualify for WIA training. Among the assessment tools used are the Test of Adult Basic Education (TABE) and WorkKeys (which was the case before Recovery Act funding). Because there was an increase in the number of individuals receiving WIA training with the added ARRA funding, the number of WIA participants assessed increased within the state (though the percentage assessed has decreased slightly).

Pennsylvania | Before the Recovery Act, the state changed its policy to ensure that eligible Pennsylvania CareerLinks customers saw a career specialist and had a one-on-one assessment and counseling session. Before receipt of Recovery Act funding, the state began working with the LWIAs to improve assessment activities. Two LWIAs began enhancing their assessment tools and were experimenting with WorkKeys and KeyTrain. Another LWIA expanded efforts to assess the workforce needs of the economically disadvantaged. From the success of these local efforts, the state and the LWIAs recently agreed to jointly purchase WorkKeys to implement its use in assessment statewide. All staff, including WIA, RES, W-P, and TAA, are being trained by one of the local WIBs to conduct the WorkKeys assessment and read and interpret the results.

(continued)

Table 3.1 (continued)

State	Assessment policies and procedures
Washington	New policies exist around basic front-end triage to determine immediate needs using an initial assessment. The initiative has included training staff on assessment tools and developing local service targets. Very little of the policy development was directly related to the Recovery Act, however, as the changes were already underway when the funding became available. Recovery Act funds simply pushed the changes farther along than they would otherwise have been at this point, given the lack of other resources. Recovery Act funds were used to make the KeyTrain assessment available for statewide use in the One-Stop centers. The only mandated assessment tool is Comprehensive Adult Student Assessment Systems (CASAS) for Adult Basic Education (ABE) and Youth. CASAS was selected because it is the tool used for ABE students in the community college system.

SOURCE: Table is based on site visits conducted in states between December 2009 and April 2012.

implementing or expanding their use of WorkKeys/KeyTrain and the National Career Readiness Certificate (NCRC) to enhance assessment procedures. These efforts were aimed at providing workers an extra credential that would be recognized by employers. Several states indicated that they were disseminating information to employers to increase their knowledge of NCRC and were attempting to make such certification an increasingly important criterion upon which employers select workers to fill job openings.

CHANGES IN TRAINING REQUIREMENTS AND POLICY

Under the Recovery Act, states were expected to use the additional workforce funding to substantially increase the number of customers served and to substantially increase the number and proportion of customers who receive training. Training services provided with Recovery Act funds include many different types: occupational skills classroom training, on-the-job training (OJT), programs that combine workplace training and related instruction (including registered apprenticeship), training programs operated by the private sector, skills upgrade and retraining, entrepreneurship training, job readiness training, adult education and literacy training, and customized training. These funds can also be used to support Adult Basic Education (ABE) training, including English as a Second Language (ESL) training. The NASWA state survey probed states on several issues related to how Recovery Act funding may have affected training policies and practices. Findings from the NASWA survey with respect to training include the following:

- Every state reported encouraging or requiring local areas to increase investments in WIA-funded training, and two-thirds of states reported significant staff efforts to encourage training.

- About one-half of the states reported having set aside—or having required LWIAs to set aside—a certain percentage of WIA Recovery Act funds for training.

- Nearly three-quarters of states reported substantial increases (greater than 10 percent) in the number of customers enrolled in training through the WIA Adult and WIA Dislocated Worker programs.

The site visits to states confirmed these key findings and provided some additional depth of information and examples of how Recovery Act funding affected training policies, number of WIA participants trained, and types of training provided under the WIA Adult and Dislocated Worker programs.

All state workforce agencies visited as part of this study indicated that they had encouraged (in their guidance, technical assistance, and discussions) LWIAs to use WIA Recovery Act funding specifically to support and expand training for the unemployed and underemployed workers served under both the WIA Adult and Dislocated Worker programs. In their discussions with local workforce agency staff, state workforce agency officials typically underscored that WIA Recovery Act funding was a one-time event, should be spent quickly and prudently, should not be used to fund permanent staff increases, and should be devoted to training. For most states, the Recovery Act funding represented additional funding to support training and other WIA activities. In a few states, however, a portion of the WIA Recovery Act funding replaced funding that had been lost because of a decrease in the state's WIA Dislocated Worker formula allocation. Wisconsin, for example, indicated that the Recovery Act WIA Dislocated Worker funds primarily brought the state back to its prior level of funding. (However, for the WIA Adult Program in Wisconsin, Recovery Act funding represented a substantial boost in funds available for training and other WIA services.)

In most states, local workforce agencies were encouraged to obligate and spend Recovery Act funds, to the extent possible, within the first program year (of the two years for which Recovery Act funding was available). Obligating funding to support training activities was generally not an issue or a challenge for most workforce areas, as many One-Stops were overwhelmed with customers who were both interested in and met requirements for training assistance. A few state agencies indicated that expenditures of Recovery Act funding on training lagged in some local workforce areas (mostly for the WIA Dislocated Worker Program) for three reasons: 1) some unemployed workers were primarily interested in finding work and were reluctant (at least until their UI benefits were exhausted) to enter training; 2) there were waiting lists (sometimes lengthy ones, especially for training for certain occupations in health careers) that made it difficult to get some individuals into occupational training that related to their interests; and 3) faced with high customer volume in One-Stop Career Centers, some One-Stops lacked staffing and resources to provide the assessment and other intensive services required prior to approval of training.

It also should be noted that several states had waivers in place in prior years that allowed the transfer of certain funds between the WIA Adult and Dislocated Worker programs. This gave states more flexibility to determine how funding for training was allocated between these two programs. During the site visits, several states indicated that changes in ETA implementation of the waiver policy limited their ability to transfer funds from the Dislocated Worker Program to the Adult Program for the Recovery Act WIA funds.[2]

As shown in Table 3.2, states adopted various policies to encourage local workforce agencies to allocate resources to training versus other allowable activities under WIA. States implemented four basic approaches to encouraging the use of Recovery Act funding for training activities:

1) They set no specific threshold or percentage that local workforce areas had to spend on training, but encouraged (through guidance, technical assistance, and ongoing discussions) LWIAs to use Recovery Act funding for training (e.g., states such as Michigan and Washington used this approach).

2) They required local workforce agencies to spend at least as much on a percentage basis on training with Recovery Act funding as they had spent in the past with their regular WIA formula funds (e.g., Colorado).

3) They applied the same threshold requirement mandated for regular WIA formula funds (e.g., that 50 percent of WIA formula funds be spent on training) to the Recovery Act funds (e.g., Illinois and Florida).

4) They mandated that local workforce areas expend at least a minimum percentage of Recovery Act funds received (ranging as high as 80 percent in states visited) on training or on training and supportive services (e.g., Maine, Montana, Nebraska, New York, Ohio, Texas, and Wisconsin).

For example, Texas mandated that 67 percent of Recovery Act funds be spent on training, including expenditures on support services

Table 3.2 Examples of Varying Approaches by States to Encourage Use of Recovery Act Funds on Training

State	State policy guidance on use of Recovery Act funds for training
Arizona	Local areas in Arizona have considerable autonomy in setting training standards and determining training expenditure levels. Prior to the Recovery Act, training was not a high priority in most local areas. Under the Recovery Act, Arizona has encouraged local areas to do more training but did not establish a statewide standard or target for training expenditures. Some local areas identified an increased training emphasis in their local plan modification, but not all. One change as a result of the Recovery Act is that individuals can access training more quickly, after only a brief connection with core and intensive services. Each local area also sets its own Individual Training Account (ITA) spending cap for individuals. In larger areas, such as the city of Phoenix, the training cap is set at $4,000 per person and also requires a participant in-kind match, which might include a Pell Grant, a federal student loan, or personal savings.
Colorado	Colorado did not require a specific percentage of ARRA funding to be used for training. Colorado required workforce regions to use a higher percentage of ARRA funds for training than their regular WIA formula funds.
Illinois	The state implemented its own policy in 2007 which required local areas to spend at least 40 percent of their Adult and Dislocated Worker allocations on training. This policy provided incentive funds to those local areas meeting this requirement and imposed sanctions on those that did not meet them. Initially there was a period of negotiation for lower limits for some of the local areas, but as of PY 2009, all LWIAs were required to meet the 40 percent minimum.
Michigan	There is no state policy requiring that a certain percentage of ARRA funds be used for training—it is left to local areas to determine what portion of ARRA funds are used for training. State administrators indicated that setting such a minimum threshold would have been difficult because of the very different sizes, context, and training requirements of the 25 MWAs across the state. The state let it be known that a high proportion (if not all) of ARRA funds should be used for training (in the form of ITAs) and that local areas should not use ARRA funding to build staff or infrastructure.
Montana	Montana responded to the Recovery Act guidance instructing states to place an emphasis on retraining unemployed workers in areas aligned with anticipated economic and job growth by dedicating 70 percent of all WIA Adult and Dislocated Worker Recovery Act dollars to training and supportive services. The estimate from the Montana Department of Labor and Industry (MDLI) is that twice as many participants received training support as in the years before the recession. The 70 percent set-aside seemed to both state and local-level administrators an effective way to support

	customers in gaining new skills while keeping administrative costs low. Administrators continue to be concerned, however (as is mentioned throughout the book), about their ongoing ability to provide support for training now that ARRA funds have been expended. "We're going to revert back to our previous levels (of providing training), maybe even a bit lower, as we carry those currently enrolled on through," said one.
Ohio	The state set a low threshold of 30 percent of ARRA funding to be spent on training activities for local workforce areas—this modest threshold was easily achieved by the state overall and by each local area within the state. For the majority of people coming in, training is often the preferred service.
Pennsylvania	The state strongly recommended that LWIAs spend at least 60 percent of their Recovery Act funds on training. Workforce Guidance Memo No. 3 stated that spending 30 to 40 percent on training was unacceptable. The memo also noted that the ultimate goal for training must be a recognized skills certification, academic credential, or employment, and that the state agency recommended that all Recovery Act funding be used to prepare and move customers into demand-driven training, postsecondary education, or employment. It also urged LWIAs to keep administrative costs to a minimum.
Texas	Texas mandated that 67 percent of Recovery Act funds be spent on training, including expenditures on support services and needs-related payments. Because of the directive in the Recovery Act legislation that the "majority" of the funds be spent on training, and because the USDOL did not establish a specific standard, the TWC determined that 67 percent would provide an aggressive focus on training while still allowing the boards to meet other needs with Recovery Act funds. Unlike formula funding, Recovery Act funding specifically defined the activities that counted as a training expenditure.
Wisconsin	The state policy required that 70 percent of Recovery Act WIA Dislocated Worker and Adult funds be spent on training. This was double the expenditure requirement for training for regular WIA formula funds (set at 35 percent) and resulted in a substantial increase in the number of WIA Adults that enrolled in training over what would have been the case without Recovery Act funding. State officials noted that Recovery Act funding was mostly a substitute for the 40 percent reduction in WIA Dislocated Worker funding that hit the state that year, and so did not result in an increase in the number of dislocated workers being trained (though without this funding source the state possibly would have enrolled fewer people in WIA Dislocated Worker training).

SOURCE: Table is based on site visits conducted in states between December 2009 and April 2012.

and needs-related payments. Because of the emphasis in the Recovery Act legislation that the majority of the funds be spent on training, and because the USDOL did not establish a specific standard, the Texas Workforce Commission (TWC) determined that a level of 67 percent would provide an aggressive focus on training while still allowing the local boards to meet other needs with Recovery Act funds. The TWC examined data on expenditures and number of customers served monthly to ensure that local boards met training and expenditure benchmarks.

Similarly, Wisconsin mandated that LWIAs spend 70 percent of Recovery Act WIA Dislocated Worker and Adult funds on training activities. This was double the expenditure requirement for training for regular WIA formula funds (set at 35 percent). In contrast, eight of the 20 states visited set no percentage requirements with regard to expenditure of WIA Recovery Act funding on training.

Recovery Act funding provided additional resources for states and local workforce areas to provide training to meet a surge in demand for training and other workforce services as a result of the deep recession gripping the nation. Table 3.3 shows data on the number of WIA Adult exiters, the number of WIA Adult exiters receiving training services, and the percentage of WIA exiters receiving training services under the WIA Adult Program for PY 2008 (July 1, 2008–June 30, 2009), PY 2009 (July 1, 2009–June 30, 2010), and PY 2010 (July 1, 2010–June 30, 2011). Table 3.4 displays this same type of data on the number of exiters and receipt of training for the WIA Dislocated Worker Program. States received Recovery Act funding allocations in the spring of 2009 (near the end of PY 2008) and planned how they would spend these added resources over a several-month period. Most, if not all, WIA Adult and Dislocated Worker Program Recovery Act expenditures on training occurred over the next two program years (PY 2009 and PY 2010). WIA Adult and Dislocated Worker Recovery Act funding was to be spent within a two-year period (with all funding to be expended by June 30, 2011—i.e., the end of Program Year 2010). With a strong emphasis placed on early expenditure of Recovery Act funding (to spur local economies and to assist the growing ranks of the unemployed as soon as possible), states expended a substantial portion of their WIA Adult and Dislocated Worker funding in PY 2009, with remaining funding allocated and spent on training services in PY 2010.

As shown in Table 3.3, across all states, the number of WIA Adult exiters receiving training increased from 109,322 in PY 2008 (the year prior to expenditure of Recovery Act WIA funding) to 152,285 in PY 2009 (the program year in which states largely expended Recovery Act WIA funding). This represents a 39 percent increase in the number of WIA Adult exiters receiving training. The number of WIA Adults enrolled in training stayed at just about the same level nationally in PY 2010 (152,813) as in PY 2009.[3] Despite the nearly 40 percent increase in the numbers trained from PY 2008 to PY 2009, the overall percentage of WIA Adults engaged in training remained relatively unchanged, increasing slightly from 11 percent of all WIA Adult exiters in PY 2008 to 13 percent in PY 2009 and 12 percent in PY 2010. This slight percentile increase (of 1–2 percentage points) in the overall number of WIA Adult exiters receiving training came about because while the number WIA Adults in training increased substantially (by nearly 40 percent), there was also an overall increase in the number of total WIA Adult exiters from PY 2008 (1,026,729) to PY 2010 (1,243,907).

Table 3.4 shows that, across all states, the number of WIA Dislocated Workers enrolled in training increased from 56,172 in PY 2008 (the year prior to expenditure of Recovery Act WIA funding) to 105,555 in PY 2009 (the program year in which states largely expended Recovery Act WIA funding), an 88 percent increase in the number of WIA Dislocated Workers receiving training. The number of WIA Dislocated Workers enrolled in training increased by another 21 percent the following program year, reaching 127,557 in PY 2010.[4] Despite the number of WIA Dislocated Workers trained more than doubling (a 127 percent increase) from PY 2008 to PY 2010, the percentage of WIA Dislocated Workers engaged in training remained relatively unchanged, increasing from 16 percent of all WIA Dislocated Worker exiters in PY 2008 to 18 percent in both PY 2009 and PY 2010. As with the WIA Adult Program, this slight change in the percentage trained resulted because while the number of WIA Dislocated Workers engaged in training increased substantially, there was also slightly more than a doubling of the number of WIA Dislocated Worker exiters from PY 2008 (358,233) to PY 2010 (719,846).

Table 3.5 provides a state-by-state breakdown of the percentage change in the number of WIA Adults and Dislocated Workers engaged in training. This table shows the sometimes very substantial changes

Table 3.3 Number and Percentage of WIA Adult Exiters Enrolled in Training

State	No. of WIA Adult exiters			No. of WIA Adult exiters in training			% of WIA Adult exiters in training		
	PY 2008	PY 2009	PY 2010	PY 2008	PY 2009	PY 2010	PY 2008	PY 2009	PY 2010
AK	369	442	312	287	354	255	78	80	82
AL	1,766	2,919	2,479	1,297	2,151	2,083	73	74	84
AR	805	1,358	1,061	692	1,132	956	86	83	90
AZ	3,147	3,005	2,767	1,056	1,542	1,627	34	51	59
CA	78,046	83,509	69,419	5,757	10,072	15,926	7	12	23
CO	2,315	2,189	2,119	1,586	1,714	1,682	69	78	79
CT	1,050	757	1,305	779	582	820	74	77	63
DC	550	862	1,191	290	516	555	53	60	47
DE	424	510	498	418	403	359	99	79	72
FL	17,911	18,309	18,707	13,943	14,380	13,402	78	79	72
GA	2,417	3,386	4,195	1,635	2,421	3,133	68	72	75
HI	188	198	264	131	126	106	70	64	40
IA	495	12,091	27,899	379	443	432	77	4	2
ID	409	610	494	326	470	414	80	77	84
IL	3,697	7,398	5,746	2,098	4,347	3,967	57	59	69
IN	126,274	132,545	114,189	4,787	6,961	8,939	4	5	8
KS	2,131	11,292	7,109	959	1,033	967	45	9	14
KY	3,760	3,842	3,426	1,982	2,757	2,552	53	72	74
LA	121,662	121,036	85,310	2,469	3,617	2,595	2	3	3

MA	1,744	2,328	3,792	1,166	1,729	3,175	67	74	84
MD	1,643	1,762	1,140	793	1,045	714	48	59	63
ME	299	347	431	220	284	359	74	82	83
MI	6,103	12,556	10,561	3,921	9,825	7,669	64	78	73
MN	1,096	1,806	1,701	361	824	928	33	46	55
MO	2,984	3,950	196,370	1,211	1,758	3,029	41	45	2
MS	29,201	29,816	15,370	3,908	4,496	2,338	13	15	15
MT	146	495	483	60	68	225	41	14	47
NC	2,322	5,100	4,016	1,924	3,939	3,486	83	77	87
ND	608	647	507	196	278	295	32	43	58
NE	388	503	452	327	424	351	84	84	78
NH	395	524	448	278	365	270	70	70	60
NJ	2,289	2,948	3,064	1,559	2,094	2,417	68	71	79
NM	1,017	2,551	1,433	637	2,118	1,268	63	83	88
NV	1,172	2,217	2,911	358	671	1,453	31	30	50
NY	326,485	333,658	271,889	9,249	17,788	15,025	3	5	6
OH	8,740	12,013	7,732	5,295	6,646	5,015	61	55	65
OK	53,848	57,398	54,140	941	1,512	1,120	2	3	2
OR	61,392	151,019	151,525	865	2,714	3,008	1	2	2
PA	4,581	4,506	6,930	1,818	2,190	2,711	40	49	39
PR	7,405	6,752	5,620	3,443	2,408	3,034	46	36	54
RI	689	861	1,148	202	482	567	29	56	49
SC	9,020	12,270	9,069	4,414	5,558	4,843	49	45	53
SD	685	597	621	322	286	364	47	48	59

(continued)

52

Table 3.3 (continued)

State	No. of WIA Adult exiters			No. of WIA Adult exiters in training			% of WIA Adult exiters in training		
	PY 2008	PY 2009	PY 2010	PY 2008	PY 2009	PY 2010	PY 2008	PY 2009	PY 2010
TN	10,263	8,812	9,159	7,152	6,732	6,791	70	76	74
TX	21,094	21,178	20,238	7,931	7,827	8,147	38	37	40
UT	96,918	94,295	104,054	6,062	7,513	6,579	6	8	6
VA	1,489	2,004	3,040	1,066	1,410	2,132	72	70	70
VI	221	518	443	109	373	321	49	72	72
VT	155	453	280	132	316	201	85	70	72
WA	2,549	2,965	3,147	1,127	1,513	1,905	44	51	61
WI	1,427	2,152	2,358	789	1,212	1,453	55	56	62
WV	714	975	955	460	582	518	64	60	54
WY	231	387	390	155	284	332	67	73	85
Total	1,026,729	1,186,621	1,243,907	109,322	152,285	152,813	11	13	12

SOURCE: Data are from the USDOL's Public Workforce System Dataset and have been assembled and analyzed by the Upjohn Institute.

between PY 2008 and PY 2010 in the overall numbers of WIA Adults and Dislocated Workers enrolled in training. At least a portion of this increase, and perhaps most of it, was a function of the added resources provided by the Recovery Act and the targeting of these added resources to training within states. As shown in the table, 11 states had a 100 percent or greater increase in the number of WIA Adult exiters enrolled in training between PY 2008 and PY 2010; and another 16 states posted a 50–99 percent increase in the numbers of WIA Adult exiters enrolled in training. Among the states with the largest percentage increase in the number of WIA Adult exiters enrolled in training were Nevada (306 percent), Montana (275 percent), and Oregon (248 percent). Ten states experienced a decrease in the number of WIA Adult exiters trained between PY 2008 and PY 2010, with the decrease reaching as much as 40 percent in Mississippi and 19 percent in Delaware. As discussed earlier, for the nation as a whole, there was an overall 40 percent increase in the number of WIA Adult exiters enrolled in training between PY 2008 and PY 2010.

The percentage increase in the number of WIA Dislocated Workers enrolled in training services was even greater than that for the WIA Adult program. As shown in Table 3.5, 36 states recorded a 100 percent or greater increase in the number of WIA Dislocated Worker exiters enrolled in training between PY 2008 and PY 2010; another six states experienced a 50–99 percent increase in the number of WIA Dislocated Workers enrolled in training. Among the states with the largest percentage increase in the number of WIA Dislocated Worker exiters enrolled in training were several fairly small states (which had a relatively small base of Dislocated Worker exiters in PY 2008), including Wyoming (a 1,200 percent increase), Montana (727 percent), the District of Columbia (681 percent), and Nevada (471 percent). However, several larger states experienced substantial increases in the number of WIA Dislocated Workers enrolled in training as well—for example, Florida (362 percent) and California (316 percent). Only three states experienced a decrease in the number of WIA Dislocated Workers between PY 2008 and PY 2010—Mississippi (−55 percent), Hawaii (−21 percent), and Louisiana (−7 percent). As discussed earlier, for the nation as a whole, there was a 127 percent increase in the number of WIA Dislocated Worker exiters enrolled in training from PY 2008 to PY 2010.

Table 3.4 Number and Percentage of WIA Dislocated Worker Exiters Enrolled in Training

State	No. of WIA DW exiters			No. of WIA DW exiters in training			% of WIA DW exiters in training		
	PY 2008	PY 2009	PY 2010	PY 2008	PY 2009	PY 2010	PY 2008	PY 2009	PY 2010
AK	267	357	216	146	223	157	55	62	73
AL	898	1,793	2,002	773	1,568	1,801	86	87	90
AR	432	745	758	280	500	577	65	67	76
AZ	1,640	2,572	2,604	460	1,182	1,631	28	46	63
CA	19,209	43,524	45,618	2,800	7,265	11,639	15	17	26
CO	611	707	1,188	388	518	863	64	73	73
CT	866	1,034	2,564	586	638	1,376	68	62	54
DC	38	227	455	21	84	164	55	37	36
DE	142	569	973	138	336	633	97	59	65
FL	2,535	4,682	8,866	1,446	3,179	6,681	57	68	75
GA	2,426	3,168	5,469	1,927	2,614	4,675	79	83	85
HI	619	741	330	179	264	142	29	36	43
IA	1,864	6,052	10,255	623	986	1,107	33	16	11
ID	552	1,065	1,287	416	913	1,168	75	86	91
IL	4,514	8,392	9,134	2,299	4,862	5,450	51	58	60
IN	14,843	26,505	24,781	1,935	3,236	4,514	13	12	18
KS	1,205	2,155	1,824	787	519	887	65	24	49
KY	1,578	2,553	3,803	845	1,527	2,374	54	60	62
LA	5,173	11,102	6,258	1,007	1,451	941	19	13	15
MA	3,015	4,723	5,104	1,787	3,043	3,445	59	64	67
MD	1,122	1,695	1,096	463	935	630	41	55	57

ME	538	1,078	1,164	346	664	908	64	62	78
MI	4,274	7,485	8,086	2,764	4,923	5,833	65	66	72
MN	1,536	4,561	4,793	424	1,767	2,272	28	39	47
MO	2,345	4,247	104,772	994	1,777	3,473	42	42	3
MS	24,650	25,732	17,457	3,258	4,487	1,478	13	17	8
MT	130	406	835	51	69	422	39	17	51
NC	2,245	6,624	6,087	1,679	5,152	5,503	75	78	90
ND	139	234	233	57	116	124	41	50	53
NE	239	485	470	185	393	412	77	81	88
NH	564	977	884	317	517	514	56	53	58
NJ	3,030	4,646	5,255	2,335	3,857	4,505	77	83	86
NM	215	277	417	191	232	346	89	84	83
NV	615	1,710	2,533	214	570	1,221	35	33	48
NY	169,956	213,289	217,888	4,659	11,106	9,467	3	5	4
OH	5,338	9,521	8,221	3,180	5,828	5,572	60	61	68
OK	3,779	20,320	15,612	467	682	502	12	3	3
OR	42,140	104,510	134,673	860	2,634	2,888	2	3	3
PA	5,273	9,292	11,959	2,331	3,885	5,379	44	42	45
PR	3,205	3,824	2,972	678	1,227	1,008	21	32	34
RI	518	1,727	1,665	271	1,001	1,018	52	58	61
SC	5,086	7,530	5,907	2,597	3,602	3,312	51	48	56
SD	189	527	516	83	252	320	44	48	62
TN	3,040	4,031	5,336	1,816	3,010	4,392	60	75	82
TX	7,804	10,825	10,669	2,901	4,410	5,953	37	41	56

(continued)

Table 3.4 (continued)

State	No. of WIA DW exiters			No. of WIA DW exiters in training			% of WIA DW exiters in training		
	PY 2008	PY 2009	PY 2010	PY 2008	PY 2009	PY 2010	PY 2008	PY 2009	PY 2010
UT	325	947	899	305	896	863	94	95	96
VA	1,741	3,084	4,296	891	1,319	2,108	51	43	49
VI	90	220	205	74	193	177	82	88	86
VT	148	389	194	135	310	161	91	80	83
WA	2,461	3,295	3,779	1,242	2,066	2,815	50	63	74
WI	2,241	4,200	5,936	991	1,869	2,905	44	45	49
WV	824	1,567	1,462	564	866	773	68	55	53
WY	6	46	86	6	32	78	100	70	91
Total	358,233	581,967	719,846	56,172	105,555	127,557	16	18	18

SOURCE: Data are from the USDOL's Public Workforce System Dataset and have been assembled and analyzed by the Upjohn Institute.

In their more qualitative assessments (offered during site visits) of the number of individuals receiving training services, officials in most of the 20 states visited indicated that the added Recovery Act funding (typically representing an almost doubling of WIA funding) increased the number of individuals in the WIA Adult and Dislocated Worker programs enrolled in training. This is similar to the results of the NASWA survey and the results shown in Tables 3.3–3.5. Despite their being able to temporarily increase the number of individuals enrolled in training, several states worried about their ability to sustain training levels once Recovery Act funding went away. Most states indicated that once Recovery Act funding had been spent, levels of training returned to pre–Recovery Act levels, both in terms of expenditures and number of participants enrolled in training. Several states indicated that as they were winding down their Recovery Act funding they worried about not meeting expectations that job seekers might have with respect to enrolling in WIA-funded training. Several states indicated that despite the end of Recovery Act funding, their local areas continued to face very high levels of unemployment and, therefore, elevated levels of demand for training and other services that could not be met post–Recovery Act. In fact, several states and local areas indicated that once Recovery Act funding had been exhausted, some of their local workforce areas imposed waiting lists for training. These waiting lists were likely to continue well into the future because local economies continued to be stressed and there was a likelihood that WIA funding would remain flat or decline in the future. Examples of states with concerns about their ability to meet demand for training when Recovery Act funding was fully expended include the following:

- **Michigan.** The main challenge with regard to training has been Michigan Works! agencies (MWAs) having sufficient resources to sustain training levels with Recovery Act funding fully spent, and needing to rely upon regular WIA funding (especially WIA Dislocated Worker Program funding, which has sharply declined). A year after ARRA funding had been fully expended, many MWAs across the state found they did not have the necessary funds to sustain training levels at the levels they were able to offer with ARRA funding. This has been a disappointment to some unemployed workers who anticipated being able to enroll in subsidized training (in part, because they had heard about

Table 3.5 Percentage Change in Number of WIA Adult and Dislocated Worker Exiters Enrolled in Training, PY 2008 to PY 2010, Sorted by Percentage Change from PY 2008 to PY 2010

	% change in WIA Adult exiters enrolled in training				% change in WIA DW exiters enrolled in training		
State	PY 2008–09	PY 2009–10	PY 2008–10	State	PY 2008–09	PY 2009–10	PY 2008–10
NV	87	117	306	WY	433	144	1200
MT	13	231	275	MT	35	512	727
OR	214	11	248	DC	300	95	681
VI	242	−14	194	NV	166	114	471
RI	139	18	181	MN	317	29	436
CA	75	58	177	FL	120	110	362
MA	48	84	172	DE	143	88	359
MN	128	13	157	CA	159	60	316
MO	45	72	150	SD	204	27	286
WY	83	17	114	RI	269	2	276
VA	32	51	100	AZ	157	38	255
NM	232	−40	99	MO	79	95	249
MI	151	−22	96	OR	206	10	236
GA	48	29	92	NC	207	7	228
DC	78	8	91	WI	89	55	193
IL	107	−9	89	UT	194	−4	183
IN	45	28	87	KY	81	55	181
WI	54	20	84	ID	119	28	181
NC	105	−12	81	ME	92	37	162
WA	34	26	69	GA	36	79	143
ME	29	26	63	TN	66	46	142
NY	92	−16	62	VI	161	−8	139
AL	66	−3	61	IL	111	12	137
NJ	34	15	55	VA	48	60	137
AZ	46	6	54	CT	9	116	135
VT	139	−36	52	IN	67	39	133
ND	42	6	51	AL	103	15	133
PA	20	24	49	PA	67	38	131
AR	64	−16	38	WA	66	36	127
KY	39	−7	29	NE	112	5	123
ID	44	−12	27	CO	34	67	122

Table 3.5 (continued)

	% change in WIA Adult exiters enrolled in training				% change in WIA DW exiters enrolled in training		
State	PY 2008–09	PY 2009–10	PY 2008–10	State	PY 2008–09	PY 2009–10	PY 2008–10
OK	61	−26	19	ND	104	7	118
IA	17	−2	14	MI	78	18	111
SD	−11	27	13	AR	79	15	106
WV	27	−11	13	TX	52	35	105
SC	26	−13	10	NY	138	−15	103
UT	24	−12	9	NJ	65	17	93
NE	30	−17	7	MA	70	13	93
CO	8	−2	6	NM	21	49	81
CT	−25	41	5	IA	58	12	78
LA	46	−28	5	OH	83	−4	75
TX	−1	4	3	NH	63	−1	62
KS	8	−6	1	PR	81	−18	49
NH	31	−26	−3	WV	54	−11	37
FL	3	−7	−4	MD	102	−33	36
TN	−6	1	−5	SC	39	−8	28
OH	26	−25	−5	VT	130	−48	19
MD	32	−32	−10	KS	−34	71	13
AK	23	−28	−11	AK	53	−30	8
PR	−30	26	−12	OK	46	−26	7
DE	−4	−11	−14	LA	44	−35	−7
HI	−4	−16	−19	HI	47	−46	−21
MS	15	−48	−40	MS	38	−67	−55
Total	39	0	40	Total	88	21	127

SOURCE: Data are from the USDOL's Public Workforce System Dataset and have been assembled and analyzed by the Upjohn Institute.

the availability of training for up to two years under Michigan's No Worker Left Behind initiative). Some MWAs had to institute waiting lists for training under the regular (formula) WIA Adult and Dislocated Worker programs as early as the first or second quarters of their program years the year after ARRA funding had been exhausted. The state indicated that all of those who had entered longer-term training with ARRA funding had been able to complete training (often with regular formula funding if ARRA funding had been exhausted during the second year). However, among those who had originally entered training with ARRA funding, sustaining some of them with regular formula funding meant that there was less available formula funding to pay for new WIA participants during the program year following exhaustion of ARRA funding (and therefore the need to institute waiting lists in some MWAs). So while there is little doubt that ARRA funding promoted the entry of many more into training than would have been the case without ARRA funding, it has been impossible for MWAs to sustain the levels of training established under ARRA.

- **Ohio.** Beginning in July 2010, when WIA funding under ARRA had been fully spent, some local workforce areas within the state implemented waiting lists. Some of these local workforce areas have continued to keep such waiting lists in effect over much of the time since ARRA funding was exhausted. There were simply not enough funds available to meet the demand for training. Some local areas had to use regular WIA formula funding to support those who had initially been funded using ARRA dollars and had not completed training by the time ARRA funding was exhausted. Overall, ARRA funding provided added resources to put substantial numbers of WIA Adults and Dislocated Workers through training, but when it was exhausted local workforce agencies reverted back to pre-ARRA training levels and even below those levels. The state expects a substantial decrease in the number of new enrollments in training in the coming year, as well as a reduction in the length of training.

- **Wisconsin.** ARRA funding was largely expended during the first year in which it was available. With ARRA funding depleted, some LWIBs found they were short on funding to cover training expenses for those already in training. This problem of running out of funds to sustain individuals in training once they were midway through training was somewhat alleviated for Dislocated Workers by the availability of additional National Emergency Grant (NEG) funding distributed to LWIBs in the state. Officials at the state and local areas visited indicated that despite the availability of NEG funding, some customers were at least temporarily unable to take additional courses to complete their degree or certification along their career pathway. Additionally, once ARRA funding was exhausted, some LWIBs had to institute waiting lists for new WIA Adults and Dislocated Workers who were eligible for and interested in entering training.

The NASWA survey results suggested that Recovery Act funding had been used to provide a variety of types of training, with a particular emphasis on using ITAs to provide classroom training. For example, survey results indicated that states had used Recovery Act funds to provide the following types of training under the WIA Adult program (with similar percentages reported for the WIA Dislocated Worker program): ITAs (95 percent of states), contracts with community or technical colleges (69 percent), on-the-job training (67 percent), registered apprenticeships (49 percent), contracts with community-based organizations (31 percent), customized training (31 percent), and contracts with four-year institutions (15 percent).

Generally, the site visits confirmed the findings of the NASWA study with respect to the types of training being provided and suggested that some states were using Recovery Act funds to emphasize (and expand) the use of certain types of training, including OJT and customized training. Table 3.6 provides several illustrations of the ways in which states used Recovery Act funds for training. States indicated that Recovery Act funding was used in most instances to support the same types of training—particularly ITAs for classroom training—at similar training institutions (selected from the state's eligible list of providers) as were being used under the regular (formula) WIA Adult and Dislocated Worker programs. It should also be noted that some states used Recovery Act funds to expand training opportunities—particularly with respect to providing increased OJT, customized training, or sectoral initiatives (for example, see Florida and Wisconsin in Table 3.6).

Table 3.6 Examples of State Approaches to Using Recovery Act Funding to Support Training Activities

State	Various state approaches to use of Recovery Act funds to support training
Arizona	Arizona used the same Eligible Training Provider List (ETPL) for both Recovery Act and formula WIA funding. State workforce staff held a training conference to help establish new relationships between the local workforce area staff and training providers on the ETPL. The intent was to improve connections between the workforce system and local training providers, with the ultimate goal of fostering more training approvals in some local areas. Targeted, shorter-term training, built upon the knowledge and skills of participants and leading to professional certifications for high-demand and emerging occupations, became more prevalent during and after receipt of ARRA funding.
Colorado	As a result of ARRA funding, the number as well as the percentage of participants in training statewide increased, both for the WIA Adult and Dislocated Worker programs. The ARRA funding has been mostly spent on ITAs, mostly for short-term training conducted at community colleges and proprietary schools. While there were no substantial changes to the types of training provided, there was an increase in the number trained as a result of additional ARRA funds and the state requirement that a higher percentage of ARRA funds than of regular formula funds be spent for training. With ARRA funding, there was some increase in both customized training and OJT (though OJT still remains a small portion of overall training provided); there was also an increased emphasis on green jobs and sector-based training.
Florida	The majority of ARRA training funds were used for ITAs, and the number of ITAs increased substantially because of Recovery Act funding. There was a push to train in green jobs occupations, emphasized by the DOL; most boards tried to reflect this, and they worked with local colleges and tech centers to implement it. A critical challenge for local workforce agencies was what to do at the end of training when there were few jobs available into which to place trainees. The majority of training with ARRA funding was in the health field (as had been the case with formula funding prior to ARRA), where jobs were projected to be available.
Illinois	Illinois reported a dramatic increase between 2007 and 2009 in the overall percentage of WIA funds spent on training. Illinois used Recovery Act funds to support all of its training services and placed special emphasis on class-size training contracts to increase the capacity of training institutions to provide sector-based training for customers. Additionally, to the extent possible, Recovery Act funding was used to prepare low-education/low-skill customers for degree/certification-based training programs by bridging the gap between their current knowledge base and the expectations and requirements necessary to enter a degree/certification training program. ARRA funding was also used to fund training for incumbent workers (i.e., training aimed at keeping people in jobs and advancing their careers).

Michigan	Most ARRA funding was expended on ITAs, which was the case prior to receipt of ARRA funds. The state also used ARRA funding to establish the "No Worker Left Behind (NWLB) Green Jobs Initiative." The goal of this ARRA-funded initiative was to focus on high demand/high growth occupations with an emphasis on green jobs. The NWLB Green Jobs Initiative increased access to training opportunities in a variety of renewable energy and energy efficiency programs focused on alternative energy production and efficiency, green building construction and retrofitting, and organic agriculture and natural resource conservation.
Ohio	State officials indicated that there were no changes in the types of training provided due to Recovery Act funding. There was continued emphasis on providing ITAs, as well as other types of training. The caps on ITAs (which are the same for Recovery Act and regular formula funding) are set by LWIBs and ranged from $5,000 to $20,000, with an average of $13,000. The data show little change in the number of WIA adults receiving training as a result of ARRA but a decrease in the percentage of adults trained. Beginning in July 2010, when ARRA funding was exhausted, some local workforce areas began to implement waiting lists for entry into WIA-sponsored training. ARRA laid the groundwork for implementing the governor's new policy to increase direct placements and reliance on OJT. With ARRA funding, the state was able to fund Project HIRE, which established links with companies interested in sponsoring OJT and in funding this OJT.
Wisconsin	The Recovery Act funding was mostly spent on ITAs, though there was also a push by local areas to use Recovery Act funding to sponsor classroom-size training programs. This was in part because there was an onslaught of unemployed individuals that sought out training at the state's technical colleges and community colleges—creating waiting lists for entry into some training programs. In addition, classroom-size training has the advantage of not needing to be timed to semester start dates/end dates (but rather to when a group of individuals can be assembled to begin a class) and offers the possibility of shortening training periods and tailoring curricula to the needs of employers and workers. It also provides an opportunity to build in remedial education or contextual learning to a curriculum tailored to the needs of the class.

SOURCE: Table is based on site visits conducted in states between December 2009 and April 2012.

LINKS TO APPRENTICESHIP

One training strategy suggested by the USDOL in TEGL 14-08 was for states and LWIAs to use Recovery Act funding for establishing new linkages and to expand existing linkages between WIA and registered apprenticeship programs. The site visits indicated that the availability of Recovery Act funding had little or no effect in terms of fostering new linkages between WIA and registered apprenticeship programs. Three-quarters of the 20 states visited indicated that the state had not established new apprenticeship linkages as a result of Recovery Act funding. A number of state workforce agencies indicated that, while they had tried to establish or expand linkages with apprenticeship programs, such efforts in the face of the recession proved to be largely fruitless. An important factor underlying the difficulties in increasing ties to apprenticeship was the poor labor market conditions in the construction sector, which traditionally has accounted for a large share of apprenticeship opportunities. Although most states visited were unable to expand linkages with apprenticeship programs, several states reported some success with regard to initiating new linkages with apprenticeship programs and indicated that when economic growth returned (especially within the construction sector) it was likely that there would be interest in increasing slots available in apprenticeship programs:

- **Arizona.** Although there has been scant construction-related apprenticeship, Arizona has experienced some expansion of registered apprenticeship in regional projects and urban areas since the receipt of ARRA funding. For example, Phoenix has seen a slight rise in precision manufacturing (related to aerospace) and sustainable energy-based occupations. Pima County bundled a $40,000 matched grant with the IBEW to develop a photovoltaic technology curriculum that may be linked to apprenticeship opportunities in the future.

- **Michigan.** In an effort to prepare Michigan's female, minority, and economically disadvantaged workforce for apprenticeship positions, weatherization projects, and other green construction jobs, Michigan launched the Energy Conservation Apprenticeship Readiness (ECAR) program in June 2009 with

ARRA funds. ECAR was based on an earlier preapprenticeship initiative—the Road Construction Apprenticeship Readiness (RCAR) program (an initiative providing tuition-paid, fast-track customized training in job-readiness skills, applied math, computers, blueprint reading, workplace safety, and an overview of the construction trades). In addition to the 240-hour RCAR program curriculum, the ECAR program included a 32-hour energy conservation awareness component. This component included curricula and training on lead, asbestos, and confined space awareness; mold remediation and safe working practices; principles of thermal insulation, geothermal, and solar energy; and principals of green construction. Similar to RCAR, ECAR offered supportive services, placement assistance, and completion certificates.

- **Ohio.** The availability of Recovery Act funding has had little or no effect on linkages with registered apprenticeship programs to date (though such links existed prior to the Recovery Act). However, a portion of the governor's 15 percent discretionary Recovery Act funds was used to fund a preapprenticeship program for youth, an initiative called "Constructing Futures." The goal of the Constructing Futures initiative was to train Ohioans of historically underrepresented populations in the building trades so that they might excel in a career in construction, ultimately leading to a family-sustaining wage and occupation. The state used $3.2 million from statewide Recovery Act workforce funds to award grants to provide preapprenticeship training. Funded programs were required to help trainees attain careers in construction occupations by preparing them to enroll and succeed in registered apprenticeship programs in those occupations. A request for proposals was released statewide to workforce investment boards (allowing for two or more workforce boards to apply together). Grant awards ranged from $400,000 to $1 million and were given to four organizations from Cincinnati, Columbus, and Toledo, with programs running from January 2010 to June 30, 2011. Eligible activities for grant funds include outreach to targeted populations, supportive services (including both before and during apprenticeship), basic literacy and GED attainment through University System of Ohio institutions, training stipends for preapprentices while in the classroom, and eligible tools and equipment.

PELL GRANT USAGE AND ISSUES

Under the Recovery Act, to maximize the reach of WIA Adult formula funds, local workforce agencies were to help eligible customers take advantage of the significant increase in Pell Grant funds also authorized by the Recovery Act. Also, subsequent to passage of the Recovery Act, the ETA sent guidance to states (USDOL 2009), encouraging them to notify UI beneficiaries of their potential eligibility for Pell Grants by letter and to broaden their definition of "approved training" for UI beneficiaries during economic downturns. (UI beneficiaries can continue to receive UI benefits while in training if the training is considered "approved training" under state laws and policies.)

As part of a NASWA 50-state survey (NASWA 2010) conducted after the ETA issued its guidance, state workforce agencies were asked about their experiences with respect to sending out a "model" letter (developed by the USDOL) to UI claimants to inform them about the Pell Grant program and to explain that they could continue to receive UI benefits while in training, with the state's approval. They also were asked about changes to USDOL policies on approved training for UI. Key findings from the survey include the following:

- Thirty-nine of 49 states (80 percent) reported sending Pell Grant letters to claimants. One additional state was about to send out letters, and four other states wrote that they had provided the information in a different format. Of the remaining five states, one state reported current workloads prohibited sending the letter, three reported current UI policies on degree-track programs were inconsistent with the Pell Grant initiative, and one reported that an insolvent trust fund prohibited a benefit expansion. Few states measured response rates, but roughly 10 states reported a heavy response.

- The types of actions states took to implement the initiative included the following: partnering with higher education to provide workshops; bringing in community college personnel to give staff and customers a better understanding of the Pell Grant process; hosting a special phone line to answer general questions regarding school attendance and UI; hosting a designated training session for local UI staff; contracting with a nonprofit to provide workshops, Pell Grants, and financial aid through the career One-Stops; and mailing letters at different stages.

- States also provided some feedback about the "model letter" provided by the USDOL to assist states in informing UI claimants about Pell Grants, including the following: suggestions to craft the letter to make it clear that no additional UI benefits would be received as a result of training and no financial aid was guaranteed as a result of the letter, suggestions that the letter was too general and did not include enough substance, and suggestions to stagger mailings.

- Forty percent of the states reported expanding the definition of "approved training" through law or interpretation since the Recovery Act.

Overall, during our site visits, states reported little change in policy or use of Pell Grants as a direct result of the Recovery Act, mostly because local workforce areas were already working under requirements that they make WIA training participants aware of and help them apply for Pell Grants. Similar to the findings of NASWA's state survey, during site visits some states indicated that they had experienced problems with the lack of clarity and substance in the model letter they distributed to UI claimants informing them about Pell Grants (see below).

Before the Recovery Act, several state workforce officials observed, the WIA program had a requirement that WIA participants enrolling in training apply for Pell Grants and use such grants first to pay for training expenses. Under WIA statutory requirements, the WIA program is to be the last payer for training after Pell Grants and other forms of student assistance. Workforce agency officials noted that while LWIA program staff notifies WIA participants of the need to apply for Pell Grants (if they are attending programs that are qualified to receive such grants), they do not usually get involved in the application for or the processing of Pell Grants. In some One-Stop centers visited as part of this study, community college staff was outstationed full-time or part-time to the One-Stop center, which facilitated WIA participants' application both to the community college and for Pell Grants. Local workforce agency officials indicated they typically were apprised of the results of Pell Grant applications by schools after a grant decision had been made. When the educational institution reported back on whether an individual had received a Pell Grant and the amount of the grant, the tuition portion of the Pell Grant was offset against the amount of tuition paid by the WIA program. From the perspective of local workforce agencies, the receipt of Pell Grants helps to spread what are often limited WIA funds so that it is possible to serve more WIA participants than would otherwise be the case. Several examples of state workforce agency experiences with Pell Grants are provided in the examples below:

- **Colorado.** Local workforce agencies experienced an increase in requests for information regarding Pell Grants as a result of the Pell Grant letters sent to UI claimants. While local workforce centers work in partnership with community colleges on Pell Grants, the community colleges are more likely to provide assistance on Pell Grant application than are workforce centers.

- **Illinois.** Coordination with Pell Grants takes place on a case-by-case basis, between individual LWIBs, WIA participants, and institutions of higher education. Where possible, the workforce agency generally aims at using WIA resources for tuition, and Pell Grants to cover living expenses. The DOL letter to UI claimants notifying them of their Pell eligibility generated some initial perplexity: despite attempts at state-level coordination, there was some confusion on the part of LWIB staff and frustration on the part of claimants who thought they were entitled to a specific cash benefit based on their reading of the letter.

- **Michigan.** Before ARRA, the WIA program already had a mandate that WIA participants must apply for Pell Grants and use such grants first to pay for training expenses. WIA funds are to be used as a last resort to pay for training (i.e., after Pell Grants and other sources). The WIA programs (and local workforce development agencies) are closely linked with community colleges, M-Techs, and other educational institutions. Many local

One-Stop centers have community college representatives co-located at the center and at the college—these representatives conduct recruitment of WIA customers (and other One-Stop customers) into their schools and can help customers prepare applications for enrollment and Pell Grants right at the One-Stop centers.

- **Montana.** Pell Grants have been widely used in combination with WIA funds to cover both tuition (for which the preference is to use WIA) and living expenses (using Pell Grants) for participants. According to one workforce agency official, "We try to use WIA for tuition so they can use Pell for living expenses. It's much more expensive for us to use needs-related payments for living expenses. We like for them to use Pell."

- **New York.** One-Stop customers are routinely provided information about how and where to apply for Pell Grants. Counselors in One-Stop centers identify Pell Grants as a source of educational assistance for qualifying postsecondary education programs and include Pell Grants in an individual's training plan for approval. In addition, UI customers have been mailed letters encouraging them to consider training and highlighting the recent changes regarding Pell Grant eligibility.

- **Ohio.** The process of applying for Pell Grants is largely under the purview of the educational institutions individuals attend, so local workforce areas do not usually get that involved in the process. Community colleges outstation staff to comprehensive One-Stop Career Centers in the state; this approach facilitates application both to training programs held at community colleges and for Pell Grants.

Finally, regarding Pell Grants, several states visited indicated they had encountered some difficulties with respect to the model letter developed by the ETA (and sent to states for dissemination). This letter was intended to notify UI claimants of the availability of increased Pell Grant funds and new rules pertaining to dislocated workers that provide for a potential reconsideration of income (i.e., providing for a "look forward" rather than a "look back" at earnings, which could potentially help dislocated workers qualify for Pell Grants). According to one state agency, when the letter was distributed to UI claimants, some UI claimants experienced confusion and difficulties. Some dislocated workers called UI offices to inquire about the possibility of obtaining Pell Grants to offset costs for education or training they were currently enrolled in—which gave rise to questions about being "ready and available" for work. This, in turn, set in motion reconsideration of UI benefits for some claimants and the eventual loss of UI benefits (and the need to repay benefits that had been paid out to the claimant). Several state agencies indicated that before sending this letter out they made some relatively minor modifications to clarify language and make sure claimants fully understood Pell Grant changes.

RELATIONSHIPS WITH INSTITUTIONS OF HIGHER EDUCATION

Under the Recovery Act, to increase state, regional, and local training capacity, states were given the authority to enter into contracts with institutions of higher education, such as community colleges, to facilitate training in high-demand occupations, so long as the contract did not limit customer choice. About half of the 20 states visited indicated that they had awarded additional contracts to institutions of higher learning since receipt of Recovery Act funding. For example, an official with the Seattle–King County Workforce Development Council (WDC) noted that the contracted classroom training "has been the most exciting, frustrating, and likely most impactful aspect of the Recovery Act. This was a real change to the system." In addition, the Washington State Legislature provided an incentive for the use of Recovery Act funds for class-size training by awarding WDCs 75 cents for every Recovery Act dollar spent on this type of training.

For the most part, state and local workforce agencies indicated that relationships with institutions of higher education were well established prior to the Recovery Act. Because local workforce agencies issue ITAs to WIA participants for coursework at these institutions, the primary linkages with institutions of higher learning occurred at the local level. Several states used Recovery Act funding to create customized, class-size training programs at community colleges or technical schools, which featured more flexible scheduling (i.e., not always tied to a semester or term schedule) and careful tailoring of the curriculum to the needs of employers in high-growth industry sectors. Such class-size programs generally led to some form of certification. Table 3.7 provides examples of how linkages between WIA programs and institutions of higher education have been affected by the availability of Recovery Act funds, including several examples of training initiatives undertaken in collaboration with educational institutions.

TARGETING LOW-INCOME INDIVIDUALS

Under the Recovery Act, priority use of WIA Adult funds must be for services to recipients of public assistance and other low-income individuals. States are particularly encouraged to provide training opportunities to these individuals. The NASWA state survey found that the vast majority of states reported that recipients of public assistance and other low-income individuals receive priority of service for WIA Adult services, including training. The visits to states and LWIAs confirmed this survey finding. During interviews with state and local workforce agencies, officials in nearly every office indicated that the Recovery Act did not usher in much of a change with regard to providing services for low-income individuals because there had always been an emphasis on giving priority to providing service for low-income individuals within the WIA Adult program.

State workforce agencies passed along Recovery Act requirements for providing priority to low-income individuals and requested that local plans reflect this priority. States typically left it up to local areas to set their own specific policies with regard to when priority of service requirements for low-income individuals came into effect. However, some states were more prescriptive about such policies. For example, in Illinois, before the Recovery Act, the state required that 51 percent of WIA funds be spent on low-income individuals. With the Recovery Act, Illinois issued a state policy requiring local areas specifically to include plans to address the workforce training and placement needs of low-income, low-skilled, and other target populations (Illinois Department of Commerce and Economic Opportunity 2009). Several other states had state policies that were explicit about providing services to low-

Table 3.7 Examples of Approaches of WIA Programs to Linking with Institutions of Higher Education

State	Various approaches to linking with institutions of higher learning
Arizona	Pima County and the Phoenix WIBS strengthened connections with community colleges, using both bundled ITAs and cohort training. Co-located and itinerant staff, as well as cross-site location of orientations and workshops, were part of service delivery practices. Pima County leveraged the community college to adopt contextual learning in its adult and developmental education classes.
Colorado	The relationship between the state's community colleges and the workforce system predated the Recovery Act, and there was no real change in linkages as a result of the Recovery Act. The state issued sector-based training grants using some Recovery Act funding. A $1.1 million sector training request for proposal (RFP) was issued, under which the training provided had to be in high-growth industry sectors and the curriculum used had to be industry-driven. Recovery Act funding was also used to provide scholarships for distance learning—payments of up to $3,000 per class were made for training that was provided remotely (via the Internet) and led to industry-approved certification in (for example) nursing and various IT occupations.
Illinois	Illinois state workforce staff reported strong relationships with institutions of higher education, especially around their sector-based efforts. With the Recovery Act, some local areas entered into class-size training contracts.
Maine	Maine attempted to use the bulk of its ARRA resources to purchase class-size training at community colleges in four key sectors: 1) health care (nursing in particular), 2) energy, 3) green energy/weatherization, and 4) information technology.
Montana	At the state level, Montana made no special arrangements with training providers or other institutions of higher learning to increase their offerings or class sizes. At the local level, the Helena Center for Technology offered a 50 percent reduction in tuition for dislocated workers on a seat-available basis. In Kalispell, Flathead Valley Community College increased both its class offerings and its class sizes. It also began a special welding track in conjunction with Stinger Welding in Libby, Montana, where an expected 250 jobs were to open up.

Ohio	The relationship between the state's community colleges and the workforce system predated the Recovery Act and remained strong. Community colleges were particularly involved in providing ITA-funded training and also were part of several special training initiatives funded with Recovery Act funds, including Project Hometown Investment in Regional Economies (Project HIRE). Project HIRE provides job-matching strategies linking employers and job seekers. Project HIRE includes hiring fairs and other outreach activities aimed at bringing employers and dislocated workers together. State and local workforce investment specialists coordinate Project HIRE events and activities.
Rhode Island	The state had started to increase coordination with community colleges before the Recovery Act, but that has now increased substantially, including an increase in contextual training programs using some Recovery Act money. The state used WIA Recovery Act state set-aside funds, issued one RFP, and the local WIBs divvied up the contractors. The RFP produced some of the same vendors, but the vendor list has expanded greatly and the programs are different, in that they are targeted to low-skilled workers. The state also used Recovery Act funds for 1,600 youth in a pilot career tech at five schools for middle-school-age youth at risk of dropping out, to expose them to a nontraditional school environment and contextual learning and to help connect them to vocational areas in which they could develop an interest.
Washington	The state legislature wanted to emphasize the importance of training, enacting the Washington State Engrossed Second Senate Substitute Bill (E2SSB) 5809, which set aside $7 million in general revenue funds to provide incentives for local councils to use Recovery Act funds for training. For every $1 a council invested in cohort training, it leveraged $0.75 from the state. For every $1 invested in an ITA, the council leveraged $0.25 from the state. After the legislature established this seed money, the governor also used Recovery Act funds to make an additional $5.5 million available for training incentives. This created intense interest in training across the state. The Recovery Act had a particular impact on the system's relationship with the community colleges because of the implementation of "cohort training." Prior to the Recovery Act, the biggest area of coordination with the community colleges was for incumbent worker training. Across the state, there have been over 100 cohort classes offered in a variety of industries—health care, business administration, information technology, manufacturing/construction, energy/green energy, and forestry—any of which can use the I-BEST model (Integrated Basic Education and Skills Training Program), which contextualizes basic and occupational skills.

SOURCE: Table is based on site visits conducted in states between December 2009 and April 2012.

income individuals but differed from the Illinois policy—for example, in North Dakota, once 70 percent of WIA Adult funds are obligated, the remaining funds must be used for providing services to low-income individuals.

In most states visited, the specific policies on serving low-income individuals were left to local workforce areas to determine. Even before the Recovery Act, local workforce areas already had such policies in place, which usually established priority for low-income individuals when funding became "limited" under the WIA Adult program for intensive and training services. Most state and local workforce officials indicated that such policies changed little or not at all in response to the Recovery Act, though in some states more funding became available, which allowed for providing WIA-funded services targeted to more low-income individuals. Several state and local workforce officials noted that co-locating TANF and Supplemental Nutrition Assistance Program (SNAP) employment and training programs at One-Stops made a difference in terms of facilitating and expanding enrollment of low-income individuals into the WIA Adult program.[5]

Overall, as reflected in Table 3.8, state workforce agencies viewed the Recovery Act as not leading to many changes in policies or practices at the state or local workforce levels related to serving low-income individuals—WIA Adult programs already were targeted to and serving substantial numbers of low-income individuals. One exception was Montana, which raised the income cutoff for being considered low-income to 100 percent of the state's self-sufficiency standard to assure that the state could spend its WIA funds.

SUPPORTIVE SERVICES AND NEEDS-RELATED PAYMENTS

The Recovery Act emphasizes the authority to use the funds for supportive services and needs-related payments to ensure participants have the means to pay living expenses while receiving training. Supportive services include transportation, child care, dependent care, housing, and other services. For individuals who are unable to obtain such services from other programs, this provision enables them to participate in activities authorized under WIA. Needs-related payments may be provided to adults who are unemployed and do not qualify for or have ceased to qualify for unemployment compensation, for the purpose of enabling such individuals to participate in training. LWIAs can take advantage of the availability of these payments so that customers can pursue their career goals, rather than allowing their short-term income needs to determine the length of their training.

In the NASWA survey, many states reported moderate (up to 10 percent) or substantial (10 percent or more) increases in WIA-related spending on supportive services since the Recovery Act on the following types of services: transportation (81 percent of states reported a moderate or substantial increase in expenditures), child care (81 percent), housing (39 percent), dependent care (36 percent), and other services necessary for participation (78 percent). In comparison to supportive services, far fewer states provided needs-related payments (45 percent) before the Recovery Act. According to this survey, slightly fewer than half the states reported having increased their funding moderately or substantially under the WIA program for needs-related payments (45 percent of states for the WIA Adult Program and 47 percent for the WIA Dislocated Worker Program).

Site visits to states indicated that states and local workforce areas had made few changes in policies with respect to supportive services or needs-related payments in response to the Recovery Act. Only three of the 20 states visited indicated they had made some changes with regard to supportive services, while five of the 20 states had made changes with regard to needs-related payments since receipt of Recovery Act funding. Even in cases where changes to supportive assistance or needs-related payments had been made, they may have not been made in direct response to the Recovery Act, or they may have been initiated by only some local workforce areas within the state. Table 3.9 provides several illustrations of the varying policies with regard to supportive services and needs-related payments across the states visited as part of this study. Anecdotal evidence from the site visits suggests that in some states, because of an increase in the number of participants flowing through One-Stop Career Centers and the WIA program (as a result of the recession and the availability of Recovery Act funding) there was at least a modest increase in expenditures on supportive services. State and local workforce agencies indicated that amounts spent on supportive services and needs-related payments, both before and since receipt,

Table 3.8 Examples of State Approaches to Targeting WIA Adult Services to Low-Income Individuals

State	Various state approaches to serving low-income individuals
Arizona	In Arizona, local areas determine the emphasis on services to low-income individuals. In those areas where the TANF Employment and Training Program is co-located in the One-Stop center, there is a higher emphasis on serving low-income customers. Local plan modification guidelines required boards to declare either limited or unlimited funding status. With limited funding, boards are required to focus on and provide priority to low-income individuals, while with unlimited funding boards have more service flexibility. WIA contracting practices in Phoenix (WIA services with CBOs) and Pima County (contracting WIA staff positions with CBOs; integration within local services continuum) help assure significant service provision to low-income as well as hard-to-serve populations.
Colorado	TANF employment and training services are often provided out of One-Stop centers, and as a result, TANF recipients have relatively easy access to WIA-funded services. The WIA Adult program, which has always served low-income individuals, issued no new policy guidance in response to ARRA. ARRA's TANF emergency funding brought subsidized employment and OJT to low-income households across Colorado through the HIRE Colorado project.
Florida	Recovery Act funds gave priority to low-income individuals and welfare recipients, and the regions were specifically notified of that. Otherwise, there were no target goals for serving low-income individuals. Florida has a federal waiver that allows WIA staff (versus human services agency staff) to provide services to SNAP recipients and TANF recipients, including eligibility determination and application for additional programs.
Illinois	Prior to the recession and the Recovery Act, Illinois required that 51 percent of WIA funds be spent on low-income individuals. With the Recovery Act, Illinois issued a state policy requiring that local areas specifically include plans to address the workforce training and placement needs of low-income, low-skilled, and other target populations. In addition to public assistance recipients, including those receiving benefits from TANF, the Food Stamp Act of 1977, and the Social Security Act, other low-income individuals who are targeted include those classified as homeless or as foster children, and individuals with disabilities who meet income requirements.
Michigan	According to state administrators, ARRA funding had no effect on the extent to which WIA resources have been targeted to low-income populations in the state. The state, which has always targeted WIA resources to low-income populations, made no policy changes related to serving low-income populations as a result of ARRA and saw no change in the

proportion of low-income individuals served. ARRA provided additional resources to serve WIA-eligible individuals, so there was an increase in the overall numbers enrolled in WIA, but the percentage of low-income recipients did not change as a result of ARRA.

Montana

Prior to the recession, Montana had prioritized WIA Adult services to those customers who fell below 80 percent of Montana's self-sufficiency standard. With the Recovery Act, Montana raised this threshold to 100 percent of the self-sufficiency standard to make more people eligible for training. Montana set up a separate program that it called the WIA Adult Recovery Act program and its regular Adult and Dislocated Worker programs to carry customers through training and supportive services once the Recovery Act had ended.

New York

Since 2008, the provision of services to low-income workers has been a priority for New York; therefore, the implementation of the Recovery Act did not change that priority, although the additional funding resources allowed the state to expand those opportunities. The state was already actively engaged in assisting this group through the WIA Adult program and through a variety of state-sponsored initiatives like the Weatherization Assistance Program, funded through the state Office of Temporary and Disability Assistance (OTDA), and the Emerging and Transitional Worker Training Program. Low-income workers are targeted in most of the other economic development training programs supported by state and federal grants.

Ohio

There has been no change with respect to providing services to low-income individuals in the WIA Adult program. There is a "limited funds policy" whereby after local areas hit a certain percentage of expenditure of WIA Adult funds, low-income individuals have priority for training and intensive services. There is a strong commitment to targeting training to low-income adults and youth; for example, one program implemented with Recovery Act funding is the Urban Youth Works program. The state workforce agency awarded $6.7 million of Recovery Act funding to urban youth programs as part of the Urban Youth Works competitive grant program. The grant addressed the needs of urban youth to successfully participate in education and training programs that lead to a self-sufficient wage and occupation based on labor market demand. Grantees included 15 organizations, two local workforce investment areas, and one state agency. TANF Emergency funding was used for Summer Youth employment in certain local areas. (About half of the counties in the state used TANF Emergency Funding to support Summer Youth Employment Programs in the summer of 2010.)

SOURCE: Table is based on site visits conducted in states between December 2009 and April 2012.

Table 3.9 Examples of State Approaches to Providing Supportive Services and Needs-Related Payments

State	Various approaches to supportive services and needs-related payments
Arizona	In Arizona, the array of supportive services prior to the Recovery Act included transportation and emergency assistance. Since the Recovery Act, housing and needs-related payments have been added to the options, though not all local areas are participating.
Colorado	Workforce regions have considerable autonomy with respect to setting policies and payments on support services, which can cover a fairly wide variety of supports necessary to find a job or stay in training (e.g., transportation, tools, work clothes, child care, etc.). In some cases local regions changed their supportive services caps but did not add supportive services, as they already were offering a wide variety. Some local regions planned for a higher level of supportive services expenditures when Recovery Act funds were available, but most did not. The state does not track these expenditures through its financial reporting system. However, based on local tracking, approximately 10 percent of local program funds are spent on supportive services in any given program year, and this percentage did not change with Recovery Act money. Both before and after the Recovery Act, there were and continue to be no expenditures made for needs-related payments. Workforce areas within the state have not used needs-related payments for at least 10 years.
Florida	There was no policy change with regard to supportive services or needs-related payments under the Recovery Act. The state encouraged regional directors to provide supportive services, but there was little response because the directors wanted to avoid such services becoming viewed as entitlements, and many were reluctant to set a precedent since after the Recovery Act they will not be able to afford generous services. The state discussed needs-related payments with local WIBs, but offering such payments is at local discretion and most have chosen not to provide needs-related payments, mainly because of limited funding.
Michigan	There has been no change since the Recovery Act in the types or amounts of WIA funds spent on support services. LWIBs within the state may cover any allowable support services, and what is covered is left to local workforce areas to decide. The state reported that there was no discernible change in expenditure patterns with regard to support services. The decision on whether to provide needs-related payments is also left to local workforce areas. Only a few local areas provide needs-related payments.
Montana	Montana has always allowed supportive service and needs-related payments but has not used them often, finding them too costly. With the extension in UI benefits during the recession, there has not been as strong a demand for such payments, though local One-Stops have issued them on an occasional case-by-case basis. There is no set cap to the amount of dollars a person might be able to draw down.

Nebraska	The State Recovery Act policy required that Needs-Related Payments (NRPs) "must be available to support the employment and training needs of these priority populations." The amount of payment was left to local discretion. None was provided in the greater Lincoln area; supportive services are deemed adequate for ongoing assistance. The remainder of the state has a $500 cap, but spokespersons indicated it was underutilized because the eligibility requirements were "too stiff"; participants had to be unemployed and ineligible for and not receiving UI, as established in the Federal Register citation 20 CFR 663.820 and state policy. Less than 1 percent of all WIA adults and dislocated workers who were served during the first five months of the calendar year 2010 received NRPs. NRPs were discontinued as of June 30, 2010.
Ohio	There has been no change since the Recovery Act in the types or amounts of WIA funds expended on support services. LWIBs provide the support services as appropriate, including transportation, work clothing, tools/equipment, and child care. Officials estimated that about 10 percent of WIA funding was spent on support services (compared to about 50 percent on training). Both before and after the Recovery Act, there were virtually no expenditures of WIA funding on needs-related payments within the state. The problem with needs-related payments is that they consume available funding quickly and, as a result, less is left to provide training and other services. Only one or two LWIBs in the state have ever provided needs-related payments.
Washington	Washington emphasized the need for local areas to leverage community support in addition to the federal and state resources available to provide wraparound services to customers. Most of the local programs have long-term relationships with community organizations and resources for supporting customers. The only new guidance as a result of the Recovery Act was to clarify the policy on needs-related payments; several areas are offering that service. Most LWIBs do not have the capacity to issue weekly checks; they are better set up to manage emergency payments.
Wisconsin	Within Wisconsin, there has been no change since the Recovery Act in the types or amounts of WIA funds expended on support services. LWIBs within the state spend only a very small proportion of their WIA allocation on support services such as transportation, child care, dependent care, and rent. Data are not tracked at the state level on expenditures for various categories of support services. Both before and after the Recovery Act, there were and continue to be no expenditures made for needs-related payments. Only one LWIB within the state has made provision for needs-based payments to WIA participants, but this LWIB has not had the available funds to make such payments. Sometimes Pell Grants that WIA participants receive cover needs-related expenses.

SOURCE: Table is based on site visits conducted in states between December 2009 and April 2012.

were a relatively small part of overall WIA expenditures (and represent only a fraction of the total amount expended on training and intensive services).

State agencies for the most part allowed local workforce agencies considerable discretion with respect to setting policies and procedures for supportive services and needs-related payments. For example, in terms of types of supportive services, local workforce agencies could to a large extent determine which supportive services were offered, under what circumstances such services would be provided and to whom, caps on such services, and overall amounts of funding that would be devoted to supportive services. State workforce agencies required local workforce areas to document in their local plans policies on providing supportive services and needs-related payments. In most states and local areas visited, most of the budget for supportive services covered expenses related to transportation, child care, clothing or tools, rent, and other emergency payments. Local workforce agencies also looked to One-Stop partners and other human service agencies where possible, asking them to pick up costs related to supportive services in order to be able to devote limited WIA funding primarily to provision of training.

Regarding needs-related payments, there was little evidence of change in policies or procedures at the state or local levels in response to the Recovery Act. State agencies made needs-related payments an option available to local workforce areas. In many of the states visited, because of limited WIA funding, local workforce areas elected not to offer needs-related payments, or, if they did make them available, they elected to spend very little on such payments. Some local workforce agency officials indicated that such payments could quickly dissipate available WIA funding and that there were clear trade-offs between providing training (and other intensive services) and making available needs-related payments to cover living expenses. Local workforce officials indicated that they mostly looked to other programs and partnering agencies to cover needs-related payments. For example, in some instances, individuals entering training had Pell Grants to cover living expenses, had remaining weeks of UI, or could obtain temporary assistance from TANF, SNAP, housing programs, or other human service programs.

Overall, with regard to both supportive services and needs-related payments, state and local workforce agencies changed little with respect to policies and the types or extent of assistance provided to WIA participants.

CHALLENGES

During the two rounds of site visits, state and local workforce agency officials were asked to discuss their major challenges with implementing the WIA provisions of the Recovery Act. As is discussed in this section, there were a number of challenges commonly identified across states and local workforce areas, including responding to Recovery Act reporting requirements and expending ARRA funding in a timely and effective manner. Table 3.10 provides several examples of implementation challenges faced by states with regard to WIA.

In adapting to WIA and other workforce programs targeted by Recovery Act funding, among the most commonly cited challenges was *dealing with the Recovery Act reporting requirements.*[6] State workforce agencies indicated that it was somewhat burdensome to set up new reports to meet Recovery Act reporting requirements (often with short notice) that were different from their regular reports in terms of schedule and, in some instances, content. The frequency of reporting—monthly rather than quarterly—also was viewed by some states as burdensome. For example, in Colorado, state officials observed that they had to scramble to set up a separate set of financial reports to meet Recovery Act requirements. This was because the timing for Recovery Act reporting was not the same as for reporting on other expenditures. The fiscal period for the state workforce agency cuts off 10 days after the end of the quarter. However, for Recovery Act fiscal reporting, the state had to develop an expenditure report for Recovery Act funds as of the last day of the month at quarter's end. In Nevada, state officials noted that reporting on jobs created and saved was essentially impossible, and that reporting on a monthly basis represented a shift from the traditional quarterly reporting system. North Dakota officials noted that the state often found itself operating Recovery Act–funded programs and activities before it knew what it would have to report on.

Second, *time issues* were frequently mentioned as a challenge with respect to expenditure of WIA funding. Some states felt intense pressure

Table 3.10 Examples of Challenges Faced by State and Local Workforce Areas in Implementing the WIA Recovery Act Provisions

State	Examples of various challenges to implementing WIA provisions of the Recovery Act
Colorado	• The state's Department of Labor had to scramble to set up a separate set of financial reports to meet ARRA requirements. This was because the timing for ARRA reporting was not the same as the state normally uses for reporting on other expenditures. The fiscal period for the state workforce agency cuts off usually 10 days after the end of the quarter. However, for ARRA fiscal reporting, the state had to develop an expenditure report for ARRA funds as of the last day of the month at quarter's end. This meant that the timing for producing the ARRA fiscal reports did not match with the timing the state normally uses for its regular reporting on other programs, such as the WIA program (i.e., the state gives local areas an extra 10 days to get fiscal information into the state computer after the end of the quarter and then closes the quarter). There was also not enough time to validate the data on the ARRA report, as is normally the case in the regular reporting system. In addition, it was burdensome for the state to report on ARRA expenditures by county and congressional district.
	• The state procurement process can be long and cumbersome. Trying to get funds out quickly and meet procurement requirements was in some cases a trial. Much of the money was allocated to local regions that did not have to deal with the procurement process.
	• The local workforce regions were trying to implement a program with little guidance from the federal level, and the state workforce agency did its best to fill in the gaps.
	• ARRA funding meant roughly a doubling of funds available under WIA, and one of the key challenges centered on timely spending of ARRA WIA-DW funding—in part because with the extensions to UI benefits, dislocated workers were not always eager to enter training.
Illinois	• The state and local workforce agencies faced difficulty in two areas: 1) maintaining the commitment and interest of clients who had completed training but still did not have a job and 2) predicting future demand for workers in the midst of a changing economy.
	• State and local workforce officials were concerned about what would happen once ARRA funds were expended, especially as the need for training and other workforce development services had not abated.
	• There were concerns with meeting WIA performance measures (especially in a challenging economy and with an emphasis on long-term training), and considerable confusion in how to report on jobs created or saved.

Michigan	• Reporting was a particular concern and burden—the state often found itself operating ARRA-funded programs and activities before it knew what it would have to report on for performance reporting. Additionally, the need to separately report on ARRA-funded activities (from regular formula-funded activities) was burdensome and, in the view of state administrators and staff, unnecessary.
	• Once WIA Recovery Act funding had been exhausted, Michigan still faced face economic headwinds (which included persistently high rates of unemployment and continuing job losses): there continued to be high demand for training slots, but there were fewer resources available compared to when Recovery Act funding was available.
	• Guidance provided by the ETA often lagged, forcing the state to make decisions about services, program operations, and reporting prior to receipt of guidance. Because of the tight timetable for spending ARRA WIA funding, the USDOL did not always have answers to questions that the state had. The state had to have ARRA funds obligated to local areas before the ETA issued guidance on ARRA.
Montana	• "We can help people be better prepared, have better résumés, get them to consider moving across or out of state . . . but we can't help much if the jobs aren't there," said one official.
	• "We're concerned about what happens come July 1, when we have folks currently enrolled in training and will have to carry them. [This] may mean we have to take fewer numbers at the front end," said another official.
	• Montana's WIA allocations dropped from $15 million in 2000 to $12 million in 2001 and then to about $6 million by 2008. The additional WIA dollars received through the Recovery Act (almost $6 million for Adults, Dislocated Workers, and Youth), when added to the annual allocation, just begin to approach earlier levels.
	• Reporting has been a challenge: there was initially a lack of clarity on definitions and what should be counted as a new job.
Nevada	• ETA guidance on reporting was delayed and IT staff at times strained to make system changes to meet ETA reporting deadlines. Data elements were not required, but then reports requested were based on these missing data elements.
	• There was pressure to spend funds on training when the economy was in such turmoil, but there was no assurance that jobs would be available at the end of training.
	• There was sometimes difficulty in convincing unemployed workers to enroll in training when they were still collecting UI.

(continued)

Table 3.10 (continued)

State	Examples of various challenges to implementing WIA provisions of the Recovery Act
New York	• Working with educational institutions to develop training programs that require accreditation or other intensive vetting is too lengthy a process to serve the immediate needs of customers and, thus, for direct engagement under the time-limited ARRA. The community college system is often not flexible enough to accommodate the immediate needs of the business community and the unemployed customer.
Ohio	• There was great pressure to spend ARRA funds quickly (but wisely), especially to get the Summer Youth Program up and running—not enough time for planning.
	• The state agency felt as though it were "under a microscope," said one official—there was lots of media and political attention paid to how Recovery funds were being expended.
Pennsylvania	• The reporting requirements under the ARRA were challenging because of the detail required and the changes USDOL made after reporting systems were implemented.
	• The implementation of the Summer Youth Program was a challenge, as the state had not operated this program since the JTPA years. Local workforce areas needed to start from scratch, and it took two months of intensive work to pull the Summer Youth Program together at the state and local levels.
Wisconsin	• An initial challenge for both the state and local workforce areas was that ARRA represented a sizable infusion of new funding and that the state and especially local areas had to ramp up services and spend ARRA resources over a relatively short period. It was necessary to ramp up services and serve more customers without making long-term commitments to hiring staff. There was a need to manage staff and expanded services (especially training offered under WIA), while recognizing that such ARRA-funded services would need to be ramped down soon.
	• For one-time funding, the reporting burden for ARRA has been considerable. With ARRA, there has been a strong emphasis on "transparency." The monthly reporting required under ARRA meant double reporting for the state—continued reporting on its regular funds and separate reporting on ARRA activities, accomplishments (e.g., job creation), and expenditures. In some instances, the ETA provided last-minute instructions on reporting requirements. Also, within the state, the TAA, Wagner-Peyser, and WIA programs are linked by a common data system, which means that reporting-requirement changes for one program have an impact on data collection and reporting for the other programs.

SOURCE: Table is based on site visits conducted in states between December 2009 and April 2012.

to quickly but prudently expend WIA funding. Several states mentioned that the need for very rapid start-up of the WIA Summer Youth Program presented a challenge because local workforce areas had not mounted such programs in many years and had to start from almost scratch in staffing and developing their programs. For example, in Pennsylvania, state workforce administrators noted that within the state, WIA Summer Youth Programs needed to be pulled together from scratch (as they had not had funding for such programs) in just two intensive months. In Wisconsin, an initial challenge for both the state and local workforce areas was that the WIA Recovery Act funding represented a sizable infusion of new resources. The state and especially local areas had to ramp up services and spend Recovery Act resources over a relatively short period, without making long-term commitments to hiring staff and maintaining expenditure levels. There was a need to manage staff and increases to services (especially training offered under WIA), while recognizing that these services would need to be ramped down in short order.

A third challenge with respect to WIA provisions under the Recovery Act was related to *funding issues*, including procurement issues and the fear of hitting a "funding cliff" once WIA Recovery Act funds were exhausted. The specific challenges identified varied among the states. One state (Colorado) said that its procurement requirements led to delays in spending some of its Recovery Act funds. The state's workforce officials observed that the state's procurement process can be long and cumbersome and that trying to get Recovery Act funds out quickly and meeting procurement requirements was at times difficult in the early stages of the Recovery Act. Two states (Colorado and Florida) stated that they experienced difficulties in spending Recovery Act funds because the ETA adjusted waivers regarding transfer of funds from the WIA Dislocated Worker Program to the Adult Program. Many of the states during both the initial and follow-up site visits expressed serious concerns about what would occur once the Recovery Act funds were spent. Some states mentioned that if customers were enrolled in long-term training, they might not be able to continue, so the following year's enrollment would drop dramatically. A common concern across states was that it was likely that demand for employment and training services under WIA would remain elevated after Recovery Act funding had been exhausted and that local workforce areas and One-Stop Career

Centers would not have sufficient WIA formula (Adult and Dislocated Worker) funding to meet demand for training and other workforce services. For example, in Michigan, a year after ARRA WIA funding had been fully expended, many MWAs across the state found they did not have the necessary funds to sustain training at the levels they were able to offer with Recovery Act funding. Some MWAs had to institute waiting lists for training under the regular (formula) WIA Adult and Dislocated Worker programs as early as the first or second quarters of their program years the year after ARRA funding had been exhausted.

Finally, many state and local workforce agency officials were challenged by *the slow pace of improvement in the economy*. Some workforce agencies worried about employment prospects for those completing WIA Adult and Dislocated Worker training, specifically whether they could find and retain a well-paying job within the field in which they were trained. For example, in Florida, the majority of ARRA training funds were used for ITAs, including a strong push to train in green jobs occupations—and local workforce agencies worried about what to do at the end of training when there were few jobs available into which to place trainees. In response to poor labor market conditions, local workforce areas focused training on industrial sectors—particularly the health care sector—where job formation continued during the recession and there were good prospects for growth in the future. Other local workforce areas worried that they would continue to be swamped with unemployed customers in search of training (and other workforce services), but that without the extra measure of Recovery Act funding they would lack the necessary resources to meet high levels of demand for training and other needed services.

ACCOMPLISHMENTS

During the two rounds of site visits, state and local workforce agency officials were asked to discuss their major accomplishments with regard to the WIA workforce provisions of the Recovery Act. As is discussed in this section, there were a number of accomplishments commonly identified across states and local areas, particularly with regard to mounting (or expanding) the WIA Summer Youth Program, enhancing training and other services, expanding the number of customers served, and improving information and reporting systems (Table 3.11).

States Administered the Summer Youth Program

The most prevalent major accomplishment in the states visited with respect to the expenditure of WIA ARRA funding was the successful development and administration of the WIA Summer Youth Program, identified by 17 of the 20 states visited as a key accomplishment.[7] Because Recovery Act funds were not available until March 2009 at the earliest, states had to act quickly to implement their Summer Youth Programs for the summer of 2009. Many states and localities had not operated Summer Youth Programs in recent years (or if they had, programs were operated on a small scale), so setting up a large program in a short period was considered a major accomplishment. Several states indicated that they had greatly expanded their Summer Youth Programs and that the programs had produced increases in work readiness and job skills. For example, Illinois workforce officials noted that 17,000 youth were served and that the program produced increases in work readiness and job skills. Workforce officials in Michigan observed that the program provided much-needed income for the youth and their families in a state with very high unemployment. And finally, Wisconsin workforce officials noted that they used the Summer Youth Program to promote green jobs and training—e.g., by initiating projects to eliminate invasive species in Wisconsin lakes and streams.[8]

States Trained More Adults and Dislocated Workers

Second, the Recovery Act added a substantial, though temporary, source of funding that enabled states and local areas to expand training slots available under their WIA Adult and Dislocated Worker programs. As discussed earlier, findings from the NASWA survey with respect to training include the following:

- Every state reported encouraging or requiring local areas to increase investments in WIA-funded training, with two-thirds of states reporting significant staff efforts to encourage training.

- About one-half of the states reported having set aside, or having required LWIAs to set aside, a certain percentage of WIA Recovery Act funds for training.

- Nearly three-quarters of states reported substantial increases in the number of customers enrolled in training through the WIA Adult and WIA Dislocated Worker programs.

The site visits to states confirmed these key findings. All state workforce agencies visited as part of this study indicated that they had encouraged (in their guidance, technical assistance, and discussions) local workforce areas within their state to use WIA Recovery Act funding specifically to support and expand training for unemployed and underemployed workers served under both the WIA Adult and Dislocated Worker programs. Some states went so far as to mandate that local workforce areas expend at least a minimum percentage of Recovery Act funds received (ranging to as high as 80 percent in states visited) on training or on training and supportive services (e.g., Maine, Montana, Nebraska, New York, Ohio, Texas, and Wisconsin). As discussed earlier (and as displayed in Tables 3.3–3.5), the number of individuals served increased fairly substantially immediately after Recovery Act funding became available to states and local workforce areas—for example, the number of WIA Adult exiters receiving training increased from 109,322 in PY 2008 (the year prior to expenditure of ARRA WIA funding) to 152,285 in PY 2009 (the program year in which states largely expended ARRA WIA funding), a 39 percent increase in the number of WIA Adult exiters receiving training.

Local Areas Expanded the Types of Training Provided

Third, the Recovery Act provided added resources to support and expand the types of training provided by local workforce areas, and to some degree allowed for experimentation with new training approaches and pilot programs. For example, Florida used Recovery Act and other funding for its Employ Florida Healthcare Initiative, which included employer-driven models for assessment and training. Illinois used Recovery Act funds to develop "bridge programs," which helped low-income workers gain basic skills and other skills to move into better occupations. Nevada issued a request for proposal (RFP) for new service providers to serve as intermediaries and expand opportunities for customers to obtain training more quickly and conveniently. Overall, the NASWA survey results as well as the site visits suggest that while states and local areas placed considerable emphasis on the use of WIA Recovery Act funding to support ITAs to provide classroom training, there were other types of training (often with an industry sector focus) that were also supported. For example, survey results indicated that states used Recovery Act funds to provide the following types of training under the WIA Adult Program (with similar percentages reported for the WIA Dislocated Worker Program): ITAs (95 percent of states), contracts with community or technical colleges (69 percent), on-the-job training (67 percent), registered apprenticeships (49 percent), contracts with community-based organizations (31 percent), customized training (31 percent), and contracts with four-year institutions (15 percent). Generally, the site visits confirmed the general findings of the NASWA survey with respect to the types of training being provided and suggested that some states were using Recovery Act funds to emphasize (and expand) use of certain types of training, including OJT and customized training.

States Expanded and Accelerated Assessment Procedures

Finally, with respect to WIA, the Recovery Act provided additional resources that helped to continue and even expand or accelerate the use of new assessment procedures for WIA participants and other unemployed or underemployed individuals. For example, several of the 20 states visited—including Colorado, Louisiana, Michigan, Ohio, Pennsylvania, Washington, and Wisconsin—were at the time of receipt of Recovery Act funding already in the process of implementing or expanding their use of WorkKeys/KeyTrain and the NCRC to enhance assessment procedures. These efforts were aimed at providing workers an extra credential that would be recognized by employers. Several states also indicated that with the help of Recovery Act funding they were disseminating information to employers to increase knowledge of NCRC and attempting to make such certification an increasingly important criterion upon which employers select workers to fill job openings.

Overall, at a time of crushing demand for training and other workforce services, the Recovery Act provided a much-needed additional

Table 3.11 Examples of Accomplishments of State and Local Workforce Areas in Implementing the WIA Recovery Act Provisions

State	Examples of various accomplishments in implementing WIA provisions of the Recovery Act
Colorado	• The Summer Youth Employment Program was a big effort because local workforce areas had either not run programs in the recent past or had very small programs. Statewide, with Recovery Act funding, over 3,000 low-income youth participated in subsidized work experience slots under this initiative.
	• ARRA provided a big increase in funding that was used to increase substantially the number of unemployed persons receiving WIA-funded training. Additionally, the Recovery Act provided extra resources to hire and deploy additional staff to One-Stop resource rooms to deal with the surge of job seekers coming into One-Stops for assistance.
Florida	• ARRA provided critical funding for the state's Summer Youth Employment Program, which provided temporary subsidized summer jobs for 14,000 youth.
	• The state used Recovery Act and other funding for the Employ Florida Healthcare Workforce Initiative, featuring employer-driven new models for assessment, training, and job placement. Additionally, ARRA funds were used to expand participation in Microsoft's Elevate America training vouchers initiative, which involved competitive awards to LWIBs for digital access and to foster community college collaborations.
Illinois	• With ARRA funding, the state was able to place 17,000 youth in subsidized jobs through the Summer Youth Program in the summer of 2009.
	• WIA state discretionary dollars were used for bridge programs for low-income workers in key sectors.
Maine	• Maine did not have a preexisting WIA Summer Youth Program and, as a result of the Recovery Act, brought partners together and was able to quickly get its Summer Youth Program up and running, reaching almost 1,000 youth across the state.
	• Maine made a clear commitment to training and supportive services by designating 80 percent of Recovery Act WIA Adult and Dislocated Worker funds for this purpose and keeping administrative costs down.
Michigan	• Many youth were served (21,000) across the state in the WIA Summer Youth Program as a result of ARRA funding. The Summer Youth Program was mounted quickly and provided much-needed income and work experience for youth enrolled in the program (at a time when there were few available Summer Youth jobs in the state). Also, the

ability to use private employers under the program for the first time was a big plus, as was the ability to serve youth up to age 24 (instead of 21, as had been the case in past years).

- WIA Dislocated Worker and Adult Recovery Act funding about doubled as a result of ARRA. This added funding was particularly helpful with regard to expanding training (and especially longer-term training) opportunities for an increased number of adults, dislocated workers, and youth. A high proportion of the Recovery Act WIA funding went to training, which has helped to boost the skills of the workforce and prepare them for new jobs.

North Carolina

- The state was proud of its successful Summer Youth Program and its use of existing staff with experience in these programs to quickly deploy efforts.
- State officials noted the success of the regional initiatives implemented. ARRA funding was able to support its ex-offender and juvenile offender initiatives and reinforced its commitment to better serving these populations. Staff believed that many of these initiatives would last beyond ARRA in some form.

North Dakota

- The state mounted a successful Summer Youth Program.
- The state purchased TORQ software and used this software to develop Skills Transferability Analysis (STA) reports for those occupations affected by layoffs. These reports were provided to One-Stop offices to be used at rapid response events and in working with laid-off workers.

Ohio

- Perhaps the greatest accomplishment with ARRA funding (according to state officials) was the successful implementation of the Summer Youth Program, which served 18,000 youth and was made possible with ARRA funding. The TANF Emergency Fund allowed some local workforce areas to continue to serve large numbers of youth the following summer (after ARRA funding had been spent the first summer).
- The state and local areas were able to substantially increase the numbers of adults, dislocated workers, and youth served and enrolled in training as a result of ARRA funding.
- ARRA funding (and particularly Project HIRE) enabled local workforce areas to test the effectiveness of OJTs and to establish linkages with employers to sponsor OJTs. This "testing out" of OJTs and establishment of linkages with employers under ARRA has meant that the state and local areas were able to respond quickly and effectively to the new governor's workforce policy, which stresses OJTs (and short-term training).
- The Recovery Act funded four training initiatives that have enhanced worker skills and employability: 1) Project HIRE, 2) Recovery Conservation Corps, 3) Urban Youth Works, and 4) Constructing Futures.

(continued)

Table 3.11 (continued)

State	Examples of various accomplishments in implementing WIA provisions of the Recovery Act
Pennsylvania	• The availability of additional funding through ARRA enabled the state workforce system to evaluate the overarching system and determine where to introduce improvements. The system served a greater volume of customers and improved efficiencies in the service delivery infrastructure.
	• Local workforce officials indicated that the greatest achievement was serving more people through training and support services during the ARRA era. Additionally, they said that employer engagement and partnerships have continued to increase and solidify. In one local area, ARRA funds were employed to build a component of an integrated advanced manufacturing employment system and career opportunity partnerships.
Rhode Island	• The state was able to quickly mount a Summer Youth Employment Program, serving 1,200 youth.
	• ARRA helped with creating a career tech program combining work readiness training and work experience in Year 1 of ARRA funding; this was expanded in Year 2 to include occupational exploration and internships for eighth-graders. Now there is a shared vision in the state regarding youth programs and an ability to move funds quickly and strategically in partnerships with technical schools, which would not have been possible without ARRA.
	• ARRA funding enabled the workforce system to serve about twice as many customers as would have been possible, expanding quality services (by providing more one-on-one attention) to substantial numbers of unemployed and underemployed individuals who had not previously interacted with the workforce system. ARRA funding also substantially increased the numbers of individuals entering training.
Texas	• The state served more than 25,000 Summer Youth, about 10 percent of all youth served nationwide.
	• Recovery Act funding allowed Texas to put more money and people into training and has increased training options.
Virginia	• The Summer Youth Program served 4,000 youth.
	• The state implemented the community college "On-Ramp" pilot for new training and career pathways in the areas of highest unemployment.
	• New VEC and UI express offices opened with ARRA funding, significantly increasing access points and a return to one-on-one assessments.

Washington	• Washington offered a Summer Youth Program for the first time in 10 years and put 5,600 youth into work experiences.
	• The Recovery Act funds enabled the state to increase its capacity to meet the greater volume of customers during the recession. The state invested ARRA funding in front-end processes, business services, and staff training—all of which will continue to pay dividends in the post-ARRA period. The Recovery Act also promoted collaboration within the broader workforce system.
Wisconsin	• Many youth were served (4,400) in the WIA Summer Youth Program. This program was mounted quickly and featured some "green" jobs and training. While this was described as a "godsend" for the state and local areas, it was a one-time provision of funds—and, post ARRA, little funding has been available within the state to provide subsidized summer jobs for youth.
	• ARRA funding brought training and other services to many adults, dislocated workers, and youth who might otherwise have not received services. Recovery Act funding in the WIA program was particularly concentrated on training: a state requirement that at least 70 percent of Recovery Act funds be expended on training (versus 35 percent for regular DW/Adult WIA funds) helped to ensure that a high proportion of Recovery Act funds were dedicated to training workers and to upgrading workers' skills.

SOURCE: Table is based on site visits conducted in states between December 2009 and April 2012.

source of WIA Adult and Dislocated Worker funding for states and local workforce agencies to expand training for WIA-eligible individuals; it also spurred testing of some new assessment and training approaches at the state and local levels.

AFTER THE RECOVERY ACT

Even at the time of the initial visits (when states were less than halfway through the two-year period available to spend Recovery Act funds), states already were anticipating and planning for when this temporary source of funding to support training and other activities no longer would be available. As shown in Table 3.12, most states indicated that with WIA Recovery Act funds exhausted, WIA participant and expenditure levels would revert to pre–Recovery Act levels. Nearly all state and local workforce agencies indicated they had not built new infrastructure and had added few (if any) permanent workers with Recovery Act funds, so it was not necessary to lay off permanent staff as a result of no longer having Recovery Act funding. However, in some instances, Recovery Act funds had been used to fund temporary workers to staff One-Stop resource rooms and otherwise provide services for WIA customers. As contracts with these temporary staff hired with WIA Recovery Act funding came to an end, some of these temporary staff were absorbed to replace permanent staff that had retired or left agencies through normal attrition; other temporary workers were laid off. None of the visited states or localities envisioned substantial layoffs of permanent staff after the Recovery Act. A key concern was whether adequate levels of resources would be available to both staff resource rooms and meet what is still expected to continue to be very high levels of demand for services and training. Several states expressed concern that WIA funding could remain flat or even be cut back. They had particular concern for WIA Dislocated Worker funding (which can fluctuate much more year to year because there is no "hold-harmless" clause, as there is under the WIA Adult Program). Several states were hopeful that other funding sources might fill the gap left by the loss of Recovery Act funding, such as added funds from an ETA competitive grant or a National Emergency Grant (NEG), though in comparison to funding

Table 3.12 State Expectations of What Will Happen to the WIA Program When Recovery Act Funds Are Exhausted

State	Expectations of state officials
Arizona	Return to pre-ARRA levels.
Colorado	Return to pre-ARRA levels.
Florida	Return to pre-ARRA levels.
Illinois	Return to pre-ARRA levels. Illinois officials, particularly those in Chicago, where nearly all ARRA WIA funds were spent by March 2010, were concerned about continuing high levels of demand for workforce services and no other funding source available to replace ARRA funds.
Louisiana	Return to pre-ARRA levels. State and local officials were concerned the need for workforce services would continue because the state and many local areas still had elevated unemployment levels. They also were concerned there would be less priority on new initiatives such as employer-based training and OJT, long-term training, and Summer Youth employment, as well as possible further reductions in staff and WIA funding.
Maine	Return to pre-ARRA levels.
Michigan	Return to pre-ARRA levels. A year after ARRA funding had been fully expended, many MWAs across the state found that they did not have the necessary funds to sustain training at the levels they were able to with ARRA funding. This has been a disappointment to some unemployed workers who anticipated entering training. Some MWAs had to institute waiting lists for training under the regular (formula) WIA Adult and Dislocated Workers programs as early as the first or second quarters of their program years. Sustaining with regular funding some of those who had originally entered training with ARRA funding meant that there was less available formula funding to pay for new WIA participants during the program year following exhaustion of ARRA funding (and therefore the need to institute waiting lists in some MWAs). So while there is little doubt that ARRA funding promoted the entry of many more into training than would have otherwise been the case, it has been impossible for the state or the MWAs to sustain the levels of training that were established under ARRA.
Montana	Montana state workforce officials were anticipating increases in WIA Dislocated Worker funding because of continued large job losses in the timber and related industries, which would help to offset, in small part, the loss of ARRA dollars—though it was not anticipated that added Dislocated Worker funding would come close to keeping pace with recession-related demands for service. Montana officials were particularly worried about having to "close the front

(continued)

96

Table 3.12 (continued)

State	Expectations of state officials
Montana (cont.)	door" to new registrants (whose numbers have yet to slow), as additional funding will be needed to continue to support those who are already registered and receiving training (and who are staying in services longer than in the past).
Nevada	Given the economy in Nevada, state officials anticipated that formula funding will be significantly higher than in pre-ARRA periods, so they will be able to continue to serve increased numbers of WIA adults and dislocated workers.
New York	Return to pre-ARRA levels.
North Carolina	Return to pre-ARRA levels.
North Dakota	Return to pre-ARRA levels or lower, given that funding does not account for state cost-of-living increases for workers.
Ohio	Return to pre-ARRA levels. There is concern ARRA funding will run out because of a continued surging demand for services at One-Stop Career Centers. State administrators noted that not only would Recovery Act funding end, but the state's allocation of formula funds (particularly for WIA Dislocated Worker funds) for the coming year would be cut. (Note: WIA formula funds to the state were cut from $140 million in PY 2009 to $127 million in PY 2010.)
Pennsylvania	Keep new staff; work with the state legislature to fund projects and industry partnerships; maintain one-on-one counseling and assessment where staff funding levels in local areas allow; maintain the use of WorkKeys.
Texas	Return to pre-ARRA levels.
Virginia	Many functions of the new Virginia Employment Commission (VEC) offices may be incorporated into One-Stops or VEC Workforce Centers. Some new offices will continue for a while if possible.
Washington	Return to pre-ARRA levels. The challenge relates to the number of customers in training during the rapid loss of ARRA funds—there is a bubble that will be difficult to manage.
Wisconsin	Return to pre-ARRA levels. LWIBs enrolled many WIA participants in longer-term training (of one and two years) with ARRA funding. However, ARRA funding was largely expended during the first year in which it was available (through January 2011). Now, LWIBs are finding they are short on funding to cover training expenses for those already in training (i.e., to cover the second year of training).

SOURCE: Table is based on site visits conducted in states between December 2009 and April 2012.

made available under the Recovery Act for the WIA program, grants made under these sources are quite small and often targeted to a locality or region of a state.

Notes

1. See Chapter 1 for additional details on the timing and methodology used in these site visits.
2. USDOL staff indicated that the waiver policy was changed in PY 2009 to ensure that the needs of both low-income workers and dislocated workers were being met while still giving state and local officials some flexibility to tailor their programs to local needs. The USDOL allowed all states to transfer up to 30 percent of their Recovery Act and WIA formula funds between the Adult and Dislocated Worker programs, and allowed states with a waiver to transfer up to 50 percent of WIA formula funds.
3. Data were not yet available for PY 2011, but they would be useful to analyze to determine whether the numbers in training were sustained when WIA ARRA funding had been fully expended.
4. See note 3.
5. SNAP was formerly called the Food Stamp Program.
6. Additional details about this challenge and other challenges are included in the book's final chapter (see Chapter 10).
7. The use of ARRA funding to support WIA Summer Youth Programs was not a focus of this study, as the USDOL funded a separate evaluation study to assess the use and effects of Recovery Act funding on the Summer Youth Program at the state and local levels. Despite the fact that this was not a topic of discussion during the two rounds of site visits, states typically cited their ability to support Summer Youth Programs as a key accomplishment.
8. Additional details about the use of ARRA funds to support WIA Summer Youth programming (and the other accomplishments discussed in this section) are included in Chapter 10.

References

Illinois Department of Commerce and Economic Opportunity. 2009. *WIA Notice No. 08-ARRA-02*. Springfield: Illinois Department of Commerce and Economic Opportunity. http://www.illinoisworknet.com/Policies/08 -ARRA-02/version_0/08-ARRA-02-PY09LocalPlanModification.pdf (accessed March 6, 2013).

National Association of State Workforce Agencies (NASWA). 2010. *NASWA Survey on Pell Grants and Approved Training for UI: Summary and State-by-State Results*. Washington, DC: National Association of State Workforce

Agencies. http://www.naswa.org/assets/utilities/serve.cfm?gid=1D066C77
-7EAE-40AB-8F57-F79696A10B26&dsp_meta=0 (accessed March 6,
2013).

United States Department of Labor (USDOL). 2009. *ETA Advisories: Training and Employment Guidance Letter (TEGL) No. 21-08 (May 8, 2009)*. Washington, DC: U.S. Department of Labor, Employment and Training Administration. http://wdr.doleta.gov/directives/attach/TEGL/TEGL21-08 .pdf (accessed March 6, 2013).

———. 2010. *Workforce Investment Act—Adults and Dislocated Workers Program*. Washington, DC: U.S. Department of Labor, Employment and Training Admnistration. http://www.doleta.gov/programs/general_info.cfm (accessed March 6, 2013).

4
Wagner-Peyser
Employment Services

Joyce Kaiser
Capital Research Corporation

BACKGROUND

The Wagner-Peyser (W-P) Act of 1933 established the Employment Service (ES), sometimes called the Job Service, which provides labor exchange services for workers and employers. As One-Stop Career Centers have become more established, in many states the Wagner-Peyser funded staff is no longer identified as the Employment Service, but simply as workforce staff whose job is to assist One-Stop customers. Services for workers include job search assistance, placement assistance, job fairs, and labor market information. Services for employers include labor market information, employee recruitment, job fairs, development of job descriptions, and assistance during layoffs and closings. The Wagner-Peyser Employment Service (W-P ES) program traditionally has funded job search assistance for UI claimants, and it serves migrant and seasonal farm workers, youth, individuals with disabilities, ex-offenders, older workers, and other special populations. In 1998, the act was amended to make the W-P ES part of the One-Stop delivery system, with the objective of having all workforce development activities easily accessible and often in the same location (USDOL 2010).

Prior to enactment of the Recovery Act, the W-P ES functions had steadily diminished because of sustained periods of federal funding cuts and static state funding. The ability of the staff funded by W-P to provide one-on-one assistance to all job seekers had all but disappeared in the early 1980s. To continue to serve job seekers, innovative modes of service delivery were developed. Today there are resource rooms for self-directed services, allowing customers to use computers with Internet access for reviewing job listings, developing résumés, and researching labor market information for any area in the country. In cases where customers are less skilled in the use of Internet tools, a second level of service includes the assistance of a resource room attendant. One-on-one services are available to customers needing an assessment of skills, abilities, and aptitudes, as well as career guidance or counseling if a career change is being considered. In addition to these kinds of services, many W-P ES offices and One-Stop Career Centers with W-P ES services offer workshops where job search techniques are discussed or where résumé preparation assistance is provided. Customers seeking job training are often scheduled into workshops where different training programs are discussed and eligibility requirements are explained.

OPERATING POLICIES AND CHANGES AS A RESULT OF THE RECOVERY ACT

General Operational Structure

State agencies administer W-P ES services, and those services are provided by state employees in all but two states in the study, Colorado and Michigan, which operate demonstrations approved by the USDOL that allow nonstate public employees to deliver W-P ES services at the local level. The majority of study states have all W-P ES services integrated into their One-Stop systems. Of the 20 states visited, 13 had no separate W-P ES offices, and all services were delivered in a One-Stop setting. One-Stops in several of these states were managed by the W-P ES, with WIA as a partner. In the remaining seven states, there were some with stand-alone W-P ES offices, but all of these states have One-Stop operations with W-P ES, WIA, TAA, and other mandatory partner workforce development programs under one roof in at least one One-Stop Career Center in each local workforce investment area, as required by the WIA statute.

Colorado and Michigan have longstanding demonstrations in which W-P ES staff are not required to be state employees. Under the demonstration rules, W-P ES staff can be employees of local public agencies such as local education authorities, county or city government, or community colleges. In addition to providing W-P ES services (including staffing of One-Stop resource rooms), staff in these states are responsible for providing direct customer services under the Trade Adjustment Assistance (TAA) and Reemployment Services (RES) programs.

With the advent of the Recovery Act, no states reported any changes to their existing W-P ES service delivery structure. However, several states (e.g., Arizona, Ohio, Texas, and Virginia) opened new offices with Recovery Act funds to accommodate increased need. Other states opened some temporary satellite operations. There were no changes in services offered in these new locations, but because of additional staff, it was possible to reduce wait times for services. With the elimination of Recovery Act funding and reductions in formula funding, temporary offices are mostly gone. Both Texas and Virginia have closed some fully functioning offices (opened as a result of the availability of Recovery Act funding), while Arizona has continued to operate the three offices originally opened with Recovery Act Wagner-Peyser funding. Ohio added ten "overflow" offices, which were expected to close by no later than August 2012.

It is important to note that Recovery Act funding for W-P ES services did not keep pace with customer demand. In the third quarter of 2006 (the low point of customer demand), slightly fewer than three million customers were registered for services at the various Wagner-Peyser funded offices throughout the country. In the last quarter of 2010 (the high point of customer registration) the number had risen by 60 percent to slightly fewer than five million customers. Regular formula funds during this period decreased by 11 percent. With the addition of Recovery Act funding there was a 13 percent increase, but certainly not enough to keep pace with the 60 percent increase in customers. Even with Recovery Act funding, expenditures per participant fell from an average of $55 during the pre–Recovery Act period to $34 in the second Recovery Act period.[1]

Coenrollment Policies

A majority of states (16) do not automatically coenroll W-P ES customers in WIA. Customers coming into the One-Stop or W-P ES office are normally first offered core services in the self-help resource rooms where they are enrolled in W-P ES. If customers are only seeking more self-directed services, such as research on labor market information, information on available jobs, or assistance in the development of a résumé, enrollment in WIA is typically not automatic. Because this is the primary pattern of service across the states visited, most WIA customers are coenrolled in W-P ES, as W-P ES services are the first offered to visitors to W-P ES or One-Stop offices.

Assessment and Counseling

Of the 20 states visited, all reported that assessment and counseling services were available before the Recovery Act but that the availability of Recovery Act funds enabled them to make improvements in how these services were offered. Montana reported that "before (the Recovery Act) we didn't offer all job seekers/claimants intensive services; now we do . . . We try and capture everybody and make sure they're getting all the assistance they need. Now we try and offer personalized services for everybody coming through."

Before Recovery Act funding, the wait time was long, and there were limited tools available to assist in the assessment and counseling process. Several states reported that at the beginning of the recession there were lines of people out the door waiting to start the process and that using resource rooms had to be done on a scheduled basis. Where possible, some One-Stop offices had evening hours to accommodate the demand. As a result of Recovery Act funding, the wait time for these services diminished and customers were being encouraged to complete enrollment documents and to utilize the counseling services. In the NASWA survey on the workforce provisions of the Recovery Act, 75 percent of states reported an increase in the number of customers being assessed or counseled. This number is consistent with comments made during the site visits, but at the site visits the increase was attributed to an increase in customer demand and not a change in policy. Increased assessment and counseling numbers can also be partly attributed to the services provided as a result of Reemployment Services (RES) funding rather than W-P increases. (A full discussion of RES services is covered in the next chapter of this book.)

Several states enhanced their assessment and counseling activities by purchasing proprietary programs to assist in determining customer skills, knowledge, and abilities for career counseling and job placement. Some of the systems mentioned were as follows:

- **WorkKeys.** This is a three-step assessment and training program matching individuals to jobs and training (ACT 2013). The first step includes assessments to measure cognitive abilities such as applied mathematics, reading for information, locating information (foundational skills), and assessments to predict job behavior (personal skills). The second step is to conduct a job analysis, and the third step is training. The training module matches the skills of the worker with selected occupations to determine if there are gaps that can be addressed by training. This final step includes KeyTrain, which offers curriculum details to address the skills gaps. Once a customer has completed the assessment, a certificate of proficiency is obtained from WorkKeys which is then used to facilitate job search activities. Related to Work-Keys, the National Career Readiness Certificate (NCRC) is an industry-recognized, portable, evidence-based credential that certifies essential skills needed for workplace success.[2] This credential is used across all sectors of the economy. Individuals can earn the NCRC by taking three WorkKeys assessments:

  - Applied Mathematics
  - Locating Information
  - Reading for Information

- **TORQ.** The Transferable Occupation Relationship Quotient is a single measurement that defines "transferability" of an individual's skills between occupations (TORQworks 2013). The tool links occupations based on the abilities, skills, and knowledge required by workers in occupations using the O*NET database. This is both a job-search and a counseling tool.

- **SMART 2010.** This is artificial intelligence software used in New York that analyzes a customer's résumé for skills, work experience, and related talents.[3] The software compares the content in résumés submitted against the content in job orders, sorting through words and similar themes. The system then recommends a number of job leads drawn from the New York State job bank. These job leads are e-mailed directly to the customer by One-

Stop staff. The appeal of this tool is that it continues to generate job leads until the résumé is removed. Changes can be made to the résumé, which, in turn, will change the focus of the search.

- **JobZone.** JobZone is an on-line resource that includes a career exploration section, a self-assessment section, and résumé preparation assistance (New York State Department of Labor 2010). The user may view occupations, training program information, and information on colleges. The self-assessment includes a review of career interests and work values as well as skill surveys. The résumé preparation section not only includes information on how to construct a résumé but allows the user to develop and store multiple résumés that can be used for different occupations. The system also includes a job search journal.

In addition, Arizona initiated a policy that customers do a "work readiness self-assessment" that now provides a basis for employment services delivery statewide. In Nebraska, customers complete a self-directed assessment on NEworks (an on-line portal to workforce services) as a first step in the customer flow process. The result of this assessment shapes the development of their Individual Employment Plan (IEP).

Some states had already implemented these programs prior to the receipt of Recovery Act funding, but Recovery Act funds allowed for increased customer usage because several newly adopted assessments have per-person charges associated with them.

The states also reported that having these systems in place will be very useful once Recovery Act funds for staffing disappear.

Staffing

According to the states visited, planning for Recovery Act implementation for W-P ES was conducted by existing staff. States generally elected to use the majority of the Recovery Act funding to increase staffing at the One-Stops or local W-P ES offices. When central office staff was hired using Recovery Act funds, generally the functions performed included program oversight, labor market information development, or special projects such as Recovery Act liaison, business development, or green jobs projects. States generally hired temporary full-time, part-time, and intermittent workers, so full-time-equivalent (FTE) information does not tell the whole story regarding numbers of new people working in W-P ES. Hiring statistics cited by the states often comingled the numbers for RES and W-P ES. The following are examples of W-P ES hires reported by the states:

- In Arizona, ARRA-related staff positions peaked at 160 seasonal and temporary workers (not FTE) prior to the expenditure of all Recovery Act Wagner-Peyser and RES allocations by September 30, 2010. Sixty permanent state W-P ES/RES positions have been retained since that time. Wagner-Peyser funding increased 3.4 percent for FY 2011, permitting continuation of these positions and the RES program.

- Nebraska reported that it hired 32 full-time personnel. The equivalent of 22 of the 32 Recovery Act W-P ES/RES FTE positions have been retained since the expiration of Recovery Act funding and are covered by formula allocations; nine positions were eliminated. To manage personnel, the state has orchestrated retirements, relied on turnover, used temporary hires, and, as a result of cross-training workers, has individuals charge time to different programs.

- Ohio initially hired between 300 and 400 intermittent staff (allowed to work up to 1,000 hours per year) using ARRA W-P funding. As of the follow-up visit, some staff remained paid from regular W-P ES funds. Thus far, no layoffs have been experienced at the state level.

- Initially, Texas hired 325 temporary staff to help meet the demand for services at One-Stop centers. Three hundred were retained for an additional program year. In Summer 2011, the Texas Workforce Commission (TWC) tentatively planned to retain 100 temporary staff in FY2012 and 50 temporary staff in FY2013 if funding was available. The planned retention was a result of customer volume in the One-Stops not dropping significantly.

- Colorado staff stated that the Recovery Act provided extra resources that enabled some workforce regions to hire and deploy additional staff to One-Stop resource rooms to deal with the surge of job seekers coming into One-Stops for assistance.

- Florida hired four staff for monitoring and two for performance measurement in W-P ES, whom it hopes to move into permanent positions.
- Montana's Department of Labor and Industry added 23 temporary employees to meet increased demand for W-P ES services. It plans to move these employees into permanent positions through vacancies and attrition.
- Virginia hired four statewide coordinators and 12 regional specialists for newly established Business and Economic Development Specialist positions. It also hired two staff in the Registered Apprenticeship Program agency.

In states such as New York, Texas, and Florida, where there is full program integration between WIA and W-P ES, core services traditionally associated with W-P ES may be carried out by WIA-funded staff, so making a distinction regarding W-P and WIA staffing (and funding for W-P ES services) is almost impossible.

The challenge facing states related to W-P ES staffing is that the W-P ES positions are generally covered by state civil service rules. According to some states, this meant that the hiring process for positions could take several months. For a program with a one-year duration, four months could be spent in the hiring process, not to mention the additional time needed for training. If there was a vacancy toward the end of the program year, there would be no point in attempting to refill the spot. Some states also faced hiring freezes (e.g., Arizona and Maine), and although they were ultimately able to move forward with recruitment, getting waivers from the appropriate state authority added additional time to the process. Some states were able to promote W-P ES staff to fill higher-level positions for one-on-one assessment and counseling and hire temporary staff to provide some staff-assisted services.

In states with high unemployment rates, finding high-quality staff was relatively easy, whereas in low-unemployment states like North Dakota, the state was in competition with a healthy private sector, which could often offer better pay and benefits. Several state officials mentioned that the recession had helped them attract better-quality staff than in periods of full employment because of the larger pool of available high-skilled workers.

CHALLENGES

Not surprisingly, the major difficulties faced by the states in the W-P ES program were staffing and turnover. As mentioned earlier, the challenges were due to operating within the confines of civil service requirements and dealing with hiring freezes. Table 4.1 provides a sample of challenges cited by the states.

ACCOMPLISHMENTS

The major achievement cited by most of the state and local respondents was their ability to serve many more customers. Some states reported that they were better prepared to meet this challenge because of changes to policies (e.g., coenrollment in WIA) or their workforce systems (e.g., integrating W-P ES and WIA services, computerized self-assessment tools) that they had implemented prior to the Recovery Act. For example, New York officials reported that the state's integration of programs at the state agency and at One-Stop offices allowed them to scale up to serve the increased number of customers. The state has cross-trained all One-Stop staff so that W-P ES and WIA staff can be deployed where needed. Other major accomplishments include improving business services and the introduction of additional labor market and assessment tools. Table 4.2 provides a sampling of the accomplishments cited by the states.

AFTER THE RECOVERY ACT

Many states are not optimistic about their ability to maintain the level of services established with Recovery Act funding. Most states hired temporary or intermittent staff for ES positions, knowing that once the Recovery Act funds were spent, the formula monies would not be sufficient to support the additional positions. In most cases, states did indicate that they would keep staff if positions became available

Table 4.1 Challenges in Implementing Wagner-Peyser Programs under the Recovery Act

Challenges	State comments
Staffing	**Arizona**—The hiring freeze required the agency to obtain specific waivers to spend Recovery Act funds on W-P ES staff, adding about a month to the process.
	Florida—Hiring additional W-P ES staff was a challenge, as was the need to train new staff.
	Illinois—There were hiring delays for new, intermittent W-P ES staff, and once hired the staff could only work for 1,500 hours per year.
	Maine—Managing the program in spite of the hiring freeze was both an accomplishment and a challenge.
	Montana—Bringing on and training new W-P ES staff at the same time the Job Service was deluged with new claimants was very difficult.
	North Dakota—At the same time North Dakota was attempting to increase the number of W-P ES staff, its Human Resources Department experienced a total staff turnover. In addition, North Dakota's unemployment rate is the lowest in the nation, which means that finding people willing to accept temporary work, or keeping temporary staff on, is more problematic than in most other states.
	Ohio—Bringing on 300–400 intermittent W-P and RES staff was inherently difficult.
	Pennsylvania—The hiring process was challenging for the state because it had to obtain exceptions to the hiring freeze and hire permanent merit staff, which was a lengthy process.
	Texas—The state had difficulty in hiring and experienced turnover in the temporary W-P ES positions funded by the Recovery Act.
	Virginia—The state experienced delays in bringing on new W-P ES staff which, when coupled with the need to train all new staff, resulted in staff shortages at the local level. The state cited background checks as a problem in the hiring process.
	Washington—Hiring and training of W-P ES staff was a challenge for the state. The Seattle–King County Workforce Development Council (WDC) noted that it was difficult to retain temporary ARRA staff, and despite an intention to convert positions to permanent it was still competing with other employers for high-quality individuals.

Funding	**Illinois**—Respondents were concerned about what would happen once Recovery Act funds were spent, especially as the need for W-P ES services had not abated.
	Louisiana—State officials expressed a need for additional funding for staff development to deal with harder-to-serve populations and continued long-term unemployment.
	Nebraska—As of March 2011, about 20–25 percent of the ARRA Wagner-Peyser and RES funds remained unexpended. Unexpended funds included, in part, obligations toward technology improvements. $1,092,623 of RES and $620,834 of Wagner-Peyser ES funding (48.64 percent of combined ARRA funding) were budgeted for the system upgrade contract; residual upgrade obligations carry forth through December 31, 2012.
	Maine—Obligating the money in a timely manner was both an accomplishment and a challenge.
	Michigan—ARRA/W-P ES funds were fully obligated by the state, but several local MWAs did not fully expend the funds obligated, [and so, as of December 2011], $109,957 [of the $5.2 million received by the state] was unspent.
Office space	**Florida**—To deal with an increase in customers, the state needed to find space without opening new centers.
	New York—Customers at some centers experienced wait times to access computers in resource rooms, wait times for appointments with counselors, and crowded orientation meetings. Some locations were able to secure donated space or short-term leases for temporary extra space, but in some areas of the state such arrangements were not possible. The major issue was that because of the temporary nature of Recovery Act funding, long-term lease arrangements were not possible.
Other issues	**Arizona**—
	• There is a need to tailor approach to meet the needs of older, longer-term workers who never thought they would be in the unemployment line searching for a job.
	• The state is developing effective procedures and informative workshops that will continue to address employment needs in a flat economy beyond the stimulus funds.
	Illinois—Purchasing a new automated labor exchange program through the state procurement process took time.
	Nevada—The state is serving large numbers of clients—19,000 as of April 30, 2011.

(continued)

Table 4.1 (continued)

Challenges	State comments
Other issues (cont.)	**New York**—Not only were there large increases in the numbers of customers coming into the One-Stop, but the characteristics of ES customers have changed. Individuals with long work histories but little experience in job search activities tended to need more assistance searching for a job and in some cases demanded more attention.
	North Dakota—Serving large numbers of clients is a major challenge.
	Texas—Officials were concerned about the impending layoff of workers on September 30, 2010.
	Colorado—
	• The state procurement process can be long and cumbersome. Trying to get funds out quickly and meet procurement requirements was in some cases a trial. Much of the money was allocated to local regions that did not have to deal with the procurement process.
	• The state Department of Labor had to scramble to set up a separate set of financial reports to meet ARRA requirements. This was because the timing for ARRA reporting was not the same as for reporting on other expenditures that the state normally uses.
	Michigan—Reporting was a particular concern and burden: the state often found itself operating ARRA funding programs and activities before it knew what it would have to report on for performance reporting. Additionally, the need to separately report on ARRA-funded activities was burdensome (and in the view of state administrators and staff unnecessary).
	North Carolina—
	• North Carolina's JobLink system, especially in certain regions, had difficulty in handling the large number of individuals coming through the doors.
	• The education and work experience of these laid-off workers were reasonably diverse, which presented a challenge to staff doing assessment and counseling.

Ohio—

- Guidance (from ETA) came at the eleventh hour or after the fact . . . Guidance and how it was issued was not as helpful as it could have been, especially on data reporting.

There was great pressure to spend ARRA funds quickly (but wisely), especially to get the Summer Youth Employment Program up and running—not enough time for planning.

Wisconsin—

- An initial challenge for both the state and local workforce areas was that ARRA represented a sizable infusion of new funding and that the state and especially local areas had to ramp up services and spend ARRA resources over a relatively short period.

- For one-time funding, the reporting burden for ARRA is considerable. With ARRA, there has been a strong emphasis on "transparency." The monthly reporting required under ARRA meant double reporting for the state—continued reporting on its regular funds and separate reporting on ARRA activities, accomplishments (e.g., job creation), and expenditures. In some instances, the ETA provided last-minute instructions on reporting requirements. Also, within the state, the TAA, Wagner-Peyser, and WIA programs are linked by a common data system; thus, reporting-requirement changes for one program affect data collection and reporting for the other programs. In addition, it may be necessary to make changes to IT systems once ARRA reporting goes away—i.e., to revert back to how reporting was conducted prior to ARRA.

SOURCE: Table is based on site visits conducted in states between December 2009 and April 2012.

Table 4.2 Achievements in Implementing Wagner-Peyser Programs under the Recovery Act

Achievements	State comments
Serving more customers	**Colorado**—The Recovery Act provided extra resources to hire and deploy additional W-P ES staff to One-Stop resource rooms to deal with the surge of job seekers.
	Montana—The Recovery Act enabled the state to have a major expansion of services without increasing the "size of the business."
	Nevada—Lines, which had once snaked around buildings, were eliminated because of additional W-P ES staffing.
	Ohio—The hiring of 300–400 intermittent W-P ES staff helped One-Stops deal with huge surges in customers and expand RES orientations for UI claimants.
	Pennsylvania—The Recovery Act funding allowed the Department of Labor and Industry to become more strategic in how it focused its workforce development investments. The key was to invest in increasing the service level (e.g., increased staffing, one-on-one assessments), not in facilities, equipment, or Web sites. There were greatly increased service levels because of Recovery Act money.
	Virginia—Several new Virginia Employment Commission (VEC) and UI Express offices increased the number of access points for ES customers and returned the system to one-on-one assessments.
	Maine—"As a result of Recovery Act funds, our ability to serve job seekers and employers will jump incredibly."
	Washington—The funds enabled the state to increase its capacity to meet the greater volume of customers during the recession. The state invested ARRA funding in front-end processes, business services, and staff training—all of which will continue to pay dividends in the post-ARRA period. The Recovery Act also promoted collaboration within the broader workforce system. The state's incentive for training and the urgency to spend the money well and quickly helped to break people out of their silos.

Program/service enhancements

Washington—The state implemented a new approach to business services with Recovery Act funding. The vision has shifted from engaging employers in the One-Stop to actively working with employers to find jobs that match the inventory of skills of the customers in the system.

New York—Use of technology tools enabled the state and LWIAs to manage workforce and UI programs and better serve customers. The SMART 2010 technology was appropriate for serving customers with Internet access, and JobZone has been successful for career exploration by adults, especially for those who may need skills upgrades and need to plan for training.

North Dakota—The state purchased TORQ software, which is used to develop STA (Skills Transferability Analysis) reports for those occupations affected by layoffs. These were provided to One-Stop offices to be used in rapid-response events and in working with laid-off workers.

Maine—The state is making infrastructure changes, including a revamped Web site to make it more user-friendly with a consistent look.

Texas—The Capital Area Board noted one accomplishment: the creation of a series of workshops for higher-earning clients—often individuals who were connecting with the workforce system for the first time after having earned a high-level salary with a single employer for a number of years. The workshops included stress management, budgeting, and how to build a consultant tool kit.

Ohio—The state implemented IT systems integration. With respect to promoting ES and UI integration, the state agency has used ARRA Wagner-Peyser funds to do the following two things: 1) create a Web site to provide an on-line orientation option for UI claimants and job seekers to introduce them to available services through the workforce development/One-Stop system and 2) create the Web site www.ohioheretohelp.com for UI claimants and job seekers, which provides a holistic overview of services available (e.g., help with housing, food, and other aspects of life as well as with getting a job). Labor market information (LMI) tools (e.g., Help Wanted OnLine technology) have been made more user-friendly and connected with job-posting sites, as well as marketed to additional employers to encourage the posting of new job openings. These technology upgrades have increased the capacity of the ES to serve more job seekers and claimants, especially by making unassisted services more readily available to claimants and job seekers. The upgrades also have made it possible to serve those who were not comfortable coming into centers.

(continued)

Table 4.2 (continued)

Achievements	State comments
Program/service enhancements *(cont.)*	**Wisconsin**—State administrators observed that the ARRA-ES funding allowed the state to cope with heightened demand within Workforce Development Centers and to implement several innovations that would not have otherwise been undertaken.

Toll-free Job Service call center implemented: ARRA-ES funding was instrumental in instituting and staffing a toll-free call center. This call center serves several purposes and is particularly aimed at dealing with changes in TAA provisions and the much higher service volumes being faced by Workforce Centers as a result of the recession. State officials note that the call center, staffed by 12 ES/TAA workers, fills a niche between in-person services and information available from the Wisconsin Department of Workforce Development's Web site. The call center also helps to provide information and referral services for job seekers located in outlying areas and has helped in responding to heightened demand for services within the workforce system. Key features and services offered through this toll-free call center include the following four: 1) the call center serves as a general job-seeker help line, answering questions and providing job leads to unemployed or underemployed individuals; 2) the call center staff includes a TAA case manager who can handle inquiries about TAA and changes to TAA provisions; 3) the call center has the capability to serve as an "employer call center"—i.e., employers can call in with questions or to place job orders; and 4) the call center serves as the central point for scheduling customers for the WorkKeys testing, a major initiative undertaken by the state and local Workforce Centers in recent years to provide customers with a transferable credential.

Expanded use of social media: ARRA funds have provided added resources (mainly in the form of staffing) to push state and local areas to increasingly use social media—such as Facebook, Twitter, and LinkedIn—as tools for better connecting with job seekers and making additional services for the customer more readily available. For example, local workforce staff can now make announcements of training and job opportunities available to job seekers instantaneously via Twitter; Facebook is being used to disseminate information on job orders and create a virtual "job club" environment. Workforce centers have also conducted workshops on how to use Facebook and LinkedIn as effective job-search tools.

IT upgrades: Some ARRA funding has been used to upgrade IT systems within the workforce system and to meet increased reporting requirements under ARRA.

One-Stop enhancements

Arizona—

- The state used ES funds to improve the infrastructure of One-Stops, including redesigning lobbies and resource rooms, increasing the size of some locations, and adding new television screens for videos and looped information.

- The state also opened three reemployment centers with ARRA funds in July 2009 in counties with high unemployment—Maricopa and Pinal (in the Phoenix metro area) as well as Pima (Tucson). Originally funded by RES, these continue to operate with regular ES funds. (Wagner-Peyser funding increased by 3.4 percent for FY 2011.)

Colorado—ARRA provided extra resources to hire and deploy additional staff to One-Stop resource rooms to deal with the surge of job seekers coming into One-Stops for assistance.

North Dakota—The state used some ARRA Wagner-Peyser funds to purchase laptops for use in the Job Service North Dakota offices. The availability of additional computers allowed more customers access to on-line services and labor market information, and it has been of substantial benefit given the decrease in staff.

Ohio—

- Computer labs: ARRA funding was used to establish seven computer labs within One-Stops across the state. Between six and 10 new computers were added to each computer lab. Software was included on the new computers to help customers develop computer skills, and the computers have been used for WorkKeys training and testing.

- The state opened ten "overflow" centers in metropolitan areas across the state, including centers in Cleveland, Dayton, Akron, Cincinnati, Toledo, and Belmont-Jefferson. The centers particularly serve UI claimants, providing UCRS and REA workshops, as well as résumé-building workshops. The centers have helped the ES meet surging demand for services among UI claimants and job seekers at the local level.

Texas—The state opened new One-Stop centers in Dallas, Tarrant County, and Alamo.

(continued)

Table 4.2 (continued)

Achievements	State comments
Other successes	**Colorado**—The efforts implemented under ARRA have helped bring the UI and workforce systems closer together. Staff on both sides are more knowledgeable about the other's programs and more willing to collaborate.
	Nevada—
	• Officials believed they were in a better position to implement the Recovery Act because of the existing structures in place in JobConnect offices and in the LWIB structure. They did not feel the need to change procedures to accommodate Recovery Act demand.
	• The state was enabled to direct Recovery Act resources into business services; this action has the potential to enhance job opportunities.
	North Carolina—ESC staff discussed the capacity-building efforts in training staff to provide enhanced assessment and counseling to customers and in developing new job-search tools as a major accomplishment.
	Michigan—
	• ARRA funding provided the MWAs across the state with the flexibility to respond to an onslaught of unemployed and underemployed workers. ARRA funding was used by MWAs to pay overtime and hire temporary (limited-term) staff at One-Stop Career Centers, to expand hours of operation, and to lease additional space (if necessary) to respond to heightened demand for services. Some areas of the state, especially those affected by the downsizing of the automotive industry, experienced unemployment rates as high as 25 percent.
	• ARRA-ES funding enabled the state to pay for costs associated with implementing National Career Readiness Certificates (NCRCs) statewide. Though the state had already made a policy shift emphasizing the use of NCRCs prior to receipt of ARRA funding, the Recovery Act provided the funding necessary for implementing this policy statewide.
	Wisconsin—
	• ARRA funding helped bring the Unemployment Insurance (UI) and workforce system programs closer together.
	• ARRA helped bring many more UI claimants into the local workforce centers for employment and training services.

- ARRA-ES funding resulted in the ability to better meet the needs of job seekers through bolstered staffing of the call center and the workforce centers.

Texas—

- It was an accomplishment for the system to put 325 temporary staff in place quickly, and a testament to the ongoing volume of customer demand that 300 of those staff have been retained for an additional program year.

- The TWC also highlighted training events held for ES staff across the state over the summer of 2010, including contractor staff and others. These events provided training on labor exchange and RES services, and they included high-level agency staff, commissioners, local board leaders, representatives of the state's Skills Development Fund, and others. The purpose of the training was to emphasize service priorities, particularly for UI claimants; highlight available tools (such as Work in Texas and LMI) and how to fully use them; identify and share best practices; and recognize One-Stop Career Center staff for rising to the current challenge.

Washington—

- Since the first-round site visit, Washington solidified the customer flow model with its emphasis on initial assessment. There is a new interest in the value-added aspect of workforce services, particularly in three key services: up-skilling, packaging (such as building résumés as a marketing tool), and job referrals. Up-skilling in particular has become the most common service at Washington One-Stop centers. Washington anticipates that the customer flow model and focus on business services will remain in place post-ARRA. The new emphasis on high-quality referrals to keep employers engaged with the system is important, though administrators noted a tension between ES staff, who want to make many job referrals, and business services staff, who only want to refer those likely to succeed.

- Washington is shifting toward functional teams over "siloed" programs. W-P provides an opportunity to improve teamwork and collaboration across the workforce system. WDC staff in Olympia noted that dedicated business services staff have made a difference in connecting with employers. The growing use of KeyTrain is another important shift, as it signals a new emphasis on career development that showcases a commitment to the value-added capabilities of the workforce system.

- Seattle–King County staff noted a need to distinguish between job-ready and non-job-ready clients. Lessons learned from ARRA have helped push the WDC toward a "career-broker model" to connect clients to training.

SOURCE: Table is based on site visits conducted in states between December 2009 and April 2012.

through normal attrition. Three states were somewhat positive about being able to retain staff after Recovery Act funding was exhausted. Three other states were more pessimistic than the rest, doubting that they would retain any staff past the initial funding cycle. Those states that have implemented additional self-help tools believe that they will be able to continue to support those activities. A few examples of post–Recovery Act actions are as follows:

- Nebraska was able to retain the equivalent of 22 full-time positions through June 2011.

- Arizona's Employment Administration indicated that Arizona will

  – make every effort to retain workers hired during ARRA;

  – continue the state's reinvigorated and more structured business services and employer engagement;

  – continue the state's use of the Virtual One-Stop (VOS) in the Arizona Workforce Connection as a major element of service delivery;

  – continue the service strategies stimulated by RES advances, including improved workshops and informed "knowledge presenters," targeted job clubs, social media networking, and better use of career guidance and labor market information (LMI) for as many clients as possible.

- Pennsylvania had anticipated retaining much of the newly acquired workforce after Recovery Act funds were no longer available; however, this is becoming a problem because of union contracts and early retirements.

- Washington's investments in front-end processes, business services, and staff training will continue to pay dividends after all the Recovery Act funds have been expended. Administrators indicated that high-quality staff was hired across the state that might never have been available otherwise. The Employment Security Department (ESD) workforce is aging, and the Recovery Act provided the state with an opportunity to bring in a significant number of new workers and expose those workers to multiple facets of the operation. The Recovery Act also promoted collaboration within the broader workforce system. The state's incentive for training and the urgency to spend the money quickly and wisely helped to break people out of their silos. Washington's ESD is now taking a close look at what services can be sustained efficiently through better collaboration and integration. There is a need to work smarter in an environment of high demand and few resources. The approach the ESD took to the Recovery Act, such as relying on the strategic leadership teams and the internal performance Web site, kept everyone involved and aware of what was going on. The ESD is using this as a lesson as it continues to explore opportunities for improved coordination within its own programs.

All states recognize that there continue to be unmet needs and that the volume of customers is still considerably greater than in the prerecessionary period, so the focus is now on how states will have to do business with fewer resources.

Notes

1. Data are from the USDOL's Public Workforce System Dataset and have been assembled and analyzed by the Upjohn Institute.
2. All customers of the Michigan Works! agencies (MWAs) are now asked to take the certification tests.
3. Information on SMART 2010 is based on interviews with state and local respondents. "SMART" stands for "Skills Matching and Referral Technology."

References

ACT. 2013. *ACT WorkKeys*. Iowa City, IA: ACT. http://www.act.org/products/workforce-act-workkeys/ (accessed March 6, 2013).

New York State Department of Labor. 2010. *Fact Sheet: JobZone—www.nyjobzone.org, Career Management for Adults*. New York: New York State Department of Labor. http://www.labor.state.ny.us/stats/PDFs/jobzone_fact_sheet.pdf (accessed March 6, 2013).

TORQworks. 2013. *TORQworks: We Build Software for Workforce Professionals*. Indianapolis, IN: TORQworks. http://www.torqworks.com/torq.html (accessed March 6, 2013).

U.S. Department of Labor (USDOL). 2010. *Wagner-Peyser/Labor Exchange*.

Washington, DC: U.S. Department of Labor, Employment and Training Administration. http://www.doleta.gov/programs/wagner_peyser.cfm (accessed March 6, 2013).

5
Wagner-Peyser Act
Reemployment Services

Tara C. Smith
University of Texas

This chapter presents findings on Recovery Act–funded Reemployment Services (RES) from site visits conducted in 20 states and roughly twice as many local areas between December 2009 and December 2011. Each state was visited twice during this period. Following a brief introduction to RES, the chapter first examines the Employment and Training Administration's (ETA's) policies for Recovery Act RES (ARRA-RES) in comparison with ETA policies for the Reemployment and Eligibility Assessment (REA) grant program. The chapter goes on to summarize ARRA-RES policy, operations, staffing, and reporting in the 20 states visited, then concludes with a discussion of recent ETA directives related to RES and REA. At the outset, it should be noted that the Recovery Act's investment in RES was a major change in emphasis for the public workforce system in many states and local areas, because prior to the Recovery Act specific grants for RES were last distributed to the states in Program Year (PY) 2005. The dedicated Recovery Act funding allowed state and local areas to deliver more integrated reemployment services to Unemployment Insurance (UI) claimants, on a larger scale, than they had since the start of the WIA program.

INTRODUCTION

As noted above, federal funding for reemployment services targeted to UI claimants has been sporadic. In recent years, however, several concerns have spurred federal initiatives focused on connecting the claimant population to workforce development services early in the claim period. These concerns include the following three: 1) the changing labor market, in which a growing percentage of the unemployed are permanently dislocated from their jobs; 2) the fact that UI claimants today apply for benefits mainly through remote methods (e.g., phone and Internet) and have no easy link to public job search assistance; and 3) concerns about UI trust fund savings.

When funded, Reemployment Services under the Wagner-Peyser Act typically are provided by the Employment Service (ES) to UI claimants to accelerate unemployed workers' reconnection in the labor market (USDOL 2009, 2010c). Services available include targeted job search assistance, counseling, assessment, and employment referrals, as well as other ES activities normally funded by the Wagner-Peyser Act. RES funds may be used to provide more one-on-one, intensive case management than is typically available with ES funding.

Through the Worker Profiling and Reemployment Services (WPRS) system, states have developed a range of statistical models and other approaches to identify specific groups of UI claimants to target for Reemployment Services. Under the 1993 amendments to the Social Security Act contained in P.L. 103-152, claimants who are identified as the most likely to exhaust UI benefits and who are most in need of Reemployment Services to transition to new employment are targeted for RES. Some states have developed models to target RES to other groups of claimants, such as those most likely to find new employment quickly. Still other states provide RES to all, or nearly all, claimants who are not returning to their previous job. Most states provide RES in One-Stop Centers or at state ES offices, though some states provide services virtually through phone- or Web-based systems.

Reemployment and Eligibility Assessment Grants

Beyond RES, many states have received Reemployment and Eligibility Assessment (REA) grants from the ETA. The goals of the program, which began in 2005 with 20 states, are to shorten UI durations and save money for the UI trust fund, both by ensuring claimants' ongoing eligibility for UI and by referring claimants to appropriate reemployment services and training. Recent studies have found that REA programs achieve these goals in a cost-effective manner and that they appear to be even more effective when integrated with RES (Michaelides et al. 2012).

During the Recovery Act period in 2010, this program funded 33 states and the District of Columbia for a total of $50 million (USDOL 2012). REA grants target requirements and services at UI claimants based on a variety of factors including benefit week, location, likelihood to exhaust, and others. The mix of required REA services has changed over time. Claimants receiving REA services were originally required to "attend one-on-one interviews in person, [including] a review of ongoing UI eligibility, provision of current labor market information, development of a work-search plan, and referral to Reemployment Services and/or training" (Benus et al. 2008, p. i).

The Employment and Training Administration expanded REA requirements in 2010, during the Recovery Act period (Workforce3One 2010). Targeted claimants were required to participate in REA activities, including developing a reemployment plan (rather than a work-search plan) and completing work search activities (e.g., accessing services at a One-Stop center, attending an orientation, or registering with the state job bank). These REA grants therefore had stronger requirements for claimants than the RES requirements in the Recovery Act (see Table 5.1 for more on this comparison).

Reemployment Services in the Recovery Act

In the Recovery Act, a total of $250 million was allocated for Reemployment Services activities. In Training and Employment Guidance Letter (TEGL) 14-08, the ETA described expectations for RES. Allowable activities for RES funds included "job search and other employment-related assistance services to UI claimants" (USDOL 2009, p. 19). States were also advised to explore technological improvements that might increase their capacity to serve UI claimants.

Recommended RES strategies included increased collaboration between the ES, UI, and labor market information (LMI) offices at the state and local level. Another recommended strategy was to provide access to a full array of Recovery Act services including activities funded by WIA, such as job clubs, targeted job development, identification of transferable skills, development of individualized reemployment plans, and soft-skills training.

The ETA also advised states to institute or expand statistical worker profiling models to "identify the most effective mix of interventions

Table 5.1 Comparison of Reemployment and Eligibility Assessment 2010 Grant Requirements and Recovery Act Requirements for Reemployment Services

Phase	REA 2010 grant requirements	ARRA RES requirements
Participant selection	• REAs target claimants based on a variety of factors including benefit week, location, likelihood to exhaust, and others.	• RES targets claimants based on likelihood of exhaustion and benefit duration.
Participation	• Identified claimants are required to participate fully in all REA components. • Claimants must report to the One-Stop Career Center in person for staff-assisted services.	• States determine participation requirements for RES; some make participation mandatory while others do not.

Activities and services	• Required activities for REA claimants:
	  – Participate in initial and continuing UI eligibility assessments.
	  – Participate in individual labor market information sessions.
	  – Participate in an orientation to a One-Stop Career Center.
	  – Register with the state's job bank.
		• Allowable activities for RES claimants:
		  – job search and placement services
		  – counseling
		  – testing
		  – occupational and labor market information
		  – assessment
		  – referrals to employers, training, and other services

Plan development	• Reemployment plan must be developed and include:
	  – work search activities
	  – appropriate workshops and/or
	  – approved training
		• Recommends reemployment plans for RES claimants who would benefit from additional RES and/or referrals to WIA, particularly those who are not a viable candidate for job opportunities in the region.

SOURCE: For REA 2010 grant requirements, USDOL (2010a); for ARRA RES requirements, USDOL (2009).

and services for different groups of UI claimants," including claimants most likely to exhaust benefits (USDOL 2009, p. 21). Recommended strategies for upgrading information technology under the Recovery Act included updating the statistical profiling model, improving communication and data sharing between UI and the One-Stop system—particularly ES/RES staff, implementing occupational coding software, integrating LMI in the service delivery model, and upgrading infrastructure to improve efficiency.

Unemployment Insurance Program Letter (UIPL) 05-10 directed states applying for FY2010 REA grant funds to document how REA and RES activities in the state would be integrated (USDOL 2010a). Eleven of the 20 states in the study (Florida, Illinois, Maine, North Dakota, Nevada, New York, Ohio, Rhode Island, Texas, Virginia, and Washington) were part of the original round of REA grants. Another six study states received REA grants in later funding rounds (Arizona, Louisiana, Montana, North Carolina, Nebraska, and Wisconsin). Arizona's REA grant was just getting started during the study period.

Figure 5.1 details REA 2010 grant recipients and the states visited for the Recovery Act study. Of the states visited, Montana, Nevada, North Dakota, and Ohio had REA grants that were described as being linked with Recovery Act RES activities. Nevada's REA and RES programs were highly integrated, which a recent study (Michaelides et al. 2012) found was a highly successful approach (see Box 5.1).

STATE APPROACH TO RECOVERY ACT RES FUNDING

The vast majority of states visited by researchers reported that they planned to spend all Recovery Act RES funds by September 30, 2010. Local areas in Colorado, Florida, Michigan, and Texas have significant control over policy, operation, and funding decisions for multiple workforce programs, including Recovery Act RES programs, but these states did not experience any expenditure issues. In Michigan, the state asked local areas to submit plans for RES activities and request funding of up to 175 percent of their Wagner-Peyser allocation. Other states distributed RES funds by formula to local areas.

Figure 5.1 Reemployment and Eligibility Assessment 2010 Grantees and ARRA Study States

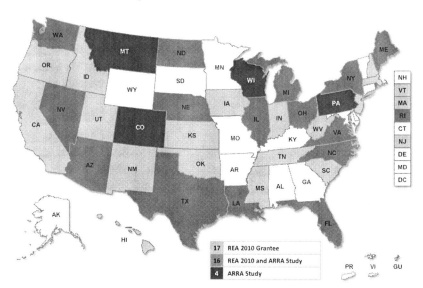

SOURCE: USDOL (2010b).

Ten states reported that additional federal funding resources were used to supplement RES activities or staffing, including the following: UI administrative funds (Colorado, Ohio, Pennsylvania, Washington, and Wisconsin), REA grants (Montana, North Dakota, Nevada, and Ohio), WIA rapid response (Ohio), W-P Act ES administrative funds (Virginia and Washington), and TANF Recovery Act emergency contingency funds (Texas). In Colorado, UI staff conducted in-person sessions with UI claimants at local One-Stop centers and trained One-Stop staff in basic UI on-line functions. Pennsylvania used UI administrative funds to hire 50 permanent RES staff. Wisconsin chose to target its Recovery Act Wagner-Peyser funds ($7.2 million) and UI administrative funds ($3.6 million) at substantially expanding RES services for UI claimants, including fundamental changes in the way UI claimants are served by the One-Stop system.

Four states (Colorado, Ohio, Texas, and Washington) invested state general revenues—some prior to the Recovery Act—to provide additional RES services, including training, for UI claimants. The Colorado

---

Box 5.1 Evaluation of REA and RES in Nevada

In a study for ETA, IMPAQ International found that "the Nevada REA program was more effective in reducing claimant UI duration and generating greater savings for the UI Trust Fund than the REA program in other states examined." The average cost per participant for integrated REA/RES was $201. On average, claimant duration was reduced by 3.13 weeks and total benefit amounts received was reduced by $873, yielding average UI regular savings of greater than two times the cost and an average total UI savings of greater than four times the cost. The program was "very effective in assisting claimants to exit the UI program early and obtain employment," and it "had a lasting effect on employment." A key feature of the Nevada program was that REA and RES services were delivered by the same staff person to a claimant in one meeting. During the Recovery Act period, Nevada RES staff was equally funded by the REA grant and Recovery Act RES funds.

SOURCE: Michaelides et al. (2012).

Enhanced Approved Training Program provides additional UI benefits to claimants in a regular state claim who are enrolled in approved training. Ohio directed $540,000 in state general revenue funds to support RES activities. In Texas, the state legislature appropriated $15 million from state general revenue funds, plus additional TANF Recovery Act emergency contingency funds, for a "Back-to-Work Initiative" that placed low-income UI claimants in subsidized employment with private sector employers. Washington State invested both Recovery Act WIA training funds and funds for state training initiatives to serve UI claimants, including the Training Benefits (TB) Program, the Worker Retraining Program, and Commissioner-Approved Training. Participation in the TB program exempts UI claimants from work search and helps them connect more quickly with longer-term training to take advantage of UI benefits extending up to 99 weeks.

Other states (Nevada, New York, Pennsylvania, and Rhode Island) used taxes on the UI tax base and other funding sources to provide RES prior to the Recovery Act. Nevada had provided RES services with state Career Enhancement Program funds, levied from a small state UI tax traditionally used to provide training for UI claimants. Nevada had been on the verge of eliminating the program because of funding constraints when the Recovery Act was passed. New York created a comprehensive program of reemployment services for UI recipients in 1998. A state UI tax on employers funds training and additional employment services for claimants. Pennsylvania's Profile ReEmployment Program (PREP) has been funded since 1995 through the state's Wagner-Peyser allocation. These states used ARRA-RES funds to expand existing operations. Rhode Island has used state Job Development funds to purchase initial licenses for software packages used in workshops and assessments.

Some states (Arizona, Florida, Louisiana, North Dakota, and Rhode Island) struggled to spend their Recovery Act RES funds or experienced delays in implementation. Louisiana did not immediately create a program in which to spend its RES funds, and ultimately the state had only six months to spend $2 million (of a total of $32 million) in Recovery Act monies. (Similar delays in spending occurred for Louisiana's other Wagner-Peyser and WIA Recovery Act funds.) Arizona also had issues when it came to spending Recovery Act funds, given the state's hiring freeze and other budget problems. In North Dakota, the RES program was slow to start, in part because of turnover within the state agency's human resources department just as the Recovery Act was beginning. Because of the ETA's delay providing guidance on reemployment services, Florida reported an initial reluctance on the part of workforce investment boards (WIBs) to spend RES funds, since they did not know how they would be measured. Rhode Island administrators reported a similar reluctance in their state.

CLAIMANTS SERVED AS A RESULT OF RECOVERY ACT RES FUNDING

Serving more claimants was the key theme of ARRA-RES programs, as 17 of the 20 states indicated that reemployment services were new or had been expanded under the Recovery Act. Twelve of the states visited (Florida, Ohio, Maine, Michigan, Nebraska, Nevada, New York,

Pennsylvania, Rhode Island, Texas, Virginia, and Wisconsin) reported that the number or share (or both) of claimants receiving RES in their state had increased under the Recovery Act. Ohio opened 10 "overflow" centers and hired 100 intermittent staff to serve UI claimants. In Michigan, RES funds were largely spent on office space and additional staff to provide RES. Montana's Recovery Act plan was to double its prerecession effort to connect UI claimants identified as most likely to exhaust their benefits with the workforce system. Montana hopes to maintain this new level of effort: "We've increased the numbers seen, and we are not going backwards. It's still to our advantage to try and see as many claimants as possible, so they don't stay on the rolls." In New York, the only claimants not required to participate in RES are those who are exempt from work search requirements; thus, increased unemployment in the state led to an increase in the number receiving RES.

Pennsylvania greatly increased RES to UI claimants, providing approximately 43 percent more assessments and 63 percent more counseling sessions in PY2009 than in PY2007. In Texas, where UI claimants have been given priority as workforce system customers since 2003, ARRA-RES was used to scale up normal business operations. Texas views claimant reemployment as a workforce system measure rather than a UI measure, including it in its performance assessment of local workforce boards.

In Virginia, ARRA-RES funds were used to open 11 reemployment offices and nine "UI Express" offices. While most have been folded back into local One-Stop centers since the end of the Recovery Act program, one center in Portsmouth has become a permanent location at which to address ongoing high levels of demand. This increase in claimant access points was identified as a key accomplishment of the ARRA-RES program in Virginia.

Prior to the Recovery Act, Wisconsin held about 10 weekly RES orientations statewide. Recovery Act funding allowed the program to expand to 80 sessions per week, with 1,300 claimants scheduled and 700–900 showing up. At the time of the second site visit, workshop offerings were down to 60–70 per week. State staff reported that claimants attending WI-RES workshops had 12 weeks' shorter duration of unemployment and obtained higher wages in subsequent employment.

These findings are similar to results reported from the NASWA survey on RES: more than half of the states (16 of 28) surveyed indicated that the proportion of claimants receiving RES services in their state had increased.

In six of the 20 study states (Arizona, Colorado, Illinois, Montana, North Carolina, and North Dakota), there was no active RES program prior to the Recovery Act. Each of those states developed a new RES program, sometimes based on prior RES efforts or REA grant activities, resulting in more claimants connecting with the workforce system. Arizona opened three dedicated reemployment centers in July 2009 in counties hardest hit by high unemployment. The state has continued to operate these centers past the expiration of Recovery Act funds through its regular W-P ES allocation.

North Carolina had not had an active RES program since the late 1990s. The state tapped staff who had been involved in that prior effort to develop the ARRA-RES strategy, coordinate programs in local areas, and train local RES staff. The best components of the prior RES program were incorporated into the new program—training on job-seeking skills and intensive follow-up with participants. RES participants were engaged early in their claim and went through an intensive 12-week program of staff-assisted services with at least three hours in person for one-on-one interviews with a job coach.

North Dakota developed a phone-based RES program to reach UI claimants in this largely rural state. All RES activities including case management and job search assistance were handled by phone. An individual plan was developed for each claimant, who was then directed to attend a mandatory interviewing-skills workshop. North Dakota also used Recovery Act RES to create a manual titled "Effective Job Search Strategies" and purchased a number of copies for future use.

Some states did not change the share of claimants receiving services as a result of the Recovery Act. In Louisiana, for example, all UI claimants not otherwise exempt have been required to come into One-Stop Career Centers since 2007. The state used Recovery Act RES funding to open overflow centers to serve claimants, as well as to upgrade the profiling model to select claimants for certain services. Recovery Act funds also helped the state expand its automated processes to extend services beyond those identified through profiling. In Washington, 60 percent of claimants are called in during their first claim week.

As discussed in more detail in Chapter 9, nationally initial claims for UI benefits peaked in the first quarter of 2009. Referrals to reemployment services did not peak until the fourth quarter of that year, and participation in services did not peak until the second quarter of 2010. Nationally, the share of claimants receiving orientation services rose to approximately 60 percent during the Recovery Act period, the share receiving assessments increased to half, and the share participating in counseling services grew to 17 percent. Referrals to education and training services were relatively flat between 2005 and 2011, at roughly 10 percent nationally.

Identifying Claimants for RES

The majority of states visited by researchers (17 of 20) use the WPRS system to statistically profile UI claimants most likely to exhaust benefits for Reemployment Services. Three states, North Dakota, Washington, and Wisconsin, also identify those least likely to exhaust benefits for either RES or REA services. Illinois and Maine also profile those most likely to remain on the caseload for an extended duration.

Washington calls in approximately 60 percent of new claimants to the One-Stop Career Center during their first claim week, including those profiled as most likely and least likely to exhaust benefits. Washington made one change to its WPRS system, extending the number of weeks a claimant is in the profiling pool from five weeks prior to the Recovery Act to 52 weeks in the extended UI benefit period.

Many states took additional factors into account when determining which clients to call in for ARRA-RES. Illinois targeted veterans and ex-offenders for enhanced services with Recovery Act RES funds. Maine served nonprofiled first-time claimants in addition to profiled claimants. In Nevada, the profiling list is prioritized based on veteran status, rapid response efforts, and other factors. In North Dakota, residents in only five counties are targeted for RES/REA; the rural nature of the state makes it difficult for rural claimants to comply with in-person meeting requirements. Colorado profiles claimants most likely to exhaust benefits and sends lists to local regions, which make decisions on whether or not to use the profiling list or to make RES mandatory (most do not require RES). Wisconsin expanded its selection of profiled claimants under the Recovery Act to include those least likely to exhaust benefits.

Two states (Arizona and Texas) updated their profiling models after 2008 (though not with Recovery Act funds) to address changing economic conditions, while others (Florida, Louisiana, North Carolina, and Nevada) worked to develop new models or systems during the Recovery Act period. Texas reevaluates its profiling model every two years. Louisiana was using Louisiana State University to develop a new profiling model to identify those who need more intensive services. North Carolina used Recovery Act funds to update its profiling model to better predict which claimants are most likely to exhaust benefits. The prior system had an accuracy of 59 percent; the new model correctly predicts exhaustion of benefits 72 percent of the time. Nevada used part of its ARRA-RES funding to merge the WPRS statistical model and selection system with the state's RES/REA claimant pool and selection system.

State and local administrators in Washington indicated they would like to update the profiling model to better identify those claimants who may need more intensive services. Washington's Olympic Workforce Development Area includes several Navy shipyards and submarine facilities. However, under the state's profiling model, recently separated veterans are not called in to make a connection with the public workforce system or to evaluate whether they may need more intensive services to find employment. State ES administrators assigned to the local area use two strategies to make up for this feature: 1) partnerships and 2) outreach. They partner with Veterans Employment and Training Services to provide a Vet Orientation/Job Club. They also partner with the Military Transition Assistance Program to provide information about One-Stop centers and services to new veterans. In addition, the area supports a Disabled Veteran Outreach Program (DVOP) specialist to provide services at transitional housing and Veterans Administration facilities.

Three sample states (Florida, Louisiana, and Ohio) at the time of the site visits did not use a statistical profiling model to identify claimants for RES services. Since 2007, Louisiana has called in all claimants but, as noted above, the state was expecting a new model for profiling from Louisiana State University. Ohio uses a characteristic screening that looks at six characteristics associated with exhausting UI benefits rather than a statistical profiling model. Florida's current system identifies all nonexempt claimants in the area and allows each local area to draw two groups based on a state formula: one is assigned to group activities, while the other participates in one-on-one sessions.

These findings are similar to findings reported in NASWA's survey. Eighty percent of the surveyed states reported that the primary mechanism for targeting RES is a statistical model to identify UI claimants. One-third of the states indicated that RES Recovery Act funding would be used to update or modify the state's profiling model.

SERVICES AND SERVICE DELIVERY UNDER THE RECOVERY ACT RES PROGRAM

Changes in RES Services Provided

Reemployment Services programs reflect the policies and workforce development philosophy of their state. Claimant experiences in RES varied widely in intensity, level of personal interaction, and opportunities to connect with other services and programs. Officials in most states remarked on the surge in claimants served and services provided as the recession deepened and programs changed (e.g., extended unemployment compensation benefits, TAA). Given the time-restricted nature of the Recovery Act funding, many states built on prior REA or state-funded reemployment programs if they were not already providing some level of reemployment service to UI claimants.

One common change in 10 of the 20 states (Florida, Illinois, Montana, Michigan, New York, North Carolina, Pennsylvania, Virginia, Washington, and Wisconsin) was to increase the number of claimants called in for face-to-face services. In Illinois, Montana, Nebraska, Nevada, New York, Pennsylvania, and Wisconsin, benefits are withheld or delayed if claimants do not come in for an assessment or other scheduled appointment. North Carolina's voluntary program is particularly intensive, with participants spending about 12 weeks in RES.

A number of states used ARRA-RES funds to create or expand workshops and orientations. Nebraska developed the Creative Job Search Workshop, which is now available to all job seekers. Maine ran a two-hour RES workshop and conducted assessments during the session. Rhode Island also ran a two-hour orientation. North Dakota developed an Intensive Reemployment Workshop. Ohio used Recovery Act funding to support additional RES orientations and created an on-line orientation Web site. Austin, Texas, developed an RES workshop targeted at higher-earning claimants. The board also identified a need to better serve claimants who may have been with a single employer for years and thus may not have done a job search in the Internet age.

Case management services were a common feature of ARRA-RES across study states, including Michigan, North Dakota, Ohio, Pennsylvania, and Washington. Several states, including Maine, Nebraska, Pennsylvania, and Virginia, also invested in RES assessments and counseling services. While Nevada did not change the state's mix of RES, officials in that state have noticed that claimants are taking more advantage of various services in the One-Stop centers.

Another key feature of ARRA-RES programs was a commitment to follow up. Illinois, Montana, North Dakota, and Rhode Island all had required follow-ups for RES activities. In Rhode Island, RES participants were expected to return to the One-Stop 30 days after their orientation and bring proof of work search activities. In Illinois, a follow-up was conducted two weeks after participation in a workshop. North Dakota conducted a follow-up by phone every two weeks.

The increase in the number of claimants receiving RES and the proportionate increase in the share that received assessment and counseling are confirmed by the NASWA survey of states. Almost two-thirds of the states (62 percent) responding to NASWA's survey of workforce administrators reported that all UI claimants are referred to a One-Stop Career Center. Seventy-four percent of the surveyed states listed as their number one priority use for Recovery Act RES funds the expansion of services to UI claimants identified through the WPRS profiling system. The majority of workforce administrators reported that RES Recovery Act funds were being targeted at increasing the number or variety of job search assistance workshops (72 percent), providing assessment and career counseling services (56 percent), or making referrals to training (54 percent).

RES Service Delivery

Service delivery under ARRA-RES was primarily at comprehensive One-Stops or satellite centers. Seven of the 20 study states opened additional offices (most temporarily) to handle the provision of RES and serve UI claimants. Arizona and Texas both opened three reemployment centers in high unemployment areas. While the Texas centers have closed, Arizona has continued to operate its reemployment centers with W-P ES formula funds. Colorado opened a joint RES/TANF office using Recovery Act funding. Virginia's RES Recovery Act funds were used to establish 11 Re-Employ Virginia! centers and nine UI Express offices to deal with the great increase in customers seeking UI and Reemployment Services. Most of these centers are now closed.

Recovery Act funding was used to open 10 temporary "overflow" centers across Ohio at which additional RES orientations and case management services were offered to claimants. Overflow centers were also opened in Louisiana and Michigan. In Wisconsin, RES activities were offered at approximately 80 community locations across the state, in addition to services available in One-Stop Career Centers.

Reemployment services in North Dakota were delivered primarily by phone. These services included job search planning, case management, and job search assistance. The RES program is under UI administration, and while claimants are referred by the UI office to the One-Stop centers in order to attend Interview Skills Workshops, visit the resource room, and explore training opportunities, their case managers are not on the staff of the One-Stop. One-Stop managers in North Dakota estimated that 55 percent of customers in the resource rooms during the recovery were UI claimants.

INFORMATION TECHNOLOGY AND LABOR MARKET INFORMATION FOR RES THROUGH THE RECOVERY ACT

Seventeen of the 20 study states reported using RES Recovery Act funds to improve or expand LMI and/or other information technology systems and infrastructure. Table 5.2 highlights each state's investment.

Many states viewed the investments in labor market information, information technology, and infrastructure as a lasting legacy of the Recovery Act, as these investments will continue to provide the foundation for workforce services into the future. For some states, ARRA-RES funding provided a real opportunity to move job search and workforce development activities for claimants into technologically current and more integrated delivery methods. As a result, the workforce system

Table 5.2 Recovery Act RES Investments in Assessment, Information Technology, and Labor Market Information

State	LMI/technology investment
Arizona	• Modified the AIRSNET system to better serve claimants in One-Stop centers.
	• Updated the case management and reporting system used in One-Stop centers.
	• Upgraded equipment in One-Stop center resource rooms.
	• Upgraded staff software and computer systems.
	• Incorporated social media networking.
	• Made better use of career and labor market information.
Florida	• Purchased access to Help Wanted OnLine (HWOL) for real-time job postings and Transferable Occupation Relationship Quotient (TORQ) for real-time LMI.
	• Every registrant has an account with HWOL.
	• Developed the new MIS case management/job matching system Employ Florida Marketplace for staff, employers, and customers.
	• Increased bandwidth and storage capacity and updated software in the state system.
	• Conducted a Job Vacancy/Hiring Needs Survey to collect information by industry and by workforce region to assist with reemployment analysis and job training needs.
Illinois	• Replaced Illinois SkillsNet with a new system based on America's Job Link Alliance (AJLA)—the new system is Illinois Job Link.
	• Upgraded state IT and LMI systems.
	• Purchased licenses for TORQ and HWOL.
	• Purchased Haver Analytics software and data warehouse tool to create customized LMI reports and clear graphics.
	• Partnered with Illinois State University to conduct research across multiple data systems on which services work with which claimants.

Louisiana
- Received $2.3 million LMI Improvement Consortium Award in 2010 to upgrade LMI.
- Purchased laptop computers for temporary RES offices.
- Purchased Micro Matrix software to improve occupational forecasting.
- Expanded automated processes; when claimants call in or file a claim on-line they are automatically registered in the Louisiana Virtual One-Stop (LAVOS) system, the state job bank system.

Maine
- Enhanced state job bank to allow customers to develop on-line résumés and catalog transferable skills targeted at job bank listings.
- The Burning Glass system also includes career pathways models to explore additional credentialing/training and an employer job/talent bank.

Michigan
- Local areas made investments in LMI/IT.

Nebraska
- Budgeted $1.09 million of ARRA-RES (and $620,000 of ES funding) for upgrades to the NEworks system. (This was approximately 49 percent of the state's ARRA W-P funding.)
- NEworks provides an access point for job seekers and employers, as well as for workforce system employees.
- NEworks autoreports required workshop attendance back to the UI system to strengthen participation and accountability.
- Purchased Kuder Career Assessment package, a Web-based self-assessment of ability, interests, work history, and LMI required of all RES clients.

Nevada
- Invested 26 percent of Recovery Act RES funds in IT.
- Purchased identity card validation equipment.
- Upgraded interactive voice response system, which automatically generates phone calls to selected claimants with appointment reminders, work status and job referral updates (with UI administrative funds).
- Purchased 20,000 Layoff-to-Employment Action Planner (LEAP) self-assessment guides from the LEAP Web site. This tool helps job seekers cope with job loss and create a reemployment plan.
- Updated system to merge WPRS modeling for RES and REA programs.

(continued)

Table 5.2 (continued)

State	LMI/technology investment
Nevada	• Created a mechanism for the UI system to provide the workforce system with potential job openings—the names of employers who have open positions because of an employee's being fired or quitting. JobConnect staff is to follow up to develop a job listing.
	• Purchased video equipment and LCD monitors to improve efficiency of communications with One-Stop center customers.
New York	• Developed a Reemployment Operating System (REOS), a scheduling and appointments tracking system that allows One-Stop staff to access information about UI customers on a daily basis.
	• Used upgrades to technology tools to enable the workforce system to manage workforce and UI programs and better serve clients.
	• Purchased SMART 2010 technology to serve customers with Internet access at home.
	• Successfully used JobZone career exploration program for claimants whose skills are no longer viable in the workforce.
North Carolina	• Developed new Web-based systems to support labor exchange services. The Job Connector system allows employers to post job openings and review potential applicants identified by the automatching function, which cross-references skills, education, and experience. Job seekers can also view available job openings matched to their résumé.
North Dakota	• State-developed enhancements to Internet-based application for Reemployment Services, including appointment scheduling and other claimant tools.
	• Purchased access to Transferable Occupation Relationship Quotient (TORQ) to identify transferability between occupations for projects and target groups.
	• Improved database to store and analyze data from Dislocated Worker Survey.
	• Supported several research projects, including: a longitudinal study of workers affected by major layoff events, a study of veterans' employment in North Dakota, a dislocated worker survey, a study of births and deaths of North Dakota businesses, and a study on the relationship of oil and gas prices to employment in that industry.
	• Integrated ES and UI information technology to better serve UI claimants through the state's on-line labor exchange system.

Ohio	• Purchased the Barriers to Employment Success Inventory (BESI), a Web-based assessment used in job search planning.
	• Purchased laptops and other IT equipment to establish overflow RES centers.
	• Created an on-line orientation option to increase the number of claimants selected for RES and provide flexibility for claimants in terms of service delivery. The on-line version is approximately two hours in length, while the in-person version is four hours.
Pennsylvania	• Purchased laptops and other technological equipment for CareerLinks offices.
Rhode Island	• Used approximately 30 percent of ARRA RES funds for LMI/IT.
	• Purchased Metrix licenses.
	• Purchased five laptops with printers to use in rapid-response outreach.
	• Purchased access to D & B Risk Management and Hoover's on-line employer information database.
Virginia	• Improved and expanded WIA/Wagner-Peyser Internet-based LMI/labor exchange/case management system to also include UI and TAA.
	• Speeded up the implementation of LMI expansion previously under way.
	• Created an interface between GEO Solutions job search, the LMI database, and UI.
Washington	• Purchased KeyTrain.
	• Conducted an analysis of extended unemployment claimants.
Wisconsin	• Purchased WorkKeys and KeyTrain.
	• Promoted WorkKeys National Career Readiness Certification.
	• Created a toll-free job service call center which included services to claimants to provide information and reschedule RES workshops and WorkKeys assessments, as well as services to employers as an information resource and a location where they could place job orders.

SOURCE: Author notes and site visit reports.

has better infrastructure and more real-time, locally relevant economic data to better serve employers and job seekers.

Findings reported in NASWA's survey also indicate that Recovery Act RES funds are being used for enhancements to assessment systems, information technology, and infrastructure. Sixty percent of state workforce administrators reported that Recovery Act RES funds were being used to integrate and improve communication or data transfer of UI claimant data between the UI information system and the One-Stop or Wagner-Peyser information system. Almost half (49 percent) were integrating LMI into strategic decision making.

Two states visited by researchers leveraged other funding to enhance Reemployment Services technology and labor market information systems. Colorado used non-RES discretionary funds to purchase Work-Keys for RES, WIA, and ES customers. Nevada used UI administrative funds to upgrade interactive voice response phone systems to remind customers of appointments and required activities, and to follow up on job referral results.

STAFFING FOR REEMPLOYMENT SERVICES THROUGH THE RECOVERY ACT

Seventeen states visited by researchers reported that Recovery Act RES funds were used to hire staff to handle the large influx of claimants. The majority of these staff members were hired as temporary employees, as Recovery Act funds for staffing ended on September 30, 2010, and payroll could not be obligated after that date.[1] Table 5.3 details each state's spending on RES staffing.

Staff in Illinois enjoyed leading the reemployment workshops, as they felt it brought the system back to directly helping claimants. As one Nevada official noted, "Having continuous, quality programs over time requires some commitment of funding . . . Given that this particular program [RES] actually results in savings to the UI Trust Fund, it would seem sensible to provide some funding guarantees so good staff and systems can be maintained."

Several states indicated that staffing was a significant challenge because of state and local government hiring freezes, bureaucratic civil service systems, need for staff training, and temporary status positions. Arizona, for example, had to request critical needs waivers from the state's Department of Administration to spend Recovery Act funds on RES and other staff, adding about one month to the hiring process. Hiring temporary Recovery Act staff was also difficult in Louisiana and Washington given those states' hiring freezes. Some states, such as North Dakota and Rhode Island, experienced hiring delays because of downsizing and turnover in state agency human resource staff.

A number of states noted that there was considerable churn in the temporary positions—many had 100 percent turnover or more during the Recovery Act period. Despite the challenges, some states reported that the temporary staff members hired were high-quality candidates, and a number have been hired into permanent ES or other workforce positions.

Findings from the site visits are also reflected in the findings from NASWA's RES Survey. Twenty-seven of the surveyed states reported that Recovery Act RES funds were used to hire RES staff, the majority of which were hired on a temporary basis. In Minnesota, the state legislature prohibited the use of Recovery Act RES funds for anything other than staff for One-Stop Career Centers. Five surveyed states (Iowa, Mississippi, Nebraska, Oklahoma, and West Virginia) reported that all RES staff hired under the Recovery Act will become permanent employees.

ACCOMPLISHMENTS

Fourteen of the 20 study states (Arizona, Colorado, Florida, Illinois, Maine, Montana, Nebraska, Nevada, North Carolina, Ohio, Pennsylvania, Texas, Virginia and Wisconsin) included RES activities among their major achievements under the Recovery Act. Table 5.4 details each state's RES accomplishments.

A local area in Colorado, the Arapahoe/Douglas WIB, highlighted a key accomplishment of its ARRA-RES activities—the creation of a three-day boot camp, which offers a series of intensive workshops aimed at helping dislocated workers and long-term unemployed persons return to work. One-third of participants were placed in jobs fol-

Table 5.3 Recovery Act RES Investments in RES Staffing

State	Staffing investment
Arizona	• Hired 160 temporary staff; 60 found permanent positions with the workforce system.
Colorado	• Spent 90 percent of ARRA-RES funds on staffing.
Illinois	• Hired 52 intermittent staff to run RES workshops. Intermittent workers are limited by a collective bargaining agreement to 1,500 hours per year, with the possibility to move into a permanent position if one should open up. • Staff were cross-trained in UI and W-P/ES.
Louisiana	• Hired 60 staff to provide RES at One-Stop centers.
Maine	• Hired 18 temporary RES staff dedicated to workshops. • Hired 18 staff across the state dedicated to intensive outreach, group session facilitation, individual guidance and counseling, and business outreach.
Michigan	• Local hiring of temporary staff—Michigan is one of three states with a waiver for W-P staff to not be state employees but rather public employees of local governments, school districts, or community colleges. • Paid overtime for existing staff working extended hours at One-Stop centers.
Nebraska	• Hired 32 permanent FTEs to provide ES/RES (63 percent of the support went to RES, as required).
Nevada	• Hired 11 FTEs and 15 temporary staff to provide RES, representing approximately 42 percent of its budget. RES and REA provided by same staff, with time charged equally. • Established one FTE RES position to provide UI program training and technical assistance, maintain tracking system, review performance measurements, and develop reporting tools.
New York	• Hired 194 temporary staff to provide RES and rapid-response services.
North Carolina	• Spent $12 million on staffing from ARRA and state funds. • Staff size grew from 650 FTEs before ARRA to 1,100 FTEs during ARRA. • Created a new position—job coach—in 63 ES centers.

North Dakota	• Hired five temporary staff for RES.
Ohio	• Hired 100 intermittent staff for the 10 overflow centers.
Rhode Island	• Hired six temporary RES staff.
Texas	• Hired 325 temporary ES staff to provide RES.
Virginia	• Hired 100 new staff to fill approximately 70 FTEs. • Opened 11 reemployment offices and nine UI Express centers. • Returned to one-on-one assessments. • Planned to keep RES staff on board with regular W-P/ES funds.
Washington	• Hired 36 reemployment specialists for One-Stop offices.
Wisconsin	• Hired 44 temporary FTEs for RES workshops. • Prior RES program run by five staff. • Used an estimated 90 percent of ARRA-RES funds for staffing. • Extended funding for temporary workers through September 2011 through another source.

SOURCE: Author notes and site visit reports.

Table 5.4 Recovery Act RES Major Accomplishments

State	Accomplishments
Arizona	• Launched a new RES program across the state. • Opened three dedicated reemployment centers in counties with significant unemployment. • Established a better service pathway for UI recipients. • Stimulated continuing improvements in ES and One-Stop services. • Changes expected to continue in the post-ARRA period with regular ES funds.
Colorado	• Brought the UI and workforce systems closer together; staff on both sides are now more knowledgeable about the other's programs and more willing to collaborate.
Florida	• New emphasis on intensive staff-assisted services for UI claimants.
Illinois	• Relaunched its RES program, last offered in 2005, with Recovery Act funding. • "We've been able to dramatically increase the number of people we're able to serve; we've developed a great set of materials and have staff trained to deliver the workshops. Customer surveys show that clients are responding positively," one Illinois official noted. • Invested in information technology (IT) and LMI upgrades that will support the workforce system into the future.
Maine	• Purchased LMI/technology improvements that strengthened infrastructure. • Expects to maintain the expanded RES program (especially the workshops and counseling features) through staff cross-training.
Montana	• Doubled the number of profiled participants receiving reemployment assessments. • Recognized the value of RES to move UI claimants off of the benefit rolls.
Nebraska	• Expanded the design of workforce services in the state. • Expects RES to continue in the post-ARRA period, given that enhanced service capacity has been structured on the state's investments in NEworks and better use of technology.
Nevada	• Saved the UI Trust Fund an estimated $9 million between February and September 2010 through shorter benefit duration. • Entered employment rates for RES claimants were higher than for the regular pool of UI claimants. • Funding enabled the reintegration of ES and UI (instead of being just for the RES program).

- Cross-training of UI and ES staff led to increased customer awareness of services and the connection between ES and UI.
- Brought in a new group of customers—a younger generation who did not know they could get services free through the JobConnect offices.

North Carolina
- Identified staff that had been involved in the state's late-1990s RES program to lead its ARRA-RES effort.
- Reinvigorated ES in the state through efforts to start and implement the state's ARRA-RES program.

Ohio
- Hired 100 intermittent (temporary, full-time) staff, who were deployed at One-Stops across the state to handle the burgeoning numbers of customers.
- Expanded the number of RES orientation sessions and one-on-one case management services available to UI claimants.

Pennsylvania
- Significantly increased the share of UI claimants receiving assessments and counseling sessions with ARRA-RES funding.

Texas
- Hired 325 temporary ES staff to scale up RES across the state.
- Trained ES and One-Stop staff across the state to better serve UI claimants.

Virginia
- Allowed the state to proceed with the institutionalization of REA, RES, UI, and WIA service integration. Prior attempts at integration had lacked sufficient staff to conduct outreach, invitations, workshops, and one-on-one assessments.
- Hired additional staff and implemented a new approach to workforce services that will carry forward in the post-ARRA period.

Wisconsin
- Substantially expanded RES in the state.
- Used Wagner-Peyser Recovery Act funds ($7.2 million) and UI Recovery Act administrative funding ($3.6 million) to expand and fundamentally change the way in which UI claimants are served by the One-Stop system.
- Provided the resources needed to reengineer and make fundamental changes to the way in which RES is provided for UI claimants.
- State staff indicated that RES/REA services appeared to make a difference in UI duration, with those attending RES workshops having 12 weeks' shorter duration and higher reentry wages than those who do not.

SOURCE: Author notes and site visit reports.

lowing the boot camp. Local administrators indicated that the boot camps would continue in the post-ARRA period, though the number of sessions was expected to decrease.

In Texas, the Capital Area Board highlighted a key Recovery Act accomplishment in the creation of a series of workshops for higher-earning claimants—often individuals who were connecting with the workforce system for the first time after having earned a high-level salary with a single employer for a number of years. The workshops included stress management, budgeting, and information on building a consultant tool kit. RES staff there also worked with claimants to understand the value of "survival jobs"—short-term, temporary jobs that could help to extend UI benefits.

In NASWA's state survey, almost half of the state respondents (46 percent) reported that their state's RES program or the UI/workforce system partnership in their state was an achievement of the Recovery Act implementation. Only 27 percent of those states, however, reported that their achievements in RES were sustainable.

AFTER THE RECOVERY ACT

Recovery Act funding had to be obligated by September 30, 2010, and fully spent by June 30, 2011. A key issue explored during state site visits concerned what the states expected would happen to their RES programs when Recovery Act funds were fully spent. In 12 of the 20 states visited (Colorado, Florida, Illinois, Nevada, Michigan, Montana, North Dakota, Ohio, Rhode Island, Texas, Virginia, and Wisconsin), administrators expected that RES programs and staffing would be cut when the Recovery Act funding expired. Eight of those states indicated that cuts would likely be to pre–Recovery Act levels.

Some states (Arizona, Florida, Maine, North Carolina, Nebraska, and Virginia) hoped to maintain RES programs (though perhaps on a smaller scale than during the Recovery Act) through trained staff, dedicated reemployment centers, or LMI/IT investments. The investments made by states to improve LMI and IT systems and infrastructure were most often cited as a means of continuing some level of RES post-

ARRA. Maine hoped to maintain its expanded RES program through staff cross-training and its LMI/IT investments.

In Nevada, New York, and Pennsylvania, RES programs will continue to operate after the Recovery Act, as these states provide state funds for RES. Nevada and New York have funded an RES program through employer taxes for a number of years. Nevada officials believe that "the annual savings to Nevada's Trust Fund have demonstrated that assisting UI claimants with their reemployment efforts has been beneficial to both Nevada's employer community and those claimants who need assistance finding employment." Pennsylvania has operated its Profile ReEmployment Program (PREP) since 1995, using its regular W-P ES funding.

ETA Guidance on RES/REA in the Post-ARRA Period

Recent program announcements by ETA highlight lessons learned from ARRA-RES and prior REA activities. In January 2011, the ETA presented the Webinar "Reemployment and Eligibility Assessments (REAs) Moving Forward" to introduce a new vision for the public workforce system—a single, integrated system with workforce services and UI as core elements (Workforce3One 2011). In an effort to improve consistency of service across the nation, the ETA identified four transformational elements to better serving UI claimants in One-Stop Career Centers: common registration forms and records systems, real-time triage to meet immediate needs, transferability of skills, and better use of social media. One of the study states, New York, was awarded a UI/WD Connectivity Pilot Grant to develop initiatives across all four transformational components.

REAs provide a key foundation for the vision of integrated service delivery. In the Webinar "REAs Moving Forward" (Workforce3One 2011), the ETA changed the vision, goals, funding model, MOU requirements, technical assistance, and measurement of the REA grant programs. There were also new requirements for REA activities, timing, and length of service: participants must be contacted to schedule REA appointment no later than the fifth claim week; all REA participants must receive one-on-one eligibility reviews and develop an individual reemployment plan; and a claimant may receive a maximum of three REA services, with subsequent interviews by phone allowable.

In February 2012, Unemployment Insurance Program Letter (UIPL) 10-12 announced, "For FY 2012, there are four additional guidelines for UI REA programs: 1) a maximum of two hours of staff time may be funded to conduct each UI REA, 2) all states that operated a UI REA program in FY 2011 must provide a narrative about their UI REA data in their proposals for FY 2012 UI REA grants, 3) all claimants selected for a UI REA must attend the UI REA, and 4) each completed UI REA must include a referral to a reemployment service or training" (USDOL 2012, p. 3).

In March 2012, the ETA announced an RES/REA program for recipients of Emergency Unemployment Compensation (EUC) (Workforce3One 2012). The program was funded as part of the Middle Class Tax Relief and Job Creation Act (Section 142). All EUC claimants beginning first-tier or entering second-tier benefits on or after March 23, 2012, are required to participate in RES/REA and to conduct weekly job search activities. EUC claimants must be notified of the requirements by the third week and appear for services by the sixth week after the EUC status change. Claimants who have previously participated in RES/REA services during their current UI claim period may be waived from further participation. The EUC program requires four elements: 1) provision of labor market and career information, 2) skills assessment, 3) One-Stop services orientation, and 4) work-search activity review.

The legacy of the ARRA-RES program appears to be a growing consensus around key reemployment services and participation requirements. These elements reflect many of the characteristics and key features of ARRA-RES programs identified as major Recovery Act accomplishments by study states. Whether a state is operating RES through its W-P ES allotment or participating in an REA grant or drawing down funds for other targeted initiatives, these key policy and program elements are now required by ETA as a means to promote service consistency and effectiveness across the nation.

Notes

1. RES services other than labor exchange services, e.g., case management, can be delivered through contracts. If the contract was in place by September 30, 2010, RES services stipulated in such contracts could be provided through June 30, 2011, when all RES funds had to be expended.

References

Benus, Jacob, Eileen Poe-Yamagata, Ying Wang, and Etan Bass. 2008. *Reemployment and Eligibility Assessment (REA) Study: FY 2005 Initiative.* Final Report. Columbia, MD: IMPAQ International. http://wdr.doleta.gov/ research/FullText_Documents/Reemployment%20and%20Eligibility%20 Assessment%20(REA)%20Study%20Final%20Report%20March%20 2008.pdf (accessed March 6, 2013).

Michaelides, Marios, Eileen Poe-Yamagata, Jacob Benus, and Dharmendra Tirumalasetti. 2012. *Impact of the Reemployment and Eligibility Assessment (REA) Initiative in Nevada.* Columbia, MD: IMPAQ International. http://wdr.doleta.gov/research/FullText_Documents/ETAOP_2012_08 _REA_Nevada_Follow_up_Report.pdf (accessed March 6, 2013).

U.S. Department of Labor (USDOL). 2009. *ETA Advisories: Training and Employment Guidance Letter (TEGL) No. 14-08 (March 18, 2009).* Washington, DC: U.S. Department of Labor, Employment and Training Administration. http://wdr.doleta.gov/directives/attach/TEGL/TEGL14-08.pdf (accessed March 6, 2013).

———. 2010a. *ETA Advisories: Unemployment Insurance Program Letter (UIPL) No. 05-10 (January 4, 2010).* Washington, DC: U.S. Department of Labor, Employment and Training Administration. http://wdr.doleta.gov/ directives/attach/UIPL/UIPL05-10acc.pdf (accessed March 6, 2013).

———. 2010b. "U.S. Department of Labor Announces $50 Million in Grants to Assist Re-employment Activities in 33 States and District of Columbia." News release, April 15. Washington, DC: U.S. Department of Labor. http:// www.dol.gov/opa/media/press/eta/eta20100488.htm (accessed March 6, 2013).

———. 2010c. *Wagner-Peyser/Labor Exchange.* Washington, DC: U.S. Department of Labor, Employment and Training Administration. http:// www.doleta.gov/programs/wagner_peyser.cfm (accessed March 6, 2013).

———. 2012. "U.S. Labor Department Awards Nearly $65.5 Million to Fund Re-employment, Eligibility Assessments for Unemployment Insurance in 40 States, Puerto Rico and D.C." News release, May 7. Washington, DC: U.S. Department of Labor. http://www.dol.gov/opa/media/press/eta/ETA20120916.htm (accessed March 6, 2013).

Workforce3One. 2010. "(Presentation Slides) Reemployment and Eligibility Assessments (REAs)." Webinar. Posted by Gary Gonzales on January 28. Washington, DC: U.S. Department of Labor, Employment and Training Administration. https://www.workforce3one.org/view/2001002843741242849/info (accessed March 6, 2013).

———. 2011. "Reemployment and Eligibility Assessments (REAs) Moving Forward (Part II)." Webinar. Posted by Margaret Lamb on January 17. Washington, DC: U.S. Department of Labor, Employment and Training Administration. https://www.workforce3one.org/view/5001101739142268395/info (accessed March 6, 2013).

———. 2012. "(Presentation Slides) Emergency Unemployment Compensation (EUC) Reemployment Services and Reemployment and Eligibility Assessments (RES/REAs)." Webinar. Posted by Gary Gonzalez on March 21. Washington, DC: U.S. Department of Labor, Employment and Training Administration. https://www.workforce3one.org/view/2001208137604189725/info (accessed March 6, 2013).

6
Trade Adjustment Assistance Program

Stephen A. Wandner
Urban Institute

The Trade Adjustment Assistance (TAA) program is a form of extended unemployment insurance (UI) that targets workers adversely affected by international trade. Fifty years ago, the TAA program was created as part of the Trade Expansion Act of 1962 to help workers and firms adjust to efforts to promote freer international trade. The TAA program stemmed from the understanding that, as trade expands, there are winners and losers, and as a policy determination, the losers should be compensated, at least in part, for the costs they experience. The program has been a continuing tool to facilitate compromise on international trade policy by lessening the impact on adversely affected workers. Since the Trade Act of 1974, TAA has provided a variety of benefits and employment services to American workers who lose their jobs because of foreign competition or imports. The primary services for workers are these three: 1) monthly cash benefits similar to, and coordinated with, unemployment insurance; 2) access to employment and training services; and 3) other services and benefits including job search assistance, relocation assistance, and a tax credit to cover the costs of health insurance.

Over the years, Congress has modified TAA many times, often in response to changing economic conditions and public policy concerns. During the time period covered by this study, three sets of TAA rules were in effect at various times during frequent and complex changes to the TAA system.

1) The Trade Act of 2002, Division A, Trade Adjustment Assistance, which may be cited as the Trade Adjustment Assistance Reform Act (TAARA) of 2002, reauthorized TAA for five years as part of legislation extending the president's expired "fast

track" authority to negotiate trade agreements. It expanded TAA in a number of ways, including making secondary or downstream workers eligible for the first time, creating a new health insurance tax credit program for dislocated workers, adding a program for farmers and authorizing a limited wage subsidy program for older workers. TAARA expired on September 30, 2007. However, the TAA program was kept afloat until February 2009 by a number or short-term bills, including the Trade Extension Act of 2007, the Consolidated Appropriations Act of 2008, and the Consolidated Security, Disaster Assistance, and Continuing Appropriations Act of 2009.

2) The American Recovery and Reinvestment Act (ARRA) was enacted on February 17, 2009. It contained many provisions, including the Trade and Globalization Adjustment Assistance Act (TGAAA) of 2009, which extended TAA for nearly two years to the end of 2010. Changes effective in May 2009 included the following: additional funding for all programs, first-time eligibility for both service workers and firms, addition of a new communities program, and an increase in the amount of the tax credit for health insurance programs for dislocated workers. The ARRA/TGAAA expired at the end of December 2010.

The AARA/TGAAA was extended through February 12, 2011, but the TAA program was reauthorized under the Omnibus Trade Act of 2010 to February 12, 2012. Under the Omnibus Trade Act, the TAA program reverted back to the pre-ARRA Trade Act of 2002. The Trade Act of 2002 provisions were then in effect again beginning on February 12, 2011, until they were superseded by provisions in the Trade Adjustment Assistance Extension Act (TAAEA) of 2011 that October.

3) Trade Adjustment Assistance Extension Act (TAAEA) of 2011 was enacted on October 21, 2011. It reflected a compromise between the provisions of the Trade Act of 2002 and the Recovery Act of 2009. This TAA program reauthorization was a condition for the simultaneous enactment of three free trade agreements with Colombia, Panama, and South Korea. It continued the worker, employer, and farmer programs from the

Trade Act of 2002 but eliminated the communities program from the Recovery Act of 2009. It also retained many of the enhanced ARRA programs and higher funding levels. While it renewed eligibility for service workers and firms, increased job training income support, and retained health insurance tax credits, it also reduced funding for job search assistance, relocation assistance, and wage supplements for older workers.

Box 6.1 summarizes when the various acts were in effect and whether study site visits were conducted during these time periods.

This chapter considers the TAA program during the period of ARRA/TGAAA implementation and operation between May 2009 and February 2011. It also covers the period of reversion to the old Trade Act of 2002 rules from February 2011 to October 21, 2011, as well as the early implementation of the expanded TAAEA program beginning on October 21, 2011.

The main focus of this chapter is on the trade provisions in the Trade and Globalization Adjustment Assistance Act of 2009 (TGAAA), contained in the Recovery Act, which significantly changed the TAA program. In addition to some alterations to the technical provisions governing eligibility determinations and employer certifications, several important programmatic changes were made that expanded eligibility and increased benefits:

- **More employers became eligible for TAA.** The kinds of employers for which workers were eligible for TAA was expanded to include service sector companies, public agencies, and workers whose jobs were offshored to other countries. Previously, eligibility was more targeted on specific trade-affected job losses, mainly in the manufacturing sector.

Box 6.1 Timeline of Laws in Effect and Site Visits Conducted

Law in effect	Time span in effect	Months	Site visits
Trade Act of 2002	8/6/02 to 2/17/09	79	No
ARRA/TGAAA	2/17/09 to 2/12/11	24	Yes
Trade Act of 2002	2/12/11 to 10/21/11	9	Yes
TAAEA	10/21/11 to date	16	Yes

SOURCE: Hornbeck (2013) and author's compilation.

- **Expanded reemployment services.** Funding increased and emphasis was placed on services to help workers become reemployed, including assessment, testing, counseling, and early employment assistance.

- **More emphasis on training.** The emphasis on and funding for job training was greatly expanded, and workers were given a longer time (26 weeks after layoff) to begin training. Workers in training could also receive TAA payments for a longer period: 136 weeks, and 156 weeks if they were in remedial education. Training could be either full-time or part-time. Previously the training period was 104 weeks and 130 for remedial education, and the training supported by TAA had to be full-time.

- **Higher subsidy for health insurance.** The Health Coverage Tax Credit for workers was increased from 65 percent to 80 percent of the monthly insurance premium.

These TGAAA provisions became effective in May 2009 and were effective through February 12, 2011. Workers and employers in companies whose TAA petitions were approved after May 17, 2009, were subject to the new rules. Firms and workers who qualified under the previous law continued to receive benefits under the old rules, except that the expanded Health Coverage Tax Credit applied to all participants. Thus, states were required to manage the program under two sets of rules because some ongoing participants were subject to the old rules, while employers and workers approved after May 17, 2009, fell under the new law.

After February 12, 2011, TAA provisions reverted to the law that had been in effect before the TGAAA, and the Omnibus Trade Act of 2010 authorized the appropriation of funds for one additional year, through February 12, 2012. However, before the February 2012 expiration of the appropriation, TAA was once again reauthorized and expanded in October 2011 by the Trade Adjustment Assistance Extension Act of 2011 (TAAEA).

This chapter synthesizes the findings from two rounds of site visits with respect to how the new TAA provisions were implemented and operated—the first one conducted in 16 states between December 2009 and June 2010, and the second conducted in 20 states between April and December 2011. Thus, the period covered during the two rounds of site visits includes the period of TGAAA implementation and operation, as well as the period of TGAAA extension and the reversion to the TAARA provisions. In addition, a few second-round visits were conducted while the states were preparing for or implementing new TAA provisions that became effective October 21, 2011, under the TAAEA.

The 20 study states had good coverage of the TAA program in the United States. Since the TAA program activity is highly concentrated among the states, the top 10 states in FY 2010 had 57 percent of the certifications. A 2011 USDOL report to Congress indicates that the 20 study states include eight of the 10 states with the most certifications: Ohio (221), Pennsylvania (208), Michigan (189), North Carolina (169), Texas (131), New York (111), Illinois (102), and Wisconsin (96).

The following four issues related to the TGAAA provisions are covered in this chapter:

1) changes made to implement the new provisions;

2) changes in the number and types of employers and workers participating in TAA;

3) changes in the types of services and training individuals receive; and

4) accomplishments and challenges in implementing the TGAAA changes, including issues relating to TAA after the TGAAA provisions expired in December 2010.

ADMINISTRATIVE CHANGES FOR IMPLEMENTING THE 2009 TAA PROVISIONS

A number of important changes in the 2009 TAA provisions required states to modify policies and procedures related to eligibility, services, and operations. Before addressing the states' implementation of the eligibility and services changes, two administrative issues of particular significance are briefly summarized, as state agencies devoted considerable time and resources to them both following the Recovery Act's enactment in 2009 and its reauthorization with somewhat different requirements in 2011. These two efforts are as follows: 1) reprogramming information technology and data systems to track the various iterations of the program, which were often operating simultaneously, as well as the new program data required to be collected; and 2) ensuring compliance with the federal regulations requiring state merit system personnel to deliver TAA benefits and services.

Reprogramming Data Systems

In Round 1 visits, all administrators noted the extensive data system reprogramming required to meet new TAA program reporting and cost accounting regulations. At that time, a few of the states (all with very small programs) were still in the process of modifying systems, but the vast majority (80 percent) of the states studied had completed the necessary reprogramming by the time of the fieldwork. In fact, as noted below, successfully making the administrative data system changes for TAA was often mentioned by state workforce agency administrators as one of their greatest accomplishments in implementing all the changes required by the Recovery Act.

However, while the reprogramming had been successfully completed, administrators and staff spoke of the magnitude of that task. In every state, administrators explained that the difficulties associated with the short time frame allowed for implementing the TAA rules were compounded by the USDOL's delayed issuing of reporting guidelines until July 2009, one month after the first enrollments commenced under the new rules and only a few weeks before the first new quarterly reports were required to be submitted to the federal government. The most burdensome TAA reporting and data systems changes mentioned were as follows:

- The requirement to report accrued as well as actual training expenditures per participant per quarter. Systems had to be reprogrammed to accurately record and track individuals enrolling and receiving services, both for those subject to the old rules and those subject to the new rules. This was seen as extremely difficult by some states like North Carolina that did not have the resources to update their systems.

- Having to maintain data systems for the dual programs for several years because workers under the old rules might still have a remaining period of training eligibility.

- The significant increase in the number of records and data fields in the data systems. For example, states had to report data on applicants as well as participants and exiters. (Under the old rules, only exiters were reported.) In one state, this reportedly increased the number of individuals in each quarterly data file by 25 times, from 1,200 exiters to approximately 30,000 applicants, participants, and exiters. Similarly, states had to track cumulative Trade Readjustment Allowance (TRA) payments over time, rather than just the payment amounts at each point in time.

Although the reprogramming was accomplished, some of the programmatic changes that were the subject of that reprogramming could continue to cause operational problems, as discussed further in the following sections. For example, administrators and staff noted the challenges in having to do the following three tasks: 1) track and report on two programs; 2) explain two sets of rules to staff, employers, and workers; and 3) reconcile costs associated with the old and new rules.

The Round 2 visits in 2011 found that all the states had implemented the Recovery Act provisions but that reporting continued to pose a challenge. Nevada, for instance, noted continued technical issues. Its state officials explained that once a TAA report was submitted through the federal Web site, the state was unable to review and correct the submission. While officials could access the site and see that there had been a successful submission, they were unable to see how the report translated onto the federal report forms that were produced. When asked at a later date why information was missing, Nevada officials indicated that it would have been difficult to retroactively supply information that they were not aware was missing. Ohio also pointed to the burdens associated with the repeated changes to the program. Officials in Ohio explained that they had invested much time and money in making changes to Ohio's data system to meet TGAAA's new requirements and noted that it required yet more staffing time and money to reprogram the system when TAA reverted back to the TAARA provisions in February 2011.

Merit Staff Rule

The second TAA administrative issue that was significant in some states concerns the recently promulgated USDOL regulation reinstituting a requirement that personnel providing TAA benefits and services must be state staff covered by formal merit system policies. In the explanations and guidelines issued by the ETA, federal officials explain that this is not a new requirement but a reinstatement of a long-standing rule in effect between 1975 and 2005, when the requirement was lifted.[1] The rationale for reinstating the rule was that the determination of program eligibility—including the eligibility for cash benefits and services—is an inherently governmental function and that in making these decisions state agency staff are, in effect, agents of the federal government. Thus, "the use of [these] public funds requires that decisions be made in the best interest of the public and of the population to be served. By requiring merit staffing, the Department seeks to ensure that benefit decisions and services are provided in the most consistent, efficient, accountable, and transparent way" (USDOL 2013).

Two exceptions to the merit staff rule are allowed. Three states (Colorado, Massachusetts, and Michigan) were operating under temporary demonstration authority approved by the USDOL in the late 1990s, which allows local merit staff to carry out Wagner-Peyser activities; that authority also applies to TAA. A second exception is a bit more nuanced—namely, that staff in partner agencies and programs, including WIA, may provide services to TAA participants, provided there are appropriately integrated state policies and procedures in One-Stop Career Centers.

According to the states from Round 1 visits, administrators were well aware of the reinstatement of the merit staff rule, and in most states there was little if any concern about it. Two states are operating under Wagner-Peyser Act demonstration authority regarding merit staffing (Colorado and Michigan), and, in nearly all the other states, either state personnel already had carried out TAA activities or the state had policies in place that would meet the second exception because of cross-program services.

Some states, however, were forced to restructure their merit staffing to better integrate services and allocate costs across programs to satisfy the federal regulatory requirement. In three states visited during Round 1 (Illinois, Louisiana, and Texas), administrators were still in the process of revising state rules and restructuring systems to come into compliance, since in all three states many local office staff members who had previously carried out some TAA activities were not state merit employees.

In Texas, over 90 percent of the staff providing TAA services before the Recovery Act went into effect were nonmerit personnel. While state personnel handled all eligibility determinations, TRA payments, and communications with employers about potentially eligible workers, nonmerit local WIB staff had responsibility for service delivery, as is the case with WIA and other workforce programs. The Texas Workforce Commission examined service delivery changes necessary to comply by December 15, 2010—the implementation date set by ETA.

In Illinois, the state employment security agency managed TRA benefits and local Workforce Investment Boards (WIBs) administered TAA benefits and services, except in Chicago, where the local Workforce Investment Board contracted out TAA functions to a nonprofit organization. State and local administrators were continuing to consider policy and service delivery changes that might be required to meet the merit staff rule.

In Louisiana, the state established regional trade coordinators that worked with local WIBs and One-Stops, and all applications were certified by these merit staff members.

At the time of the Round 1 site visits to these three states, no final policies had been established, as they were awaiting final ETA guidance, and there was continuing concern about how the merit staff rule would affect the TAA programs.

By the time of the Round 2 visits, however, the merit staff issue had been resolved. In order to comply with the requirement that merit staff deliver TAA services and benefits, Illinois hired several new state staff members through the state merit system to oversee the TAA approval and certification process. Texas used the one-third of its administrative dollars designated for case management to hire 23 new full-time state staff through the state's merit system. These staffers were placed in the areas with highest trade activity, with two staff members remaining at the Texas Workforce Commission to provide technical assistance and allow flexibility in case of increased activity in other areas of the state. Louisiana had met the merit staffing requirement and provided training to merit-staffed personnel.

States where Wagner-Peyser services are delivered by local merit staff employees, such as Michigan, did not use Recovery Act funds to increase state staff. Instead, Michigan distributed the Recovery Act funds to the Michigan Works! agencies, which could themselves use the funds to hire limited-term temporary staff. Colorado, like Michigan and Massachusetts, continues to operate through demonstration authority, using approved staff arrangements to carry out the government functions of its TAA program.

Changes in Employers and Workers in TAA

Perhaps the most important change introduced through the 2009 act was the substantial expansion of eligibility for TAA, for both employers and workers. At the time of the first site visits, the message from the field was that while the number of employer petitions for TAA and the number of workers enrolled might be increasing (in some cases, substantially increasing), states believed that most of the increases were due to the recession much more than they were to the new eligibility provisions. There were some notable exceptions, as discussed below, but at that time the new changes only had been in effect for a few months. By the second site visit a somewhat different picture emerged, due in part to the ETA's clearing its backlog of certification petitions.

While the numbers of employer petitions and TAA worker enrollments generally increased, there was great variation across states. It is somewhat difficult to compare participation trends over time and across states, in part because federal reporting rules have changed. For example, before the Recovery Act reauthorization, states had to report to ETA the number of individuals who exited the TAA program but not their applications or enrollments. Some states in this field study were able to provide more detailed information, though. This (when combined with the statistics in the federal reports) suggests the following general patterns: More than half the states visited during Round 1 had experienced at least a 50 percent increase in petitions and active participant enrollments, but there was considerable variation across states—see Table 6.1. Included in the group of states that had experienced the most substantial increases were four states that reported that their participants had more than doubled since 2007 (Florida, Ohio, Texas, and Virginia), and seven states where petitions had more than

Table 6.1 Percentage of Study States Visited Where Administrators Reported Increased TAA Activity in the First Year after Enactment of the Recovery Act

Reported change compared to prior years	Increase in number of TAA petitions	Increase in number of TAA participants enrolled
Small or no change (<10%)	10% of states	10% of states
Moderate increase (~10–50%)	40% of states	40% of states
Substantial increase (~50–200%)	50% of states	50% of states

SOURCE: Site visit interviews conducted in states.

doubled (Florida, Michigan, Ohio, Virginia, Wisconsin, and two states with smaller programs, Montana and North Dakota). To give a sense of the scale, in Ohio, petitions increased from about 85 in 2007 to more than 300 between May 2009 and May 2010, when several thousand individuals were reportedly active in TAA (including 1,700 from one GM plant alone). In Michigan, the state that led the nation in TAA activity and TAA participants, 28,752 TAA participants enrolled in PY 2009, while 33,015 enrolled in PY2010, of which 11,980 received training services (36.3 percent). By mid-2011, 11,000 Michigan workers had received training and support, including approximately 3,000 in long-term training. In Texas, the number of TAA participants being served also more than doubled, increasing from approximately 3,000 to over 6,500. In Montana, a small state, the number of petitions rose from six in 2007 to 30 in the first 12 months of the new program, while in North Dakota the number of petitions rose from one to three between PY 2008 and PY 2009, doubling the number of employees in training. Two other small programs, however, Nevada and Arizona, reported having little or no change in activity. In North Carolina, the state with the largest number of trade-affected workers after Michigan, 3,000 TAA workers took advantage of the health care tax credit.

During the Round 1 visits, state and local administrators attributed these increases in petitions and enrollments primarily to the recession and its aftermath, and considerably less to the changes in the law. But they also noted that this could change in the coming year for various reasons. Administrators in several large states, including New York, expected to see the petition numbers increase in 2010. Administrators in nearly all states also explained that once ETA cleared its backlog of petitions, the number of certified employers also would increase, as would the number of workers from the certified employers. At the time of the Round 1 fieldwork, state officials indicated that on average it was taking 9–10 months for the ETA to make a decision on petitions.

Part of the early increase in TAA in some states, however, also reflected concentrated efforts to market the new rules to employers. A few states were developing marketing and public information campaigns to reach out to potentially eligible workers and employers. Florida, for example used its data system to generate phone calls to specific employers (see Box 6.2).

In addition, the U.S. Department of Labor reports that it encouraged firms and employees to withdraw petitions in early 2009 and resubmit them after May 17, 2009. The response was large. There was a surge in petitions filled in the last five months of FY 2009 because of the Recovery Act program provisions, while certifications reached a maximum the following year because of the time it took to review cases. The number of petitions and certifications, however, declined sharply after their peak (see Table 6.2).

Types of Employers and Workers

There is some indication that part of the increase in petitions may more directly reflect the changes in the statute, particularly the expansion of sectors eligible for TAA, which may have changed the mix of employers and workers in TAA. During the Round 1 visits, many

---

Box 6.2 State TAA Outreach Effort: Florida Marketing to Firms

To build its capacity to reach more TAA-eligible firms, the state of Florida purchased a module from Geo Solutions, the vendor that developed the Employ Florida Marketplace (EFM) integrated labor market information and job matching program. The module generates lists for biweekly calls to firms that may be likely to petition or that already have petitioned, to make them aware of TAA services for firms and workers.

SOURCE: Site visit interviews conducted in states.

Table 6.2 TAA Petition Filing and Determination Activity, FY 2008–2011

	2008	2009	2010	2011
Petitions filed	2,224	4,889	2,542	1,347
Petitions certified	1,471	1,887	2,810	1,115
Percentage of certifications in service sector	0	19[a]	35	39

[a]Between May 18, 2009, and September 30, 2009, 19 percent of certifications were in the service sector. (The service sector was not covered until TGAAA implementation on May 18.)
SOURCE: USDOL (2009, 2010, 2012).

states noted little evidence in the first year of implementation that the increases in petitions were disproportionately from employers in the newly eligible sectors. However, in some states, it appeared that TAA petitions from employers and employees in the service sector increased. In Florida, for example, which experienced a very large increase in TAA activity, administrators reported that in 2010 approximately one-third of TAA participants were from the new sectors. In Wisconsin, there were 120 new petitions from service firms, and approximately 15 percent of all certifications were from the service sector. In Illinois, nearly 2,000 service sector workers from 42 certified locations received TAA benefits and services. In Montana, where past activity came mainly from timber, transportation, and related industries, the expansion of eligibility to service sector firms, along with the recession, led to many more petitions, a greater interest from firms than in the past, and an increased number of actively served workers (700 in Kalispell alone). In contrast, in Pennsylvania, administrators indicated there were no service sector petitions at that time, but state officials expected future service sector petitions, and they noted that some firms that had already filed petitions might have been mixed-sector (e.g., pharmaceutical companies). Officials in several other states noted that there were reports of some firms "switching" their sector of record specifically to qualify for TAA.

In Round 1 visits, states indicated that the new law had little impact on the characteristics of workers in TAA. A number of administrators reported that the education level of TAA enrollees was somewhat higher than in the past in states where service sector and government petitions had been certified. But in most states, administrators and staff reported that the types of workers had not changed since the new TAA rules went into effect.

For the United States as a whole, there was a dramatic increase in the participation of service sector firms and workers in the TAA program over a short period of time. Between 2008 and 2011, the percentage of certified firms from the service sector went from zero (when the service sector was not covered) to nearly 40 percent, as was shown in Table 6.2. On the other hand, the USDOL reported little change in the characteristics of participants in the program. Table 6.3 provides TAA participant characteristics: older, primarily male, less educated, and longer tenured.

CHANGES IN TAA SERVICES

During the implementation of the 2009 provisions, a couple of patterns emerged regarding two categories of services: 1) counseling, assessment, and case management; and 2) emphasis on training.

Counseling, Assessment, and Case Management

Given the emphasis on counseling and assessment and the 2009 legislative change that allowed TAA funds to be used for these services, it is not surprising that in nearly every state visited, there was a greater focus on these activities. As required, there was more emphasis on case management, although some states continued to be confused about what exactly counted as case management for TAA cost-accounting purposes. Many states reported that they were starting the counseling and assessment process earlier, and a number were using new assessment and case management software technology or expanding its use to include TAA participants in computer program applications that they already were using for participants in other workforce programs.

The Recovery Act reauthorization emphasized providing counseling and assessment services up front to "threatened workers." Some states, like Illinois, actively sought lists of such workers to notify them of the benefits available under the TAA program, but staff explained that such efforts were very challenging because it was difficult to get an accurate list of these workers. The intent, nevertheless, was to engage workers sooner and provide them with one of the several case management

Table 6.3 New TAA Participant Characteristics, FY 2010 Average

Age	Gender: male	Education: h.s. diploma, GED, or less	Race: white	Tenure in trade-affected employment
46.7 yrs.	60.7%	64.1%	66.5%	13.8 yrs.

SOURCE: USDOL (2012).

activities required in TAA, including testing, assessment, the development of an Individual Employment Plan, and employment counseling.

Even in states where there was little or no increase in the number of people receiving assessment and counseling, there is evidence that the changes to TAA had the indirect effect of increasing overall counseling and assessment throughout the workforce system. This occurred in large part because many states used other sources of funds (mainly WIA–Dislocated Worker and Wagner-Peyser funds) to pay for counseling and assessment, case management, and support services for TAA participants. Many staff and administrators explained that one of the main reasons they coenrolled individuals into TAA and into WIA Dislocated Worker programs was to provide the TAA clients with counseling and assessment. The new rules meant that agencies could distribute the costs across programs for individuals enrolled in multiple programs to more accurately reflect the costs of services. And the end result was that

---

Box 6.3 Counseling, Assessment, and Case Management in the TAA: The Perspective of One Administrator

"We always provided case management and related services [to TAA clients], and our standard expectation is that folks are coenrolled as Dislocated Workers. It's great that funding is now set aside for case management in TAA . . . this has been a big change. We didn't want to continue to rob Dislocated Workers to pay for case management for TAA clients. It's allowed us to do a better job for TAA and to serve more Dislocated Workers."

SOURCE: Site visit interviews conducted in states.

a larger number of individuals in total (i.e., across programs) received testing, assessment, and counseling (see Box 6.3).

Administrators in several states asserted that the new TAA rules had a secondary effect of allowing the state agencies to streamline and improve service delivery systems, not only with respect to assessment and case management, but also with respect to improving their administrative and technology resources to support service delivery, driving down the cost of program delivery. This included, for example, expanding the use of testing and assessment software and allowing the enhancements to integrated data systems that already had been underway but had not been included in TAA. The following cases provide illustrations:

- Wisconsin enhanced its TAA intake and assessment process, including expanding its use of WorkKeys and KeyTrain for TAA participants, which can lead to National Career Readiness Certification.

- Virginia improved its Internet-based labor market information/case management system, already used in Wagner-Peyser and WIA programs, to also include TAA participants and UI recipients.

- Phoenix, Arizona, added a computer literacy assessment to Dislocated Worker services and LinkedIn training to job search/job readiness services.

- North Carolina developed a new information strategy to better reach trade-affected workers. It used a combination of media and direct contact to inform workers of the services available to them.

- In Ohio, IT staff used ARRA workforce funds to make programming changes to the state's automated case management system so that the client's record was fully integrated with the WIA and Wagner-Peyser client record, which allowed tracking of demographic characteristics and services received across the three programs.

- Washington strengthened electronic access to TAA resources for staff.

A few state administrators noted that even with the new TAA rules that allowed the program funds to cover assessment and case management, the total amount of funding for these services across all programs was inadequate. One also suggested that ETA should consider revising the allocation of funds for case management ($350,000 to each state) more equitably since some states had very high program levels and others had minimal programs. The interest in case management was high in nearly all states visited, although several administrators and staff said that there was still confusion about what exactly could be counted as case management for reporting purposes. Given the expanding interest, states were looking for guidance in this area.

Training

In the states included in this study, administrators reported that there was an increase in the number of TAA participants entering training, including more participants who were in training for six months or longer. However, administrators were careful to note that most of the increase was consistent with the entire public workforce system, including WIA; it had increased the emphasis on training, which tends to increase during periods of high unemployment. They cautioned that it was not clear if the increase in TAA training (where it existed) was due to the changes in TAA itself (e.g., allowing longer-term training and allowing a longer time to initiate training). One state, however, noted that, under the Recovery Act TAA rules, the ability to provide TAA-funded training prior to separation was a useful device where firms staged layoffs prior to closure.

There were a few issues related to TAA training that are important to note. First, there was considerable variation both in the types of training providers that TAA participants could access and in the maximum tuition that would be allowed. Not only did Recovery Act provisions allow a longer period of training, but also the training providers and institutions were not limited to those on the state's Eligible Training Provider List (ETPL), and there was no specific cap on the cost of training per participant. States had discretion, which led to variation across the study sites. In some states, such as Arizona and Florida, TAA and WIA training used the ETPL established for WIA, generally limiting individual enrollment to the programs of providers on the list.

Most states visited, though, including Nevada, Texas, and Washington, did not limit TAA training to the providers on the ETPL. There was also variation in the amount of tuition that could be covered by TAA; Washington State, for instance, had a cap of $22,000–$25,000 (it was $12,000–$16,000 pre–Recovery Act), while Florida had no cap.

Second, the delay in processing petition decisions at the national level had an unintended and negative effect on training. The Recovery Act rules both encouraged programs to begin to work with participants as soon as possible and to encourage them to enroll in training. Recovery Act provisions also permitted TAA customers to obtain longer-term training and gave them a longer period of time after they were laid off in which to begin that training. However, during the transition to the Recovery Act rules, USDOL approval of petitions was taking as long as 12 months (though by mid-2010 the delay was reduced to approximately seven months). This meant that individuals who had exhausted UI benefits and then, after certification, had begun receiving TRA and long-term training, might nevertheless exhaust their combined UI and TRA weeks of benefits before completing training. While no such cases were identified, several administrators and staff noted their concerns (Box 6.4).

A third issue concerns the interest in training. While the program's emphasis on training, especially long-term training, increased in about two-thirds of the states visited, there is little evidence that there were

---

Box 6.4 Unintended Effects on Training of Delays in Approving Petitions: The Concern of a State Administrator

"[We are worried that] the delay in petition approvals, along with the natural inclination of some trade-affected workers to delay their decisions to enter training, will mean that some workers will run out of TRA benefits before they finish the training. They can run through their UI, which counts against their TRA weeks, while their company's petition is being approved, and then they might delay starting a program. The result could be that a TAA participant might run out of TRA also and still have six months or a year to go in their program."

SOURCE: Site visit interviews conducted in states.

any changes in the level or length of training entered by TAA participants. In some of the states, the number of participants in training increased, but staff felt that those numbers reflected the total number of individuals in TAA and did not represent an increase in the percentage of individuals who entered training. There also is no evidence that the duration of training entered was any longer than in the past. In general, the length of training was about the same as before the Recovery Act (averaging six months to two years). Staff suggested that this was partly due to continuing low interest in long-term training. Some states began to ramp up on-the-job training (OJT) for TAA, and that form of training might have been more attractive to unemployed workers, but no data was collected on that option.

In the other third of the states visited, there was some evidence that training was increasing and that those who were going into training were more often choosing long-term training. Pennsylvania, for example, had over 4,000 in training, and two-thirds of them were in long-term programs taking over six months to complete. In Montana, officials indicated that most TAA participants were entering training, and that over two-thirds of them were in long-term training, with many "taking advantage of what they perceive to be a once-in-a-lifetime opportunity." The story was similar in Florida, where state and local administrators indicated that training was increasing and most in training were in long-term programs (usually 9–24 months). The pattern was generally similar in Washington State, where officials further explained that there was significant variation by type of worker and by region (since local workforce investment boards had discretion on many issues). Workers in mining and timber, for example, were less interested in pursuing training or education than workers from service sectors. However, in Arizona, staff reported that while displaced workers, including engineers, from the Phoenix-area microelectronics industry benefited from the available training, workers were often reemployed at lower wages (unlike in the past, when employees usually moved from lower to higher wages).

Thus, the effect of the Recovery Act and its extension until February 2011 on training and long-term training was mixed. Most states saw no major difference in training rates or types of training entered into, but in a number of states there was a clear trend toward more and longer training.

ACCOMPLISHMENTS AND CHALLENGES

Both the number of employers petitioning for TAA and the number of workers enrolled in TAA increased considerably among the study states. In approximately half the states, activity levels were reported to be up substantially in 2010, and in several states both the number of petitions and the number of participants more than doubled. State and local administrators and staff, however, felt that most of the increase was attributable to the recession and that a small part, in some states, might reflect the Recovery Act's changes to the program, including the coverage of service sector workers. In general, state administrators felt that their greatest accomplishment had been handling the substantial increase in workload stemming from the TAA and other workforce investment programs. Several states pointed to the TAA health coverage and tax credits as having the greatest positive effect on their recipients.

The administrators also pointed to the rapid implementation of the changes to TAA as a major accomplishment. The president signed the law in February 2009, and the first workers became eligible in May. It was a major effort for state agencies to reprogram their data systems to accommodate the changes, both for determining eligibility and providing services as well as for complying with federal program and cost accounting reporting. This huge effort was made all the more challenging because states did not receive implementing regulations or guidance from the USDOL until after the program went into effect. And both the data systems and reporting procedures had to be revamped—and then revamped again after new TAA rules became effective in February 2011—to maintain records under what became, in effect, three different TAA programs. Despite the considerable reprogramming achievements, the reprogramming also presented the most significant challenge states faced in implementing the Recovery Act provisions and then the act's 2011 modification.

The states faced great administrative complexity starting in 2011. Three separate TAA programs had to be maintained in tandem—one for those subject to the TGAAA (those who entered the program after May 2009), another for those subject to the law as it existed prior to TGAAA, and yet another for those subject to the reversion to pre-TGAAA provisions starting in late February 2011. There continued to be uncertainty about some issues that affected the programs, including how to define and allocate case management costs and alternative structures that could meet the merit staff rule. States were also unsure of ways to reach the potential pool of employers and workers eligible for TAA to ensure that they were made aware of the services, for which they were eligible.

Additional challenges identified by the states included

- lengthy delays between the filing of a petition and certification, resulting in loss of benefits and services;
- the difficulty in explaining to customers from employers certified under one program why they were not eligible for benefits under one or more of the other programs;
- uncooperative employers who refused to provide, or delayed in providing, worker lists;
- difficulty in determining in which state outsourced teleworkers, who did not report to a physical location, should be certified;
- multiple state certifications and confusion over which state should contact the employer to get the worker list;
- loopholes in the implementing regulations, which allowed employers to lay off employees and then hire them back as temporary workers, shifting the cost of health benefits to the state, as well as a 45-day limit on the waiver of the deadline for health benefit enrollment when there might be many legitimate reasons why a worker missed the deadline.

In addition, one state noted that many participants from the manufacturing sector did not want to reveal to agency staff that they did not have high school diplomas or GEDs, which made it difficult to direct those participants to training. A community college offering remedial classes (e.g., GED and computer literacy) using course names that minimized embarrassment was deemed to be helpful.

CONCLUSION

The Trade and Globalization Adjustment Assistance Act of 2009 (TGAAA) was enacted under the Recovery Act and significantly expanded the TAA program. State agencies had considerable difficulty implementing the program, particularly as it related to developing new automated systems and, for a small number of states, converting to merit staffing for TAA administration. TAA petitions and certifications increased greatly upon implementation, but they have since declined. Under TGAAA, service sector certifications grew dramatically, reaching 39 percent of the caseload by FY 2011. The characteristics of workers participating in the TAA program, however, do not appear to have changed a great deal with the implementation of TGAAA.

Notes

1. For the employment services, merit staffing provisions have been in effect under the Wagner-Peyser Act since its enactment in 1933. For Unemployment Insurance, merit staffing provisions were in effect under administrative grant rules from the outset of the program in 1935 and were codified under the Social Security Act in 1940. Merit staffing rules were applied to the TAA program when it became effective in 1975.

References

Hornbeck, J. F. 2013. *Trade Adjustment Assistance (TAA) and Its Role in U.S. Trade Policy.* Washington, DC: Congressional Research Service.

United States Department of Labor (USDOL). 2009. *Trade Adjustment Assistance for Workers: Report to the Committee on Finance of the Senate and Committee on Ways and Means of the House of Representatives.* Washington, DC: U.S. Department of Labor, Employment and Training Administration.

———. 2010. *Trade Adjustment Assistance for Workers: Report to the Committee on Finance of the Senate and Committee on Ways and Means of the House of Representatives.* Washington, DC: U.S. Department of Labor, Employment and Training Administration. http://www.doleta.gov/tradeact/docs/AnnualReport10.pdf (accessed March 4, 2013).

———. 2012. *Trade Adjustment Assistance for Workers: Fiscal Year 2011 Report to the Committee on Finance of the Senate and Committee on Ways and Means of the House of Representatives.* Washington, DC: U.S. Department of Labor, Employment and Training Administration. http://www.doleta.gov/tradeact/docs/AnnualReport11.pdf (accessed March 4, 2013).

———. 2013. *Questions & Answers—Trade Adjustment Assistance Final Rule on Merit Staffing of State Administration and Allocation of Training Funds to States.* Washington, DC: U.S. Department of Labor. https://www.dol.gov/regulations/taa-qa.htm (accessed March 6, 2013).

7
Other Related Initiatives

Labor Market Information, Green Jobs, and Subsidized Employment

Joyce Kaiser
Capital Research Corporation

The Recovery Act affected many aspects of the workforce invest-ment system. This section summarizes provisions that were separate from but interacted with the act's provisions for Workforce Investment Act (WIA), Wagner-Peyser, Trade Adjustment Assistance (TAA), and Unemployment Insurance (UI) programs in at least some of the states included in this study. The three areas discussed here are 1) labor mar-ket information (LMI) improvements, 2) green jobs initiatives, and 3) implementation of the subsidized employment programs authorized under the Temporary Assistance for Needy Families (TANF) Emer-gency Fund.

LABOR MARKET INFORMATION SYSTEM IMPROVEMENTS

The Recovery Act, along with formula funding, provided either new resources or new motivations to improve, expand, or upgrade automated labor market information systems in many of the study states. Major motivations for the Recovery Act initiatives around LMI were to encourage states to upgrade their LMI systems and to improve their overall workforce investment systems to incorporate emerging or expanding green jobs occupations and industries related to renewable energy and energy efficiency. State Labor Market Information Improve-ment Grants, funded by the Recovery Act, were awarded to individual states and consortia of states to enhance and upgrade their LMI infrastructure in various ways, as well as to improve the technology. The grants are listed in Tables 7.1 and 7.2.

All but two study states (North Dakota and Wisconsin) participated in the Recovery Act LMI Improvement Grants. A few examples of how these funds were used follow:

- **Colorado** (consortium participant). Colorado received $245,000 in grant funds, aimed at providing timely and comprehensive information on current and future industry workforce supply and demand conditions. Licenses for the Help-Wanted OnLine (HWOL) Data Series from the Conference Board were procured in June 2010. The LMI Gateway Web site was updated during the past year and now includes a number of additional features including Help-Wanted OnLine job, occupation, and employer data for Colorado. HWOL data has been referenced in LMI economic analyses and presentations.

- **Michigan** (consortium participant). Under the LMI Improvement grant (on which Indiana and Ohio collaborated), there were a number of important achievements, including the following four:

  1) LMI staff in Michigan and Ohio produced a Green Jobs Report, which assessed the types of green jobs emerging in the consortium states and skills required of workers to fill these jobs (including transferable skills that auto workers have, allowing them to make the transition to employment within the green jobs sector).

  2) The consortium staff developed a Web site, which it called www.drivingworkforcechange.org. This site disseminates information about the initiative and is a resource on green jobs for employers, job seekers, and workforce development professionals.

  3) The Michigan Workforce Development Agency purchased a one-year subscription to the Conference Board's HWOL data. This LMI system provides administrators and staff (including staff in One-Stop Career Centers) with real-time data on job openings, including those in high-demand and emerging occupations. The data from the Help-Wanted OnLine

Table 7.1 **State Labor Market Information Improvement—Consortium Awards (study sites in bold)**

Organization	City	State	Additional consortium members	Amount ($)
Indiana Department of Workforce Development	Indianapolis	IN	**Michigan, Ohio**	4,000,000
Louisiana Office of Occupational Information Services (OOIS), Research & Statistics Division	Baton Rouge	LA	Mississippi	2,279,393
Maryland Department of Labor & Industry	Baltimore	MD	District of Columbia, **Virginia**	4,000,000
Montana Department of Labor & Industry	Helena	MT	Iowa, **Nebraska, North Dakota** (opted out), South Dakota, Utah, Wyoming	3,877,949
Nevada Department of Employment Training and Rehabilitation	Carson City	NV	**Colorado, Florida, Illinois, New York, North Carolina, Texas,** Utah	3,753,000
Vermont Department of Labor	Montpelier	VT	Connecticut, **Maine,** Massachusetts, New Hampshire, New Jersey, **New York, Rhode Island**	3,999,923

SOURCE: USDOL (2009).

Table 7.2 State Labor Market Information Improvement—Individual State Awards, Study Sites

Organization	City	Amount ($)
Arizona Department of Economic Security	Phoenix	1,211,045
Florida Department of Economic Opportunity	Tallahassee	1,250,000
New York State Department of Labor	Albany	1,112,207
Employment Security Commission of North Carolina	Raleigh	946,034
Ohio Department of Job and Family Services	Columbus	1,015,700
Pennsylvania Department of Labor & Industry	Harrisburg	1,250,000
Washington State Employment Security Dept.	Olympia	1,060,910

SOURCE: USDOL (2009).

system was found to be extremely helpful and, as a result, the state workforce agency decided to continue its subscription with the Conference Board after American Recovery and Reinvestment Act (ARRA) funding was exhausted.

4) The Michigan Workforce Development Agency held a green jobs conference ("Driving Workforce Change") in Dearborn, Michigan, in May 2009. A total of 225 people attended this conference, including representatives of Michigan Works! agencies, academia, employers, and economic and workforce development officials. A focus of this conference was on the greening of the automotive industry.

• **New York State.** New York received funds under three LMI Improvement Grants to participate in two multistate consortia to develop forecasting methodologies and real-time supply-and-demand modules for green jobs and the skills required for the jobs.

• **Nevada** (consortium participant). In Nevada, funds were used to make technical improvements to the LMI system and to upgrade the state's projection systems. No staff was added with Recovery Act funds. In order to generate money to support LMI activities in general, the state agency has begun to offer LMI services to other state agencies on a fee-for-service basis. Currently, the state agency has a fee-for-service arrangement with the state treasurer's office.

- **Nebraska** (consortium participant). Five contiguous states (North Dakota dropped out) joined together to improve LMI and research for enhancing the labor exchange system for careers within the green economy. Nebraska's LMI group completed its survey work and analysis, and those activities have helped shape NEworks, an on-line information site providing a complete set of employment tools for job seekers in Nebraska, improving the state's capacity to provide better and more targeted information related to green jobs employment.

In addition to the Recovery Act LMI grants, most states have been improving their automated information systems used for program management, job matching, and case management, relying on regular annual LMI grants as well as WIA and Wagner-Peyser funds. For example, North Dakota (Box 7.1) and Wisconsin, while not recipients of LMI grant funds, did use other Recovery Act funds and formula funds to initiate improvements to their LMI systems and to conduct important research.

Based on discussions with administrators and staff in the study states, a couple of points can be made about LMI support for green jobs in the Recovery Act period. First, the 2009 LMI grants are being primarily used, as intended, to support research and analysis necessary

---

Box 7.1 North Dakota's Use of Other Recovery Act Funds

The state initiated research related to the burgeoning oil and gas extraction efforts taking place in the state and produced *Bakken Oil Formation*, a Web publication that explores the relationship between the price of oil and its influence on employment levels in the state's mining and extraction industry sector. *Business Survivability in North Dakota* is a research publication exploring the relationship between the trends in business survivability in the state. This is also a Web publication. These are only two examples of LMI activities, with many more located on the labor market information Web site http://ndworkforceintelligence.com.

SOURCE: State and local office site visit reports.

for defining green job occupations, establishing a baseline number of current green jobs in the state, and upgrading forecasting models to project future demand for workers in green jobs. About one-third of the workforce development agencies of the states in the sample are sponsoring surveys of green jobs, engaging in statistical analysis to develop or upgrade forecasting models, or conducting other research to define occupations and skills needed to integrate information on these jobs into existing LMI systems (Colorado, Illinois, Michigan, Montana, Ohio, Pennsylvania, and Washington). Louisiana and Illinois intend to conduct research and analysis to improve their LMI systems, including new forecasting analysis for Louisiana done by Louisiana State University researchers. Second, many states already had fairly sophisticated LMI systems because of the high federal and state investment in this area over the past decades (e.g., Florida, Michigan, New York, Ohio, Texas, and Wisconsin). In general, administrators in many of these states indicated that little if any of the Recovery Act or LMI grant funds are being used to improve the hardware or technology of those systems. However, in several of these advanced LMI states, there are some notable examples of information technology (IT) enhancements related to program services and management systems that are being made with Recovery Act funds or had been planned prior to the Recovery Act. In several states, improvements are now being accelerated because available resources have allowed investments in one-time upgrades, particularly for improving job matching and integrating more programs into a single system. Some examples of these efforts are as follows:

- **Washington State** is integrating green jobs components into its SKIES system, upgrading the link to UI systems, and upgrading data access and quality control procedures to allow businesses expanded job-matching queries.

- **Virginia** has integrated TAA and UI into the Virginia Workforce Connection's Web-based LMI/job matching/case management system already used for WIA and Wagner-Peyser.

- **Florida**, which also has an integrated LMI/case management system, used Recovery Act funds to increase its available bandwidth and storage capacity, refine job matching, and integrate real-time LMI tools that line staff can use in counseling customers.

Several staff and administrators noted that such upgrades in the LMI systems are especially important now because many more higher-skilled customers are unemployed and seeking employment services than in the past. Having more sophisticated LMI tools allows the workforce investment system to better serve these customers.

Along with the LMI improvements being made in nearly every state, several administrators discussed constraints that have affected some planned LMI-related initiatives. For example, a state hiring freeze in Arizona led the state workforce agency to revise its plan for conducting in-house most of the analysis to improve projections. And North Dakota had been notified by the Employment and Training Administration (ETA) that the state could receive an LMI green jobs grant, but the legislature voted not to accept the grant.

In summary, almost every state in this study has made improvements in LMI systems to support services in workforce investment programs, such as career counseling, occupational assessment, case management, and job matching. And most states report making substantial progress in defining and incorporating occupational information on green jobs into their LMI systems.

GREEN JOBS INITIATIVES

The national priority on the energy efficiency and renewable energy sectors was reflected in the Recovery Act provisions that specifically authorized funds to develop the green jobs workforce. Over the past few years, the federal government has placed a high priority on increasing the number of workers who have the skills needed for various high-demand occupations and industries, and green jobs are among the highest priority for industry-focused training. A number of ETA grant programs have been established to fund the development and implementation of skills training for jobs in these emerging and growing sectors. The main grant programs authorized in the Recovery Act that can be used to develop or expand green jobs training were the following:

- **State Energy Sector Partnership and Training Grants** ($190 million in 2010) for state workforce boards to establish partnerships to develop workforce strategies targeted to energy efficiency and renewable energy industries.

- **Energy Training Partnership Grants** ($100 million in 2009) for cross-agency partnerships to develop training and employment programs for individuals affected by the broader energy and economic situation, including workers formerly in the automotive sector.
- **Green Capacity Building Grants** ($5 million in 2009) were awarded to existing USDOL grantees for local green jobs training programs. Local organizations in 14 of the 20 study states received these grants.
- **Pathways Out of Poverty Grants** ($150 million in 2009) for local programs and local affiliates of national organizations to expand training and employment services for low-income individuals to move into expanding energy-efficiency and renewable-energy jobs.

In all but one of the 20 study states, some funding was received under one or more of these grant programs (the exception is North Dakota). Over half of the state workforce agencies visited had received State Energy Sector Partnership and Training Grants, and in most states, some local Workforce Investment Boards (WIBs) or community-based organizations received Green Capacity Building or Pathways grants. Several national grantees also served areas in some of the study states—for example, grants to industry organizations such as the International Training Institute for Sheet Metal and Air Conditioning, and nonprofit entities with local affiliates like Goodwill Industries and SER–Jobs for Progress.[1] Several states used the LMI and Energy grants to develop or expand comprehensive integrated state energy workforce strategies (Arizona, Illinois, Nevada, and Florida).

A number of states have implemented major green jobs initiatives using a variety of federal grants and, in many places, WIA and state funds. Interviews with state and local administrators and staff indicate that at least half of the states in this study have major statewide initiatives related to the green jobs economy, and that the Recovery Act funds were leveraged to support and expand those initiatives. A few examples that illustrate how Recovery Act funds were used for different green jobs efforts include the following:

- **Montana** is using federal Energy Training Partnership and LMI grants to expand the state's green economy efforts, particularly as related to renewable energy. The effort started before the Recovery Act with Workforce Innovation in Regional Economic Development (WIRED) grants from the ETA and state funds. Montana was successful in its application for the Energy Training Partnership discretionary grant, which was developed with state Joint Apprenticeship and Training Committees representing 10 trades and was used to prepare workers for green jobs in renewable energy and energy efficiency.

- **Wisconsin** has set green jobs training as a priority for training under WIA for the Adult, Dislocated Worker, and Youth programs. State Energy Grant funds along with WIA funds and governor's discretionary funds for WIA are being used, for example, to expand apprenticeship and preapprenticeship training programs as part of a statewide strategy established by the governor.

- **Ohio** has a statewide focus on green jobs, particularly for youth, and used the LMI and State Energy Grants to promote an integrated strategy, including establishing the Recovery Conservation Corps. The state agency also encouraged and supported collaborations between local WIBs and Energy Partnership Grants in the state, including several industry training and apprenticeship programs for youth and dislocated workers.

- **Colorado** is leveraging several funding sources for green jobs training as part of the state's high-priority New Energy Economy initiative (e.g., WIA Adult, Youth, and Dislocated Worker, State Energy Grant, and governor's discretionary funds). Recovery Act funds were used to hire a state green jobs coordinator to facilitate cross-program partnerships and initiatives (e.g., workforce development, registered apprenticeship, economic development, and human services). Funds from several federal Recovery Act funds from ETA and the Department of Energy were used to implement special projects (Green Careers for Coloradans and the Denver Green Jobs Initiative). The Colorado State Energy Sector Partnership (SESP) team developed projects that by their nature are sustainable, including the following five:

1) The Clean Energy Business Colorado model has been adopted as the entrepreneurial development model by the Colorado Center for Renewable Energy and Economic Development (CREED). CREED is a cooperative program between Colorado and the National Renewable Energy Lab (NREL).

2) An entrepreneur vetting tool developed by a volunteer of the Clean Energy Business Colorado project has been commercialized under the company Valid Eval, and an unlimited license has been purchased by the Colorado Workforce Development Council (CWDC) for use statewide in helping assess viability of entrepreneurial proposals.

3) GreenCareersCO.com, a career and vocational advisory Web site, was released for public use during the first quarter of 2011. The workforce system, high schools, and colleges use the site to guide individuals interested in careers in energy efficiency and renewable energy. The site is hosted on e-Colorado.com, is maintained by Colorado Department of Labor and Employment (CDLE) staff, and is designed to be current and without need of updating for several years.

4) The Green Jobs Workforce Collaborative has led to the development of new partnerships among various community organizations engaged in green jobs. Examples of projects that the groups are likely to continue working on together are the formation of preapprenticeship programs, outreach to employers through customized recruitment events, and continued networking.

5) The Colorado SESP Business Advisory Council was featured in an NGA report on best practices. The Business Advisory Council concept is being adopted around the country as a benchmark for business engagement.

- **Texas** has an increasing emphasis on green jobs, particularly in the area of wind power, and the state workforce agency is supporting several industry training partnerships with governor's discretionary funds as well as Recovery Act funds and grants.

- **New York** has placed a high priority on supporting the state's green economy, making green jobs one of the three top sectoral priorities. There are at least 12 Pathways, Green Capacity, and Energy Training Partnership grants in the state, in which the state workforce agency collaborates with other agencies and leads multiagency state initiatives. Investments in green jobs training are occurring across agencies (labor, human services, transportation, and education). These efforts include new green jobs Web sites and cross-departmental collaborative grant programs, which are funding local programs such as the Green Jobs Corps and providing training and subsidized employment in green industries (using TANF emergency funding).

- **Michigan** directed resources toward preparing women, minorities, and disadvantaged individuals for apprenticeship opportunities in a variety of green jobs. This program was called Energy Conservation Apprenticeship Readiness (ECAR—see Box 7.2).

Box 7.2 Recovery Act–Funded Green Jobs Project: Michigan's Energy Conservation Apprenticeship Readiness (ECAR) Program

ECAR is an effort to prepare women, minorities, and economically disadvantaged individuals for apprenticeship positions, weatherization projects, and other green construction jobs. ECAR builds on the Road Construction Apprenticeship Readiness (RCAR) Program, which was an earlier preapprenticeship program providing tuition-paid fast-track customized training in job readiness skills, applied math, computer skills, blueprint reading, workplace safety, and construction trades. In addition to the 240-hour RCAR Program curriculum, the ECAR program has a 32-hour energy conservation awareness component that includes the following: training on lead, asbestos and confined space awareness; mold remediation and safe working practices; principles of thermal insulation, geothermal energy, and solar energy; and principles of green construction. ECAR and RCAR both also offer supportive services, job placement assistance, and completion certificates.

SOURCE: State and local office site visit reports.

- **Wisconsin** used receipt of the national ARRA discretionary competitive grant of $6.0 million from the USDOL to fund the Sector Alliance for the Green Economy (SAGE)—an initiative to provide training (with a focus on apprenticeship) in green energy sectors.

During the first round of visits, state staff expressed a concern about the push for green jobs as a means to lift states' economies out of the downturn. This is still a concern. While many believe the focus on green jobs can be a viable long-term strategy, they do not see efforts to train and place customers in green jobs as an immediate solution to unemployment because there are few available jobs. Several state representatives pointed out that in many instances, current occupations are evolving into green jobs; thus there is more of a need to "upskill" workers. Some state staff also mentioned the challenge of defining green jobs accurately and the challenge of avoiding making decisions regarding what industries and occupations should be included as a result of political pressure.

Based on the state visits, it seems clear that green jobs are a high priority in nearly every state visited and that the Recovery Act funds, which include special grants, WIA supplemental funds, and Recovery Act funds from other agencies (e.g., Energy and Health and Human Services [HHS]), are being used strategically to both develop statewide approaches and, more commonly, enhance and expand state green jobs initiatives that had begun before the recession. In addition, many of the projects and initiatives are focusing on providing training and apprenticeship opportunities for dislocated workers (especially from the automotive and steel sectors), minorities, women (in nontraditional occupations), and low-income youth.

SUBSIDIZED EMPLOYMENT THROUGH THE TANF EMERGENCY FUND

The workforce investment system and the work programs associated with TANF have close linkages in some but not all states. Recovery Act provisions for TANF, therefore, can also affect workforce agencies and local programs. One of the most significant Recovery Act provisions under TANF is the TANF Emergency Fund (EF). The scale of the program and its interaction with the workforce investment systems make it a unique part of the story of the implementation of the Recovery Act. States were allowed to draw down as much as 50 percent of the TANF block grant amount in emergency funds, which could be used for three purposes: 1) to cover additional TANF benefit costs, 2) for one-time nonrecurrent benefits, and 3) for subsidized employment. The subsidies are not limited to TANF recipients but can be used to subsidize jobs for low-income parents with children under 18, with the states determining monetary eligibility requirements. Most states used the same eligibility requirements for TANF services (aside from cash benefits), which is usually either 200 or 225 percent of poverty.

Subsidized employment has been an allowable expenditure in TANF, but it was not a high priority at the federal or state levels because subsidized employment programs are usually cost-prohibitive. Thus, the Recovery Act guidelines and the amount of funds potentially available to states for subsidized employment created considerable interest. After enactment of the Recovery Act, states were encouraged to submit plans to the national TANF agency, the Administration for Children and Families (ACF) at the U.S. Department of Health and Human Services. States were required to submit their plans for TANF-EF subsidized employment to the ACF for approval. The TANF Emergency Fund ended on September 30, 2010, with states having received the full $5 billion authorized.

Some states (e.g., New York and Florida) submitted plans in late 2009, but most states submitted plans in early to mid 2010. Much of the increased emphasis on TANF-EF subsidized employment occurred after January 2010, when joint guidance was issued to the field by ETA and ACF (TEGL 12-09). As of July 8, 2010, ACF had approved subsidized employment plans from 31 states, with potential expenditures ranging from $15,000 in Utah to over $190 million in Illinois. Fifteen of the 20 states in this study were approved by ACF to operate TANF-EF subsidized employment programs. Table 7.3 details the TANF-EF funding in the 15 states.

Where the program was operational, it was a high priority and the workforce investment system and One-Stop Career Centers usually played a major role.

Table 7.3 TANF Emergency Fund–Subsidized Job Placements (state estimates of total placements with funds available through September 30, 2010)

State	Year-round program (Adult)	Summer Youth	Total
Colorado	1,724	0	1,724
Florida	5,588	0	5,588
Illinois	29,092	6,624	35,716
Michigan	1,365	0	1,365
Montana	444	374	818
New York	4,217	0	4,217
North Carolina	1,036	0	1,036
North Dakota	600	0	600
Ohio	1,759	15,034	16,793
Pennsylvania	14,000	13,000	27,000
Rhode Island	735	0	735
Texas	2,594	22,305	24,899
Virginia	340	0	340
Washington	7,200	0	7,200
Wisconsin	2,500	0	2,500
U.S. total	124,470	138,050	262,520

NOTE: Programs may be funded in whole or in part with TANF emergency funds.
SOURCE: Information was collected directly from state officials or from published documents by the Center on Budget and Policy Priorities and the Center for Law and Social Policy. Data as reported by January 31, 2011.

- **Illinois's** program, Put Illinois to Work, was second only to that of California in size (California placed a total of more than 47,000 people in jobs, but more than half were summer youth.) The Illinois program planned to draw down over $194 million and to subsidize 15,000 jobs statewide by September 30, 2010. By hiring for short periods (e.g., three months), each job slot might potentially be filled over time by more than one worker. As of the end of the program, the state had placed over 29,000 adults and over 6,600 summer youth. The initial enrollees in the program were individuals already enrolled in WIA. The program was administered statewide by Heartland Alliance, a large non-profit agency with extensive experience operating transitional jobs programs, particularly for ex-offenders and homeless individuals. Many local WIBs and nonprofit program providers were subcontractors for the program.

- **Pennsylvania's** Department of Labor and Industry administered the TANF-EF program and issued the request for proposals to local WIBs interested in operating the program.

- **New York's** Office of Temporary and Disability Assistance (OTDA) administered the state's TANF-EF program, with a collaborative role for the Department of Labor. Locally, several WIBs in New York, along with several nonprofit organizations, received OTDA grants for TANF-EF funded subsidized employment programs in early 2010.

- In **Florida**, the state workforce agency, the Department of Economic Opportunity (DEO), administers the TANF work program and was responsible for the TANF-EF subsidized employment program called Florida Back to Work. WIBs operated the program locally. Eligibility for Back to Work jobs extended to families whose income was up to 200 percent of poverty with a dependent child. The subsidy model is similar to on-the-job training, with 100 percent of the wage subsidized, for a length of time determined by the local One-Stop center (usually through September 2010). Individuals applied on-line through the Department of Children and Families (DCF) Web site. There was an expectation that private sector employers would attempt to retain the person after the subsidy ended; public and nonprofit employers did not have to make such a commitment.

- The **Texas** Back to Work program was authorized by the legislature in 2009 to subsidize jobs for UI claimants who previously had earned less than $15 per hour. In collaboration with the Texas Health and Human Services Commission, the Texas Workforce Commission planned the TANF-EF subsidized employment program by modifying the Back to Work program to also serve as the TANF-EF subsidized employment program. This allowed the state to provide assistance to additional low-income residents.

A few insights emerged from the visits to the study states:

- In some states, the state workforce agencies had operational and administrative responsibility for the subsidized employment programs, as they did for TANF work programs. In states such as Florida, much of the responsibility for the success of the program fell to the workforce investment system.

- In several states, workforce development staff at the local level administered and delivered program services, but some initially raised concerns about whether enough employers would sign up to meet the goals set by the state agencies.

- Some staff members were troubled by having to shift their priority to the new program when so many other customers were seeking employment services in the local offices because of the recession.

- Aspects of many of the subsidy programs are similar to OJT. Some states, such as Illinois, have specifically incorporated provisions into the contracts whereby the employer agrees to provide some training. Illinois, along with a few others, had a cap on the wages that could be subsidized. In other states, the training might have been implied but not in the contract per se, and there was no cap on the amount of the wage subsidy.

- In some states, such as Pennsylvania, the TANF-EF subsidized program served youth as well as adult participants. A considerable amount of TANF-EF funds were used to supplement and expand the 2009 and 2010 Summer Youth Programs.

- In August 2009, the Colorado Department of Human Services (DHS) created a subsidized employment program (HIRE Colorado) with $11.2 million in Recovery Act supplemental TANF reserve funds, which provided a safety net for individuals who had exhausted their UI benefits. The funds were given to workforce centers to implement the program.

- About one-half of the counties in Ohio used TANF emergency funding to support Summer Youth Employment Programs in Summer 2010.

According to administrators and staff in locations where the workforce development system was involved, the majority of adults in TANF-EF funded subsidized jobs were not TANF cash recipients; all were unemployed and many were UI claimants or recent UI exhaustees. Some states have consciously made UI claimants the top priority for subsidized jobs, and staff noted, off the record, that this was considered a way to reduce the cost burden on the UI Trust Fund, even if only temporarily.

Note

1. "SER" stands for "Service, Employment, Redevelopment."

Reference

U.S. Department of Labor (USDOL). 2009. "U.S. Department of Labor Announces Nearly $55 Million in Green Jobs Training Grants through Recovery Act." News release, November 18. Washington, DC: U.S. Department of Labor. http://www.dol.gov/opa/media/press/eta/eta20091439.htm (accessed March 4, 2013).

8
Unemployment Insurance

Yvette Chocolaad
NASWA

Wayne Vroman
Urban Institute

Richard A. Hobbie
NASWA

BACKGROUND ON THE UNEMPLOYMENT INSURANCE (UI) SYSTEM

From its beginning, the Unemployment Insurance (UI) system has served two purposes—1) economic stabilization and 2) temporary and partial wage replacement for most workers who have lost their jobs. During recessions, policymakers historically have relied on expansions to unemployment insurance benefits to assist not only individuals but also the economy more broadly, since benefit expansions help sustain purchasing power and thereby minimize the depth and duration of recessions (Blaustein 1993).

The UI system is a unique federal-state partnership, grounded in federal law but administered through state law by state officials. Created by the Social Security Act of 1935, it has been a successful social insurance program for many years. The system is decentralized at the state level to address the varying economic conditions among the states. State unemployment benefits are financed through state payroll taxes, which are held in individual state trust fund accounts in the federal Unemployment Trust Fund in the U.S. Treasury. State UI agencies are responsible for both the tax and benefit functions necessary to administer their UI programs.

Administering unemployment benefits involves four core business processes, which are displayed in Figure 8.1: 1) intake, 2) adjudication, 3) continuing claims, and 4) appeals. These are complicated and time-consuming tasks, each involving numerous subprocesses, which have been made harder by a record number of claimants during and after the "Great Recession." Taking and responding to initial claims for UI benefits (intake) involves not only making a determination of eligibility but also detecting issues and referring cases for adjudication, tracking claims, communicating with claimants, and connecting some or all claimants to workforce services designed to speed reemployment. Adjudication involves assigning cases to staff, processing information from employers, conducting fact-finding, and making eligibility determinations. For continuing claims, states must determine continued weekly eligibility, detect issues and refer cases for adjudication, process claims, and connect some or all claimants to workforce services designed to speed reemployment. Claimants or employers may file appeals regarding a state's determination of an individual's eligibility for benefits. Nearly all states have both lower and higher authority appeals processes, which involve subprocesses related to recording the appeals, assigning cases, conducting discovery, providing notices of hearings, conducting hearings, implementing decisions, and possibly preparing for appeals of final agency orders through the court system.

THE UI PROVISIONS OF THE AMERICAN RECOVERY AND REINVESTMENT ACT

The Recovery Act's main objective was to provide economic stimulus that would "save and create jobs immediately" (whitehouse.gov 2009). Other objectives were to provide aid to individuals affected by the recession and to invest in improving schools, updating infrastructure, modernizing health care, and promoting clean energy. At the time of passage in February 2009, the cost of the economic stimulus package, which included both spending and revenue provisions, was estimated by the Congressional Budget Office (CBO) to be $787 billion over the 10-year period from 2009 through 2019. By February 2012, the CBO had revised the estimate to $831 billion and reported that "close

193

Figure 8.1 Core Business Processes for UI Benefits Administration

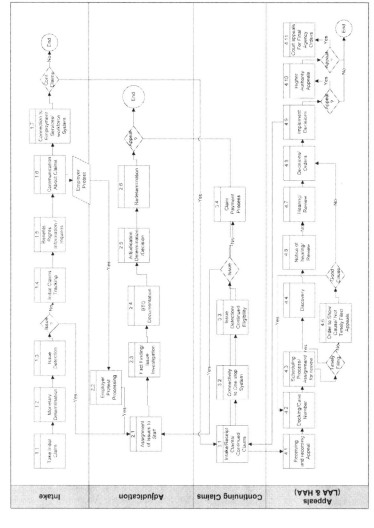

SOURCE: NASWA, UI Performance and Accountability Project for the U.S. Department of Labor, March 2011.

to half of that impact occurred in Fiscal Year 2010, and more than 90 percent . . . was realized by the end of December 2011" (CBO 2012).

The unemployment insurance provisions of the Recovery Act included both tax and spending provisions. Major provisions included a $500 million supplemental distribution to states for UI administration, a provision temporarily waiving interest on federal loans to state UI trust funds, funding to encourage state UI program "modernization," UI benefit extensions, a temporary $25 weekly UI benefit enhancement, and a provision temporarily suspending federal income tax on a portion of UI benefits. As Table 8.1 shows, the CBO estimated that these provisions would result in federal outlays totaling approximately $45 billion over 10 years, with almost all the funds projected to be spent quickly—in fiscal years 2009 and 2010. However, the estimates were made in the early months of 2009, well before the depth and duration of the Great Recession were widely understood, and they substantially underestimated actual costs. The estimates also do not include subsequent extensions related to the Great Recession. Estimates of all benefit extensions subsequently totaled more than $200 billion for the 2008–2012 time period.

Additional detail on the Recovery Act's UI provisions is provided in Table 8.2, and information on other UI legislation enacted in response to the Great Recession in Table 8.3.

THE RESEARCH PLAN

As noted above, the main objectives of the Recovery Act's UI provisions were to provide relief to out-of-work Americans and to help stabilize and stimulate the overall economy. This study discusses challenges states faced in getting UI benefits into the hands of customers quickly, to ensure not only that customers got the assistance they were due but also that the program worked as timely economic stimulus. It also presents recent summary evidence of the UI system's macroeconomic and antipoverty impacts and administrative performance during the recession. The study also documents the effect of the Recovery Act legislation in achieving secondary objectives more specifically related to the UI program. These secondary objectives include eligibility expansions,

ANTLR

Table 8.1 Estimated Budget Effects of the UI Provisions of the Recovery Act

Recovery Act provision	Explanation of provision	Estimated budget effects, FY 2009–2019 ($ billions)
Interest-free loans	Temporarily waived interest payments and the accrual of interest on federal loans to states through December 31, 2010.	1.1
Administrative funding	Transferred $500 million to the states for administration of their unemployment programs and staff-assisted reemployment services for claimants.	2.6
UI modernization	Provided up to a total of $7 billion as incentive payments for states to "modernize" state UC benefit provisions. Payments were available through September 30, 2011, and states could use them for UI benefits or UI or ES administration.	
Benefit extensions	Extended the Emergency Unemployment Compensation (EUC) program for new claims from March 31, 2009, to December 31, 2009 (subsequently extended through the end of 2012). Provided 100% federal financing of the Extended Benefits (EB) program for weeks of unemployment beginning before January 1, 2010 (subsequently extended through the end of 2012).	27.0
Benefit increase	Provided a temporary $25 per week supplemental unemployment benefit, known as the Federal Additional Compensation (FAC) program, for weeks of unemployment ending before January 1, 2010 (subsequently extended through beginning of June 2010); prohibited states from reducing average weekly benefit amount for regular compensation below level of December 31, 2008.	8.8
Suspension of federal income tax	Temporarily suspended federal income tax on the first $2,400 of unemployment benefits (per recipient) received in 2009.	4.7
Total		44.7

NOTE: Figures do not sum to total because of rounding.
SOURCE: U.S. Joint Committee on Taxation (2009); votesmart.org (2009).

Table 8.2 Detailed Explanation of the UI Provisions of the Recovery Act

Temporary interest-free loans on outstanding state trust fund balances

The Recovery Act temporarily waived interest payments and the accrual of interest on loans received by state unemployment trust funds through December 31, 2010. This provision was not renewed.

A special $500 million transfer to states for UI administration

The Recovery Act provided a $500 million special UI administrative distribution to states. Each state's share was deposited in the state's account in the Unemployment Trust Fund on February 27, 2009, where it is available for
- implementing the state's UI modernization provisions;
- improving outreach to individuals potentially eligible under the state's UI modernization provisions;
- improving UI tax and benefit operations, including responding to increased demand for UI; and
- administering staff-assisted reemployment services for UI claimants.

Funds may not be used for the payment of UI. Each state's share was based on its proportionate share of Federal Unemployment Tax Act (FUTA) taxable wages multiplied by the $500 million. Most state laws require appropriation of these funds by the state legislature.

UI modernization provisions and incentive payments

The Recovery Act made a total of $7 billion in UI modernization incentive payments available to states that included certain eligibility provisions in their state UI laws. States received one-third of their share of the payments for using more recent wages (the alternative base period provision) to determine UI eligibility if a claimant was not eligible using the normal base period. States received the remaining two-thirds of their share for adopting two of the following four eligibility provisions:
- Pay UI to individuals seeking only part-time work.
- Ease qualifying requirements for workers who quit their jobs because of certain family responsibilities. These relate to workers who leave work because of domestic violence or sexual assault, to care for an ill family member, or to accompany a spouse who moves to a new job.
- Extend benefits to workers in approved training who exhaust regular UI.
- Add dependents' allowances to weekly benefits.

The maximum incentive payment allowable for a state was distributed to the state Unemployment Trust Fund accounts based on the state's share of estimated federal unemployment taxes (excluding reduced credit payments) made by the state's employers. States had to apply, and applications were due to the U.S. Department of Labor by August 22, 2011. Incentive payments were available through September 30, 2011.

States may use incentive payments for
- the payment of UI; or
- upon appropriation of the state legislature, administrative costs for the UI and employment services programs.

There is no time limit on the use of the incentive payments for benefit or administrative purposes.

Table 8.2 (continued)

Extension of the Emergency Unemployment Compensation (EUC) Program

Under Recovery Act provisions, the Emergency Unemployment Compensation (EUC) program, created in June 2008 and expanded in November 2008, provided up to 20 weeks of benefits to eligible jobless workers in all states and up to 13 additional weeks of benefits in states with high unemployment. The Recovery Act extended the date for new EUC claims from March 31, 2009, to December 31, 2009, with payments on those claims ending on May 31, 2010. The EUC program was extended in subsequent legislation through the end of 2012.

Temporary full federal funding of extended benefits

The Extended Benefits (EB) Program is a permanent federal-state program that provides up to 13 or 20 additional weeks of unemployment benefits to eligible jobless workers in states with high and rising unemployment. At state option, workers in some states with very high total unemployment rates (TUR) are eligible for 20 weeks of EB rather than the standard 13 weeks. Costs of EB under permanent federal law are split equally between the federal government and the states.

The Recovery Act provided 100 percent federal funding of EB for weeks of unemployment beginning before January 1, 2010. This provision, which was extended in subsequent legislation through the end of 2012, gave states an incentive to adopt an optional "trigger" based on the state's three-month average TUR. It is easier for many states with relatively low insured unemployment rates to trigger on the TUR instead of on the insured unemployment rate.

Increased UI benefit amounts—Federal Additional Compensation

The Recovery Act created a new, temporary Federal Additional Compensation (FAC) program providing a 100 percent federally funded $25 add-on to all weekly UI payments for weeks of unemployment ending before January 1, 2010. (This provision was subsequently extended three times for new claims through June 2, 2010, and for weeks compensated through the end of 2010.) All states signed agreements to pay FAC effective February 22, 2009, the first week for which FAC was payable.

A temporary suspension of federal income tax on unemployment benefits

By law, all federal unemployment benefits are subject to income taxation. The average unemployment benefit is approximately $300 per week. Effective for taxable year 2009, the Recovery Act temporarily suspended federal income tax on the first $2,400 of unemployment benefits per recipient. This provision was not extended in subsequent legislation.

SOURCE: NASWA staff, based on summaries of the legislation from the NASWA Web site.

Table 8.3 Other UI Legislation Related to the Great Recession (as of June 30, 2012)

Law	Approval date	Explanation of provisions
P.L. 110-252 Supplemental Appropriations Act of 2008	06/30/2008	Provided $110 million of contingency funding to states for UI administration; authorized EUC through March 31, 2009.
P.L. 110-328 SSI Extension for Elderly and Disabled Refugees Act of 2008	09/30/2008	Permitted states to use the Treasury Offset Program (TOP) to recover covered unemployment compensation (UC) debts through offset from federal income tax debts.
P.L. 110-449 Unemployment Compensation Extension Act of 2008	11/21/2008	Increased the basic EUC entitlement by up to 7 weeks, for a total of up to 20 weeks of benefits; created second tier of benefits of up to 13 additional weeks.
P.L. 111-5 American Recovery and Reinvestment Act of 2009	**02/17/2009**	See Table 8.2.
P.L. 111-92 Worker, Homeownership, and Business Assistance Act of 2009	11/06/2009	Extended second tier of EUC to 14 weeks and to all states, and created a third tier (of up to 13 weeks) and a fourth tier (of up to 6 weeks)
P.L. 111-118 Department of Defense Appropriations Act of 2010	12/19/2009	Extended the EUC program, 100% federal financing of the EB program, and the $25 FAC benefit through the end of February 2010.
P.L. 111-144 Temporary Extension Act of 2010	03/02/2010	Extended the EUC program, 100% federal financing of the EB program, and the $25 FAC benefit through April 5, 2010.
P.L. 111-157 Continuing Extension Act of 2010	04/15/2010	Extended the EUC program, 100% federal financing of the EB program, and the $25 FAC benefit through June 2, 2010.
P.L. 111-205 Unemployment Compensation Extension Act of 2010	07/22/2010	Extended the EUC and EB programs again, until the end of November 2010 (the FAC program was not extended); provided rules for coordinating EUC with regular compensation; imposed a nonreduction rule on states for regular UI compensation.

Public Law	Date	Description
P.L. 111-291 Claims Resolution Act of 2010	12/08/2010	Made amendments to the TOP regarding the collection of certain UC debts; required employers to report to the National Directory of New Hires (NDNH) the first services remuneration date of each newly hired employee.
P.L. 111-312 Tax Relief, Unemployment Insurance Reauthorization, and Job Creation Act of 2010	12/17/2010	Extended the EUC and EB programs to early January 2012 and made changes through December 31, 2011, to the EB look-back enabling states with declining unemployment rates to continue to trigger on EB.
P.L. 112-40 Trade Adjustment Assistance Extension Act of 2011	10/21/2011	Imposed a mandatory penalty assessment on UC fraud claims; prohibited non-charging in certain cases of employer failure to respond adequately or in timely fashion to requests for UC claim-related information; included certain retired employees in the definition of "new hires" for the NDNH.
P.L. 112-78 Temporary Payroll Tax Cut Continuation Act of 2011	12/23/2011	Extended the EUC and EB programs to early March 2012 and extended through February 29, 2012, the changes to the EB look-back made by P.L. 111-312.
P.L. 112-96 Middle Class Tax Relief and Job Creation Act of 2012	02/22/2012	Extended the EUC and EB programs through the end of 2012; extended through December 31, 2012, the changes to the EB look-back made by P.L. 111-312; provided funding for reemployment services and reemployment eligibility assessments; and other provisions.

SOURCE: USDOL (2013a).

improved state trust fund positions, improved UI tax and benefit operations, and a renewed emphasis in the UI program on reemployment. These program-specific objectives are outlined in Table 8.4.

This study also documents some of the operational and administrative challenges states faced in implementing the new benefit expansions and other provisions, as well as some of the state innovations and sustainable improvements to UI operations resulting from the demands of the recession or the availability of new Recovery Act funding (specifically, the Recovery Act funding for UI administration and the incentive payments for implementing UI modernization provisions).

To gather information for the study, the research team conducted in-depth teleconference interviews with key UI administrative, tax, benefits, and information technology (IT) staff in the 20 sample states during the fall and winter of 2011–2012. A pilot teleconference interview was held with officials in the state of Florida on October 7 and another on October 27, 2010.

To prepare for the teleconference interviews, the research team assembled and shared with the states an interview guide that included questions about states' experiences with the recession and with Recovery Act implementation (see Box 8.1). The research team also developed individual state case studies and used these studies to customize the interview guide for each state interview. The state case studies recorded individual state UI program conditions and actions before and after the Recovery Act, incorporating information on each state's

- UI program structure and economic environment;
- historical UI program performance;
- historical and current UI program financial conditions;
- response to a 50-state NASWA survey on the recession and the state's experiences in implementing the Recovery Act (NASWA 2010a);
- tax and benefits IT systems, based on a NASWA-funded survey (NASWA 2010b); and
- legislative actions, if any, regarding the UI modernization provisions of the Recovery Act and to address trust fund solvency.

In addition to the results from the 20 state interviews, the research team drew on numerous USDOL and NASWA sources for this report,

Table 8.4 Legislative Intent of UI Recovery Act Provisions

Recovery Act provision	Economic stimulus/state fiscal relief	Relief to individuals	Permanent expansions of UI eligibility	Improved state trust fund positions	Improved state UI tax and benefit operations	Emphasis on reemployment
			Legislative intent			
EUC extension	X	X				
Interest-free loans	X			X		
Extended benefits	X	X		X		
Benefit increase (FAC)	X	X				
Temporary suspension of federal income tax	X	X				
UI modernization	X		X	X	X	X
Administrative funding	X				X	X

SOURCE: Authors' compilation.

**Box 8.1 Interview Guide Questions for Recovery Act Study,
UI Provisions**

1. What was the status of state UI administrative performance before the recession, and how was state UI administrative performance affected by the recession? What were the implications for states' decision-making as they dealt with the caseload surge of the recession and implemented the Recovery Act's UI provisions?

2. Before passage of federal stimulus legislation in February 2009, what adjustments did states make to their UI operations to handle the overwhelming numbers of new and continued claims filed by jobless workers? How were these process improvements and technology upgrades funded, and did they result in any sustainable improvements to UI operations?

3. On what did states spend or plan to spend the $500 million allocation for UI administration? What has been the timetable for the expenditure of these funds?

   a. Did states spend or plan to spend UI administrative funds to improve tax and benefit operations, and if so, what process improvements or technology upgrades were or will be implemented? Are these improvements or upgrades sustainable?

   b. Did states spend or plan to spend UI administrative funds to improve the connection between the UI and workforce systems and the availability of reemployment services, and if so, what improvements and services were or will be implemented? Are any of these improvements or services sustainable?

   c. Did states spend or plan to spend UI administrative funds to implement the modernization provisions of the Recovery Act?

   d. Did states combine or plan to combine new UI administrative funds with other funds (e.g., UI contingency funds, Reed Act funds, state funds) to achieve their goals?

4. What administrative and operational challenges and successes have states encountered in implementing the UI benefit expansion provisions, including:

   a. the Emergency Unemployment Compensation (EUC) provisions;

   b. the Extended Benefit (EB) Program provisions;

    c. the Federal Additional Compensation (FAC) provision; and

    d. the provision temporarily suspending federal income tax on certain benefit payments?

5. What changes did states make to state UI laws as a result of the Recovery Act's modernization act provisions?

    a. Did states without an optional trigger for the EB program enact one, and if not, why not?

    b. Did states expand eligibility for UI through the modernization incentive provisions?

    c. What was the nature of the debate on these provisions? Are statutory changes likely to be sustained?

6. What are states spending or planning to spend UI modernization payments on employment services administration; or to improve the connection between the UI and workforce systems or the availability of reemployment services? If so, what improvements and services were or will be implemented? Are they sustainable?

    a. Are states spending or planning to spend UI modernization payments to pay benefits?

7. What was the status of state UI trust funds before the recession, and how did states' trust fund positions change during the recession? How have states responded?

SOURCE: UI teleconference interviews conducted for the study by researchers from the Urban Institute and NASWA.

which are documented in footnotes. These sources provide historical data on UI program performance, the financial status of state UI trust funds, funding for UI administration (including state supplemental funding), UI claims activity, and expenditure patterns for Recovery Act UI administrative grants.

SETTING THE STAGE: UI ADMINISTRATIVE FINANCING AND UI CLAIMS WORKLOAD BEFORE AND DURING THE GREAT RECESSION

Before the Great Recession in December 2007, many states were struggling to administer their programs even at a time of high employment. Federal base funding for UI program administration had been declining since the mid-1990s, adjusting for inflation and workload. Despite hoped-for improvements in productivity from the adoption of remote methods (i.e., telephone call centers and the Internet) for taking UI claims, many states faced steep challenges when the recession brought a three-fold spike in initial UI claims and a more than doubling of continued UI claims. They were not in a position to expand capacity dramatically without engaging in substantial reallocations and triaging of existing resources. Fortunately, the UI system was designed to respond to such increases in demand for unemployment benefits with additional administrative funds, but not without critical time lags and much scrambling by states as they awaited additional resources.

Funding for State UI Administration before the Recession

In the federal-state UI system, one of the roles of the federal government is to provide grants to states to fund the administration of state UI programs. In part, Title III of the Social Security Act says the following:

> The Secretary of Labor shall certify . . . for payment to each state which has an unemployment compensation law . . . such amounts . . . necessary for the proper and efficient administration of such law during the fiscal year . . . The Secretary of Labor's determination shall be based on (1) the population of the State; (2) an estimate of the number of persons covered by the State law and the cost of proper and efficient administration of such law; and (3) such other factors as the Secretary of Labor finds relevant.

Figure 8.2 shows federal base funding for state administration of UI programs from 1986 to 2007, adjusted for both inflation and workload. The solid line graph shows a substantial decline in real resources for base funding in the period before the recession, from about $2.2 billion per two million in average weekly insured unemployment (AWIU) in

Figure 8.2 UI Base Funding, 1986–2009 (inflation-adjusted dollars, per 2 million AWIU)

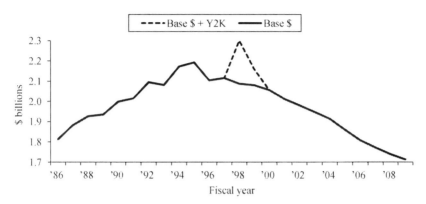

NOTE: Dotted line shows added federal funding to aid states in making software adjustments for the year 2000 changeover.
SOURCE: U.S. Department of Labor, Employment and Training Administration, Office of Unemployment Insurance, Division of Fiscal and Actuarial Services staff.

1995 to less than $1.8 billion per two million in AWIU in 2007. AWIU of two million claimants is a rough USDOL measure of the base workload that would exist nationally to maintain operations of all state UI programs even at very low unemployment levels. Note that the dotted line shows added federal funding to aid states in making software adjustments for the year 2000 changeover.

Although some of the decline in funding might be due to adjustments that occur automatically as state programs become more efficient, states have long said they have not received enough base-level funds to administer their programs in a proper and efficient manner even during periods of relatively low unemployment, much less to make many necessary longer-term capital investments (NASWA 2012). Historically, many states have adjusted for insufficient funds by adding state funds, but recently their ability to supplement is dwindling as states cut their own UI spending to balance their annual budgets. To illustrate this, in the aggregate states added about $180 million of their own funds to the federal grants for administration of UI in 2007, but this total declined to about $135 million in 2010.

The status of state UI IT systems at the start of the recession reflects the insufficient capital investment. The average age of UI IT systems for both tax and benefits administration was over 20 years in 2009, and only eight states had a modernized benefits system (NASWA 2010b). Without a modernized benefits IT system, states face difficulties in addressing caseload surges, implementing federal law changes, and automating and redesigning processes of UI benefits administration. Among the interview states, only two had a modernized benefits system entering the Great Recession—Nebraska and Ohio. Illinois recently completed a modernization effort. While numerous other states are engaged in consortia or single-state efforts to modernize their benefits systems, many are in the planning stages. The ability to produce an efficient and responsive system will depend on the availability of funding (costs to develop a full UI IT system are estimated to range from roughly $40 million upwards), as well as other factors such as the quality of project technical requirements and vendors' ability to deliver.[1]

The Effect of the Great Recession on UI Claims Workload

Figure 8.3 shows the effect of the Great Recession on weekly initial claims and continued claims workload for regular state UI benefits (excluding Emergency Unemployment Compensation [EUC] and Extended Benefits [EB]) at four-month intervals from January 2007 through midyear 2012. The number of weekly initial claims for state benefits (unadjusted for seasonal variations) was about the same in July 2008, six months after the start of the recession, as it was in July 2007, before the beginning of the recession.[2] Unemployment usually lags behind the initial stages of a recession. Between July 2008 and January 2009, weekly initial claims more than tripled, from around 300,000 to around 900,000. The number of weekly continued claims for state benefits also rose, in response to more and more claimants entering the system and staying on UI for longer durations than had been experienced historically in the program.[3] Weekly continued claims nearly doubled, from about 3 million in July 2008 to about 6 million in July 2009.

As the economy began recovering, from 2010 to 2012, weekly initial claims and continued claims activity showed gradual declines. As employer layoffs declined, the number of initial claims declined, but growing long-term unemployment and extensions of unemployment

Figure 8.3 Numbers of Unadjusted Initial and Continued UI Claims

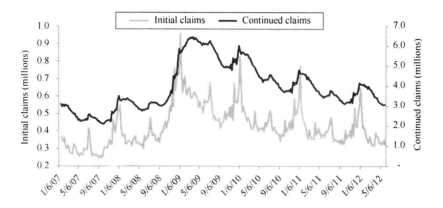

SOURCE: U.S. Department of Labor, Employment and Training Administration, Office of Unemployment Insurance, Division of Fiscal and Actuarial Services staff.

benefits led to longer durations on regular state benefits and higher numbers of weekly continued claims than would have existed in a stronger economic recovery.[4] At the beginning of 2012, the number of weekly initial claims was nearly back to normal, but the number of weekly continued claims remained high at about four million.

The Responsiveness of UI Administrative Funding during the Great Recession

As the prior two subsections document, base funding for administration of the UI program was low before the recession, and when the recession began to take effect the UI system was confronted with a threefold spike in initial claims activity. An unforeseen increase in service demand of this magnitude and over such a short time period is extraordinary by the standards of most business or government agency operations, and perhaps the best comparison can be made to the resource allocation and upscaling issues that some businesses and agencies (such as insurance and utility companies) confront after a natural disaster. To address the new workload demands with additional service capacity, the main sources of funding available to states were federal grants for above-base and contingency funding.[5] Whereas base funding is, in a sense, how much USDOL determines a state needs to keep its program running at or near full employment, above-base funding is distributed annually by USDOL to states processing workloads that exceed those funded by base funding. Conceptually, this allows USDOL to distribute funds to states that need funds above the base funding level, but only after the threshold workload has been experienced and reported by the individual state.

Contingency funding is activated automatically at the national level when the average weekly insured unemployment exceeds the level of AWIU that was funded in the federal budget. When a recession begins, contingency funding usually activates after the beginning of the recession when unemployment increases. The formula provides USDOL with $28.6 million per 100,000 additional AWIU above the level funded in the budget, which USDOL then distributes to states that have experienced the increased unemployment.

Figure 8.4 shows federal grants to states for above-base and contingency funding for UI administration from fiscal years 2000–2011. These data are not adjusted for either inflation or workload. Significant increases for above-base and contingency funding helped states cope

Figure 8.4 Federal Grants to States for UI Administration—Above-Base and Contingency Funding (by quarters—FY 2000 to FY 2011)

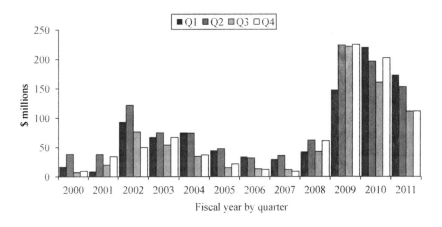

SOURCE: U.S. Department of Labor, Employment and Training Administration, Office of Unemployment Insurance, Division of Fiscal and Actuarial Services staff.

with the recession that began in December 2007, the last month of the first quarter of Fiscal Year 2008. The substantial increases in above-base and contingency funding began in Fiscal Year 2009 (which started October 1, 2008) and continued in 2010 and 2011. Note that because funds are distributed as states experience and report increased caseloads (above-base funding) and after unemployment rises at the beginning of a recession (contingency funding), the increase in funding follows the pattern of the historically steep increase in claims activity that began in September 2008. Many states reported having little to no lead time or funding to prepare for the unprecedented increases in claims activity through new investments in labor and other resources, or through the streamlining of business processes.

UI PROGRAM PERFORMANCE BEFORE AND DURING THE GREAT RECESSION

Performance Related to Economic Impacts

Much has been written about problems states encountered with unemployment insurance call centers and online claims processing at the beginning of the recession, but at the level of broad program indicators, state UI programs were successful in reacting and adapting to the unprecedented challenges of the Great Recession, and in paying out a record increase in benefits within a short time period. From 2008 to 2010, benefits paid to UI claimants more than tripled, from roughly $42 billion in Fiscal Year 2008 to $143 billion in Fiscal Year 2010, before falling to $113 billion in Fiscal Year 2011. As will be documented in later sections of this chapter, the rapid and unprecedented increases in workload on state workforce agencies since 2008 presented numerous challenges and required significant adjustments. Some state programs, heavily reliant on outmoded computer systems for payment processing, were brought nearly to a breaking point. However, the UI system met the broad objectives of the Recovery Act to stabilize the economy and help individuals sustain their incomes.

Several recent studies using different analytical and modeling approaches have estimated these economic impacts.[6] One study by

Impaq, commissioned by the USDOL in 2004, estimated the macro-economic impacts of the UI expansions that occurred with the Recovery Act and other UI legislation enacted before July 2010. The study (Vroman 2010) found the following:

- The UI program (both regular and extended benefits) "closed 0.183 [18.3 percent] of the gap in real GDP [gross domestic product] caused by the recession." As the USDOL noted in announcing the study, this translated into "nominal GDP being $175 billion higher in 2009 than it would have been without unemployment insurance benefits. In total, unemployment insurance kept GDP $315 billion higher from the start of the recession through the second quarter of 2010" (USDOL 2010).

- The "early intervention with EUC and EB caused these extended benefits to add a large element to the stabilization effect of UI . . . The UI program provided stronger stabilization of real output than in many past recessions because extended benefits responded strongly."

- Notable effects on employment included the effects of both regular and extended benefits on employment: In 2009Q2, the trough quarter, real regular UI benefits raised total employment by 1.050 million, while extended benefits caused an additional employment increase of 0.748 million and UI taxes had a negligible effect (a reduction of 0.002 million). During the eight quarters from 2008Q3 to 2010Q2, the estimated effects on employment were an increase in real regular UI benefits of 0.891 million and in real extended benefits of 0.714 million and a decrease in real UI taxes of 0.015 million.

The USDOL estimates these increases in employment yielded a reduction in the unemployment rate of 1.2 percentage points during the low point of the recession (USDOL 2010).

A January 2012 study by the Congressional Research Service analyzed the antipoverty effects of the UI program and found that the antipoverty effect of UI doubled during this latest recession compared to the last peak years of unemployment in 1993 and 2003, likely due to the Recovery Act expansions and related legislation. The estimated effect of UI benefits (both regular and extended benefits) on the poverty status of individuals and families was large (Gabe and Whitaker 2011):

- In 2010, well over one-quarter (27.5 percent) of unemployed people who received UI benefits would have been considered poor prior to counting the UI benefits they received; after counting UI benefits, their poverty rate was cut by well over half, to 12.5 percent.

- Because the U.S. poverty measure is based on the income of all coresident related family members, UI receipt affects not only the poverty status of the person receiving the benefit but the poverty status of all related family members as well. In 2010, while an estimated 12.4 million people reported UI receipt during the year, an additional 19.4 million family members lived with the 12.4 million receiving the benefit. Consequently (with rounding), UI receipt in 2010 affected the income status of some 31.9 million persons.

- The poverty rate for persons in families who received unemployment benefits in both 2009 and 2010 was approximately half of what it would have been without those unemployment benefits.

- In 2010, UI benefits lifted an estimated 3.2 million people out of poverty, of which well over one quarter (26.8 percent, or 861,000) were children living with a family member who received UI benefits.

Performance Related to Program Administration

The unprecedented increase in claims activity and benefit payments of the Great Recession caused a decline in key areas of state UI administrative performance.[7] While every state's recession experience is unique, some general national themes emerge from a review of both state performance data and the qualitative information relayed through the interviews of state UI officials. At a national aggregate level, the timeliness with which states conduct processes, the quality of eligibility determinations, and the accuracy of benefit payments all are sensitive to the volume of claims, and so they generally deteriorate during recessions; unsurprisingly, this analysis of USDOL data shows that the high volume of UI claims from 2008 through 2011 affected performance in all three areas.

Updating an earlier unpublished analysis (Vroman 2011), national data on state UI administrative performance from 1997 through 2011 were analyzed. Included were measures of timeliness for states' handling of first payments, continued claims, nonmonetary adjudication determinations, and appeals, as well as measures of the quality of adjudication determinations. Except for the continued claims measures, these timeliness and quality measures are part of the USDOL's "UI Performs" core performance measurement system, under which the USDOL has established uniform national acceptable levels of performance (ALPs). As such, they are considered "representative of the health of the entire unemployment insurance system" (USDOL 2013b). Also analyzed were the national data the USDOL currently uses to estimate and evaluate state performance in the area of benefit payment accuracy. These data are available through the Benefit Accuracy Measurement, or BAM, program. The BAM program "is designed to determine the accuracy of paid and denied claims . . . The results of BAM statistical samples are used to estimate accuracy rates for the population of paid and denied claims" (USDOL 2011).

Timeliness of Performance

Figure 8.5 displays five series showing timeliness performance from 1997 to 2011. Each series is a simple average across 52 regular UI programs—i.e., the 50 states plus the District of Columbia and Puerto Rico, but excluding the Virgin Islands. The series track the following categories:
- The percentage of first payments made within 14/21 days
- The percentage of continued claims made within 7 days
- The percentage of continued claims made within 14 days
- The percentage of nonmonetary determinations made within 21 days
- The percentage of lower authority appeals decided within 30 days

The USDOL's acceptable levels of performance (ALPs) for the series are as follows: 87 percent of first payments within 14/21 days, 80 percent of nonmonetary determinations within 21 days, and 60 percent of lower-authority appeals decided within 30 days. As noted above,

Figure 8.5 National Trends in UI Program Timeliness Performance

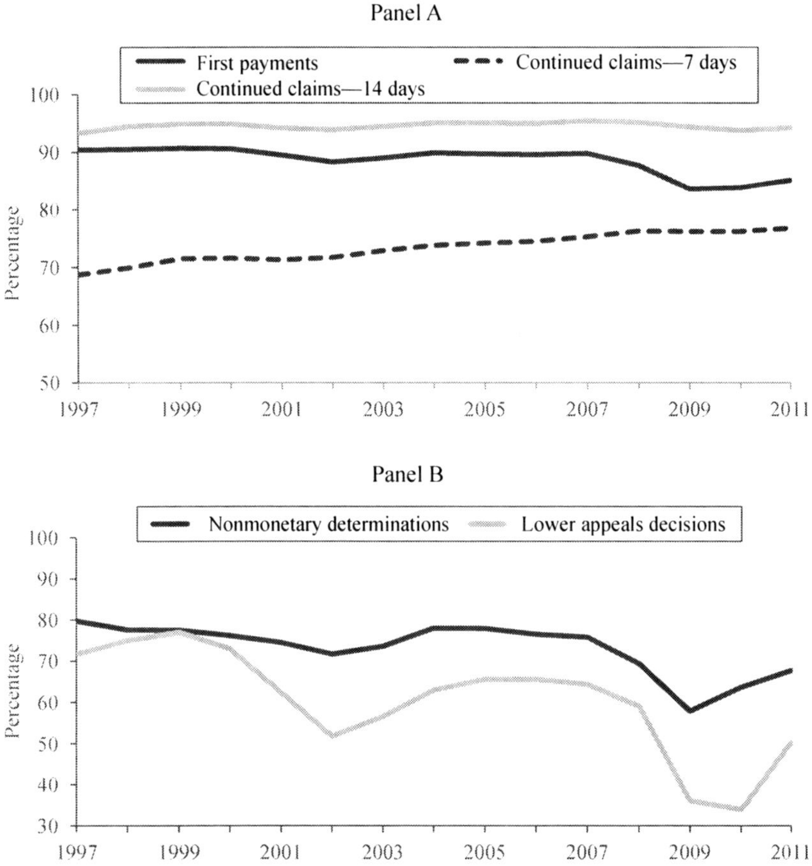

Panel A

Panel B

SOURCE: Time-lapse data from USDOL ETA reports 9050, 9051, 9052, and 9054L.

there is no USDOL performance standard for continued claims timeliness, but this measure and the measure of first payment timeliness are of importance. These measures show how quickly recipients actually receive payments, and the Social Security Act and related regulations require states to determine eligibility and make payments "with the greatest promptness that is administratively feasible."[8]

Figure 8.5 shows that, averaging across states, state administrative performance is affected negatively by recessions. Because of the severity of the Great Recession, the decreases between 2008 and 2011 were much larger than during 2001 and 2002. Note also that decreases in timeliness were much larger for nonmonetary determinations and appeals than for first payments and continued claims. In fact, the percentage of continued claims made within seven days increased measurably between 1997 and 2011 (from 68.7 percent to 76.8 percent). Observe also in Figure 8.5 that the timeliness measures were uniformly higher in 2011 than in 2009. Timeliness in performance clearly improved in the later stages of the Great Recession. Continued improvement in 2012 probably can be anticipated.

The series traced by Figure 8.5 were also examined with multiple regressions. Two principal findings from those regressions should be noted. First, while there were trends in performance between 1997 and 2011, most trends were small. Only for lower authority appeals was there a downtrend that amounted to more than 5 percentage points per decade. A large positive trend was realized in continued claims made within seven days. This positive trend probably reflects greater reliance on telephone claims and Internet claims in more recent years. Second, all performance series showed a strong effect of the business cycle. The cycle was measured in three different data series: the total unemployment rate, weeks paid for regular benefits, and weeks paid for all three tiers of UI benefits. The three cyclical variables were all highly significant, showing a large negative effect of recessions on time-lapse performance.[9] The cyclical variables accounted for most of the time series variation in time-lapse performance. Generally, the cyclical effects on performance were much larger than the trends included in the same regressions. After controlling for the cycle, the trend effects between 1997 and 2011 were generally modest, less than 2 percentage points per decade for first payments, continued claims paid within 14 days, and nonmonetary determinations. The downward trend for timeliness of lower-authority appeals, however, was close to 5 percentage points per decade.

Evidence from teleconference interviews with state UI officials corroborates these administrative performance trends: state UI officials generally said they faced more difficulty with timeliness performance in the areas of appeals and nonmonetary adjudication determinations than in claims-taking, although trends varied by state and all three areas were affected by the recession.

These interviews suggest that several factors contributed to the general decline in state UI administrative performance. Some states noted that they were underfunded for UI administration before the recession, and, as noted earlier, many experienced a lag between the workload increases of the recession and the availability of additional funds for UI administration necessary to address the workload. In addition, UI officials mentioned the complicated and unpredictable federal law changes of the Recovery Act and subsequent UI legislation, outmoded state UI information technology systems that were inflexible and required "work-arounds," a need to hire quickly and the resulting inexperienced new staff, and high staff turnover. Obviously, many of these factors were interrelated.

The interviews suggest many state UI officials were more likely to maintain—or address declines in—claims-taking timeliness than timeliness in the other two functional areas, for several reasons. Many state officials reported deliberate action to make claims-taking a priority to respond to the economic needs of individuals and communities in their states. As noted earlier, states also are required by federal law to ensure prompt benefit payment. Often during the caseload surge, this emphasis on claims processing came at the expense of performance in another functional area—such as adjudications and appeals—through staff reassignments, for example. Other factors states mentioned include a higher degree of automation (i.e., less labor dependence) in initial and continuing claims functions, and less training needed when moving or hiring staff into the claims-taking area than in the more complex areas of adjudication and appeals.

Quality of Performance: Adjudication Determinations

The quality of UI agency nonmonetary adjudication determinations was adversely affected by the Great Recession, but at a national aggregate level the change was small, a peak-to-trough decline of about 4 percentage points. In fact, in the teleconference interviews with the states, when asked how state administrative performance had changed with the recession, only a few state UI officials mentioned issues with performance in the area of quality of determinations, and most tended to see these issues as a natural consequence of the recession.

The quality of state determinations for both separation and non-separation issues is measured on a scale whose maximum value is 100 when the determination is judged to be fully satisfactory. Figure 8.6 traces developments in the quality of nonmonetary adjudication determinations from 1997 to 2011. It displays two quality series, providing separate scores for separation and nonseparation determinations. Both series are simple averages of 52 scores from the individual programs (the 50 states plus the District of Columbia and Puerto Rico).

Three features of Figure 8.6 are noteworthy. First, the series trend strongly upward between 1997 and 2008, but then decrease during 2009 and 2011. Second, quality is significantly higher for nonseparation determinations than for separation determinations. The difference in their scores averaged 6.5 percentage points during the 15 years spanned by the data. Third, the average quality scores decreased by about 4 percentage points during 2009 and 2011, showing a cyclical effect on performance.[10]

Payment Accuracy Performance

Data to estimate payment accuracy in the regular UI program have been collected for 25 years. Figure 8.7 displays the estimated overpayment rate for regular UI benefits from 1988 to 2011. Four features of the chart are noteworthy. First, in most years the estimated overpayment rate was between 7.5 and 10.1 percent of benefits. Second, there is an upward trend in the estimated rate. Most rates were less than 9.0 percent before 2000, while all exceeded 9.0 percent after 2000. Third, the highest estimated overpayment rate occurred in 2010, at 11.45 percent.

Fourth, the estimated overpayment rate decreased in 2011, to 10.67 percent. The high overpayment rate in 2010 might be linked to the high continued claims volume of that year. A specific feature of 2010 was the number of changes in EB and EUC eligibility (refer to Table 8.8). These stops and starts in extended benefit eligibility, along with three "reach-back" periods in 2010, could have affected operations in the regular UI program.

A regression analysis of the BAM overpayment rate yielded three findings of interest. First, the uptrend in the error rate seen in Figure 8.7 was confirmed by regressions. The trend was estimated with greater precision when the regression excluded 1988 and 1989, the first years

**Figure 8.6 Quality of Nonmonetary Determinations, 1997–2011 (% of
determinations)**

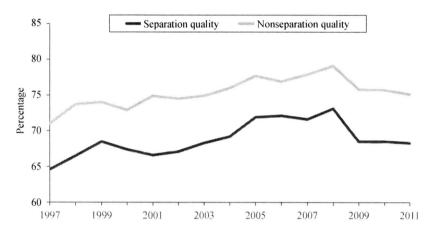

SOURCE: Quality data from USDOL ETA Report 9056.

of BAM measurements. Second, no systematic effect of cyclical variables was found despite the obvious spike in the error rate in 2010.
The upward deviation above the regression line of the data point for
2010 is about 0.8 percentage points. The increase over 2009 so appar-
ent in Figure 8.7 partly reflects a negative regression residual in 2009,
when the error rate was almost 1.0 percentage point below the regression line. This statistical noise from 2009 and 2010 partially reflects the
fact that the BAM samples are small, yielding variable BAM estimates
for individual years. Third, estimates of trend and cyclical effects did
not change when the data points for 2010 and 2011 were either included
or excluded from the regressions. The upward trend in the estimated
payment error rate ranged from 1.0 to 1.3 percentage points per decade.
The absence of a strong cyclical effect stands in contrast to the cyclical effects found in the timeliness and quality regressions discussed
previously.

Figure 8.7 is helpful for assessing recent discussions about the size
of UI payment errors during the Great Recession. Estimated overpayment error rates have exceeded 9.0 percent in every year since 2002.
Between 2009 and 2010 the overpayment error rate increased from 9.28
percent to 11.45 percent. The popular discussion of payment errors has

Figure 8.7 National Trends in Estimated UI Overpayment Rates

SOURCE: Annual Benefit Accuracy Measurement (BAM) reports.

often emphasized the volume of erroneous payments. Although the error rate did increase in 2010, most of the recent increase in erroneous payments reflects growth in total benefit payments. Erroneous payments totaled $6.65 billion in 2010, out of regular UI benefits of $58.1 billion. With an error rate of 9.0 percent, the average between 1997 and 2005, this total would have been $5.39 billion. The principal determinant of the growth in the dollar amount of payment errors is the growth in the underlying volume of benefit payments, not the growth in the error rate.

STATE UI AGENCY OPERATIONAL ADJUSTMENTS DURING THE GREAT RECESSION—BEFORE IMPLEMENTATION OF THE RECOVERY ACT

During the period of the recession before implementation of the Recovery Act, states were wrestling with rising caseloads for regular benefits. They also struggled with additional caseload growth and implementation issues because of UI legislation approved in June and November 2008 authorizing and extending the EUC program. In most states, the major keys to addressing the surging caseloads were the hiring and training of staff. Also important in many states was automating or otherwise streamlining certain UI processes. This section provides detail on these staffing, technology and business process adjustments. Of course, states continued making adjustments throughout the remainder of the recession and beyond, especially in response to the provisions of the Recovery Act, and some of these are discussed in a later section of this chapter. This section is organized by types of adjustments, not by the core UI processes. However, Box 8.2 illustrates the types of adjustments states made in what was for many a challenging core UI process—appeals. The box highlights how investments in technology, staff, staff training, and business process changes were all potentially important to addressing appeals caseloads and backlogs.

Box 8.2 How Technology, Training, and Business Process Changes Addressed Appeals Caseloads and Lessened Backlogs

- Arizona: New technology for the first-level appeals process was planned before the recession and implemented successfully during the recession. This technology is Web-based and provides more functionality for customers, adjudicators, and administrative law judges (ALJs) on the front end. The combination of this new appeals system, the bringing back of retirees, and the hiring of temporary ALJs has enabled the department responsible for this function (which is outside the UI area) to address appeals time-lapse issues.

- Louisiana: The state reorganized its lower authority appeals processes as a result of a backlog. A new head of the appeals division was appointed, an outside consultant hired, and an improved division of labor implemented. Previously, ALJs performed tasks more appropriate for clerical staff, so a new clerk of court was established. Also, to help clear the backlog, 150 appeals cases were transferred to an alternative division (Administrative Law) for resolution. The state hopes eventually to move away from dependence on its legacy IT system and toward a Web-based approach.

- Michigan: The state addressed a trend upwards in the age of lower-authority appeals by centralizing appeals and setting up a separate postal box and fax line for appeals. Appeals work now is kept separated, saving days.

(continued)

Box 8.2 (continued)

- Montana: In training adjudicators, the state focused on training them well in fact-finding and decision-making, which slowed claims-processing times for adjudications but ultimately reduced the number of appeals. A backlog in adjudications also reduced the number of cases making it to appeals to begin with.
- Nevada: To help maintain timely appeals performance the agency got permission to hire additional referees in 2009, but the positions were hard to fill because they required significant UI experience, lacking in many new UI hires. The agency officials noted the volume of appeals increased sharply in part because the appeals rate rose due to the lack of jobs in the economy. Even relatively straightforward monetary determinations were being appealed by some unemployed workers desperate to get assistance, despite an absence of sufficient base period earnings.
- Ohio: To address delays in appeals, both the numbers of hearing officers and cases decided per officer have increased. By 2011 most of the backlog was eliminated, but it remains an area of concern. Modernizing the benefits system has helped to improve appeals timeliness.
- Virginia: Increased number of appeals (due, in part, to the lack of training among new hires handling first determinations) coupled with staff turnover and the reassignment of staff to other UI functions meant ALJs had a sharp decrease in average years of experience. The appeals function was strengthened by increasing overtime hours, hiring more staff (including some retirees) and training.

SOURCE: UI interviews conducted by Urban Institute and NASWA researchers.

Staffing Adjustments

States made numerous adjustments to staffing in response to the caseload surge, not only to meet the growing UI claims demand during regular hours, but also to allow for extended hours of operation. Staffing adjustments included hiring new staff, rehiring retirees, requiring or allowing staff overtime hours, and reassigning existing staff. Training new staff was necessary and often challenging, and hiring and keeping qualified staff was often a challenge as well. The story told by officials in one state—Virginia; see Box 8.3—provides an example of the significant scaling up of, and shift in, staff resources during the recession.

Table 8.5 describes some of the staffing adjustments each of the other interview states made before enactment of the Recovery Act.

New hires and training. Nearly every state reported hiring new staff members, and in the vast majority of states many or all of these new staff were temporary hires. New staff hiring presented both opportunities and challenges. Several states volunteered that the quality of new hires was above average because of the recession-related supply of available labor, and they expressed hopes that new hires could eventually become permanent staffers as other staff retired. For example, Nebraska officials remarked that the new staff came through the administrative services office that provides temporary staff, and that they were of higher caliber than is typical, with even lawyers and accountants in the mix. Maintaining temporary staff was sometimes a challenge; officials in several states volunteered that recruiting was a continuing

---

Box 8.3 Staffing Adjustments: A Virginia Example

Normally, in the Virginia Employment Commission, the breakdown of staff resources is about an even 50-50 split between UI and worker adjustment services at the One-Stops. With greatly increased UI caseloads during late 2008 and throughout 2009 the de facto allocation of Commission staff between UI claims and "everything else" changed to a roughly 80-20 split. A large element of the adjustment was the hiring of temporary staff for UI, but other adjustments included reassigning staff to UI claims, working increased overtime hours, and rehiring some recent retirees. The staff reassignments occurred both within UI (from functions like nonmonetary determinations and appeals to claims activities) and from the One-Stops to UI. Staff had previously been cross-trained, so reassigned workers were able to perform claims functions. Despite or because of these reallocations, performance decreased in first-payment promptness and nonmonetary determinations, and the volume of worker adjustment services in the One-Stops was drastically curtailed.

SOURCE: UI interviews conducted by Urban Institute and NASWA researchers.

Table 8.5 Examples of State UI Staffing Adjustments in Response to the Recession, before the Recovery Act

State	UI program staffing adjustments
Colorado	The agency made staffing increases in most functional areas, including initial claims, adjudication and fact-finding, first-level appeals, and continued claims. Weekly hours were adjusted in adjudication and fact-finding.
Florida	The state made an aggressive effort to hire and train additional staff, with the number of staff increasing from 400 to 1,700. These were overwhelmingly new employees hired on a temporary, contractual basis.
Illinois	Illinois was aggressive in staffing up. The state always maintains a pool of intermittent employees, many of whom are cross-trained for UI and Employment Services. The state increased the hours of many intermittent employees. The flexibility provided by these employees, both to scale up operations as well as to move staff between functions, proved very helpful as the number of UI claimants rose. The state also hired and trained new staff, and it temporarily rehired retirees. Staffing also was increased by extending staff hours.
Louisiana	New staff was hired to process initial claims in call centers and conduct monetary determinations and appeals. Total adjudication staff was expanded from 30 to 40, with plans to add 15 more by late fall of 2011. The state created a special training series for the new adjudicators. The shortage was exacerbated in mid-2011 through buyouts and retirements when agency downsizing was mandated.
Maine	Prior to the recession, staffing levels were at a low. About 40 to 45 claims takers were needed but only 18 were on staff, less than 50 percent of need. Even then, the agency was not able to handle the current workload as efficiently as it would have liked. Staffing levels were low for several reasons: attrition and retirements, a state hiring freeze, and funding declines. When the recession hit, pressure from the legislature and the public led to the tripling of claims staff, including the rehiring of retirees. Training was a challenge, even though the quality of hires was high. Some staff was reassigned within the agency; e.g., some quality-control staff, fraud adjudicators, and tax staff were moved to claims. The assignment of staff for nonmonetary determinations was modified, to ensure newer staff worked on simpler issues (quits rather than misconduct). Training was needed because adjudication was increasing due to increased volume; often claims staff were elevated to adjudication with limited experience.
Michigan	The state implemented voluntary and mandatory staff overtime, hired between 100 and 150 new temporary employees for a new call center (a 10 percent increase in agency staff), and reassigned staff, mostly from support activities to telephone claims filing for both initial and continued claims.

Montana	Montana offered compensatory time and overtime to existing staff, rather than hiring and training new staff, to maximize efficiency (the state later hired new staff).
Nebraska	As the recession hit, the state nearly doubled its claims-taking staff, from 60 to over 100. The new staff was mostly agency temporary staff traditionally allowed to work one year before taking a break and acquiring a new assignment. During the recession the agency got an exemption from this requirement to implement a break period. The new staff came through the administrative services office that provides temporary staff, and was of higher caliber than is typical, with some lawyers and accountants in the mix. The training schedule was intensive despite the quality of the new hires. New temporary staff also was hired for adjudications and first-level appeals work.
Nevada	Forty-four new UI staff were hired, a 5 percent increase. The new workers were temporary intermittent employees whose weekly hours could vary between 0 and 40. The state also reassigned 15 to 25 staff from outlying offices to UI operations and increased staff overtime hours (with regular staff working up to four hours' overtime each day).
New York	The state hired both temporary and permanent staff and reallocated existing staff to claims functions.
North Carolina	The state added staff in its adjudication unit, initial claims unit, and appeals. The state was understaffed in the adjudication unit prior to the recession. New hires were recruited from outside the agency and required training. The state sought hires with experience in the insurance industry. These were temporary positions, and turnover was an issue. The state was not able to hire up to the numbers it needed to address the workload. For appeals, the state hired lawyers from outside, which worked well since many of them were out of work but had high skill levels. While they were hired into time-limited positions, some have become permanent staff, and the appeals staff has been upgraded as a result. Hires for initial claims were primarily new, temporary staff, but some have been kept on as permanent staff. The state had an established training program it used for these new hires.
North Dakota	North Dakota hired temporary staff. Because the agency already used temporary staff to handle seasonal workload variation, the established pattern was followed but hiring volume was increased.
Ohio	Staff was approved for overtime hours. Prior to the recession, Ohio's agency was at full staffing levels, in part because officials began an early internal campaign for new hires and intermittent employees as the caseload began to grow. Local library staff was trained in on-line benefit applications so they could serve as a resource for persons wishing to file on-line who did not have computer access at home.

(continued)

Table 8.5 (continued)

State	UI program staffing adjustments
Pennsylvania	Before the recession, UC benefits staffing was at a low point of 700 employees, due primarily to limited federal administrative funding, so the initial focus as the recession hit was to hire staff as expeditiously as possible. Staffing increases were needed in all UC benefit functions, particularly those relating to new and continuing claims. Pennsylvania also temporarily reassigned staff from other UC functions (such as UC tax and fraud investigations), recalled annuitants, and used optional and mandatory overtime. Staffing increases took time because of state civil service rules and training capacity issues. Many of the new hires were temporary employees.
Rhode Island	Before the addition of new staff with the passage of Recovery Act legislation, people from outlying workforce development offices with UI knowledge were reassigned to UI and allowed to work up to four hours of overtime a day.
Texas	By November 2008, 110 additional staff members were hired and trained to work in the state's telecenters.
Washington	The state increased staff significantly beginning in February 2008, and by December 2010 it had boosted staff by 51 percent. These were both permanent and temporary hires.
Wisconsin	Before the recession, in the second half of 2007, the state agency lost 20 percent of its UI staff. As the workload increased with the recession, staff increases included long-term temporary (two-year) project staff, limited-term temporary (six-month) staff, and contract staff (temp agency staff). The agency also rehired some retirees and moved part-time staff between activities (to adjudication from nonclaims activities like IT and management). The agency also authorized overtime work.

SOURCE: UI teleconference interviews conducted for the study by researchers from the Urban Institute and NASWA.

need because of high turnover of temporary staff. Virginia officials noted, for example, that temporary employees often leave to take other jobs, an "ongoing problem in UI administration," as they put it. Several states also mentioned hiring was a challenge, because of a lag between caseload increases and increases in UI administrative funding (Rhode Island), state civil service rules (Pennsylvania), or hiring freezes. Problems with training capacity or long lead times for training also hindered some states' ability to place staff into positions.

Training new staff members was both important and a major challenge in many, if not all, states, as evidenced by the number of times state officials brought up training despite the interview protocol having no direct questions about training. Florida officials reported, for example, that training new staff was the biggest challenge they faced in ramping up. Nebraska, which nearly doubled its claims-taking staff as the recession hit, described its training schedule as "intensive." Rhode Island officials noted that when the number of staff tripled in February 2009, the state faced significant challenges with training.

Training was necessary not only for staff coming in the door, but for staff moving among positions, and training staff in more specialized areas could require a significant investment of time. For example, officials in Montana noted the state couldn't staff up fast enough in the nonmonetary determinations area because it takes four to six months to train a new hire adequately. Maine officials said newly hired staff worked on simpler issues at first, but it often was necessary to elevate these staff with little experience to high-skilled positions, such as adjudication, and more training was then required. This was mirrored in Nevada, which received permission to hire additional referees in 2009 to maintain timely appeals performance, but struggled filling positions because these referees require significant UI experience. Thus, recent hires were often promoted from examiner to adjudicator after just one week of agency experience. Rhode Island officials noted that during 2010 performance improvements in adjudications were smaller than in some other areas because more than half the persons doing adjudications were recent hires with limited initial knowledge of UI and no initial adjudication knowledge.

Insufficient staff training could have implications for both customer service and a state's performance relative to federal standards, but getting staff into jobs quickly also was a priority. States sometimes had to make trade-offs between training staff quickly and training them well. Montana officials noted, for example, that training adjudicators "well" in fact-finding and decision-making slowed the state's claims processing times but ultimately reduced the number of appeals.

To the extent some states innovated in scaling up training capacity, it was not a focus of the study; this suggests a possible area for follow-up, given the challenge training presented to so many states. Louisiana responded to the difficult time frames and trade-offs by creating a new, shortened training series. Officials in Texas mentioned that the state did a good job of anticipating the training needs of new hires (and these new hires worked out well). In North Carolina, the state was able to rely on an already-established training program for new hires for the initial claims function. Illinois may present a special case: as part of normal operations, the state maintains a pool of intermittent employees, many of whom are cross-trained for UI and ES, so when the recession hit, the state was able to increase the hours of these intermittent employees without great investments in training, which provided unusual flexibility to scale up operations as well as move staff among various functions.

Staff reassignment. During the teleconference interviews, a majority of the interview states reported reassigning staff among UI functions, or from other agency functions to UI, usually with an emphasis on maintaining timeliness of claims-processing or adjudications. Staffing trade-offs sometimes resulted in performance declines in UI or workforce functions of lower priority for resources. Many states facing short- or long-term resource constraints coupled with high customer needs found it necessary to triage in this way. Some examples follow (Box 8.4):

Retiree hires. Many states reported temporarily rehiring retirees as a complement to other hiring; no state reported rehiring retirees as the only way to increase staff. Rhode Island, for example, enacted legislation in February 2009 allowing the state to rehire recent retirees for eight weeks, which allowed the state some lead time to train new hires so they would be more proficient when they started to perform claims-related and other activities. Arizona hired new staff generally, but hires of administrative law judges came from among retirees.

Box 8.4   How States Reassigned Staff to Maintain Timeliness of Claims-Processing and Adjudication in the Face of High Demand

- In Florida, the state received a waiver allowing the agency to reallocate staff resources from fact-finding to adjudication; this was in effect for 2009 only.

- Montana reassigned staffers from the Benefit Accuracy Measurement (BAM) area to work on adjudications, calling it "a finger in the dyke." But after six months the state was sanctioned for this reallocation of staff, even though state officials thought the reallocation ultimately would enhance integrity (by allowing for more accurate determinations).

- Pennsylvania reassigned staff to claims processing from other UI functions, including tax and fraud investigations.

- Prior to the addition of new hires, Rhode Island reassigned staff with UI knowledge from outlying workforce development offices to work in UI, and allowed them to work up to four hours of overtime a day.

- Wisconsin moved staff to adjudication from "nonproduction" activities like information technology and management, on a part-time basis.

SOURCE: UI interviews conducted by Urban Institute and NASWA researchers.

Staff overtime. States often had to implement aggressive measures as they strove to meet customer needs and performance standards, and as a result longer work hours came into play for some, if not many, employees. A majority of states reported encouraging or requiring staff overtime, at least temporarily. Several examples follow (Box 8.5):

Separately, many states reported tremendous efforts, including overtime on weekends, holidays, and through some nights, by IT and high-level administrative staff even before implementation of the Recovery Act, to help implement process adjustments dependent on technology changes as well as the early EUC legislation. Similar efforts followed with implementation of the Recovery Act provisions, as the report later documents.

Box 8.5 How States Met Increased Customer Demand by Encouraging or Requiring Employee Overtime

- Until later in the recession, when new hiring became a necessity, Montana found it more efficient to offer compensatory time and overtime to existing staff, rather than hire or train new staff.
- Nevada increased staff overtime hours, with regular staff working up to four hours' overtime each day.
- Ohio began an "early internal campaign" for new hires and intermittent employees as the caseload began to grow, and was able to reach full staffing levels early in the recession; the state approved these staff for overtime hours.
- Pennsylvania and Michigan relied on voluntary and mandatory overtime to increase staff capacity.

SOURCE: UI interviews conducted by Urban Institute and NASWA researchers.

Outside staff support. Many states undoubtedly undertook initiatives to reach out in the community for resources to support UI claims processing. In Ohio, for example, local library staff members were trained on how to apply for UI benefits over the Internet so they could serve as a resource for claimants wishing to file on-line who did not own a computer. The teleconference interviews did not collect systematic information on the use of outside staff resources.

Adjustments to hours of operation. All but a few states mentioned extending hours of operation in order to meet the needs of UI customers during this period. Some states kept a Monday-through-Friday schedule but extended the day, while others implemented weekend hours, and still others did both. Some states also expanded call center hours of operation. Examples of specific adjustments include those listed in Box 8.6.

Adjustments to call center capacity and phone lines. Nearly every state added one or more call centers or upgraded its phone lines to increase capacity during the recession. Even states shifting claims-

---

**Box 8.6 How States Extended Hours of Operation to Meet the
Needs of Customers**

- Arizona opened offices earlier and closed them later, but remained with Monday-through-Friday hours.

- Florida extended hours of operation on weekdays, from 7 a.m. to 9 p.m., and established weekend hours of operation on both Saturdays and Sundays. Weekend operations were devoted to the processing of Internet claims; informational calls were accepted only on weekdays.

- Illinois increased the hours of interactive voice response (telephone IVR) availability from 12 hours (7:00 a.m. to 7:00 p.m.) to 16 hours (5:00 a.m. to 9:00 p.m.) per day.

- In Louisiana, office hours were extended by three hours, from 8:00 a.m.–5:00 p.m. to 7:00 a.m.–7:00 p.m.

- In Maine, career centers were opened on Saturday mornings to accommodate claims and information inquiries.

- Michigan extended both in-person and phone customer service hours, with phone hours increasing from 8:00 a.m.– 4:30 p.m. to 7:00 a.m.– 6:30 p.m.

- Washington opened its call centers for four hours on Saturdays for two months during winter peak, and later opened centers an hour early during weekdays.

SOURCE: UI interviews conducted by Urban Institute and NASWA researchers.

---

taking heavily toward the Internet usually found it necessary to revert in part to this older technology as One-Stop staff were overwhelmed by large numbers of UI claimants arriving with UI claims questions. Unlike most of the staffing adjustments states made, some of these technology-supported upgrades to IVR systems and call centers are sustainable. Of particular note, several states mentioned that adopting "virtual hold" or similar technology markedly improved call center efficiency during the recession. This technology allows a claimant calling the center a choice to either remain on the phone in a queue or be called back by an automated computer system that assigns a call-back time based on call volume (Box 8.7).

**Box 8.7 How States Increased Call-Center and Phone-Line
          Capacity during the Recession**

- In Arizona, which had shifted claims-taking primarily to the Internet before the recession, the surge in UI claimant calls negatively impacted other Arizona agencies because of a shared phone system. After a number of cross-agency meetings, phone lines were added and the interactive voice response (IVR) system was reworked (e.g., to allow lines to switch from one agency to another depending on slack and peak demand times).

- Florida increased the number of phone lines by contracting out call center services for the overflow of calls.

- Illinois upgraded its IVR system and added new telephone lines, increasing IVR capacity by one-third. This required nine new T1 fiber-optic telephone lines and three new servers.

- In Maine, the scripting of the IVR for taking claims was streamlined to address the backlog in phone claims stemming from a high volume of information inquiries being served on the same lines as claims.

- Michigan implemented a new call center in January 2009, increasing the number of centers to four. The state also purchased new IVR boxes for continued claims before and again after Recovery Act implementation.

- North Carolina relied on an already-established, contracted call center overflow unit to handle high initial and continuing claims volume. The unit was set up prior to the recession in case the call center went down.

- Texas's telecommunications provider began installing additional telephone lines in August 2008. By October 2008, the agency had 168 additional lines, growing to 336 by January 2009. In September 2008 the IVR systems were modified to allow claimants to submit payment requests on any available day (previously such requests were limited to specific days). A temporary call center was opened.

- Washington funded a new call center. It also modified its IVR system by implementing virtual hold technology. Implementation of this technology increased the quality of call experience, reduced wait times and freed up intake agents. A significant minority of the interview states adopted this technology at some point during the recent recession.

- Wisconsin increased phone-line capacity for both initial and continued claims.

SOURCE: UI interviews conducted by Urban Institute and NASWA researchers.

Other technology upgrades. Overall, a majority of the technology updates the interview states implemented were motivated by caseload pressures and designed to allow for more self-service over the Internet, with a goal of reducing the need for staff involvement. The updates were fairly narrow in scope, although they were key to automating or otherwise streamlining certain operations. For example, Rhode Island implemented technology changes allowing a greater percentage of claims to be completed at initial application over the Internet without the need for follow-up involvement of UI staff. Other state examples appear in Box 8.8.

In many states, the recession exposed broader weaknesses inherent in outmoded large-scale state IT systems for UI benefits administration, and in related software applications. But modernizing UI IT systems is a costly and challenging task and not a short-term option to address the unexpected caseload demands of a recession. As noted earlier in this chapter, Illinois was the one state to complete an IT modernization effort during the recession, but its effort—focused on the IT benefits system—was initiated and in process before the recession. The section below on the Recovery Act's $500 million supplemental distribution to states for UI administration reveals that many states are using or planning to use these supplemental administrative funds to plan or help execute major, multiyear IT benefits or tax system upgrades. Illinois relied on these Recovery Act funds to help complete its modernization effort.

Other (nontechnology) business process improvements. In the teleconference interviews, many states mentioned making business process improvements that did not involve technology investments, and some are captured in Box 8.9.

Recovery Act UI Provisions: State Implementation Experience

$500 million for UI administration. The Recovery Act legislation included a supplemental grant of $500 million to states for UI administration. Funds were allocated to states without the need to apply or take other action, and based on each state's proportionate share of taxable wages under the Federal Unemployment Tax Act (FUTA). Unlike most Recovery Act grants, states were not required to obligate or spend these funds by a particular date. The strains the recession put on state UI programs and the competing needs—to shore up outmoded infrastructure,

**Box 8.8 How States Updated Technology to Meet Increased
Caseload Pressures**

- In Arizona, a new technology for the first-level appeals process was planned before the recession and implemented successfully during the recession. This technology is Web-based and provides more functionality for customers, adjudicators and administrative law judges on the front end, although it still is tied to the old mainframe system.

- Colorado enhanced its on-line capabilities for completing fact-finding and adjudication. In addition, its outmoded computer system could not automatically pay EUC benefits on anything other than the most recent claims, causing the state to have to process an "extraordinary" number of claims manually. The state developed an automated solution for this manual process, allowing claims to be paid automatically but outside the existing payment system.

- Florida's technology innovations included putting more self-service online, with the capability for claimants to change their PINs and check claims; developing a refinement in the mainframe computer system that enables the computer to identify new employers; and developing an informational customer service e-mail system for claimants in order to reduce phone calls and address a problem of incoming emails containing no identifying information. The e-mail system includes identifier information from the claimant and the claimant's question, and e-mails are served by a callback team (to the extent possible, responses come from local One-Stop offices). The system eliminated some backlog, and 90 percent of e-mails were handled within two hours.

- Illinois reworked Internet certification processes and technologies.

- Maine implemented programming modifications for initial claims, continued claims, and adjudication activities. Also, the state was switching to debit cards at the time the caseload increased. Debit cards proved to be time savers and facilitated the servicing of the increased claims volume. (Nevada switched from paying claims by mail to the use of debit cards before the recession, in 2006 and 2007, and staff indicated the increased volume of calls during the recession could not have been addressed as well if payments were still made by mail.)

- In order to free up more telephone lines for incoming EUC and regular claims, Nebraska purchased cell phones for the adjudicators to use for fact-finding. It was much quicker to switch to cell phones than it would have been to install land lines, and to downscale once the extra capacity is not needed at the end of the recession. Using cell phones also made it possible for the state to be more flexible in utilizing office space, as using the cell phones meant adjudicators could relocate to another building to free up space for claims takers at the call center.
- New York responded to the claims volume by making programming modifications for initial and continued claims.
- North Dakota implemented a visual calendar to reduce claimant confusion caused by all the benefit extensions. The calendar gives claimants a highlighted date range for certifications.
- A big system adjustment for Ohio gave staff access to the benefits system even while batch processing was occurring. Previously, staff was not permitted to access the system during batch processing, and was forced to conduct certain business processes (both IVR and Internet) via paper during those times. The adjustment allowed certain business entries on a 24/7 basis, including filing initial claims, additional/reopened applications, filing of continued claims, fact-finding, entering appeals, claimant affidavits, and employer responses to requests for separation.
- Texas allows some claims examiners and appeal hearing officers to telecommute. The telecommuting staff members get their assignments and perform the work the same as staff located in the office. Telecommuting claims examiners have local and toll-free numbers that claimants and employers can use to return their calls, and they conduct their hearings telephonically utilizing Clear2There (C2T), a conferencing technology.

SOURCE: UI teleconference interviews conducted for the study by researchers from the Urban Institute and NASWA.

**Box 8.9 How States Made Improvements to Their Business
Processes to Meet Increased Demand**

- Louisiana reorganized its lower-authority appeals processes. A new
  head of the lower-authority appeals division was appointed who previously had headed higher-authority appeals and accomplished process
  improvements there. With the aid of recommendations from an outside consultant, the state implemented an improved division of labor.
  Previously, administrative law judges (ALJs) were doing some clerical work, so a new clerk of court was established. Also, to help clear
  an appeals backlog, 150 appeals cases were sent to the Division of
  Administrative Law for resolution.

- Louisiana created a special training series for new adjudicators after
  experiencing a staff shortage.

- Michigan instituted business process changes to address a 15-
  percentage-point decline in performance related to quality of determinations. Originally, incoming cases were distributed to call centers on
  a first-come, first serve basis. Under the changes, officials organized
  work by areas of specialization, allowing for continuous training and
  process improvement, as well as greater staff accountability.

- Michigan made an effort to increase employer-filed claims to reduce
  individual claims (mostly in mass layoff situations).

- Michigan addressed an upward trend in the average age of lower-
  authority appeals by centralizing appeals and setting up a separate
  postal box and fax line for appeals.

- New York streamlined claims-taking with innovations such as identifying callback times when claims volume was lower and spreading
  claims more evenly over the week.

- In Ohio, local library staff was trained on online benefit application so
  they could serve as a resource for persons wishing to file on-line who
  did not have computer access at home.

- Washington formed a team to develop mitigation strategies for times
  when the caseload surged. The team was composed of subject matter
  experts from each of the call centers, so solutions were designed with
  desk-level input. The state also relied on business consultants to get

respond to increased claims demand, streamline operations, address the reemployment needs of claimants, modernize eligibility provisions, and protect trust fund balances—are reflected in the purposes to which states were allowed to dedicate the special distribution for UI administration:

- Implementing and administering the provisions of state law that qualify the state for the UI modernization money
- Improved outreach to individuals who may be eligible by virtue of the modernization provisions
- The improvement of UI benefits and tax operations, including responding to increased demand for UI
- Staff-assisted reemployment services for UI claimants

Note that unlike the Recovery Act's incentive funding for modernizing UI eligibility provisions, which also may be used for UI administration as well as employment services, the Recovery Act grant for UI administration could not be used to pay benefits.

During our teleconference interviews with UI officials in 20 states, we asked on which activities states had used or planned to use their share of the funding, the funding breakdown by activity, and how much of each state's share of these funds was already spent or obligated. Subsequent to these state interviews, additional information became available through a survey conducted by NASWA. The January–February 2012 NASWA survey was designed to gather information from all states on the status of these Recovery Act funds for the period ending December 31, 2011. Forty-eight states and the District of Columbia, representing 98 percent of total national allocations, responded to the survey. The NASWA survey did not gather data on how states allocated funding across allowable activities, but it did provide more recent information for some of the states on spending decisions and time frames.

How states are using the $500 million special distribution for UI administration. Findings from NASWA's national survey reveal on which activities states had obligated or spent *any* funds as of December 31, 2011:

- Over 80 percent of the 49 reporting jurisdictions had obligated or spent funds to improve UI benefits and tax operations (including both technology and staffing investments).

- Forty percent had obligated or spent funds on staff-assisted reemployment services for UI claimants.

- Nearly 30 percent had obligated or spent funds to implement and administer provisions of state law to qualify for UI modernization incentive funds.

- Close to 25 percent had obligated or spent funds to reach out to individuals who might be eligible for UI based on the modernization provisions.

In order to estimate the share of funding in the 20 interview states that will flow to various investments, information for these states from both the NASWA national survey and the state teleconference interviews were combined. Overall, the 20 states fell into three general categories:

- Approximately half of the states reported they would spend or had spent all or a large majority of funds on technology improvements. These improvements include large-scale IT benefits or tax system enhancements or overhauls; smaller-scale technology projects (e.g., implementation of debit-card technology for UI payments, improved IT security, and upgraded interactive voice response systems); or computer programming to accommodate law changes.

- About one quarter of the states had spent or planned to spend all or a majority of funds on staffing for basic UI operations or for reemployment services (and in all but one case these were temporary staff).

- In the remaining one-quarter of states, funds were more evenly divided between investments in technology and staffing.

Louisiana and North Dakota are examples of states with a heavy technology focus. Louisiana chose to spend a fraction of its funds during the recession to increase staffing but reserved the majority for longer-term investments in information technology. North Dakota was engaged in a state consortium project to upgrade its tax and benefits IT system before the recession and is dedicating the majority of its funds to this effort. In contrast, Ohio is an example of a state spending with a focus on staffing. Ohio spent its UI administrative funds quickly to fill a funding gap that resulted when its administrative grant for base funding was reduced by 11 percent at the beginning of the recession. The funding allowed Ohio to maintain staff throughout all UI operations. Texas's funds were split more evenly between technology investments and staffing. The state has emphasized UI claimant reemployment and directed over half its funds to improving reemployment services, with another large amount directed at technology improvements.

Table 8.6 summarizes the results for 19 of the 20 states interviewed (representing 95 percent of the funds allocated to the 20 states). The table shows that these states have spent or plan to spend approximately 60 percent of the funds overall on technology investments. The remaining 40 percent of funds have been or will be dedicated mostly to staffing for both basic UI operations and reemployment services. State-by-state details for all 20 states appear in Table 8.7.

It is not surprising these states are targeting the majority of funds toward technology-related projects, given the old age of many state UI IT systems, the desire to streamline processes as a result of both the recession and budget constraints, and the need to program computers for law changes. Some of the interview states are using (or planning to use) some or all of the funds to plan or execute major IT benefits or tax system upgrades, often looking to cobble together the funds with other funding sources, such as Reed Act monies and special funding from supplemental budget requests (SBRs). However, the availability of sufficient funding to complete major IT systems upgrades is an ongoing issue for many states.

Given the other funding available to states for reemployment initiatives under the Recovery Act's Wagner-Peyser Act provisions, the

Table 8.6 Summary Estimates of State Investments from the $500 Million Recovery Act Grant for UI Administration (data from 19 interview states)

Type of investment	$ millions	% of total
Technology-related investments	153	60
Major system or small-scale upgrades	137	54
Programming for EUC/EB/modernization provisions	16	6
Staffing and infrastructure	99	40
Staffing of general UI operations (client services, administration)	45	18
Infrastructure	5	2
Staffing of reemployment initiatives	49	19
Total Recovery Act grants to 19 states for UI administration	252	100

NOTE: Percentages of subcategories in second column do not sum to 100 because of rounding.
SOURCE: UI interviews conducted by Urban Institute and NASWA researchers.

allocation of roughly a fifth of the UI administrative funding for reemployment staff is interesting, and possibly reflective of several states' focused emphasis on this area, as well as the heavy demand for One-Stop center services in the face of limited funding available through Wagner-Peyser Act and WIA programs. Texas, Washington, Michigan, and Pennsylvania are allocating roughly a third to a half of their grants to the hiring of reemployment staff. Texas, with a large total allocation, represents nearly half of the UI administrative funds states have used or plan to use for staffing of reemployment initiatives.

How quickly funds have been spent or obligated. As noted above, the Recovery Act did not require states to spend or obligate the special distribution for UI administration by a certain date. This funding is available to tend to the infrastructure and integrity needs of the UI system, and is key to enabling prompt and accurate payments to eligible individuals. States' priorities for the funding, outlined above, varied significantly, and therefore spending patterns did too, with some states focused on longer-term capital investments and others on nearer-term needs.

Based on public accounting methods, the major categories of state spending for UI administration—staffing and technology—generally ensure a fairly significant lag between the time funding is obligated and when it is actually spent.[11] Capturing information on both obligations and expenditures is important to understanding the full stimulus effect of the grant. Data from the NASWA survey of January–February 2012 show that, as of December 30, 2011, states had spent approximately 40 percent of the grant and obligated another 26 percent. Six states had spent all their funds, 13 had not yet spent any, and 34 had spent a portion.[12] The survey found that nearly all states had plans to spend or obligate any remaining funds. More recent data from the USDOL shows that six months later (through July 6, 2012), states had spent more than 50 percent of the grant. (Information on obligations was not available.) Seven states had spent all their funds, seven had not yet spent any, and 39 had spent a portion.

Emergency Unemployment Compensation and Extended Benefits. During 2009, 2010, and 2011, total UI benefit payments to unemployed workers exceeded $380 billion. Benefit payments in both 2009 and 2010 were more than four times their level in 2007, while payments in 2011 were more than triple those of 2007. Benefit extensions for claimants who had exhausted their regular UI entitlements were a major part of the increased payments. Federal Emergency Unemployment Compensation has been making payments to exhaustees in all states since July 2008, while Federal-State Extended Benefits were available in about three quarters of the states between mid-2009 and early 2012. The combined sum of EUC and EB payments exceeded $180 billion during 2009–2011. In fact, their combined totals in both 2010 and 2011 exceeded regular UI benefits for the first time in the history of benefit extensions that have been activated in all recessions since 1958.[13]

Administering benefit extensions has presented numerous challenges for the states. In contrast to regular UI, which operates continuously, EUC and EB are governed by federal legislation and trigger calculations that determine when they are "on." During the Great Recession the "on" periods for both programs have been determined by a series of federal enactments that the states had to implement, often on short notice, and sometimes with retroactive provisions that require states to reach back into the past to make appropriate benefit determinations and payments. EUC and EB were able to make payments until the last week of 2012. Absent further federal legislation, by December 2012 the statutory provisions affecting EUC benefits will have been in

Table 8.7 States' Investments from the $500 Million Distribution for UI Administration (planned and actual, as of January 2012)

State	Distribution amount ($ millions)	State investments from the $500 million special distribution for UI administration under the Recovery Act
Arizona	10.7	Arizona is one of four states in a consortium project to replace both the tax and the benefit automated systems that are currently in use. While funding was received from the USDOL to fund the majority of these system replacement costs, the state will use a large portion of the remaining balance of Recovery Act administrative funding on this consortium effort. In addition, the state will use a portion of the funding to gradually reduce staffing after EUC and EB are phased out in order to maintain client services during the phaseout period.
Colorado	9.1	About 83 percent was appropriated for UI workload support. As of April 30, 2011, 96 percent of these funds have been expended, while the remaining will be expended by the end of June 2011. In addition, 12 percent was appropriated and expended for costs associated with implementing the federal-state EB program. Specifically, the funds were used to program the agency's UI computer system to pay extended benefits. The remainder was appropriated for outreach and marketing of enhanced unemployment benefits to allow an individual enrolled in certain approved training programs to receive an additional 50 percent of the original weekly benefit amount for up to 20 weeks while enrolled in training. The majority of the UI administration money was used to pay for additional staff, which is not sustainable.
Florida	31.7	Florida's share of the new administrative funding will be used to implement an integrated claims/benefits/appeals IT system, to include also adjudications, charging and benefit payment control (BPC). The state will supplement the administrative funds with set-aside contingency funds. Florida plans to expend $10 million of the $31.7 million in FY 2012; $5 million will be expended by February 29 and $5 million more before September 30, 2012, for UC automation.
Illinois	21.5	The majority of Illinois's $21.5 million share of the new administrative funding was used to support the upgrade of the benefits IT system. The money has been largely spent. Other monies were also used to improve IT associated with benefits administration: a USDOL SBR, state penalty and interest (P&I) funds,

241

		and EUC caseload administrative monies. These changes will permanently enhance administrative capacity in the area of benefits administration, and state officials expressed confidence that the state is better poised to handle the next downturn.
Louisiana	7.0	Roughly 21 percent of Louisiana's $7.0 million share of the new administrative funding was spent on the hiring of additional staff. The remainder will be spent pending decisions regarding possible areas for IT improvements: basic tax and benefit processes, technical support for REA activities and support for more effective employment services. To improve basic tax and benefit processes, a new CISCO IT support software system will be implemented to help upgrade the call center. Replacing the legacy IT system will be a high priority.
Maine	2.0	Several technology initiatives are under way using these funds and a variety of funding sources. To date, all funds have been obligated but not fully expended. Other funding sources include SBR grants, contingency funds, and monies from the Reed Act distribution of 2002. Technology projects include instituting debit cards, improving overpayment recovery, improved IT security, and enhanced procedures for tax audits. When finished, all of these changes will permanently enhance the IT capabilities of the UI program. The biggest challenge in IT is to secure adequate resources to implement desired changes.
Michigan	14.9	Half of Michigan's $14.9 million share of the new administrative funds went to the workforce agency for reemployment services. The other half will be used for an interactive voice response (IVR) upgrade, which is part of UI IT modernization. The funds will be used in combination with UI Modernization Act incentive funds. The UI IT upgrades will involve an overhaul of front-end and back-end benefits and tax systems which will retire the state's old mainframe system. Rollout will occur in two phases, with tax and wage occurring by Fall 2012, and benefits by Fall 2013. Contracts are in place for spending all of the technology monies. The state hasn't faced any barriers to spending or planning to spend the UI administrative funds.
Montana	1.4	After first relying on UI above-base funding, the state has used the UI administrative funds to pay for staff to catch up on the claims backlog. The majority of funds will be used on staff and will be expended by June 2011. The additional staffers hired are temporary. The state used a small portion of the funds to improve Internet filing when EB was programmed, and the improvements to the Internet filing system will be permanent features of the state process. The improvements allow claimants to file redeterminations and appeals on-line.

242

Table 8.7 (continued)

State	Distribution amount ($ millions)	State investments from the $500 million special distribution for UI administration under the Recovery Act
Nebraska	3.1	To date, all expenditures of funds have been dedicated to IT projects needed to modify the benefit payment IT system to accommodate new legislation. Ten percent was spent to upgrade the benefit payment system platform, hardware, and software to accommodate the newly enacted provisions passed in order to qualify for UI modernization incentive funds. Nearly half has been budgeted for additional IT programming changes needed to accommodate the additional benefits related Modernization Act provisions (40 percent had been spent at the time of the interview). Once the state is certain all modernization IT projects are completed, the remaining funds will be used for improvements to the UI benefits and tax systems. To date, the state has not combined these funds with other funding streams. But other funds would be needed to complete improvements to the UI benefits and tax systems. All of the changes made with the Recovery Act UI administrative funds will be sustainable improvements.
Nevada	5.5	The state has spent or obligated most of its share of the new administrative funding. $1.5 million allowed the state to expedite planned technology changes for the call centers, including a virtual call center that dynamically routes calls to the state's call centers as individual claims examiners become available. The telephonic system the state is replacing prioritized the claimant queues by region, which led to an imbalance in wait times. The adoption of the virtual call center/virtual hold system was a permanent modification to the UI telephonic infrastructure. Some of the funds ($1.2 million) have been or will be used to continue RES, which the state implemented in coordination with its existing REA program. RES and REA generate savings to the trust fund of about $5 for every $1 spent. Remaining funds will be used to upgrade the agency on-line registration system ($1.2 million), upgrade technology in One-Stop centers in order to enhance services in the resource centers statewide ($32,000), and make additional system enhancements for the prevention and detection of UI fraud ($940,000).
New York	29.5	The money will be used for large-scale IT upgrades for tax and benefits administration, as well as for staffing needs. Priorities and timing of future IT improvements are still under discussion. Monies for IT improvements also will be derived from other sources, such as contingency funds and Recovery

243

State		
		Act UI modernization monies. When the upgrading has been completed, it will represent a sustainable improvement in administrative capacity. Staff members noted the existing IT systems are old and take time to modify.
North Carolina	14.6	The state will use $10 million for time-limited (two year) positions dedicated to adjudications, appeals, integrity, and claims-taking through the call centers. The remaining $4.6 million will be used for infrastructure improvements in the facilities.
North Dakota	1.0	This funding is being used for staffing and costs associated with WyCAN, a state consortium project to improve the benefits IT system. Because of this, the funds have a specific intended purpose but do not fall into the DOL obligation definition. The state used about 34 percent to hire temporary staff. The remainder of the funds will fund future IT upgrades, especially for the consortium modernization project, in combination with funds from several sources: remaining monies from the 2002 Reed Act distribution, and anticipated monies from the consortium.
Ohio	18.9	The state experienced a significant reduction in base grant funding. The state's share of the new administrative funding helped correct the shortfall. The state was able to maintain staff. The funding for these FTEs was spread throughout all operations and enabled the state to maintain its existing staff. In total, the new administrative funding was used for state payroll costs associated with improving outreach to claimants, payroll costs for improving tax and benefit operations, and reemployment services (internal administrative hires). The state did not combine these funds with other funds to implement these services, and all funds were spent on temporary efforts. State officials report no barriers to spending the funds.
Pennsylvania	19.5	About one-quarter of Pennsylvania's share of the administrative funds was allocated to hire new staff to support increased reemployment of claimants. The majority of the rest was utilized for programming modifications to the new computer system to accommodate new federal law changes, including building EUC functionality. Since EB had not been activated for over two decades, new programming for EB payments was also needed. About 6 percent was obligated and spent for programming in 2012. The upgrading of the computer systems represents a permanent increase in IT capacity. No impediments to spending administrative funds have been experienced.

(continued)

Table 8.7 (continued)

State	Distribution amount ($ millions)	State investments from the $500 million special distribution for UI administration under the Recovery Act
Rhode Island	1.7	The UI Division is in the process of finalizing statements of work for technological improvement projects in UI and tax on the balance of the funds. We anticipate work to begin on the projects during PY 2012. The state has spent about 30 percent of funds developing a new IT application for weekly certifications. Prior to September 30, 2010, claimants whose claim was pending could not use the automated payment system. Thus, once their claims were authorized, a certification mailing was sent out and back via mail. All customers now can certify on a weekly basis, even those in pending status, so funds can be released when payments are due. Before last September, weekly certifications were done by mail. They also used some of the funds to update their telephone system. Other planned IT uses include: automate the entire Web certification, upgrade aspects of tax operations, automate applications and payments in the STC (workshare) program, and automate the process of mass filings. The various IT activities are to be financed by at least three sources of money: Recovery Act administrative monies; SBR from national office; an anticipated workshare administrative cost allocation from the national office. When the automated weekly certification process is in place it will reduce the mail costs. Challenges to spending administrative funds on IT improvements include: numerous EUC bills that resulted in few administrative staff available for other functions and the centralization of IT in the state government. Even with good support from staff transferred from UI to central IT, access can be restricted because staff allocations and priorities are set outside the UI agency.
Texas	39.7	The state has obligated its $39.7 million share of these monies for use in UI benefit and tax operations and for reemployment services. Forty-three percent has been directed at tax and benefit automation improvements, while the remaining has been obligated towards improvements in reemployment services.
Virginia	13.5	Our plan has been to use this funding in FY 2012 and FY 2013 for base UI administrative activities. This looks achievable because of the progress of our UI modernization project. These augmentations will enable an increased focus on national and state integrity initiatives and the prevention and minimization of UI overpayments. We plan to have the funds fully expended by September 30, 2013.

| Washington | 10.5 | The department has increased staffing and is currently utilizing these funds to address the high demand for reemployment services and the Unemployment Insurance claims center. According to TEGL 28-10 the department cannot obligate staff salaries; therefore, the obligation at this time is zero. The department began expending these funds as of January 1, 2012. The split is $4.14 million for core UI staffing, and $6.33 million for reemployment staffing. |
| Wisconsin | 9.6 | Two-thirds of Wisconsin's $9.6 million share has been/will be used for reemployment services. The remainder is allocated for technical modernization efforts. Of that amount, 44 percent was used for data base conversion. The remaining allocation will be used for benefits and modernization projects. The first phase will be the claimant portal, scheduled for completion in the fourth quarter of 2012. The claimant portal project will involve modernizing security so all applications are wrapped under one "security umbrella," and adding new services such as electronic correspondence so they can e-mail claimants. The state will use other funds to supplement these projects. The funds were received from an SBR for "state-specific solutions." UI grant funds will be used for the remaining costs for a series of multiple projects over a period of 3 to 5 years. The technical improvements are sustainable. The RES funding is for staffing and will be exhausted. The state has not faced any barriers to spending the UI administrative funds. |

SOURCE: UI teleconference interviews conducted for the study by researchers from the Urban Institute and NASWA.

place for 54 months and Recovery Act–related EB provisions for 46 months.

Between June 2008 and February 2012, ten different federal laws were enacted that affected eligibility for benefit extensions. Table 8.8 identifies each law, along with the intake dates and end dates for EUC and EB. Four laws included reach-back provisions that required the state UI programs to examine earlier periods for purposes of determining extended benefit eligibility and payments. The longest reach-back period was 14 months, in the June 2008 legislation that created the EUC program. However, three bills enacted in 2010 also included reach-back provisions because eligibility for new claims lapsed before the legislation could be enacted. The longest break was an eight-week period during June–July 2010. Typically the states advised claimants to remain in active claims status during these periods so that they would be eligible for the full retroactive payments after new legislation extended the intake and eligibility dates.

The amount of detail in Table 8.8 provides insight into the degree of administrative complexity associated with the benefit extensions during 2008–2012. Besides the various start, stop, and reach-back dates shown in the exhibit, the individual bills also addressed the possible continuation, modification, or termination of other elements in the Recovery Act legislation of February 2009, such as maximum potential benefit duration, the tax treatment of benefits, the payment of federal additional compensation, and the calculation of weekly benefits (see the earlier Table 8.3). The Recovery Act legislation also facilitated the temporary expansion of the EB program by allowing the states to use total unemployment rate (TUR) triggers and providing full federal financing of EB payments.

For both EUC and EB, the potential duration of benefits was linked to each state's unemployment rate—i.e., higher unemployment triggered longer potential duration—but with a key difference in their triggers. The EUC trigger used only the level of the state's unemployment rate (the total unemployment rate, or TUR). Thus during 2010 and 2011, states with a TUR of 8.5 percent or higher could pay up to 53 weeks under four tiers of EUC, while states with an unemployment rate of 6.0 percent or below could pay only up to 34 weeks under EUC's first two tiers. The EB program, in contrast, has a two-part trigger: 1) the level of the unemployment rate and 2) the ratio of the current unem-

Table 8.8 Important Dates Affecting Eligibility for EUC and EB Since 2008

Law	Legislative date	EUC intake, last date	EUC benefit, last date	EB intake, last date	EB benefit, last date	Reach-back date
PL 110-252	6/30/2008	3/31/2009	6/30/2009			5/1/2007
PL 110-449	11/21/2008	3/31/2009	11/27/2009			
PL 111-5	2/17/2009	12/31/2009	5/31/2010	1/1/2010	6/1/2010	
PL 111-118	12/19/2009	2/28/2010	7/31/2010	2/28/2010	7/31/2010	
PL 111-144	3/2/2010	4/5/2010	9/4/2010	4/5/2010	9/4/2010	
PL 111-157	4/15/2010	6/2/2010	11/6/2010	6/2/2010	11/6/2010	4/5/2010
PL 111-205	7/22/2010	11/30/2010	4/30/2011	12/1/2010	5/1/2011	6/2/2010
PL 111-312	12/17/2010	1/3/2012	6/9/2012	1/3/2012	6/11/2012	11/30/2010
PL 112-78	12/22/2011	3/6/2012	8/15/2012	3/7/2012	8/15/2012	
PL 112-96	02/23/2012	12/29/2012	1/5/2013	12/29/2012	1/5//2013	

NOTE: Blank = not applicable.
SOURCE: Table assembled from entries in the UWC publication "Highlights of State Unemployment Compensation Laws" and UIPL No. 04-10 (USDOL 2009).

ployment rate to the rate for the same three months one and two years previously.[14] Because the period of high unemployment following the Great Recession lasted so long in most states, in early 2011 the look-back for the EB triggers was extended from two years to three years to prevent EB from ending too soon.[15] Even with a three-year look-back, EB ended in nearly all states in mid-2012. During April and May 2012, the number of states paying EB decreased from 31 to seven.

Our sample states provide a good representation of the differing unemployment rates faced by state UI programs during the Great Recession. For example, across all 51 "states" in 2010,[16] the annual unemployment rate exceeded 10.0 percent in 16, fell below 7.0 percent in 10, and there were 25 state TURs in the intermediate range between 7.0 and 9.9 percent. In the interviewed states, the counts in the same high, medium, and low TUR intervals were respectively seven, eight and five states.

The interviewed states also present a varied picture in terms of experiences with EB and EUC, closely mirroring national experiences. During 2010, for example, 40 of 51 states paid EB, as did 17 of 20 in our sample. Of the 17, all but three paid EB for 20 weeks during at least part of 2010. Nationally, 47 states paid Tier 3 EUC benefits (47 weeks) during 2010, as did 18 of the 20 states we interviewed. The respective counts of states that paid Tier 4 EUC benefits (53 weeks) were 27 nationwide and 11 in our sample.

Both benefit extensions presented multiple administrative challenges for the states. During most weeks between June 2009 and March 2012, most states paid EB as well as EUC. Because nearly all states elected to pay EUC prior to EB, the sequencing of benefits was most commonly regular UI, then EUC, and finally EB, for persons eligible for all three types of benefits. Three factors explain why total EUC benefits were much larger than EB benefits: maximum duration of EUC was longer, more states paid EUC, and many EUC claimants returned to work before exhausting EUC and ever claiming EB. In 2010, for example, total weeks compensated under regular UI, EUC, and EB were respectively 200.7, 228.9, and 30.9 million.

Because nearly all states experienced major increases in weeks claimed, our interviews identified several common administrative problems. Communication problems with claimants were identified by all states. Claimant inquiries about eligibility frequently were made (or attempted) on phone lines intended for initial claims or continued claims. Modes of agency outreach such as public service announcements, agency splash pages on their Internet sites, and mailings were all used to disseminate information, but phone volume was frequently so large that it interfered with the prompt processing of claims.

Communication problems within UI program administration were also encountered. After federal legislation extending benefits was passed, the states frequently sought guidance from the national office regarding the interpretation and implementation of new provisions. After guidance was received, the information had to be communicated to agency staff so that correct information could be shared with claimants. Individual states offered differing opinions as to the timeliness of the federal guidance.

As states increased staffing to handle the increased volume of claims, those newly hired and reassigned from other agency divisions required training in their new responsibilities. This needed to be accomplished quickly because of the pressure of high claims volume.

New legislation often required rewriting IT programs related to benefit delivery. Writing and testing these programs was done under intense time pressure. Legislation passed in 2010 gave the states and claimants a choice in the calculation of the weekly benefit amount (WBA) when large WBA reductions were otherwise implied. While this favorably affected benefits for many claimants, it also presented programming challenges for the agencies in making appropriate calculations. Overall, many of the states reported that the recession exposed broader weaknesses inherent in outmoded state information technology systems for benefits and tax administration and related software applications. In many states, IT staff dedicated a tremendous number of hours, including time after-hours and during holidays, to "working" these systems and related applications to ensure customer needs for benefits administration were met.

During 2010 there were three separate periods with breaks in new intake for EUC and EB. Most states advised claimants to keep filing during the breaks, even though benefits were not being paid, so that payments could be made expeditiously once new intake resumed. Claimants found this confusing, and agency suggestions were not always followed, leading to payment delays when eligibility resumed.

The extension of EUC potential duration in November 2009 created four separate tiers of eligibility, with maximum potential duration of 20, 14, 13, and 6 weeks for tiers one through four, respectively. This legislation also created a fourteenth-week problem for the second tier of EUC benefits in several states. Many states had been paying 33 weeks of EUC (20 plus 13) and therefore needed to add a fourteenth week to the second tier of expanded eligibility. Several states mentioned that they had developed an IT "work-around" to pay the fourteenth week of Tier 2, necessitating programming and testing, again under severe time pressure.

Several states mentioned problems in administering payments when more than one type of UI benefit or earnings from more than one state was involved. These interfaces could involve Trade Adjustment Assistance (TAA) benefits and interstate claims as well as interfaces between regular UI, EUC (with its four tiers after November 2009), and EB.

The Recovery Act legislation reactivated the federal-state EB program, which had been largely moribund for 25 years. Between 1984 and 2008 EB was paid in very few states—e.g., the highest annual numbers were eight states in 1991 and five states in 1994 and 2003. After the Recovery Act, the state counts were 40 in 2009 and 2010, 37 in 2011, and 34 in 2012. Administering the revived EB program presented several challenges. EB has more stringent work-search requirements than EUC. Storage of work-search declarations (frequently received as paper declarations) as well as verification of them presented challenges in several states.

Because EB triggers include a look-back comparison of current state unemployment with unemployment one and two years earlier, several states would have triggered "off" in early 2011. This was avoided by allowing states to enact a three-year look-back early in 2011. Most states that paid EB enacted the extended look-back. The states that paid EB were mainly states that had established the temporary TUR triggers allowed under the Recovery Act. Following the Recovery Act, the number with TUR triggers increased from 12 to 39, and all 27 states that adopted the TUR trigger adopted temporary triggers. Under current legislation, the number of states with a TUR trigger will revert to 12 in January 2013.

While EB could be activated using either a TUR trigger or an IUR trigger, the vast majority of EB benefits were paid under TUR-based calculations. Only during March–June 2009 were IUR triggers of any importance—i.e., they were active in from four to 12 states. In the months between September 2009 and May 2012 no more than two states made weekly EB payments under an IUR trigger. Almost all EB payments during the Great Recession were paid under TUR triggers.

Federal Additional Compensation (FAC)

The Recovery Act created a new, temporary Federal Additional Compensation (FAC) program providing a 100 percent federally funded $25 add-on to all weekly UI payments for weeks of unemployment ending before January 1, 2010. The provision was subsequently extended three times for new claims through June 2, 2010, and for weeks compensated through the end of 2010. The FAC was unprecedented in that it made the same weekly payment to persons for partial weeks as it did for full weeks of benefits. All states signed agreements to pay FAC effective February 22, 2009, the first week for which FAC was payable.

Among the Recovery Act UI benefit provisions, the FAC stands out for presenting enormous administrative challenges relative to the size of total payouts. The FAC required states to do something outside of normal processes that they were not equipped to do, and to do it quickly. As a result, only one of the states we interviewed found the FAC relatively straightforward to administer. Most states faced multiple administrative challenges in the area of computer programming or systems development, with strong negative implications for the recovery of overpayments as well as for customer communications and service. Federal reporting and income tax withholding also presented challenges in many states.

Most states' IT benefits systems lack the flexibility to easily accommodate a simple-seeming add-on payment like the FAC. To implement the FAC provision in a short time frame, most states had to develop a separate computer program or even a separate payment system outside the main IT benefits system, or to pursue a manual payment process. Programming this new payment type into the existing benefits program (or system) was either impossible or would have resulted in great delays. For example, Maine officials reported that their IT system was not structured to handle the FAC, and they had to use an off line payment module usually reserved for special UI programs. Texas officials noted IT staff estimated it would have taken six months to incorporate FAC payment and overpayment processes into the state's automated benefits system, so the state chose to pay FAC as a supplement outside the system. Nevada officials mentioned they had to treat the FAC as a separate payment outside their regular UI programming, which substantially increased the administrative workload, and "several aspects of workload essentially doubled due to FAC payments," they said. Developing and testing the new programming or system was important to ensuring accuracy of payments, but it was also time-consuming.

North Carolina appears to have been unique among interview states in having a programming mechanism available to help administer the FAC. According to officials there, the benefits IT system allows for adjustments to UI payments when there is a change in the amount due a claimant. The state was able to treat the FAC as an "adjustment payment" in its system, which required some initial programming but did not create any major programming challenges.

Ohio and Nebraska, the only two states in the interview sample with a modernized benefits system at the beginning of the recession, reported significant challenges in implementing the FAC. In Ohio, implementation of the FAC required "drastic" system enhancements since it was a completely new type of enhanced benefit foreign to the state's IT benefits system. Officials there report that many processes were affected, including benefit payments, continued claims, employer charging, overpayments, repayments, reporting, and pay adjustment. The state was concerned about avoiding payment errors and devoted significant resources to testing the FAC programming prior to implementation. In Nebraska, also, the FAC was foreign to the state's modernized IT benefits system, and the state faced significant challenges with programming and overpayment recovery. Both states began paying FAC beyond the allowable first date of February 22, 2009, with Ohio reporting that it was one of the last states to begin payment, and Nebraska reporting that it worked until April 1 to implement needed programming changes.

Nearly all states reported difficulties identifying and recovering FAC overpayments. States often had to develop a new program to handle overpayments, since the payment of the FAC occurred outside the normal benefits program or system. Manual adjustments for overpayments were required in some states. One state official expressed the frustration typical of many of those interviewed, saying "the legacy of programs like this is that overpayments tend to be out there long after the program is exhausted."

In the majority of states, the FAC also created challenges with customer communications and service, as delays or administrative difficulties resulted in less-than-smooth FAC payment and overpayment recovery processes. Some states reported that they staggered FAC implementation because they could not implement it for all claimants on the same starting date, which created confusion and resulted in calls from claimants.

In many states, the FAC also created communications issues when it was phased out, as claimants did not understand why their benefit amount had been reduced. In a couple of states, communications lagged, but even in states that reached out aggressively through mailings and the Web site, claimant confusion was sometimes an issue that created a workload burden for state staff. Why this was a greater issue in some states than in others is not clear from the interviews.

To sum up, while several state officials noted that claimants benefited from the additional financial resources of the FAC, these benefits must be lined up against significant administrative costs. Most states reported that it was grossly inefficient to deliver these additional resources to claimants through an add-on payment, with costs spilling over to both claimants and program administration, including costs not accounted for here that resulted when states had to divert resources from other UI activities to handle FAC administration.

Income Tax Withholding

The state interviews revealed that UI programs did not face significant challenges in implementing the provision of the Recovery Act that provided a temporary suspension of the first $2,400 of UI benefits for taxable year 2009. Generally, states followed normal processes allowing claimants to decide whether to apply withholding and implementing claimant preferences. Many states did report initiating special communications to claimants. All claimants in Michigan received a mailing, for example. Arizona used the mail system and its agency Web site to inform claimants of the provision. Louisiana created a pop-up box as part of its Internet application. Montana placed information on its Web site. In New York, information was communicated using press releases, scripts added to the phone system's interactive voice response (IVR), and the Internet application. Generally, claimants made only a limited number of phone inquiries, except in Colorado, which reported significant claimant confusion and many calls.

UI Modernization

One innovative feature of the Recovery Act encouraged the states to broaden regular UI eligibility by adopting so-called modernization features. The legislation set aside $7.0 billion for distribution to the states whose UI laws included specific benefit provisions. Each state's proportional share of the $7.0 billion was determined by its share of federal taxable UI payroll. To receive its share, a state had to pass new legislation or demonstrate the presence of designated modernization features by late August 2011. Of the 53 state programs, 41 received either part or all of their shares of these funds.

Five aspects of benefit availability were the focus of Recovery Act modernization:

- The alternative base period (ABP)
- Part-time availability
- Enhanced eligibility for job-leavers who quit because of family responsibilities
- Eligibility for training support after exhausting ui benefits
- Paying the dependents' allowance

To receive any money, a state first had to have an ABP. States with an acceptable ABP received one-third of their total allocation for modernization. To receive the remaining two-thirds of modernization funds, a state had to have two of the remaining four features. Across the 53 UI programs, 41 received compensation for the ABP ($1.64 billion) and 36 received compensation for having at least two other modernization features ($2.78 billion). Thus, of the $7.0 billion total set aside for modernization, $4.42 billion (63 percent) was paid to the states.

The majority of states in our interview sample received modernization funds. Fourteen had an acceptable ABP and received one-third, and 11 of these received the remaining two-thirds. Modernization payments to the 20 states totaled $1.74 billion. Table 8.9 shows the breakdown for the 20 states by individual modernization feature.

The most obvious feature of the exhibit is the small number of states compensated for their dependents' allowance—only seven in the entire state UI system and just two of the 20 interviewed states. Nationally, 28 programs were compensated for their part-time provisions, 21 were compensated for quits for family reasons, and 16 were compensated for training support of exhaustees. In our sample of 20 states, these three provisions were of roughly equal prevalence, with counts of between five and eight states.

The states compensated for modernization usually applied for and were approved for payments shortly after the enactment of the Recovery Act in February 2009. Thirty-two of 41 approvals for ABP-related compensation occurred before December 31, 2009, and just two were approved after January 2011. Of the 32 approvals in 2009, 26 occurred before July 1. In nearly all instances, the states already with an ABP did not have to modify the ABP to receive approval.

One strong determinant of the timing of the applications and approvals was the presence of modernization provisions before the Recovery Act. Twenty-one of 41 programs with ABP compensation already had their ABP at the end of 2008. Table 8.9 shows that 10 of the 14 states in the interview sample had the ABP before the Recovery Act. The exhibit also shows that most of the states compensated for the individual two-thirds provisions had their provisions before the Recovery Act.

The intent of Recovery Act modernization was to broaden access to UI benefits. Among the 20 states interviewed, and more broadly within the set of 53 state programs, two factors have limited the actual expansive impact of modernization. First, several state programs—six of 20 within our sample and 12 of 53 among all state programs—did

Table 8.9 Recovery Act Modernization Payments in 20 Interview States

Time frame	ABP	Part-time	Quits for family reasons	Support for exhaustee training	Dependents' allowances
20 states, as of September 2011	14	7	8	5	2
20 states, before Recovery Act	10	5	7	3	2
Impact of Recovery Act	4	2	1	2	0

SOURCE: Counts based on data from the Office of Unemployment Insurance.

not enact any modernization provision. Second, several states that were compensated under Recovery Act modernization already had the specific provisions before the Recovery Act. For the latter states, the modernization payments were a windfall that did not lead to increases in weeks compensated or higher weekly benefits.

After the Recovery Act was enacted, nearly all 20 states in the sample made estimates of the cost of adopting each of the five individual modernization provisions. The states indicated that cost calculations strongly influenced decisions on whether to adopt any of the provisions (if not already present). Cost calculations also strongly influenced the selection of the detailed modernization provisions in the states that received the two-thirds compensation.

In states without the ABP there were two elements to the cost calculations. The modernization payment could be compared with the expected increase in the stream of future benefit payments. Among all six states that did not receive any modernization funds, state administrative staff said these calculations showed that the modernization payment would be used up in less than four years. This short period of positive impact on the trust fund balance was cited by many opponents as arguing against adopting UI modernization. Since employer payroll taxes support UI trust funds, the argument was ultimately about possible increases in future UI taxes. This cost argument was supplemented in three of the six states by the argument that adopting modernization would expand UI beyond its present scope, which was already deemed appropriate. Two of these states also expressed concern that UI modernization would increase the scope of federal influence in the UI system. These latter responses show that opposition and nonadoption were based on more than just cost considerations.

Cost comparisons were also important in states adopting two-thirds provisions. Given the strains on UI trust fund balances, the states were influenced to select the low-cost provisions among the four possibilities. Since several states were already paying dependents' benefits, there was probably greater certainty in budgeting for the cost of this modernization provision than the others. The increase in potential costs probably influenced a few states not to select this provision. Just one of the 53 programs (Tennessee) adopted a new dependents' allowance. In the sample of 20, two (Illinois and Rhode Island) were paid for having an appropriate dependents' allowance. Both already had the allowance but needed to make small modifications to satisfy Recovery Act requirements.[17] Their modifications left total benefit costs for dependents unchanged.

Several states reported that estimating the cost of the modernization training element posed great uncertainty. The uncertainty arose from at least three identifiable factors: 1) uncertainty about future take-up among those eligible, 2) uncertainty about future availability of extended benefits (and an associated effect on regular UI exhaustions), and 3) uncertainty about alternative future sources of support for training. Despite this uncertainty, the training for exhaustees was adopted by 16 states nationwide and by five in the sample. One explicit reason given for selecting training in two of the five states was that it was appropriate for the needs of the state's future economy.

Funds raised through UI taxes on employers and deposited into state trust funds can be used only for a single purpose: to pay regular UI benefits. Modernization funds under the Recovery Act could be used by the states for UI administration, claimant training, and IT upgrading, as well as for paying for benefits. The 14 states (out of 20 sampled) that received modernization funds indicated they would use the money in a variety of ways. The most frequent use (seven states) was to deposit the money into the trust fund to pay benefits. Thus, a total of seven out of the 20 state UI agencies had access to modernization funds to make investments in IT or staffing. Five states indicated they would use some of the funds to upgrade their IT systems, and one (Michigan) planned to use it all for IT upgrading. Four states said that some monies would be used to defray staffing costs. Although modernization funds have a wider set of potential uses than UI tax receipts, no state indicated that this greater flexibility was an important reason for adopting its modernization provisions.

Most states that have needed recent Treasury loans saw their trust funds descend to zero and to negative balances during 2009. Adopting an approved UI modernization package would have provided an immediate infusion into the trust fund and slowed its rate of decline. In interviews with the 14 states that received modernization payments, this positive short-run effect on trust fund balances was not mentioned by any state as a determinative factor in adopting modernization.[18]

One question that has been posed about UI modernization actions concerns the permanence of the changes. While the Recovery Act was in force, a state could not make temporary changes to enlarge access to benefits and receive modernization funds. The expansions, in other words, could not automatically sunset after a specific future date.[19] However, a current federal law such as the Recovery Act cannot prohibit future state legislation that might undo the modernization provisions. Eight states responded clearly to a question regarding serious state-level discussions about reversing their modernization provisions. Seven stated there had been no serious discussions, while just one indicated such discussions had been held. From information received in the interviews, it appears that the modernization provisions of the Recovery Act will not be reversed.

Trust Fund Loan Provisions and Status of State UI Trust Funds

The unprecedented increase in claims and benefit payments brought on by the Great Recession caused serious problems for most states in financing their regular UI benefit programs. State UI trust fund reserves held at the U.S. Treasury, the source for benefit payments in the regular UI program, declined sharply.[20] Between mid-2008 and the end of 2011, net reserves of the 53 programs in the state UI system decreased by more than $60 billion, with each state having a much lower fund balance at the end of 2011 compared to June 2008. At the end of December 2011, only 14 of the 53 programs had reserves equal to half or more of their reserves at the end of June 2008. The loss of reserves has caused widespread and large-scale borrowing. While this decrease in net reserves is an intentional aspect of UI program design and has helped to stabilize the economy, the states face major challenges in rebuilding their reserves.

To date, 36 of the 53 state programs have secured loans from the U.S. Treasury to help finance benefit payments. As a group, the 17 programs with indexed taxable wage bases have fared much better than the other states: loans have been made to 7 of 17 indexed programs, compared to 29 of 36 nonindexed programs. At the end of March 2012, 30 state programs owed nearly $41 billion to the Treasury. When loans obtained in the private bond market are included in the calculations, the March 2012 totals are 32 programs, having debts of roughly $46 billion.

The Recovery Act included a provision to reduce the immediate cost of state trust fund indebtedness. Loans by the Treasury to the states during 2009 and 2010 were made interest-free. Usually a state receives an interest-free loan only if all borrowing before September 30 of a given year is fully repaid by that date and no additional loans are secured from October to December of the same year. These are called "cash flow" loans. The states that borrowed during 2009 or 2010 did not meet this requirement in either year. The Recovery Act relieved debtor states of two years of interest charges, at an original estimated cost to the federal budget of $1.1 billion (see Table 8.1).

The states surveyed in phone interviews have shared fully in the financing issues of the state UI system. Fourteen of the 20 have needed loans, and many have large-scale debts. At the end of 2011, for example, 11 of these states had debts that represented at least 0.5 percent of covered payroll. For all 14 that have borrowed, loans have been outstanding for more than two years, and eight programs have been continuously in debt since the end of March 2009. The indexed states in the sample have generally fared better than the nonindexed states—e.g., two of the five indexed states have borrowed, compared to 12 of the 15 nonindexed states.

With large-scale and long-term debts, the states have been required to make interest payments to the Treasury starting in 2011. Also since 2011, automatic repayment has started to occur through increased FUTA tax credit offsets. These offsets start at 0.3 percent of federal taxable payroll in their first year of applicability and grow by at least 0.3 percentage points in each successive year that loans remain outstanding. Of the 14 debtor states in the sample, 12 were subject to FUTA credit offsets in 2011.

The interest charges and increased FUTA tax credit offsets provide financial motivation for states to repay their loans. Our interviews found the states have responded in a variety of ways. The imposition of the credit offsets has been automatic, a matter of adhering to federal requirements governing loan repayments. States have used different mechanisms to finance their interest charges. In some instances they also have acted to repay part of the principal on the loans. For most of the states, however, the response in repaying the principal has been slow as states struggle to recover from the effects of the recession. Several have relied on the workings of federal law to repay the principle of the loans and have not yet acted to improve their long-run situation. Others have borrowed or plan to borrow in the private bond market as part of their repayment strategy. During 2011, several also enacted legislation to reduce future benefit outlays. Thus, the states in the sample present a mosaic of responses that are still unfolding and were not completed in 2012. The full responses to their financing challenges may not be completed by the end of 2013 or longer.

To describe the state responses, let's begin with UI taxes. Annual revenue across the 20 states in 2011 averaged 38 percent higher than in the prerecession year of 2007. This average increase masks wide diversity. In six states total revenue increased by less than 25 percent, while one experienced a doubling of revenue. The modest responses in many states might reflect hope in those states for some form of financial relief from their debt obligations during 2009–2010, which did not occur. Also, while profits as a share of GDP were very high in both 2010 and 2011, there were concerns among many policymakers about the effect of revenue increases on employment growth and labor market recovery. [21]

Contrary to what might have been expected, slow revenue growth has characterized most of the 10 states with large debts in the sample. Just two of the 10 had 2011 revenue of at least 50 percent above their revenue in 2007. Thus, big revenue responses (i.e., 50 percent or more in 2011 compared to 2007) were more typical of the states that did not borrow (four of six) and the states with small loans (three of four). The interview responses did not suggest much larger revenue increases would occur during 2012.

At least to date, there has been reluctance to respond to financing challenges by undertaking large increases in the UI taxable wage base. While the tax base has increased in 11 of the 20 states at least once during 2010, 2011, and 2012, the changes have been largely automatic or due to prerecession legislation. The bases in the four indexed states have increased automatically, as have the bases in two other states where the base increases when the trust fund decreases (Louisiana and Rhode Island). Just three of the 11 with higher bases in 2012 achieved the increase through recent legislation. Colorado increased its base from $10,000 to $11,000, Florida raised its base from $7,000 to $8,000, and Michigan increased its base from $9,000 to $9,500. These changes are relatively modest, although Colorado's base will increase automatically in the future after the trust fund achieves a positive balance. [22] The interviews found that legislative proposals to raise the tax base faced strong opposition in the sample of 20 states.

Some states also have passed legislation to keep experience rating from operating as specified in the state UI statutes, when the statutory provisions would have resulted in an increase in UI taxes. In six of our 20 interview states, laws have been passed that either have limited the automatic movement to a higher tax rate schedule or have prevented the automatic full imposition of a statutory solvency tax. One obvious effect of these measures has been to slow the recovery of trust fund balances.

Eight states in our sample enacted measures in 2011 to limit future benefit payouts. The changes included reducing maximum potential duration (three), imposing a waiting week (two), increasing the monetary eligibility requirement (one), instituting a severance pay offset (one) and strengthening the work-search requirement (one). Several of the states have passed laws and administrative requirements to improve payment accuracy and reduce overpayments. Increased federal concern in this area is reinforcing state developments related to payment accuracy. We also found that the pace of benefit reductions in the states increased noticeably during 2011. For example, all three states in the sample that reduced maximum benefit duration for regular UI benefits did so in 2011.

The states have used a variety of strategies to pay interest on loans outstanding during 2011. These interest charges must be financed separately from the state's UI trust fund. The most common method, used in seven states, has been to levy a flat rate assessment distinct from the regular state UI taxes but collected through the UI tax apparatus. Other methods, used in a total of seven states, have included the use of general revenue (two), penalty and interest receipts (one), funds from a tobacco settlement (one), payments from a state reserve fund (one), and the use of proceeds from a private bond issuance (two).

The annual interest rate on loans from the Treasury was 4.09 percent in 2011, but it decreased to 2.94 percent in 2012. Because interest rates in the private bond market are lower than these rates, several states have explored issuing private debt to repay their Treasury loans. Two states have already borrowed in the private market (Michigan and Texas). Michigan has borrowed with very short-term instruments but expects to convert to longer-term bonds later this year. Illinois has authorized a bond issuance and is also expected to issue bonds later in 2012. At least three other states in the sample are exploring this option. The intent is to repay the principal owed the Treasury and to have the bonds cover not only private bond interest charges but also interest obligations related to Treasury loans. Repaying the principal owed the Treasury also will eliminate future FUTA tax credit offsets.

State officials recognize that issuing private bonds does not "cure" their financing problem. In effect, it changes the appearance of the debt because it no longer explicitly appears in reports of the Treasury or the USDOL. To assess the net trust fund situation of individual states and of the overall UI system, the principal on the private issuances must be subtracted from the balances held by each state at the Treasury. Current and future private debts are likely to extend to the end of the present decade.

Future developments related to private bond issuances will undoubtedly be influenced by the interest rate differential between Treasury loans and private loans. The differential decreased by more than 1 percentage point in 2012 compared to 2011, and the reduced spread may discourage the volume of future private bond issuances. At this time, however, several states are holding active discussions with investment banks about issuing private debt instruments.

To summarize, the interviews with the 20 states had four main findings related to trust fund solvency:

1) The states have exhibited a variety of responses to their trust fund indebtedness. Besides the response of their experience rating systems, some have overridden their tax statutes to retard the pace of tax increases, while others have reduced future benefits.

2) Several debtor states have yet to undertake measures to repay their loans and improve their long-run solvency prospects.

3) The states have used several methods to pay the interest charges on their UI loans from the Treasury.

4) Two states have already entered the private bond market, and others are likely to do so in the near future.

Notes

1. Cost estimate provided by the Information Technology Support Center at NASWA in an e-mail dated October 5, 2012.
2. We use seasonally unadjusted data because we are discussing "real-time" workload here.
3. Average duration for regular UI benefits was about three weeks greater than in any prior recession, topping out at 20.2 weeks in 2010.
4. Economists are still developing an understanding of the impact of the benefit extensions on unemployment and benefit receipt. Two studies that evaluate this are Grubb (2011) and Rothstein (2011).
5. In addition to the federal grants, states can receive funds through supplemental budget requests (SBRs), which fund irregular activities, such as implementing the State Information Data Exchange System (SIDES), Reemployment and Eligibility Assessments, or information technology modernization projects. States also can add their own funds for UI administration.
6. Examples of other studies and reviews not detailed in our report are Blinder and Zandi (2010); Hungerford (2011); and Rothstein (2011).
7. A few points about administrative performance should be made. First, the analysis refers to time lapses, quality, and accuracy in only the regular UI program. Second, details on the reasons for payment errors were not examined, neither with regard to the parties responsible for the errors (claimant, employer, or agency) nor with regard to which UI processes caused the errors. Third, no state-level analysis of time-lapse performance or payment accuracy was attempted.
8. CFR (Code of Federal Regulations) 640.3, interpretation of section 303(a)(1) of the Social Security Act.
9. Details of the regressions are available from the authors.
10. The aggregate quality indicators displayed in the chart were also examined with regression analysis. The regressions showed large and significant upward trends in quality performance as well as a measurable cyclical effect on performance.
11. Obligations are legal commitments to spend funds that occur at the time services are rendered, or before services are rendered when a binding agreement has been entered into.
12. Data were included for the District of Columbia, Puerto Rico, and the Virgin Islands.
13. Throughout the discussion the term "extended benefits" will be used to refer to the combined EUC and EB programs that pay benefits to regular UI exhaustees. When the individual programs are being discussed the abbreviations EUC and EB will be used.
14. The look-back provisions differ in EB depending upon the trigger used to activate EB—the trigger being either the TUR (total unemployment rate, from the Current Population Survey) or the IUR (insured unemployment rate, computed using UI claims data).
15. This extension was authorized by federal law, but it required state legislation to change the EB trigger.

16. The count includes the District of Columbia but not Puerto Rico and the Virgin Islands.
17. The Recovery Act required that the weekly allowance be at least $15 per dependent up to a family maximum of at least $50.
18. The short-run effect during the first three years would be positive even if the longer-run effect was not clear. For states with the indicated provisions already in place, the effect even in the long run was positive.
19. Prospective modernization legislation enacted in Missouri in 2009 included a sunset provision. It was not approved by the U.S. Department of Labor.
20. Long-term UI benefits—Emergency Unemployment Compensation (EUC) and Federal-State Extended Benefits (EB)—have both been fully financed by the federal partner since the enactment of the Recovery Act. Thus the discussion in the text is restricted to just the regular UI program.
21. The profit shares in the two years were 0.124 and 0.129, respectively, the highest shares in the past 25 years and much higher than the average of 0.086 during 2004–2007.
22. Rhode Island's base will also be indexed after 2012, but the changes will start from the $19,000 base present in 2011 and 2012.

References

Blaustein, Saul J. 1993. *Unemployment Insurance in the United States: The First Half Century.* Kalamazoo, MI: W. E. Upjohn Institute for Employment Research.

Blinder, Alan S., and Mark Zandi. 2010. "How the Great Recession Was Brought to an End." Working paper. Princeton, NJ: Princeton University; and New York: Moody's Analytics. http://www.economy.com/mark-zandi/documents/End-of-Great-Recession.pdf (accessed March 7, 2013).

Congressional Budget Office (CBO). 2012. *Estimated Impact of the American Recovery and Reinvestment Act on Employment and Economic Output from October 2011 through December 2011.* Washington, DC: Congressional Budget Office. http://www.cbo.gov/sites/default/files/cbofiles/attachments/02-22-ARRA.pdf (accessed March 5, 2013).

Gabe, Thomas, and Julie M. Whitaker. 2011. *Antipoverty Effects of Unemployment Insurance.* Washington, DC: Congressional Research Service. http://digitalcommons.ilr.cornell.edu/cgi/viewcontentcgi?article=1858&context=key_workplace (accessed March 7, 2013).

Grubb, David. 2011. "Assessing the Impact of Recent Unemployment Insurance Extensions in the United States." Working paper. Paris: Organisation for Economic Co-operation and Development. http://www.iza.org/conference_files/UnIRe2011/grubb_d6938.pdf (accessed March 7, 2013).

Hungerford, Thomas L. 2011. *The Effect of Unemployment Insurance on the Economy and the Labor Market*. CRS Report R41676. Washington, DC: Congressional Research Service. http://economic-legislation.blogspot .com/2011/03/effect-of-unemployment-insurance-on.html (accessed March 7, 2013).

National Association of State Workforce Agencies (NASWA). 2010a. *NASWA Survey Shows Implementation of UI Recovery Act Provisions Posed Challenges to States*. Washington, DC: National Association of State Workforce Agencies, Center for Employment Security Education and Research (CESER). http://www.naswa.org/assets/utilities/serve.cfm?gid=F5551335 -A3C1-4CA8-9FD5-983567CCF269 (accessed March 7, 2013).

———. 2010b. *A National View of UI IT Systems*. Washington, DC: National Association of State Workforce Agencies. http://www.naswa.org/assets/ utilities/serve.cfm?gid=8E0228AE-7341-42EE-9E62-97269BFDC447 (accessed March 7, 2013).

———. 2012. *NASWA Policy and Resolution Notebook*. Washington, DC: National Association of State Workforce Agencies. http://naswa.org/assets/ utilities/serve.cfm?gid=0090443d-2a76-4ea5-a7db-986a16c2e759&dsp _meta=0 (accessed March 7, 2013).

Rothstein, Jesse. 2011. "Unemployment Insurance and Job Search in the Great Recession." NBER Working Paper No. 17534. Cambridge, MA: National Bureau of Economic Research. http://www.nber.org/papers/w17534 (accessed March 7, 2013).

U.S. Department of Labor (USDOL). 2009. *Unemployment Insurance Program Letter No. 04-10*. Washington, DC: U.S. Department of Labor, Employment and Training Administration. http://wdr.doleta.gov/directives/attach/UIPL/ UIPL4-10.pdf (accessed March 14, 2013).

———. 2010. *Summary: The Role of Unemployment as an Automatic Stabilizer during a Recession*. Washington, DC: U.S. Department of Labor. http://www.dol.gov/opa/media/press/eta/eta20101615fs.htm   (accessed March 7, 2013).

———. 2011. *Calendar Year 2010 Benefit Accuracy Measurement Data Summary*. Washington, DC: U.S. Department of Labor, Employment and Training Administration. http://www.ows.doleta.gov/unemploy/bam/2010/ bam-cy2010.pdf (accessed September 16, 2013).

———. 2013a. *Chronology of Federal Unemployment Compensation Laws*. http://www.ows.doleta.gov/unemploy/pdf/chronfedlaws.pdf (accessed September 16, 2013).

———. 2013b. *Unemployment Insurance Performance Management*. Washington, DC: U.S. Department of Labor, Employment and Training Administration. http://www.ows.doleta.gov/unemploy/performance.asp (accessed March 6, 2013).

U.S. Joint Committee on Taxation. 2009. *Estimated Budget Effects of the Revenue Provisions Contained in the Conference Agreement for H.R. 1, the "American Recovery and Reinvestment Act of 2009."* Washington, DC: U.S. Joint Committee on Taxation. http://www.jct.gov/x-19-09.pdf (accessed March 5, 2013).

votesmart.org. 2009. "Baucus Hails Senate Passage of Bill Creating Jobs, Cutting Taxes for America's Working Families and Small Businesses." Press release, February 10. Philipsburg, MT: votesmart.org. http://votesmart .org/public-statement/407786/baucus-hails-senate-passage-of-bill-creating -jobs-cutting-taxes-for-americas-working-families-and-small-businesses (accessed March 5, 2013).

Vroman, Wayne. 2010. *The Role of Unemployment Insurance as an Automatic Stabilizer during a Recession.* ETAOP 2010-10. Columbia, MD: IMPAQ International. http://wdr.doleta.gov/research/FullText_Documents/ ETAOP2010-10.pdf (accessed March 7, 2013).

———. 2011. "Time Lapse Performance in Unemployment Insurance Administration." Unpublished paper. Washington, DC: Urban Institute.

whitehouse.gov. 2009. *About the Recovery Act.* Washington, DC: White House. http://www.whitehouse.gov/recovery/about (accessed March 5, 2013).

9
Data Analysis of the Implementation of the Recovery Act Workforce Development and Unemployment Insurance Provisions

Randall W. Eberts
Upjohn Institute

Stephen A. Wandner
Urban Institute

OVERVIEW

This chapter uses administrative data to examine the response of the nation's workforce system to the needs of workers during the recent recession and the Recovery Act funding period.[1] The Recovery Act provided funds so that states could respond to worker needs at two levels. The first level expanded the short-term capacity of the workforce system to meet the surge in demand for reemployment services and training. This required more staff and office space and often an upgrade of telephone and Internet capabilities. The second level of response required strategic decisions to improve the infrastructure of the nation's workforce development system. This included reshaping and improving the capacity of the system to meet future needs more efficiently and developing innovative service delivery systems that attempt to anticipate the changing structure of the workforce and the economy (USDOL 2009).

Using state-level administrative data, this chapter examines the response of state workforce agencies in providing public workforce and unemployment insurance services to unemployed workers before, during, and after the recent recession. It tracks participant flows, service receipts, expenditures, and outcomes of the major workforce programs during this period. It also compares changes in the flow of services with changes in expenditures. In particular, it analyzes total expenditures and expenditures per participant, highlighting the reduction in expenditures per participant compared with prerecession levels, as the workforce programs were inundated with new participants. While the analysis is conducted at the state level, the results are aggregated to the national level in order for the chapter to fit within the page constraints.[2]

The chapter begins with a short review of the programs and data used for our analysis, described in the next section. The third section traces the flow of workers through the unemployment insurance (UI) system, the Employment Service, and the two adult WIA programs. The fourth section examines program expenditures and participation for the various programs. It specifically analyzes the difference between expenditures before the recession and during the Recovery Act period. The final section offers concluding remarks. Appendix B, starting on page 391, contains tables of the data used in the figures and tables in this chapter.

WORKFORCE PROGRAMS AND DATA SOURCES

During an economic downturn, the unemployed rely heavily on three basic workforce services for assistance in finding reemployment—1) unemployment compensation, 2) labor exchange and reemployment services, and 3) job training. The federal government, in partnership with states and local entities, provide these services through the Unemployment Insurance (UI) system, the Wagner-Peyser Act Employment Service (ES), and the Workforce Investment Act (WIA) programs. The UI system offers eligible unemployed workers cash assistance for up to 26 weeks in normal times and longer during recessions while they look for work. The Wagner-Peyser Act Employment Service provides job search assistance, such as help with writing résumés and accessing job postings. The WIA programs provide more intensive job search assistance and job training to dislocated workers and economically disadvantaged adults. Additional federally funded programs, including WIA Youth and Job Corps for youth, Trade Adjustment Assistance programs for workers displaced by foreign competition, and the Community Service Employment Program for Older Americans (also known as the Senior Community Service Employment Program) for low-income workers over the age of 55, offer assistance, but these are not included in the analysis.[3]

This chapter uses administrative data from the U.S. Department of Labor's reporting system.[4] The data set covers participant and expenditure data for the three largest federally funded workforce programs: Unemployment Insurance (UI), the Wagner-Peyser Act Employment Service (ES), and the Workforce Investment Act (WIA) programs for Adults and for Dislocated Workers (DW).[5] The data are collected quarterly for each state, the District of Columbia, and territories and are compiled in a database called the Public Workforce System Dataset (PWSD). For this analysis, the original database was updated to 2011Q3 for UI and the Employment Service and to 2011Q1 for the two adult WIA programs, the most recent data available at the time.

TRACKING THE FLOW OF PARTICIPANTS THROUGH THE WORKFORCE SYSTEM

This section provides a framework for tracking the flow of participants through the workforce system. The flow diagrams displayed in Figures 9.1, 9.8, and 9.11 offer graphical representations of the three major workforce programs: the Unemployment Insurance system, the Wagner-Peyser Employment Service, and the WIA Adult and Dislocated Worker programs. While each program is considered separately in the analysis, they are interconnected as well as overlapping through referrals and coenrollment. Programs overlap when they have responsibilities for delivering similar services, such as occurs between adult WIA programs and the Employment Service. Moreover, the practice of coenrollment in ES and WIA, which began around 2006, has had a large impact on the number of participants in WIA, particularly the Adult Program. The number of entrants into the WIA Adult Program jumped 125 percent in one quarter, from 67,000 in 2006Q2 to 151,000 in the next quarter. In New York alone, the number of entrants into the WIA Adult Program increased tenfold between those two quarters, accounting for a large share of the nationwide increase.

Unemployment Insurance System

According to data on initial claims and benefit payouts, the unemployment insurance program was severely tested during the recent recession. It paid out more benefits to more unemployed workers for longer periods of time than it ever had in its 80-year history. Benefit payments quintupled from $31 billion in Fiscal Year 2006 to $156 billion in FY 2010. The unemployed receiving first payments doubled from 7.4 million in FY 2006 to 14.4 million in FY 2009. The number of regular UI beneficiaries exhausting their entitlement to benefits increased from 2.6 million in FY 2006 to 7.0 million in FY 2010. The dramatic increase in the use of the UI system obviously reflects the surge in the number of unemployed during the recession. Nearly 8 million people joined the ranks of the unemployed from the beginning of the recession in December 2007 to October 2009, pushing up the unemployment rate to a high of 10.0 percent. During that same period, the economy lost 8.5 million payroll jobs. The combination of fewer jobs and more people looking for work increased the need for reemployment services for UI beneficiaries, both when they first became unemployed and during the unprecedented length of time they remained unemployed.

Figure 9.1 shows the flow of unemployed workers into and through the UI system, as well as through the process of referral to and receipt of reemployment services. The process begins when unemployed workers file an initial claim for UI benefits. UI beneficiaries are then screened through the basic Worker Profiling and Reemployment Services system to determine their likelihood of exhausting regular benefits—that is, their likelihood of not finding a job during the time they are eligible for regular benefits. Most states use a statistically based screening tool based on a recipient's employment history, education, and barriers to employment. Those who are identified as likely to exhaust their benefits are then referred to orientation and other reemployment services shortly after they first receive benefits.[6] Most of the reemployment services, such as assessment, counseling, job placement, and job-search workshop, are provided through the Wagner-Peyser Act Employment Service and are not necessarily delivered in any particular sequence, as indicated by the absence of arrows in that part of the diagram.

The following figures show the flow of participants through the UI system as depicted in the diagram above. The strong seasonality in

Figure 9.1 Flow Diagram of the Unemployment Insurance System

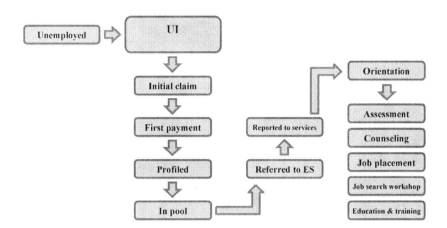

SOURCE: Authors' calculations of the PWSD, updated from the data at USDOL (2010).

both initial claims and first payments obscures this relationship to some extent. To gain a better perspective of the ability of the UI system to process initial claims and send out first payments, we eliminated the seasonality by using a four-quarter moving average. Figure 9.2 displays the seasonally adjusted data and reveals that the ratio of initial claims to first payments has actually increased throughout the recession. A similar increase is observed during the previous recession. Some of the increase may reflect the increase in eligible claimants as a result of more claimants losing their jobs through no fault of their own.

Figure 9.3 shows the flow of services from the worker profiling process to the referral and reporting-to-services stages. Worker profiling takes place near the time of first UI payment, and consequently the observed influx of profiled beneficiaries occurred at approximately the same time as the sharp increase in the number of laid-off workers receiving first payments. However, the referral to services and the receipt of services did not occur simultaneously, as shown in more detail in Figure 9.4. Three quarters elapsed (2009Q1 to 2009Q4) between the peak in first payments and the peak in referrals to services; two more quarters elapsed before the number of beneficiaries receiving services peaked in 2010Q2. The sequence of events resulted in a total lag of five quarters

**Figure 9.2   Unemployment Insurance: Number of Initial Claims and
First Payments**

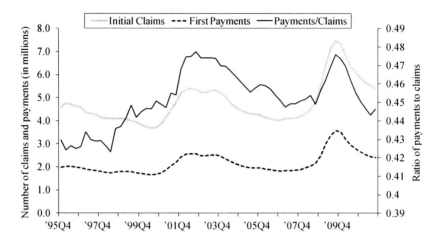

NOTE: All three series seasonally adjusted using the average of four lagging quarters.
SOURCE: Authors' calculations of the PWSD, updated from the data at USDOL (2010).

**Figure 9.3   The Worker Profiling Process and Referral to Services in the
UI System**

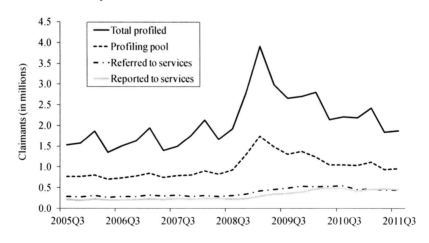

SOURCE: Authors' calculations of the PWSD, updated from the data at USDOL (2010).

Figure 9.4 Relationship between Initial Claims and Reporting to Services

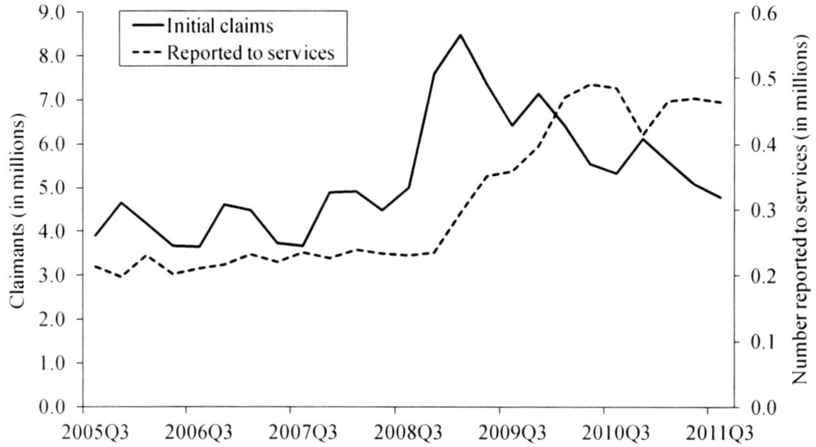

SOURCE: Authors' calculations of the PWSD, updated from the data at USDOL (2010).

between the receipt of first payments and receipt of services (2009Q1 to 2010Q2).

The number of UI-profiled claimants referred to and reporting to services increased during that time, as shown in Figure 9.5. Low-cost services—orientations and assessments— received the largest enrollments; the more expensive and intensive services of education, training, and counseling experienced the smallest enrollments.[7] Figure 9.6 shows the distribution of services before and during the recession (profiled claimants could enroll in more than one service). Of those profiled claimants referred to and reporting to services, the percentage receiving orientations increased from approximately 50 percent to slightly over 60 percent during the recession and the period of Recovery Act funding. The percentage of profiled claimants receiving assessments increased as well, jumping sharply from 30 percent to 50 percent within two to three quarters following the availability of Recovery Act funds. Referrals to education and training remained at roughly 10 percent throughout the entire period, and counseling increased from 10 percent to 17 percent during that same period.

The average duration of regular UI benefits and the exhaustion rate increased during the Recovery Act period. Both peaked in 2010Q1, as

Figure 9.5 Number of Profiled Claimants Referred to and Reporting to Various Reemployment Services

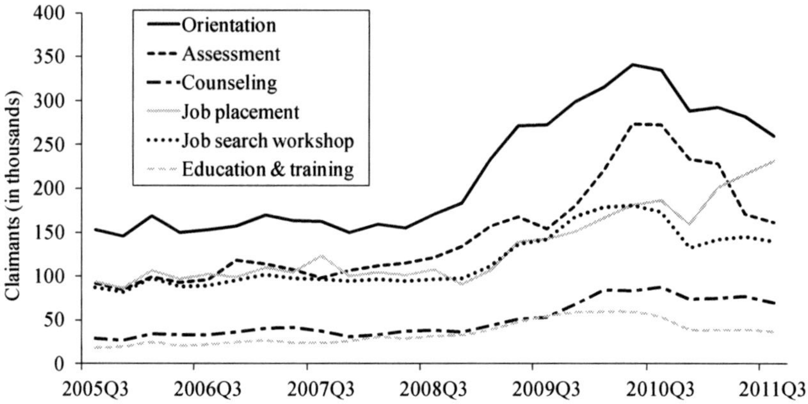

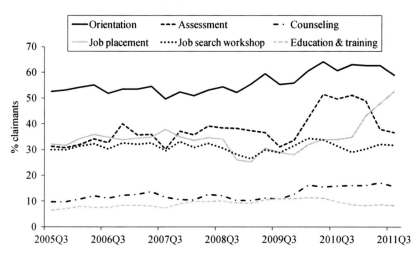

SOURCE: Authors' calculations of the PWSD, updated from the data at USDOL (2010).

Figure 9.6 Percentage of Profiled Claimants Referred to and Reporting to Various Reemployment Services

NOTE: The denominator underlying this figure is the number of profiled claimants who were referred to and reported to services in general, and the numerator is the number of profiled claimants who were referred to and reported to that specific service, such as orientation.

SOURCE: Authors' calculations of the PWSD, updated from the data at USDOL (2010).

shown in Figure 9.7. The exhaustion rate peaked at 56 percent, and the average duration of UI receipts reached its maximum of 20 weeks' duration that quarter.

The Employment Service

The Employment Service (ES) provides a variety of labor exchange services, including but not limited to job search assistance, job referral, and placement assistance for job seekers, reemployment services to UI claimants, and recruitment and screening services for employers with job openings. Services are delivered in one of three modes: 1) self-service, 2) facilitated self-help services, and 3) staff-assisted. Depending upon the needs of the customers, other services may be available. They include an assessment of skill levels, abilities and aptitudes, career guidance when appropriate, job search workshops, and referral to training. These reemployment services overlap with the core and intensive services provided by WIA programs, and many ES participants are also WIA participants because of coenrollment between the two programs.

The flow diagram in Figure 9.8 depicts the basic steps in receiving these services. Participants enter the ES system either through a

Figure 9.7 Average Duration of UI Benefits and the Rate of Exhaustion of Regular UI Benefits

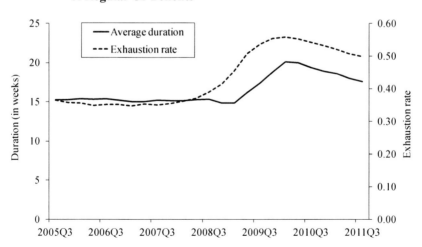

SOURCE: Authors' calculations of the PWSD, updated from the data at USDOL (2010).

Figure 9.8 Flow Diagram of the Wagner-Peyser Employment Service System

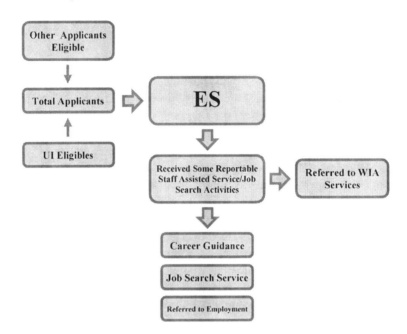

SOURCE: Authors' calculations of the PWSD, updated from the data at USDOL (2010).

referral from the UI system or on their own. Under federal law, the UI "work test" closely links the ES system to the UI system. In order to be eligible for UI benefits, claimants must be able and available to work, and in most states they must demonstrate that they are actively looking for employment. Consequently, UI recipients are required to register for work and are referred to local workforce offices. However, a large majority of ES participants enter the system on their own. They can be employed and looking for a better position or unemployed and seeking help to find employment. All are eligible to receive basic reemployment services.

As shown in Figure 9.9, the increase in the number of ES participants accelerated near the end of 2007 and continued to climb until cresting in 2010Q3 at nearly 5 million individuals. The number of participants receiving staff-assisted services followed closely but at a

Figure 9.9 Wagner-Peyser ES Participants, Number of UI-Eligible Participants, and Those Who Received Services

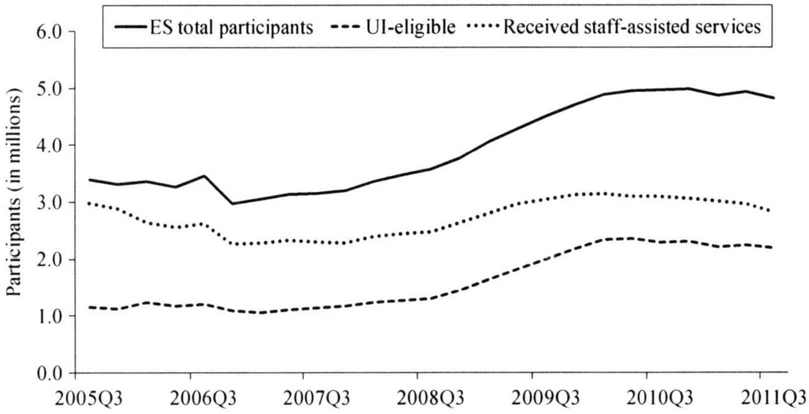

SOURCE: Authors' calculations of the PWSD, updated from the data at USDOL (2010).

slower pace. It leveled off at 3.1 million a few quarters before the peak in participants and slowly declined throughout the remainder of the recession and the Recovery Act funding period. With the sharp increase in unemployment and the number of job seekers and the drop in the number of people hired during that period, it is not surprising that the percentage of exiters finding employment fell. As shown in Figure 9.10, the ES entered employment rate (the percentage of exiters who were employed the first quarter after exit) dropped from around 60 percent to under 50 percent between 2009Q2 and 2010Q2.

WIA Core, Intensive, and Training Services

The Workforce Investment Act system (WIA) provides core, intensive, and training services to eligible adults and youth. Services range from basic reemployment services, such as assistance with résumé writing and job interviewing, to occupational training. While WIA is the main provider of training for the workforce system, only a quarter of adults who leave the program (exiters) received training services. The large majority received core and intensive services. WIA also includes a Youth Program, which is not included in the analysis. Most of the

**Figure 9.10 Number of ES Participants and Exiters and the Entered
          Employment Rate**

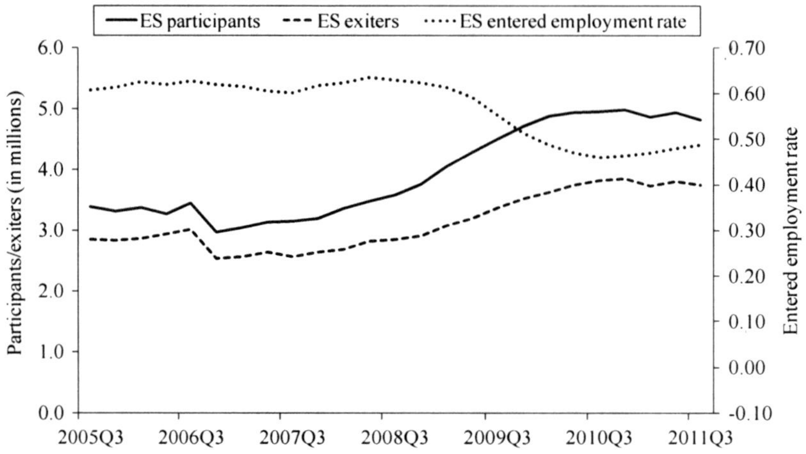

SOURCE: Authors' calculations of the PWSD, updated from the data at USDOL (2010).

Recovery Act funding for the Youth Program was used for temporary employment of economically disadvantaged youth in the summer of 2009. Recovery Act funding for the adult WIA programs, on other hand, was used to help the unemployed find more permanent employment.

The flow of participants through the WIA Adult and Dislocated Worker programs is depicted in Figure 9.11. WIA participants can be referred from the ES program or can come into the program on their own. In either case, they must meet specific eligibility criteria for enrolling in the WIA Adult and the WIA Dislocated Worker programs. As previously mentioned, some states coenroll ES program participants in WIA programs. All workers are eligible to receive core self-assisted services or staff-assisted services.[8] Once enrolled in WIA, participants can be referred to more intensive staff-assisted services, which include reemployment services and job training programs. Each successive level of service, from core self-assisted through job training, requires progressively greater staff intervention and consequently is more expensive to provide. WIA was initially designed so that participants would progress sequentially from the least staff-intensive to the most staff-intensive services until they succeeded in finding employment. In recent years,

Figure 9.11 Flow Diagram of the WIA Adult and WIA Dislocated Worker Programs

SOURCE: Authors' calculations of the PWSD, updated from the data at USDOL (2010).

many states have changed to a more customized approach. While many participants were still referred to core services when they entered the program, One-Stop Career Center staff was more likely to refer participants directly to services that best meet their needs, hence the omission of arrows in Figure 9.11.[9]

For the following analysis of the WIA programs, the reference point for counting the number and percentage of services is the entrant into the program. That is, when we refer to the number of services received, we refer to the services received by the individual who enters the program. We identify the date at which an individual enters the program, and then we look forward to see whether or not that person received a service. In some USDOL publications, the reference point is the exiter. In that case, they identify a person who exits the program and then they look back in time to see whether or not that person received a service and what type of service he or she received. Since the purpose of this analysis is to examine the response of the workforce system to the needs of people entering the system, we contend that entrants, not exiters, are the appropriate point of reference. The difference is significant. The average length of time between registering for the program and first receiving training, for example, is 38 days for the WIA Adult Program and 58 days for the WIA Dislocated Worker Program. In contrast, the number of days between receiving training and exiting the program is 300 days for the WIA Adult Program and 378 days for the WIA Dislocated Worker Program. These averages are computed for the period 2005Q3 through 2011Q2. Furthermore, the pattern of length of time between entrants to service and service to exiters is also different. The length of time between registration and receiving training peaks in 2008Q4, and the length of time between receipt of training and the time of exit peaks in 2011Q1. These time intervals are obtained by analyzing the individual participant data from the WIASRD files. The one exception in using entrants as the reference point is the reporting of outcome measures, such as the entered employment rate. In this case, the reference is the exiter, and the denominator in the entered employment rate calculation is the adjusted number of exiters.

WIA Adult Program

Figure 9.12 shows the increase in the number of entrants, participants, and exiters, which began in 2006, long before the recession and the enactment of the Recovery Act.[10] The primary reason for the increase was the issuance at that time of reporting instructions by the U.S. Department of Labor that permitted states to coenroll ES participants (and other program participants) in WIA programs. Several large states coenrolled all ES participants, swelling the number of participants not only within those states but nationally as well. Nonetheless, between 2008Q3 and 2009Q3, the gap between the number of entrants and exiters widened, leading to a surge in the number of participants. During that time, the number of exiters continued to climb, but not as fast as the number of new entrants. Shortly after 2009Q3, however, the number of entrants and exiters leveled off and remained flat at about 300,000 new entrants and exiters thereafter, except for a spike of entrants in 2010Q3.[11]

Figure 9.12 Number of Participants, Entrants, and Exiters in the WIA Adult Program

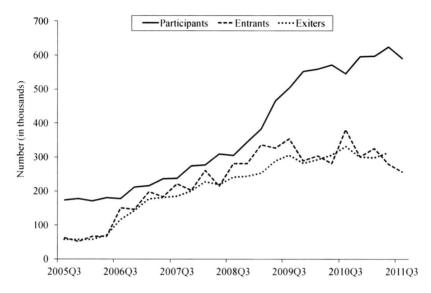

SOURCE: Authors' calculations of the PWSD, updated from the data at USDOL (2010).

The number receiving WIA Adult staff-assisted services quickly increased as the recession deepened, even before Recovery Act funds became available. As shown in Figure 9.13, intensive services receipts increased abruptly in 2008Q3 from 63,000 per quarter to 104,000 per quarter, peaking a year later (2009Q3) at 156,000. The number receiving training and supportive services also doubled, but within an even shorter time period, beginning in 2009Q1 and peaking in 2009Q3. Between 2008Q4 and 2009Q3, the number receiving training increased from 30,000 a quarter to 60,000 a quarter. However, the heightened service receipt lasted only one quarter before starting to decline. By the following quarter, service receipt among the three services fell by as much as 30 percent and continued declining throughout the remainder of the Recovery Act period. The surge in services, particularly training services, is consistent with the U.S. Department of Labor's directive to states at the time the Recovery Act was enacted for them to use the

Figure 9.13 Number of Entrants Receiving WIA Adult Intensive, Training, and Supportive Services

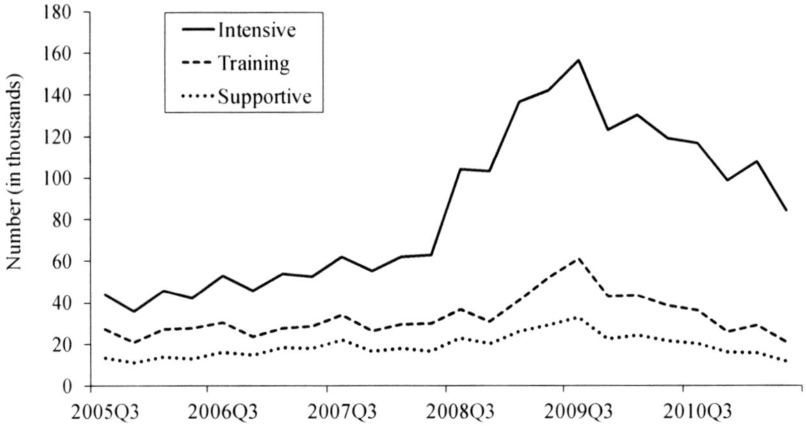

SOURCE: Authors' calculations of the PWSD, updated from the data at USDOL (2010).

available funds expeditiously to make services available to participants as quickly as possible.

The rapid increase in the number receiving services in the latter half of 2008 led to a higher percentage of entrants receiving services than during the year before. From 2008Q1 through 2009Q3, as shown in Figure 9.14, the percentage of entrants receiving intensive services rose from 23.8 to 44.1 percent, a much greater increase than the increase in WIA Adult funding (as shown in a later chart).[12] The percentage of entrants receiving high-cost job training services reached 17 percent as Recovery Act funds became available in the middle of 2009, and the share of entrants receiving supportive services peaked at 9 percent. However, within a year after the peak, the percentage of entrants receiving training fell to 9 percent and that of supportive services to 5 percent. By 2010Q3 the share of each service was below its rate before the Recovery Act was instituted, because of a combination of reduced services and a continued high level of entrants. The share of those receiving intensive services, on the other hand, remained about the same at the end of the Recovery Act period as before the act was passed. The percentage receiving staff-assisted services is also included in the analysis. However, the percentage of entrants receiving these services is

Figure 9.14 Percentage of WIA Adult Entrants Receiving Various Services

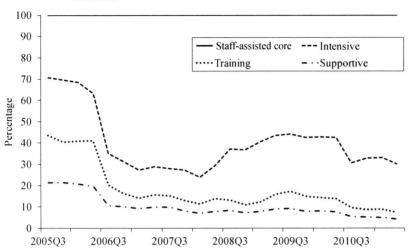

SOURCE: Authors' calculations of the PWSD, updated from the data at USDOL (2010).

always 100 percent, since WIASRD reporting definitions count all new entrants as receiving staff-assisted core services.

As the number of entrants into the WIA Adult Program started to increase significantly in 2008Q3, state and local workforce agencies may not have had the capacity to respond quickly to the increased demand for services. The lack of capacity may be reflected in the number of days between the point of registration and the receipt of services, particularly training services. From 2008Q1 to 2008Q4, the number of days between registration and commencement of receiving the first training services increased precipitously, from 36 days to a peak of 65 days (Figure 9.15). However, after 2008Q4, the length of time between registration and training start-time began to decline, and the decline continued throughout the remaining period in which Recovery Act funds were available. The shortening of the waiting period around the time Recovery Act funds became available suggests that Recovery Act funding provided resources necessary to increase the capacity of state and local workforce agencies to provide additional services.

At about the time of the uptick in the number and percentage of entrants receiving the various staff-assisted services, the average num-

Figure 9.15 Number of Days between Registering for a Program and First Receiving Training

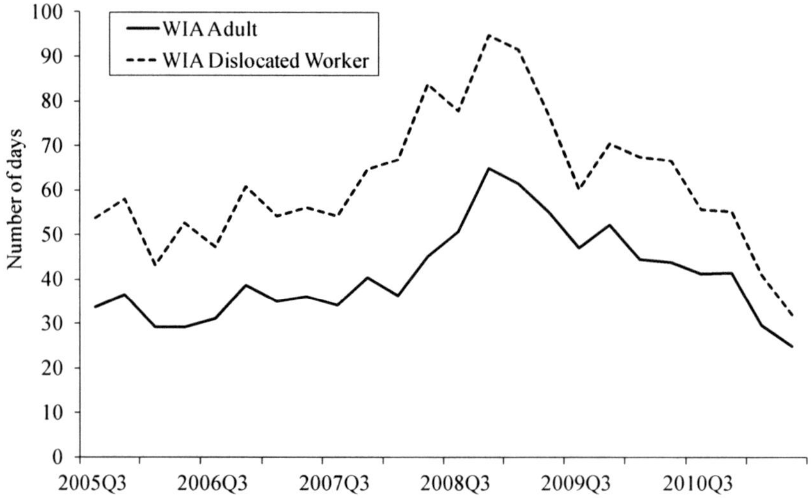

SOURCE: Authors' calculations of the PWSD, updated from the data at USDOL (2010).

ber of services received by entrants also started to increase. As shown in Figure 9.16, the average number of services per entrant climbed from 2.2 in 2008Q1 to 2.9 in 2009Q3, indicating that not only were entrants moving into services that required more staff time but they were also receiving a greater number of services on average.[13] Another indication of the greater number and intensity of services was the increase in the number of days in the program. This increase occurred about four quarters after the number of services started to rise. However, the increase in average duration in the program could also be attributed to the difficulty in finding employment, as the number of days continued to climb even after the number of services received began to decline.[14]

As the unemployment rate continued to climb in 2008, WIA Adult participants had increasing difficulty finding employment. As shown in Figure 9.17, the percentage of exiters moving immediately into employment (as measured by the entered employment rate) fell from 73 percent to 53 percent in that one year. From that point on, the entered employment rate remained virtually flat. However, during that period of a constant entered employment rate, the number of exiters

Figure 9.16 Average Duration and Average Number of Services Received by WIA Adult Program Entrants

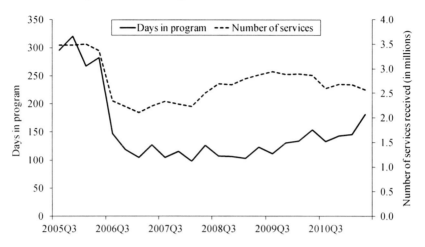

SOURCE: Authors' calculations of the PWSD, updated from the data at USDOL (2010).

Figure 9.17 WIA Adult Entered Employment Rate and Its Components

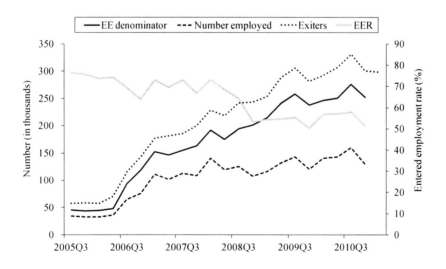

SOURCE: Authors' calculations of the PWSD, updated from the data at USDOL (2010).

who found employment rose by 52,000, from 107,000 in 2008Q3 to 159,000 in 2010Q3, an increase of nearly 50 percent. This increase can be explained to a large extent by the greater number of participants in the program. The number of exiters rose at roughly the same rate, which kept the entered employment rate constant throughout this period.

WIA Dislocated Worker Program

The WIA Dislocated Worker (DW) Program provides services to experienced workers who permanently lose their jobs through no fault of their own. Consequently, as the unemployment rolls swelled during 2008, the number of entrants into the WIA DW Program also increased. Figure 9.18 shows the flow of new entrants into the program. From 2005 to the middle of 2008, the number of new entrants averaged approximately 61,000 per quarter. As the recession set in, the number of new entrants increased sharply. Between 2008Q2 and 2009Q2, the number of unemployed increased by 6 million, swelling the ranks to 14.3 million in that one-year period, an increase of 74 percent. During that same period, the number of entrants into the WIA Dislocated

**Figure 9.18 Number of Entrants, Exiters, and Participants in the WIA
Dislocated Worker Program**

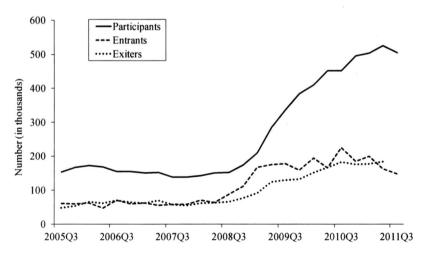

SOURCE: Authors' calculations of the PWSD, updated from the data at USDOL (2010).

Worker Program increased by 110,000 per quarter, which was a much larger percentage increase (173 percent) than the percentage increase in the unemployed. In contrast, entrants into the WIA Adult Program increased by a much larger percentage, but the upward trend started long before the recession began, as shown in Figure 9.19. As previously noted, the increase in WIA Adult entrants resulted primarily from the decision by several populous states to coenroll all ES participants as WIA Adult participants.

The influx of entrants into the program was promptly met by an increase in the number of services provided. Figure 9.20 shows that the increase in intensive, training, and supportive services at least doubled for each of these services between 2008Q3 and 2009Q3. As with the WIA Adult Program, state workforce agencies responded strongly to the USDOL's call for increased training and other intensive services. For all three types of services, the number receiving the services started to increase even before the Recovery Act funds became available in 2009Q2. During this period, the number receiving intensive services grew from 46,000 to 114,000, those receiving training jumped from

Figure 9.19 Comparison of Entrants and Exiters in the WIA Adult and WIA Dislocated Worker Programs

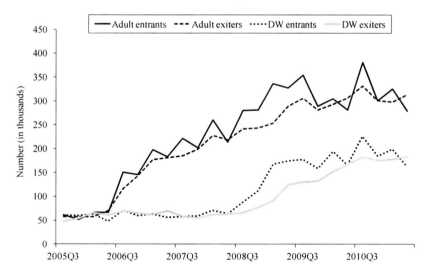

SOURCE: Authors' calculations of the PWSD, updated from the data at USDOL (2010).

**Figure 9.20 Number of Entrants Receiving WIA Dislocated Worker
Intensive, Training, and Supportive Services**

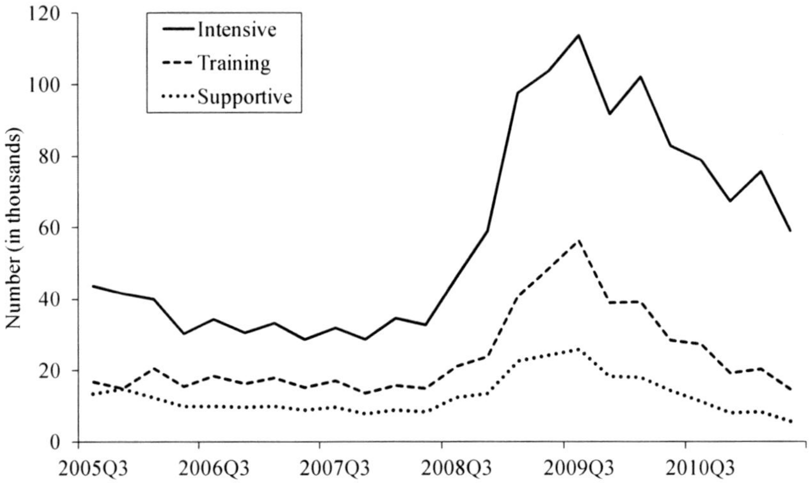

SOURCE: Authors' calculations of the PWSD, updated from the data at USDOL (2010).

21,000 to 56,000, and those receiving supportive services increased
from 12,500 to 25,700. The surge in services lasted only a few quarters,
however. Immediately after peaking in 2009Q3, the number receiving
services declined and continued a downward trend through 2011Q3.

During the initial quarters of the Recovery Act period, the WIA DW
Program appeared to have the capacity to provide services to the influx
of entrants. As shown in Figure 9.21, the percentage of entrants receiving intensive services, training, and supportive services increased during the two quarters prior to 2009Q3, the quarter in which the percentages peaked. However, for the remainder of the Recovery Act period,
the percentages trended downward and ended in 2011Q3 below what
they were before the Recovery Act period began.

As with the WIA Adult Program, state and local workforce agencies
did not respond immediately to the increased demand for WIA Dislocated Worker services. The number of days between the time a person
registered for the WIA Dislocated Worker Program and the time that
person first received training services increased dramatically beginning
in 2007Q3 (shown in Figure 9.15). The number of days increased from

Figure 9.21 Percentage of WIA Dislocated Worker Program Entrants Receiving Selected Services

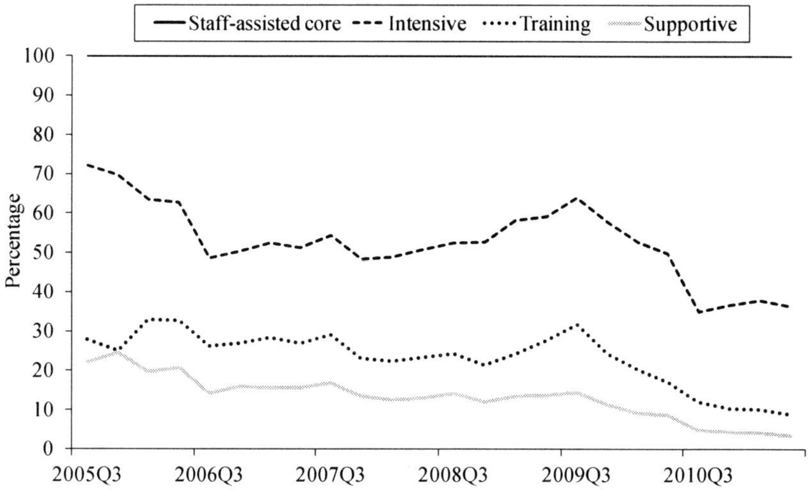

SOURCE: Authors' calculations of the PWSD, updated from the data at USDOL (2010).

54 in 2007Q3 to 95 in 2008Q3. From that quarter on, and throughout the time Recovery Act funds were available, the number of days steadily declined until it reached a low of 31 in 2011Q2. It is interesting that the number of days between registration and service receipt began to increase at least three quarters before the number of entrants into the program started to increase. This could suggest a diminished capacity to provide services during that time, a period that corresponded to a 9 percent reduction in WIA Dislocated Worker funding (PY2007 through PY2009).

Starting in 2009Q2, the average duration of entrants in the WIA DW Program began to increase, as displayed in Figure 9.22.[15] This occurred at the same time Recovery Act funding became available, but the upward trend continued throughout the entire funding period, long after the number and percentage of exiters receiving training declined. Moreover, the average number of services received by DW entrants also trended downward during most of that period.

While the increased usage of more intensive services may have contributed to the increased duration in the program, at least in the early

Figure 9.22 Average Duration and Number of Services Received by
Entrants in the WIA Dislocated Worker Program

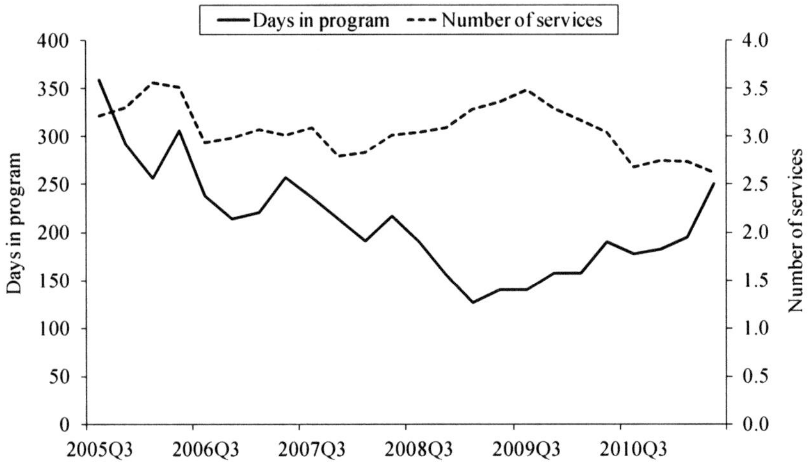

SOURCE: Authors' calculations of the PWSD, updated from the data at USDOL (2010).

part of the Recovery Act funding period, this cannot explain the continued increase in length of time in the program, since the percentage of entrants receiving intensive services and training fell after 2009Q3.

Another explanation for the increased duration may be the reduction in job prospects. The percentage of WIA DW exiters finding employment immediately after leaving the program (defined as the entered employment rate) dipped during the recession. As shown in Figure 9.23, the entered employment rate fell from 70 percent in late 2007 to around 50 percent by 2008Q4. It remained at that rate until the beginning of 2010, when it began to increase, although it only reached 60 percent before falling back to 55 percent at the end of 2010Q4, the last quarter for which these data are available.

Despite the lower entered employment rate, the number of exiters finding employment steadily increased throughout the Recovery Act period. From 2009Q1 through 2010Q3, the number employed grew from 45,000 to 106,000, an increase of 135 percent. This increase stands out, as the number of hires nationwide declined by 2.8 percent and the number of private sector jobs fell by 2.2 percent during that period.[16] Part of the explanation is in the greater number of exiters during that

Figure 9.23 WIA Dislocated Worker Entered Employment Rate and Its Components

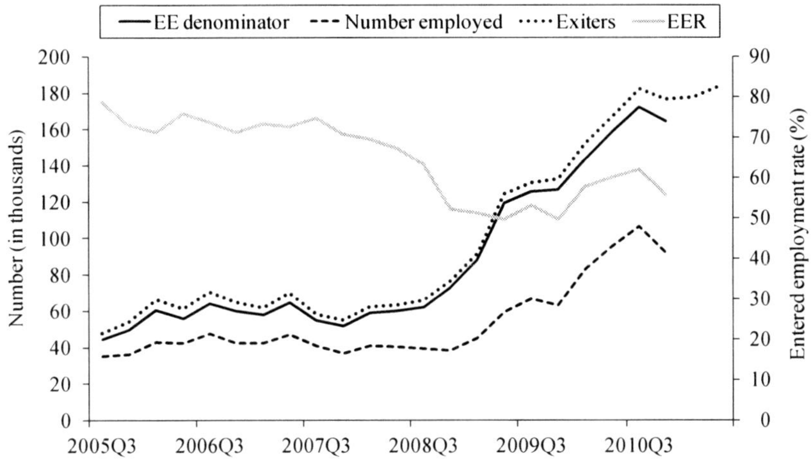

SOURCE: Authors' calculations of the PWSD, updated from the data at USDOL (2010).

period, an increase of 86 percent, but at a lower rate than the number finding employment. It may also be explained by an improvement in the effectiveness of the services and the qualifications of participants.

EXPENDITURES AND PARTICIPATION

Recovery Act appropriations for workforce programs were intended to support the increased need for reemployment and training services as unemployment climbed during the recession.[17] Total Recovery Act funding for the three workforce programs—the Employment Service, the WIA Adult Program, and the WIA Dislocated Worker Program— amounted to $2.35 billion. The Employment Service and the WIA Adult programs received roughly 55 percent of their 2009 fiscal year budget, and the WIA Dislocated Worker Program received 108 percent of its 2009 fiscal year budget. The act provided funding for two years, but as an economic stimulus program, the administration encouraged its agencies to spend the funds as quickly as prudently feasible. The U.S.

Department of Labor's (USDOL's) March 2009 field guidance directed states to spend the Recovery Act funds "expeditiously and effectively," which resulted in many states spending a majority of the funds in the first year (USDOL 2009b, p. 3). The Employment Service responded the fastest of the three programs. By 2010Q2, a year after Recovery Act funding began, the Employment Service had spent 85 percent of its available Recovery Act funding, the WIA Adult Program had spent 72 percent, and the WIA Dislocated Worker Program had spent 60 percent of its funds. While helping to accommodate the influx of participants into the three programs and to provide more intensive services, the speed at which funds were used in the first year left disproportionately fewer funds for the second year, even as the number of participants in the three programs remained high.

The Relationship between Expenditures and Participation

Figures 9.24 through 9.29 show the patterns by which the three workforce programs spent the Recovery Act funding. Expenditures for all three workforce programs are expressed in current dollars. Annual appropriations and expenditures for the three workforce programs were mostly flat before and after the Recovery Act funding period. For example, FY2009 funding for the three programs amounted to $3.09 billion compared with FY2011 funding of $3.00 billion, a reduction of 3.0 percent. For all three programs, Recovery Act funding provided additional resources during a time of increased program participation, which was more than enough to raise expenditures per participant for the first year of Recovery Act funding. However, the Recovery Act funds that remained for the second year were not enough to offset the continued increase in the number of participants in each program, and consequently expenditures per participant fell in the second year of the Recovery Act funding period. Despite increased dollars, funding per participant (in current dollars) of the three workforce programs was lower throughout the Recovery Act funding period than it had been before the recession. Recovery Act funds filled a portion of this difference, but appropriations were not sufficient to keep up with the increase in enrollments and to return expenditures per participant to prerecession levels.

Figure 9.24 Wagner-Peyser Act ES Expenditures and Participants by Quarter, with and without Recovery Act Funding

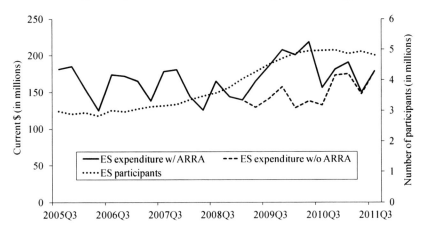

SOURCE: Authors' calculations of the PWSD, updated from the data at USDOL (2010).

Figure 9.25 Wagner-Peyser Act ES Expenditures per Participant, with and without Recovery Act Funding

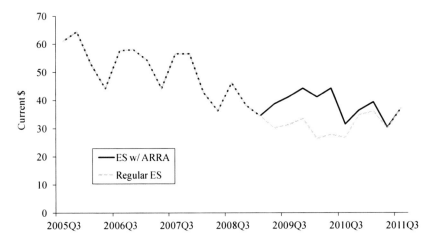

SOURCE: Authors' calculations of the PWSD, updated from the data at USDOL (2010).

Figure 9.26 WIA Adult Participants and Expenditures, with and without Recovery Act Funding

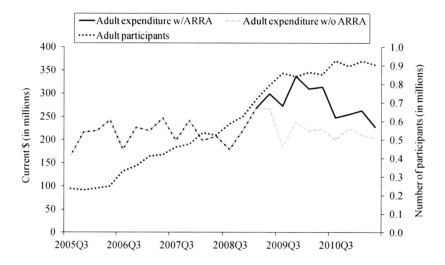

SOURCE: Authors' calculations of the PWSD, updated from the data at USDOL (2010).

Figure 9.27 WIA Dislocated Worker Participants and Expenditures, with and without Recovery Act Funding

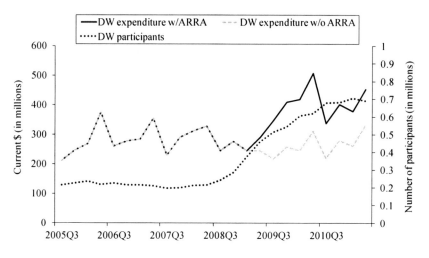

SOURCE: Authors' calculations of the PWSD, updated from the data at USDOL (2010).

Figure 9.28 WIA Adult Expenditure per Participant, with and without Recovery Act Funding

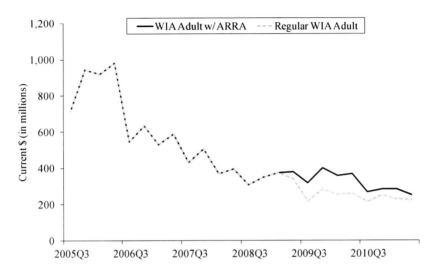

SOURCE: Authors' calculations of the PWSD, updated from the data at USDOL (2010).

Figure 9.29 WIA Dislocated Worker Expenditure per Participant, with and without Recovery Act Funding

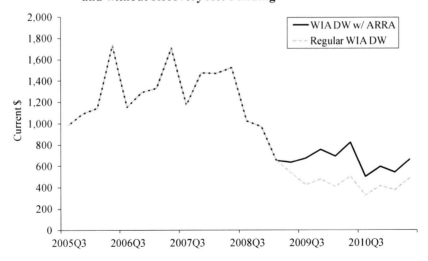

SOURCE: Authors' calculations of the PWSD, updated from the data at USDOL (2010).

Comparison of Per Participant Expenditures before and during the Recovery Act Funding Period

This section provides estimates of the level of funding required to restore per-participant expenditures in each of the three programs to prerecession levels. The estimates are intended to illustrate the cost of accommodating the influx of participants during the recession at levels of service that were provided before the recession began. For this analysis, average expenditures per participant may be viewed as an approximation of the level and type of services. However, various factors may confound the linkage between per-participant expenditures and the level and type of services. One is inflation, which over time increases the cost of providing a unit of service. Expenditures are expressed in current dollars for ease of presentation, so the estimates underestimate the expenditures required to maintain the level of service that was provided before the recession during the Recovery Act period.[18] Another factor may be a shift in need or preference of participants and workforce staff for the types and levels of services offered. The types of reemployment services required by workers during an economic expansion may be different from those needed during a recession. A third factor, particularly for the WIA Adult Program, is coenrollment, which started during what we defined as the prerecession period. Despite these confounding factors, expenditures per participant can serve as a rough proxy for levels of service.

Two types of comparisons are presented. First, we estimate the additional funding required to accommodate the increase in the number of participants during the Recovery Act period at prerecession average-per-participant expenditures. More succinctly, we calculate the difference in the average number of participants between the Recovery Act period and the prerecession period $(x_1 - x_0)$ and multiply that difference by the average per-participant expenditure in the prerecession period $[(x_1 - x_0)b_0]$. Second, we estimate the amount "saved" due to a lower expenditure per participant during the recession than before the recession $[(b_1 - b_0)x_1]$. The notion of cost savings is only in the context of the difference in providing services at higher prerecession expenditure-per-participant levels versus lower Recovery Act levels for the additional participants enrolled in the programs during the Recovery Act period. Adding together these two weighted differences provides an estimate of the average difference in expenditures between the prerecession period and the Recovery Act period $(x_1b_1 - b_ox_o)$. Therefore, the two comparisons provide a way of decomposing the difference in expenditures between the differences in the number of participants and the differences in the average per-participant expenditures. It should be noted that the second comparison does not presuppose that a particular per-participant funding target was set for the Recovery Act period. Setting such a target would have been difficult since it would have required an accurate forecast of the number of participants entering the programs, which in turn depended upon the depth and length of the recession. Rather, the average expenditure per participant during the Recovery Act period was the product of the confluence of the severity of the recession and the enactment of federal legislation.

Both of these comparisons are motivated by the following question: "What additional funds would be required to provide participants with the same level of services during the Recovery Act period (as measured by expenditures per participant) as had been provided before the recession?" The first comparison shows that the regular budgeting process had not kept pace with the increase in participants during the recession. The second comparison highlights that the Recovery Act funding, although intended to provide additional funding to accommodate the increase in enrollment and the greater need for intensive services, provided a lower per-participant expenditure level than was attained before the recession.

To compare per-participant expenditures before and during the Recovery Act funding period, we estimated the average expenditure per participant for two time periods. We defined the prerecession period as having extended from 2005Q3 through 2007Q4 and the Recovery Act period as having extended from 2009Q2 through 2011Q2. We also computed the average expenditure per participant with and without the Recovery Act funds.

Table 9.1 shows the relationship between percentage change in participants and expenditures between the Recovery Act and the prerecession period that resulted in the decline in per-participant expenditure. For example, the number of participants of the WIA Adult Program grew by 157 percent, while total expenditures without Recovery Act funds increased by only 1.7 percent and with Recovery Act funds grew 30.3 percent. In both cases, expenditures grew at a slower pace than

Table 9.1 Percentage Changes in Number of Participants and Expenditures from Prerecession Period to Recovery Act Period, by Program

% change from prerecession period to Recovery Act period	Program		
	ES	WIA Adult	WIA DW
Participants	58.9	156.7	183.5
Avg. expenditure/participant without Recovery Act funds	−44.1	−60.4	−66.8
Avg. expenditure/participant with Recovery Act funds	−30.0	−49.3	−50.3
Expenditures without Recovery Act funds	−11.2	1.7	−5.9
Expenditures with Recovery Act funds	11.2	30.3	40.7

NOTE: Percentage changes are calculated between the time periods 2005Q3–2007Q4 and 2009Q2–2011Q2, based on quarterly averages within each period.
SOURCE: Authors' calculations of the PWSD, updated from the data at USDOL (2010).

the number of participants, resulting in a decline in the average per-participant expenditures of 60 percent when Recovery Act funds are not included and a decline of 49 percent when the funds are included.

Table 9.2 displays the quarterly average per-participant expenditures along with the quarterly average number of participants in each of the three programs for these time periods. Multiplying the average number of participants by the average per-participant expenditures yields the average quarterly expenditure for a specific program. Multiplying the average quarterly expenditure by the nine quarters of the Recovery Act period provides an estimate of the total expenditure for that nine-quarter period. We use the nine-quarter period to compare the expenditures during the Recovery Act period with expenditures during a nine-quarter period before the recession.

The basic question of this section is what amount of additional funds are required to accommodate the increase in enrollment at prerecession levels of per-participant expenditures. To address this question, we consider the hypothetical increase in expenditures if the level of per-participant expenditures stayed at prerecession levels. For example, as displayed in Table 9.2, the average prerecession per-participant expenditure for the WIA Adult Program was $633; the per-participant expenditure during the Recovery Act period was $251 without the Recovery Act funds. The average quarterly number of participants increased from 340,231 before the recession to 873,324 during the Recovery Act period. In order to provide the same level of services, as measured by per-participant expenditures, expenditures would have increased by the difference in participants times the prerecession per-participant expenditures (i.e., $[x_1 - x_o]b_o$ times nine quarters). For the WIA Adult Program, the increase would have amounted to $3.04 billion (i.e., [873,324 − 340,231] × 633 × 9). Based on average quarterly estimates, the program actually spent $33 million more from the annual appropriations (not including Recovery Act funds) during the nine-quarter Recovery Act period than in an average nine-quarter period before the recession. The difference was due to the lower average per-participant expenditures in the Recovery Act period, which amounted to a hypothetical reduction of $3.0 billion. This latter reduction is calculated as the difference in the per-participant expenditures between the two periods times the number of participants during the Recovery Act period (i.e., [$251 − $633] × 873,324 × 9). Factoring in the Recovery Act funds expended during that period, the program spent $586 million more during the nine-quarter Recovery Act period than in an average nine-quarter prerecession period. This increase included the $33 million increase from annual appropriations, with the remainder coming from Recovery Act funds. Nonetheless, an additional $2.45 billion would have been required to bring the participants during the Recovery Act period to the per-participant expenditure during the prerecession period.

Changes in the WIA Dislocated Worker Program between these two periods followed patterns similar to those of the WIA Adult Program. The number of participants of the WIA Dislocated Worker Program increased by 184 percent between the two periods, while the average expenditures without Recovery Act funds fell by 5.9 percent (Table 9.1). The infusion of Recovery Act funds increased total expenditures by 40.7 percent, but this increase fell far short of the nearly tripling of the number of participants, resulting in a decline in the average expenditures per participant of 49 percent. Recovery Act funds inserted an additional $1.17 billion into the program over the nine-month period, raising the average per-participant expenditure from $432 without the funds to $646 with the funds. This per-participant spending level was still half of the amount of the prerecession period. To reach that level for the number of participants in the program during the Recovery Act period, an additional $3.6 billion would have been required.

Table 9.2 Hypothetical Funds Needed to Maintain Prerecession Per-Participant Expenditure Levels during the Recovery Act Period

Period	Average quarterly participants (x)	Avg. \$ expenditure/ participant w/o recovery funds (b)	Avg. \$ expenditure/ participant w/ recovery funds (b_R)	$(x_1 - x_o)b_o$ (\$ millions)	$(b_1 - b_o)x_1$ (\$ millions)	$(b_{1R} - b_o)x_1$ (\$ millions)
Panel A: Employment Service						
Prerecession						
2005Q3–2007Q4	3,008,622	55				
Recovery Act						
2009Q2–2011Q2	4,781,915	31	38	877	−1,032	−731
Panel B: WIA Adult						
Prerecession						
2005Q3–2007Q4	340,231	633				
Recovery Act						
2009Q2–2011Q2	873,724	251	321	3,037	−3,003	−2,450
Panel C: WIA Dislocated Worker						
Prerecession						
2005Q3–2007Q4	215,099	1,301				
Recovery Act						
2009Q2–2011Q2	609,832	432	646	4,622	−4,770	−3,595

SOURCE: Authors' calculations of the PWSD, updated from the data at USDOL (2010).

Although the ES program boasted the largest number of participants of the three programs, it experienced the lowest rate of increase in participants between the two periods. Between the prerecession period and the Recovery Act period, the number of participants increased by 59 percent (Table 9.1). Total expenditures, without including Recovery Act expenditures, decreased by 11.2 percent. Consequently, the decline in per-participant expenditures was the least of the three programs, exhibiting a 44 percent decrease. To bring the Recovery Act period per-participant expenditures up to the prerecession level would require an additional $877 million, as shown in Table 9.2. Recovery Act expenditures infused an additional $333 million into the ES program, which raised the average expenditure per participant from $31 to $38. This level is still $17 below the prerecession level of $55. Another $731 million would be required to bring the per-participant expenditure up to the prerecession level.

The previous analysis averaged expenditures per participant over the entire nine-quarter period in which Recovery Act funding was available. However, as we have shown in a previous section, a greater proportion of these funds were spent in the first half of that period than in the latter half. Since the number of participants in the programs remained high throughout the Recovery Act period, expenditures per participant fell. Table 9.3 shows the expenditures per participant for the three time periods: the prerecession period (2005Q3–2007Q4), Recovery Act Period One (2009Q2–2010Q2), and Recovery Act Period Two (2010Q3–2011Q2), in which the Recovery Act period was divided into the first five quarters and the latter four quarters. The ES spent the Recovery Act funds the fastest, with 85 percent of the available funds expended in the first five quarters. If the funds were spent evenly over the nine quarters, 55 percent of the funds would have been expended during the first five quarters. The WIA Adult Program spent 72 percent of available Recovery Act funds the first five quarters, and the WIA Dislocated Worker Program spent 60 percent.

Figure 9.30 shows the distribution of states by the percentage of Recovery Act funds that they spent during the first five quarters of the Recovery Act period. The distribution reflects the national percentages, described above. Thirty-two states spent 80 percent or more of their ES Recovery Act funds within the first five quarters, whereas only 17 and nine states spent 80 percent or more of their Adult and DW Recovery

Table 9.3 Participants and Expenditures by Prerecession and Recovery Act Periods

Period	Avg. quarterly number of participants	Avg. quarterly expenditures per participant without Recovery Act funds ($)	Avg. quarterly expenditures per participant with Recovery Act funds ($)	% Recovery Act funds expended in period
Panel A: Employment Service				
Prerecession (2005Q3–2007Q4)	3,008,622	55		
Recovery Act 1 (2009Q2–2010Q2)	4,661,847	30	42	85
Recovery Act 2 (2010Q3–2011Q2)	4,931,999	32	34	15
Panel B: WIA Adult				
Prerecession (2005Q3–2007Q4)	340,231	633		
Recovery Act 1 (2009Q2–2010Q2)	841,581	269	364	72
Recovery Act 2 (2010Q3–2011Q2)	912,800	230	272	28
Panel C: WIA Dislocated Workers				
Prerecession (2005Q3–2007Q4)	245,099	1,301		
Recovery Act 1 (2009Q2–2010Q2)	547,975	466	720	60
Recovery Act 2 (2010Q3–2011Q2)	687,153	398	571	40

SOURCE: Authors' calculations of the PWSD, updated from the data at USDOL (2010).

Act funds, respectively, during the first five quarters. For the WIA Adult and WIA DW programs, the largest number of states spent between 60 and 80 percent of their Recovery Act funds in the first five quarters.

For all three programs the number of participants was higher on average in the second half of the Recovery Act period than in the first half, and expenditures per participant (including the Recovery Act expenditures) were lower in the second half. While still higher than expenditures per participant from regular appropriations, in all cases expenditures per

Figure 9.30 The Number of States that Spent Various Percentages of their Recovery Act Funds during the First Five Quarters of the Recovery Act Period

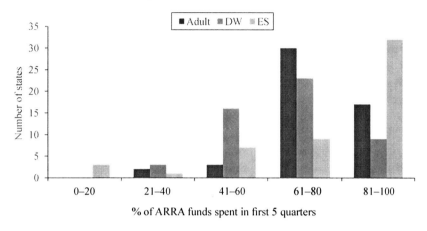

% of ARRA funds spent in first 5 quarters

NOTE: The District of Columbia and Puerto Rico are included along with the 50 states.
SOURCE: Authors' calculations of the PWSD, updated from the data at USDOL (2010).

participant in the second half of the Recovery Act period approached expenditures per participant without Recovery Act funding. Therefore, as the Recovery Act funds were spent down and the number of participants remained high, the level of service as measured by expenditures per participant continued to decline.

CONCLUSION

This chapter demonstrates that the American workforce system responded to the needs of workers during the recent recession by spending available Recovery Act funds expeditiously to provide re-employment and training services to the influx of participants into three workforce programs—Employment Service, WIA Adult, and WIA Dislocated Worker. However, increases in the number of participants were greater than increases in funds available through the Recovery Act and regular appropriations, forcing states to substitute proportionately more lower-cost services for higher-cost staff-assisted services such as training and counseling.

Overall, we found that the flows of workforce services did not keep pace with the needs of unemployed workers. Recovery Act funds only partially compensated for the increase in participants during and immediately after the recession. As a result, workforce programs did not serve participants with the same level or type of service that was provided before the recession. This is evidenced by the reduction in expenditures per participant and in the lower percentage of workers receiving more intensive services and training.

In general, funding for public workforce services was inadequate to avoid a substantial decline in nominal per-participant spending, which had already been developing before the recession and which continued during and after it. Recovery Act funding countered part of the decline, but mostly during parts of 2009 and 2010. For the Recovery Act period as a whole, an additional $8.5 billion would have been needed to accommodate the influx of participants into the three programs during the Recovery Act period at the prerecession level of service, as measured by expenditures per participant. The Recovery Act provided $2.03 billion, which was about a quarter of the funds needed to maintain the prerecession expenditure per participant. When we split the Recovery Act period in two, we found that the gap in funding was much greater in the second Recovery Act period than the first. The results confirm that the state workforce agencies took seriously the U.S. Department of Labor's March 2009 field guidance that the Recovery Act funds should be spent "expeditiously and effectively," so the great majority of the funds were spent in the first year.

Considering the supplemental funding appropriated through the Recovery Act for all workforce programs and the UI system, our findings are not surprising. Federal policymakers put almost all of the new money into the UI program for income maintenance purposes and relatively little into reemployment and training services. Policy emphasis was heavily placed on what the Organisation for Economic Co-operation and Development (OECD) calls "passive labor market policy" rather than on "active labor market policy." As a stimulus initiative, this may have been an appropriate decision, since the intent was to put money in workers' pockets to provide a temporary, timely, and targeted stimulus to the economy.[19]

Our analysis covered only up to 2011Q2, because of the lack of more recent data when the report was prepared. However, it is important to understand what happened afterward, when unemployment and program participation remained high while funding was reduced to prerecession levels. To continue the analysis, the Public Workforce System Dataset (PWSD) should be updated and used to examine what happened after Recovery Act funding terminated. An extension of this study could analyze the flow of unemployed workers into and through reemployment services and training, examining the funding of the workforce system and determining the extent to which limited funding might constrain the ability of the system to provide adequately for those workers who continue to become and to remain unemployed.

Notes

1. This chapter contains portions of a larger, forthcoming report funded by the U.S. Department of Labor that provides data analyses with respect to the workforce system's response to ARRA supplemental funding.
2. State-level analyses will be included in a separate report.
3. The primary reason for the omission of these programs from the analysis is the unavailability of data at the time the study was conducted.
4. A fuller description of the data will be included in the separate final report that we will produce.
5. This analysis does not include Trade Adjustment Assistance program data from the Public Workforce System Dataset (PWSD), since it has not yet been updated and made available to the authors. The WIA updates were generated from the WIA Standardized Record Data (WIASRD).
6. The basic WPRS system is mandated by federal statute. States are free to expand WPRS to target the provision of reemployment services in other ways. The Department of Labor encouraged states to try other targeting approaches in its March 2009 Recovery Act guidance.
7. As shown in Figure 9.5, some services, including education and training, experienced a bigger increase in service provision than the increase in ARRA funding for the WIA Dislocated Worker Program, indicating a substantial effort by state workforce agencies to use ARRA funds to increase training.
8. Recognizing the reporting problems associated with self-served services, particularly at the national aggregate level, we have elected to omit these services from the national-level analysis presented in this chapter. While it is generally recognized that a large number of participants receive self-served services, some states do not record them in WIASRD and thus they are underreported at the national level. One issue contributing to underreporting is the way in which states enroll WIA

participants. In some states, people can use services without registering, whereas in other states everyone using services is required to register. For staff-assisted services, the recording procedure is uniform across all states and straightforward. The WIASRD reporting system counts everyone enrolled in WIA as receiving staff-assisted services, which leads to 100 percent of WIA exiters receiving such services. We will include self-served services in the analysis presented in the full report for selected states that are considered to accurately record the receipt of these services.

9. This may explain why the number of services received and the average duration in the program were greater in the early years of WIA than more recently, as discussed later in this section. However, coenrollment of ES participants in the WIA programs confounds this interpretation.

10. The terms "entrants" and "exiters" measure the flow of individuals into and out of the program, whereas the term "participants" measures the stock of workers in the program.

11. According to the Job Openings and Labor Turnover Survey (JOLTS) data compiled by the Bureau of Labor Statistics (BLS), the average number of hires each month during the second half of 2009 was 1.6 million below the average monthly number of hires from 2005Q3 through 2007Q4, a 30 percent reduction.

12. It should be noted that prior to 2006 and before coenrollment, the share of participants receiving intensive services reached a high of 70 percent. Again, the abrupt decline in the percentage receiving intensive services after 2006 can be attributed to coenrollment.

13. The number of services received is by registration quarter, while days in program is by exit quarter.

14. As with the other trends in services, the average duration in the program and the number of services appear to be influenced by the advent of coenrollment in 2006. Immediately prior to that time, the average number of services was around 3.5 and the average duration in the program was around 300 days. By 2006Q4, these numbers had fallen to 2.2 and 119, respectively.

15. The number of services received is by registration quarter, while days in program is by exit quarter.

16. The number of hires is from the BLS JOLTS data, and the number of private sector jobs is from the BLS.

17. The American Recovery and Reinvestment Act of 2009, which we refer to as the Recovery Act, provided additional budget authority to federal agencies to obligate funds above the levels provided in the previously enacted Fiscal Year 2009 budget. Much of the spending, particularly for workforce programs, was based on preexisting formulas or mechanisms. The March 18, 2009 Training and Employment Guidance Letter (TEGL 14-08) states, "Recovery Act funding may only be used for authorized WIA and Wagner-Peyser Act activities as provided in this TEGL. ETA expects states and local areas to fully utilize the additional workforce funding to substantially increase the number of customers served, and to substantially increase the number and proportion of those customers who receive training. These funds must be used to supplement annual WIA/Wagner-Peyser appropria-

tions and must only be used for activities that are in addition to those otherwise available in the local area (WIA sec. 195[2]). To that end, Recovery Act funding is to be spent concurrently with other WIA and Wagner-Peyser funding, and should not be used to replace state or local funding currently dedicated to workforce development and summer jobs" (USDOL 2009).

18. The expenditures are in nominal terms. If converted to constant dollars, the difference would be even greater, as the consumer price index grew by 10 percent from 2005 through 2011, even though it took a sizable dip in 2008.

19. In testimony before the Joint Economic Committee on January 18, 2008, Lawrence Summers, Harvard University professor and former secretary of the Treasury, echoed his previous call for a fiscal stimulus that was "timely, targeted, and temporary," which for many became the basic principles for an effective stimulus package.

References

U.S. Department of Labor (USDOL). 2009. *ETA Advisories: Training and Employment Guidance Letter (TEGL) No. 14-08 (March 18, 2009)*. Washington, DC: U.S. Department of Labor, Employment and Training Administration. http://wdr.doleta.gov/directives/attach/TEGL/TEGL14-08.pdf (accessed March 6, 2013).

———. 2010. *Public Workforce System Dataset (PWSD)*. Washington, DC: U.S. Department of Labor, Employment and Training Administration. http://www.doleta.gov/reports/pwsd/ (accessed September 10, 2013).

10
Challenges and Accomplishments

States' Views

John Trutko
Capital Research Corporation

Burt S. Barnow
George Washington University

This chapter summarizes the visited states' views on the most significant challenges and greatest achievements in implementing the Recovery Act workforce and UI provisions. During the two rounds of site visits (workforce development programs) and the teleconference interviews (UI programs), UI and state and local workforce agency officials were asked their views on their greatest overall challenges and accomplishments in dealing with the Recovery Act, as well as challenges and achievements for specific programs. The previous chapters summarized challenges and accomplishments for specific programs or provisions, and this chapter describes the challenges and accomplishments most frequently noted by states visited.

CHALLENGES AND ACCOMPLISHMENTS—WORKFORCE DEVELOPMENT PROVISIONS

Challenges

An important objective of the site visits involved identifying challenges that states and local workforce areas encountered in planning and implementing Recovery Act requirements. During two rounds of site visits, states and local workforce areas were asked to identify and discuss their greatest challenges and major accomplishments with respect to the Recovery Act. The most commonly cited challenges are listed in Table 10.1.

The most commonly cited challenge, mentioned by 17 of the 20 states visited, was *dealing with the Recovery Act reporting requirements*. Many of the comments by state workforce agencies focused on the need to set up, with little notice, new reports that were different from their regular reports in terms of schedule and, in some instances, content. The frequency of reporting—monthly rather than quarterly—also was viewed by some states as burdensome. One state official indicated that reporting on jobs "saved" or "created" was challenging because it was difficult to know which jobs really fit into that category. Several state officials commented that they did not have enough time to complete the software programming to generate required reports; some of the initial definitions of data items were unclear to some states (Illinois and Montana); and, at least in the case of TAA, a few states believed that ETA did not issue guidance sufficiently in advance of when the reports were due (Colorado, Michigan, and Ohio). Several of the specific concerns identified by states with regard to reporting are illustrated below:

- **Colorado.** Reporting on Recovery Act expenditures has proved to be burdensome for the state. The state workforce agency had to scramble to set up a separate set of financial reports to meet Recovery Act requirements. This was because the timing for Recovery Act reporting was not the same as for reporting on other expenditures. The fiscal period for the state workforce agency cuts off 10 days after the end of the quarter. However, for Recovery Act fiscal reporting, the state had to develop an expenditure report for Recovery Act funds as of the last day of the month at quarter's end. This meant that the timing for producing the Recovery Act fiscal reports did not match with the timing of what the state normally uses for its regular reporting on other programs, such as the WIA programs. There also was not enough time to validate the data used to meet Recovery Act reporting requirements, as is normally the case with the regular reporting system. In addition, it was burdensome for the state to report on Recovery Act expenditures by county and congressional district. The state had to move very quickly with existing IT staff to meet the Recovery Act reporting requirements. This effort was fur-

Table 10.1 Challenges Most Commonly Cited by States

Challenge	No. of states citing
Recovery Act reporting requirements	17
Time issues	13
Funding issues	12
Staffing issues	12
The bad economy	11
Guidance	10

SOURCE: Site visit interviews conducted in states.

ther complicated because guidance from the ETA on reporting requirements came very late. For example, guidance on financial reporting was issued in mid-September (of 2009), and the report was due to the USDOL about two weeks later (September 30).

- **Michigan.** One of the larger and more burdensome aspects of TAA reauthorization was the new reporting requirements. The USDOL issued final guidance on reporting only a few weeks before reports were due, which made it difficult for states to meet the new requirements. One of the most burdensome reporting elements was the need to report accrued expenditures on training per participant per quarter—this necessitated the entry of accrued and actual expenditures for each TAA participant into the system each quarter.

- **Nevada.** Reporting was a nightmare. More state participation in the development of reporting requirements would have been useful. States could have provided information on current data collection and systems in place to see if existing reports could be modified to meet ARRA data requirements. Reporting on jobs created and saved was essentially impossible. Reporting on a monthly basis was a shift from the traditional quarterly reporting system, and given that there had been no investment in data collection mechanisms this was a serious burden. The sheer volume of applicants also made reporting a major burden at the local level.

- **North Dakota.** Reporting was a particular concern and burden—the state often found itself operating Recovery Act–funded programs and activities before it knew what it would have to report on. Additionally, the need to separately report on Recovery Act–funded activities (from regular formula–funded activities) was burdensome (and in the view of state administrators and staff unnecessary).

- **Ohio.** State workforce officials observed that guidance on reporting requirements was delayed and, in some cases, issued after reports were due to the ETA. There were new data items to report on—in particular, there was quite a bit more of a burden to report on the TAA. In addition, the state had to move quickly to make changes to its automated data systems to meet ETA reporting requirements. At times, IT resources were strained in making changes to systems to meet ETA requirements in a timely manner (especially for the TAA).

- **Wisconsin.** The monthly reporting required under the Recovery Act meant double reporting for the state—continued reporting on its regular funds and separate reporting on Recovery Act activities, accomplishments (e.g., job creation), and expenditures. According to state officials, Recovery Act reporting differed somewhat from WIA Common Measures reporting: Recovery Act reporting was more process- than outcome-oriented—e.g., reporting on numbers served, services provided, and expenditures. In some instances, ETA provided last-minute instructions on reporting requirements. For one-time funding, the reporting burden for the Recovery Act was considerable. Also, within the state, the TAA, Wagner-Peyser, and WIA programs are linked by a common data system, since any changes in reporting requirements for one program will affect data collection/reporting for the other programs.

Second, *time issues* were mentioned as a challenge in 13 states, often in conjunction with staffing and reporting issues. Some states felt that the pressure to spend Recovery Act funds quickly was more difficult because of changes in ETA implementation of waiver authority, which states previously used to transfer funds from the WIA Dislocated Worker Program to the WIA Adult Program. As discussed below, some states had problems in hiring the staff needed to run the programs (including Illinois, Colorado, and New York). The TAA was cited by a number of states for timeliness issues (for example in Wisconsin, New York, and Michigan) regarding publishing regulations and providing guidance (especially related to reporting) and approving TAA petitions in a timely manner. Finally, with respect to timeliness, several states mentioned the WIA Summer Youth Program, because they did not have long to mount the program and many states (and local areas) had not run a summer program for many years (Ohio and Pennsylvania). The following bulleted paragraphs provide several illustrations of the strain that state and local workforce agencies were working under to quickly mount, administer, and report on Recovery Act–funded activities:

- **Ohio.** A key overall challenge was that the planning period was very short, particularly with respect to getting the Summer Youth Program up and running. Many local areas did not have an active Summer Youth Program, and so it was considerable work to get programs up and running. The state was under a lot of pressure to spend quickly and wisely. There was little time available for planning—and so the state had to work with existing programs and structures. It was not possible to be exceedingly creative at times because of the very short time period for implementation and the temporary nature of the funding. As one agency official noted, "The federal government gave us the money and then expected it to be spent immediately—there was no time to really spend it! There was a focus on expenditure rate. We were under the microscope to prove this was successful, but you cannot have success in 24 hours!"

- **Pennsylvania.** State workforce administrators noted that the implementation of the Summer Youth Program was a challenge, as they had not operated this program since the JTPA years. They needed to start from scratch, and it took two months of intensive work to pull the Summer Youth Program together at the state level. More broadly with respect to the Recovery Act, the expectation that additional resources and infrastructure would be immediately implemented was a persistent challenge at the state and local levels. Agency officials indicated that the regulatory processes required by the funding commitment were at times at odds with the requirement to exhaust the funds within a short time period. The focus on exhausting the funds to avoid penalty stunted opportunities for innovation and restructuring.

- **Wisconsin.** An initial challenge for both the state and local workforce areas was that the Recovery Act represented a sizable infusion of new funding and that the state and especially the local areas had to ramp up services and spend Recovery Act resources over a relatively short period. It was necessary to ramp up services and serve more customers without making long-term commitments to hiring staff. There was a need to manage staff and increases to services (especially training offered under WIA), while recognizing that these services would need to be ramped down.

The next most frequently identified challenge with respect to the Recovery Act implementation was *funding issues*, mentioned by 12 of the 20 states visited. The specific challenges identified varied among the states. One state (Colorado) said that its procurement requirements led to delays in spending some of its Recovery Act funds. The state's workforce officials observed that the state's procurement process can be long and cumbersome and that trying to get Recovery Act funds out quickly and meeting procurement requirements can (in some cases) be a great difficulty. Two states (Colorado and Florida) stated that they had experienced difficulties spending Recovery Act funds because the ETA adjusted their waivers and limited the amount by which they could transfer their WIA Dislocated Worker funds to the Adult Program.

Many of the states during both the initial and follow-up site visits expressed serious concerns about what would occur once the Recovery Act funds were spent. Some states mentioned that if customers were enrolled in long-term training, they might not be able to continue, or the following year's enrollment would drop dramatically. Even a state like North Dakota, with the lowest unemployment rate in the nation, was concerned about the "funding cliff." A common refrain across states was that it was likely that demand for employment and training services would remain elevated for at least several years after Recovery Act funding was dissipated and that One-Stop Career Centers would not have sufficient staffing and funding to provide the training and other services needed by unemployed and underemployed customers. This is reflected in the following examples from site visits:

- **Louisiana.** State workforce officials were concerned about whether the program systems and processes they had developed in whole or in part with Recovery Act funds would be continued once Recovery Act funds were exhausted. Newer state priorities funded by the Recovery Act, such as employer-based training, OJT, Summer Youth employment, long-term training, and developmental education could be dropped. Some local areas were concerned about whether they would have enough funds to continue standard workforce development services. A few, for example, were considering incorporating with another LWIB. The 60 staff members hired as a result of the Recovery Act were all temporary employees. Recovery Act funds postponed the staff reductions the state was going to have to make because of its shrinking WIA and Wagner-Peyser funding, but the increasing fiscal pressure in the state was likely to require more staff cuts.

- **Michigan.** After the first summer, the state (and local Michigan Works! agencies) had nearly exhausted Summer Youth funding. This program was a key accomplishment under the Recovery Act—providing valuable skills development, experience, and wages for youth involved—and according to state administrators it was unfortunate that a second year of funding was not made available for Summer Youth activities. The state's welfare agency did not elect to use Recovery Act funding the second summer to support the Summer Youth Employment Program—and so Michigan Works! agencies were left with only year-round Youth money to use for Summer Youth activities (if they chose to use funding for this purpose).

- **Montana.** Prior to receipt of Recovery Act funding, Montana's WIA allocations had fallen by more than half, from $15 million in PY 2000 to about $6 million by PY 2008. The additional WIA dollars received through the Recovery Act (almost $6 million for Adults, Dislocated Workers, and Youth), when added to the annual allocation, just began to approach earlier levels. Montana officials were particularly worried about having to "close the front door" to new registrants (whose numbers had yet to slow), as a larger percentage of available funds would be needed to continue to support those already registered and receiving training (and who were often staying in services longer than in the past). An official observed, "We're concerned about what happens come July 1, when we have folks currently enrolled in training and will have to carry them, which may mean we have to take fewer numbers at the front end."

- **Ohio.** From the beginning, state workforce officials feared that Recovery Act funding would be fully spent but that economic conditions would not turn around quickly enough in the state to dent Ohio's very high unemployment rate. In addition, as state administrators looked forward, they saw that not only would Recovery Act funding end, but the state's allocation for formula funds (particularly for WIA Dislocated Worker funds) would likely be cut. There was a lot of concern in the state that there would still be surging unmet demand for employment and training services at many One-Stop Career Centers. As noted by one workforce official, "Stimulus dollars are gone before the needs are gone—public perception is that the money is still there, but it's gone already, given time constraints to spend the funds."

Tied with funding issues as the third most identified challenge with regard to the Recovery Act—mentioned by 12 of the 20 states—was *staffing issues*, particularly related to bringing on new staff and providing necessary training. For example, Louisiana workforce officials indicated that it was a challenge to train state and local staff on new procedures resulting from the Recovery Act, particularly because there was a change in state administration. One state indicated it had run into hurdles in bringing on new staff because of issues with the state human resources department. Several states indicated that hiring was slowed because of civil service hiring procedures at the state or local level (New York and Colorado experienced problems at the local level, and Virginia at the state level). Although not noted as a major challenge, Illinois could only hire intermittent staff for Wagner-Peyser positions (i.e., within the constraints of working no more than 1,500 hours per year). Finally, several states reported hiring freezes or staff furloughs that complicated efforts to bring on new staff—for example, Pennsylvania had a hiring freeze and had to get an exemption to use Recovery Act funding to hire new staff. Several illustrations of the specific staffing issues encountered by states follow:

- **Florida.** According to state workforce officials, the real challenge since receipt of Recovery Act funding was that every local WIB had to increase staff because the One-Stops were overwhelmed with customers. They had to find and train new staff and find space (there was not sufficient funding to open new One-Stop centers) to increase services. They had to retrain existing staff in order to change the skill sets of workers to address the needs of new UI claimants and long-term claimants who often had higher-level skills and higher incomes than many past customers.

- **New York.** While the "functional alignment" of workforce programs helped to alleviate the issue of handling the increased volume of customers, it could not solve logistical issues such as having enough space and One-Stop staff to serve everyone. Customers at some centers experience lengthy wait times to access computers in resource rooms and for appointments with counselors, as well as sometimes-crowded orientation sessions. Some locations were able to secure donated space or short-term leases for temporary extra space, but in some areas of the state such arrangements were not possible. Hiring new permanent staff also required changes to budgets and a lengthy process if the position had to be approved through government channels.

- **Rhode Island.** The Recovery Act funds arrived when the state was in the throes of major staff downsizing. Because state hiring rules required that all hires be handled by a centralized Human Resources system, there were also delays in filling the positions created using Recovery Act funds. Interagency dynamics between WIA and UI were further complicated because the classifications for UI and workforce positions were the same and UI staff began applying for Recovery Act jobs in WIA.

- **North Dakota.** Given the state of the economy in North Dakota, hiring temporary ARRA workers to staff the Job Service North Dakota (JSND) was more difficult because workers had other employment options in North Dakota, and some were not interested in temporary work when permanent work was available. In addition, if staff resigned late in the program year, it was not possible to find new people and get them trained in time to be of assistance.

- **Virginia.** The speed with which the state had to ramp up for the Recovery Act was considerable, and the staffing and facilities issues were critical because the Virginia Employment Commission (VEC) had closed offices, in part because the Wagner-Peyser program had been flat-funded for more than a decade. Hiring with Recovery Act funding meant mainly bringing back laid-off agency employees, but challenges were encountered in staffing up because of delays in the civil service hiring procedures and the need to train new or returning staff while local offices were responding to surging customer volumes brought on by the recession.

- **Washington.** State workforce officials reported the most difficult aspect related to the Recovery Act was hiring staff, given the state's existing civil service system and ongoing hiring freeze. Administrators noted it was easier to get approval to hire front-line staff than human resources staff, even though the HR staff was needed to help bring the front-line staff on board. Washington added some direct-service staff to provide reemployment services to UI claimants, using both Recovery Act and UI contingency funds. In addition, the state added business outreach managers in each local area to develop job leads. Washington also hired three Summer Youth managers on a temporary basis and one MIS person. The challenge was in retaining these temporary hires. One issue was that the state workforce agency wanted to focus on hiring high-quality applicants, but many workers with high-quality skills did not want temporary employment. If they took a position, the newly hired workers often continued to look for regular employment and moved on when they found it.

Eleven states mentioned that the *bad economy* was a major challenge to effectively mounting program activities funded by the Recovery Act. For example, Nevada and Michigan, with among the worst unemployment rates in the nation, were concerned that they would have trouble placing people into jobs once they had completed training. Florida workforce officials also expressed general concerns about the state's economy. With leading industries such as tourism and housing in decline and a weak economy overall, it was very hard to place customers in jobs.

Finally, half of the 20 states visited found *guidance from the ETA* to be a challenge. Issues included timeliness of guidance and getting responses in a timely manner that addressed specific questions states and local workforce agency staff had with respect to implementing workforce provisions of the Recovery Act. As noted earlier, guidance on the TAA was considered to be late in coming. The states recognized that the ETA had very little time to develop and disseminate guidance, and they expressed the view that the ETA did quite well given how rapidly the guidance to states had to be issued. Some specific examples of challenges with respect to guidance were the following:

- **Ohio.** At times, the state had to plan Recovery Act spending and activities based on what the ETA said rather than formal written documentation. Guidance on reporting requirements was delayed and in some cases was issued after reports were due to the ETA. There were new data items to report on—in particular, there was quite a bit more burden in reporting on the TAA. In addition, the state had to move quickly to make changes to its automated data systems to meet ETA reporting requirements. At times, IT resources were strained in making changes to systems to meet ETA requirements in a timely manner (especially for the TAA).

- **Rhode Island.** There were conflicting concerns that the state workforce agency needed to move quickly to allocate the funds but also to move cautiously in the absence of detailed guidance from the DOL national and regional offices. For example, state officials cited the lack of clarity and instructions on how to allocate costs between regular funds and the Recovery Act and how to "count" which customers were Recovery Act versus regularly (through the WIA formula) funded individuals. Around the SYEP, there were restrictions on work sites and paying wages versus stipends, and on interpretation of needs-related payments.

- **Wisconsin.** In planning for ARRA implementation, the state reviewed TEGLs as they were released by DOL. These were very helpful, though not always released in a timely manner and sometimes later clarified or revised. State officials also sat in on DOL webinars—which they found to be extremely useful initially but over time less helpful and, at times near the end, repetitive. The state issued administrative memos to pass on information to local workforce areas (similar to TEGLs issued by the

ETA). Overall, given the extremely tight time constraints on Recovery Act rollout, state agency officials credited the ETA with doing a "good job given the circumstances" of issuing directions and guidance to states on implementing the Recovery Act.

- In conclusion, it is important to note that although state and local workforce agencies faced significant challenges, for the most part states were able to achieve their goals and serve their customers with Recovery Act funding. Ideally, they would have liked more time, more flexibility, and better guidance, but states and local workforce areas generally recognized that the ETA was under intense pressure to get things going, and they did not view the challenges faced as fatal flaws in moving forward with rapid and effective implementation of Recovery Act requirements and activities.

Accomplishments

During the two rounds of site visits, state and local workforce agency officials were asked to discuss their major accomplishments with Recovery Act funding. As is covered in this section, there were a number of accomplishments commonly identified across states and local areas, particularly with regard to mounting (or expanding) the WIA Summer Youth Program, enhancing training and other services, expanding the number of customers served, and improving information and reporting systems. Table 10.2, below, lists the major accomplishments cited by the states visited, and Table 10.3, following this section, provides an overview of the accomplishments identified by each state.

Table 10.2 Accomplishments Most Commonly Cited by States

Accomplishment	No. of states citing
Successful development and administration of the WIA Summer Youth Program	17
Serving more customers	16
Changes to the state's training programs	15
Significant service enhancements	13
Reemployment services and enhanced relationships between the Employment Service and UI	10

SOURCE: Site visit interviews conducted in states.

The most prevalent major accomplishment in the states visited was the *successful development and administration of the WIA Summer Youth Program*, identified by 17 of the 20 states visited. That so many cited the Summer Youth Program as a major accomplishment is impressive because the site visits were not intended to cover the WIA Youth programs, so this program was not the subject of questions asked during site visits. Because Recovery Act funds were not available until March 2009 at the earliest, states had to act quickly to implement their Summer Youth Programs (for the summer of 2009). Many states and localities had not operated Summer Youth Programs in recent years (or if they had, programs were operated on a small scale), so setting up a large program in a short period was considered a major accomplishment. Several states indicated they had greatly expanded their Summer Youth Programs and that the programs had produced increases in work readiness and job skills. For example, Illinois workforce officials noted that 17,000 youth were served, and the program produced increases in work readiness and job skills. Louisiana workforce agency officials referred to the Summer Youth Program as the "hottest thing in the Recovery Act," as it had provided many youth with their first paid work experience. Workforce officials in Michigan observed that the program provided much-needed income for the youth and their families in a state with very high unemployment. And finally, Wisconsin workforce officials noted they used the Summer Youth Program to promote green jobs and training—e.g., by initiating projects to eliminate invasive species in Wisconsin lakes and streams. Below are several illustrations of the ways in which Recovery Act funding made a critical difference with regard to enabling states to substantially expand Summer Youth enrollment and employment experiences:

- **Florida.** The highlight of the Recovery Act spending in Florida was $42 million for its Summer Youth Program, which employed 14,000 youth in the summer of 2009. The state had not been able to fund a summer program since the Job Training Partnership Act (JTPA) in the 1990s. It was a challenge, requiring local WIBs to start from scratch to redevelop partner relationships. For the summer of 2010, the state used unspent funds from 2009 as well as some state funds for a modest program. State officials moved some funds (about $1 million in WIA Youth funds and $1 million in WIA Adult funds) to jump-start a program for the five or six regions that requested it. About half the WIBs had funds to run a program for the summer of 2010.

- **Louisiana.** One of the main accomplishments under the Recovery Act, according to state officials, was the implementation of the Summer Youth Program in 2009. It was done well and had a substantial impact on the economy of the state by investing in students who might not have otherwise had this type of experience. In addition, many working in the workforce investment system had been frustrated and discouraged with so many unemployed, and introducing the Summer Youth Program and the momentum needed to implement it increased morale.

- **Ohio.** Perhaps one of the greatest accomplishments under the Recovery Act, according to state officials, was successfully mounting a Summer Youth Program that served a total of 18,000 youth. Local areas implemented programs in a timely and effective manner, even in areas where there had not been Summer Youth Programs for years.

- **Wisconsin.** Many youth were served (4,400) in the WIA Summer Youth Program. This program was mounted quickly and featured green job activities and training. The state used Recovery Act discretionary funds to conduct two special projects, one in energy conservation and the other in aquatic invasive species. The "energy auditors" initiative provided 19 WIA youth in five communities across the state with 40 hours of training on going into homes to conduct energy audits to identify ways in which homeowners could conserve energy. Under an "invasive aquatic species" initiative, a total of 49 WIA youth received training and then accompanied Department of Natural Resources staff at lakes around the state to advise boat owners about how to take precautions to halt the spread of invasive aquatic species in Wisconsin's lakes. An estimated 5,000 recreational boats were inspected across the state as they were pulled from the water— and, when appropriate, youth helped to clean off mud from the bottom of boats that could be harboring invasive species.

Sixteen of 20 states visited cited *serving more customers* as a major accomplishment. During state and local interviews, agency officials often observed that One-Stops in their state were "overwhelmed" or "swamped" with unemployed and underemployed customers in need of employment, education, training, and a range of supportive services. For example, officials at one state, Colorado, responded, "The Recovery Act provided extra resources to hire and deploy additional staff to One-Stop resource rooms to deal with the surge in customers." In Montana, state workforce officials said One-Stops were able to expand staff and the number of customers served with added Recovery Act funding. State officials in Nevada indicated that they had been able to use the extra resources provided by Recovery Act funding to eliminate lines in the One-Stops. With Recovery Act funding, Ohio was able to hire 100 intermittent Wagner-Peyser staff to help deal with the surge in customers at the One-Stops and to expand RES to a much larger number of UI claimants than would have been the case without Recovery Act funding.

Fifteen states cited *changes to their training programs* as a major accomplishment of the Recovery Act. For example, Florida used Recovery Act and other funding for its Employ Florida Healthcare Initiative, which included employer-driven models for assessment and training. Illinois used Recovery Act funds to develop "bridge programs," which helped low-income workers gain basic skills and other skills to move into better occupations. Nevada issued an RFP for new service providers to serve as intermediaries and expand opportunities for customers to obtain training more quickly and conveniently. Finally, in Wisconsin, Recovery Act funding brought training and other services to many adults, dislocated workers, and youth who might otherwise have not received services. A state requirement in Wisconsin that at least 70 percent of Recovery Act WIA Adult and Dislocated Worker funds be spent on training (versus 35 percent for regular WIA formula funds) helped to ensure that a high proportion of Recovery Act WIA funds allocated to local workforce boards was dedicated to training and upgrading worker skills.

Thirteen states cited *significant service enhancements* as a major accomplishment made possible with the availability of the Recovery Act resources. These service enhancements came in a variety of services offered to One-Stop customers. For example, Wisconsin was able to use Recovery Act RES funds to pursue its goal of providing a rich array of reemployment services using WorkKeys and KeyTrain that helped claimants work toward the National Career Readiness Certifi-

cate (NCRC). North Dakota used Recovery Act funds to purchase software (TORQ) to develop skills transferability reports for occupations
affected by layoffs. These reports were provided to One-Stops to be
used in rapid response services. Florida used Recovery Act funds to
fund Florida Back to Work, the state's return-to-work program, enabling
TANF recipients to get subsidized employment and improve their prospects for an unsubsidized job. Montana used discretionary Recovery
Act grant awards to pursue strategies to advance the state's renewable
energy strategy. And finally, in Nevada, Recovery Act funding was used
to make major improvements in the state's UI system.

Half of the 20 states visited cited *RES or improved UI/ES relationships* as a major accomplishment. Colorado workforce officials stated
that the Recovery Act activities helped to bring UI and workforce staff
closer together. Staff members on both sides are now more knowledgeable about the each other and more willing to collaborate. Several states,
including Florida and Illinois, said that Recovery Act funds enabled
them to reinstate RES. As noted earlier, Wisconsin conducted a major
upgrade of its RES services, which the state hopes to make available to
an increasing share of its customers. Two more detailed illustrations of
the ways in which RES services have been expanded or UI/ES relationships improved are highlighted below (and in Table 10.3):

- **Colorado.** The efforts implemented under the Recovery Act
  helped to bring the UI and workforce systems closer together.
  Staff members on both sides are more knowledgeable about the
  other's programs and are more willing to collaborate. One-Stops
  and workforce regions had reached near-crisis levels in responding to UI claimant concerns (e.g., delayed checks, could not get
  through on the telephone to a call center, etc.). The Recovery Act
  funding helped the state to conduct special UI workshops in various regions (referred to as "road shows") that helped to alleviate
  stress on the One-Stop system to address UI claimant concerns.

- **Wisconsin.** One of the biggest changes in the workforce system
  that resulted from the Recovery Act was the substantial expansion in RES services for UI claimants. Wagner-Peyser Recovery
  Act funds ($7.2 million) and UI Recovery Act administrative
  funding ($3.6 million)—for a total of nearly $11 million—were
  used to expand and fundamentally change the way in which UI

claimants are served by the One-Stop system. The state was able to vastly expand the number of UI claimants attending orientation services, as well as the number receiving one-on-one services. Having experimented with the "Career Pathways" model for several years under a Joyce Foundation–funded grant, Recovery Act funding provided an opportunity to take this model and apply it to UI claimants.

While states and local areas were able to identify various short-term accomplishments made possible with Recovery Act funding, some of the effects of the Recovery Act may not be fully felt or known for some years to come—particularly with respect to investments that have been made in long-term training and in work experiences provided through the Summer Youth Programs, efforts to expand RES to unemployment insurance claimants and to better connect the One-Stop system with the UI system, and technological upgrades to improve tracking of services and employment outcomes for individuals served by workforce development programs.

After the Recovery Act

During the second round of site visits, state and local workforce agencies were asked to reflect on the differences that the Recovery Act had made, as well as their plans and priorities after the Recovery Act funds were spent. By the time the second round of visits under this study was completed, states had exhausted or nearly exhausted their Recovery Act funds and had already entered a post–Recovery Act period. According to both state and local workforce agency staff across virtually all 20 of the states visited, despite returning to pre–Recovery Act funding levels in their WIA and Wagner-Peyser programs, demand for workforce services at One-Stop centers remained at elevated levels, approximating (or just below) those experienced during the 2007–2008 recession. This was because local economies across many states had not as yet recovered from the deep recession and remained stressed by stubbornly high unemployment and underemployment levels (e.g., particularly with regard to some workers who had joined the ranks of the long-term unemployed).

According to many state and local agencies in the 20 states visited, the Recovery Act had provided a temporary (and desperately needed)

Table 10.3 Major Accomplishments with Recovery Act Funding as Identified by State Workforce Agencies

State	Major accomplishments
Arizona	• Recovery Act funding helped to retain, improve, and expand services during the initial shock waves of the economic crisis and restructure service delivery to more efficiently serve the large numbers and various employability profiles of job seekers. • The state reinstituted an RES program using Recovery Act funds. Three Reemployment Centers were opened in areas of high unemployment. RES was incorporated as a regular feature of One-Stop local service delivery—ARRA resulted in enhanced coordination between the One-Stop and UI systems through such practices as ES and WIA coenrollment for UI claimants and more open access for claimants to work-readiness workshops held at One-Stops. • The workforce system has adapted and become more responsive to a broader client base including incumbent workers, long-term and skilled/semiprofessional workers displaced by the recession who have had little or no prior contact or knowledge of the public workforce system, and the rising tide of unemployed seeking employment assistance. • The state used ARRA-ES funds to improve the infrastructure of One-Stops, including redesigning lobbies and resource rooms, increasing the size of resource rooms in some locations, and adding new television screens for videos and looped information.
Colorado	• The Summer Youth Employment Program was a big effort because local workforce areas had either not run programs in the recent past or had very small programs. Statewide, with Recovery Act funding, over 3,000 low-income youth participated in subsidized work experience slots under this initiative. • ARRA provided a big increase in funding that was used to increase substantially the number of unemployed receiving WIA-funded training. Additionally, the Recovery Act provided extra resources to hire and deploy additional staff to One-Stop resource rooms to deal with the surge of job seekers coming into One-Stops for assistance.

- With its Recovery Act funds, UI initiated a road show of UI staff that conducted in-person sessions with UI claimants at local workforce centers to respond to questions that claimants had about their claims and resolve outstanding issues in an expedited manner. In addition, UI trained key workforce center staff in basic UI on-line functions so that the local staff could handle basic on-line needs for claimants.

- The Colorado Department of Human Services (DHS) created a subsidized employment program (HIRE Colorado) with $11,200,000 in ARRA supplemental TANF Reserve Funds that provided a safety net for individuals who had exhausted their UI benefits. The funds were given to workforce centers to implement the program.

- Recovery Act funding was very helpful in terms of modernizing data systems, particularly in handling extended benefits under the UI program.

Florida

- ARRA provided critical funding for the state's Summer Youth Employment Program (SYEP), which provided temporary subsidized summer jobs for 14,000 youth.

- The state used Recovery Act and other funding for the Employ Florida Health Care Initiative, featuring employer-driven new models for assessment, training, and job placement. Additionally, ARRA funds were used to expand participation in Microsoft's Elevate America training vouchers initiative, using competitive awards to LWIBs for digital access and to foster community college collaborations.

- The state used Recovery Act funds to staff the Florida Back-to-Work/TANF subsidized employment program.

- The state improved RES services, with more emphasis on intensive staff-assisted reemployment services targeting many more UI claimants.

- Using ARRA funds, a major LMI expansion was undertaken—bandwidth and storage capacity expansions, and software to enhance real-time information for front-line staff.

Illinois

- With ARRA funding, the state was able to place 17,000 youth in subsidized jobs through the Summer Youth Program (in the summer of 2009).

- WIA state discretionary dollars were used for bridge programs for low-income workers in key sectors.

- The state reinstated Reemployment Services (especially via Reemployment Workshops) that had been discontinued in 2005.

(continued)

Table 10.3 (continued)

State	Major accomplishments
Louisiana	• SYEP was the "hottest thing in Recovery Act spending"—it was a learning experience and implementation success, placing 5,000 in Summer Youth jobs the first year; 50% of participants were out of school and most had never worked before. Also, ARRA helped in connecting older youth with services.
	• Interdepartmental collaboration was a direct result of the Recovery Act; departments had to scramble to spend money, find partners, and push in same direction. "Before, there were silos; now there is more cooperation," one official said.
	• "ARRA kept us afloat," allowing state and local areas to retain staff that would have otherwise been lost through attrition, cuts and office closures, said another source.
Maine	• Maine did not have a pre-existing WIA Summer Youth Program, and as a result of the Recovery Act, brought partners together and was able to quickly get its Summer Youth Program up and running, reaching almost 1,000 youth across the state.
	• Maine made a clear commitment to training and supportive services, designating 80% of Recovery Act WIA Adult and Dislocated worker funds for this purpose and keeping administrative costs down.
	• Maine maximized the influx of resources via coordination across agencies and funding streams. One example is the weatherization program; another was a combined LMI and U.S. Department of Education effort to create a longitudinal student database of resident educational experiences including K-12 and postsecondary education and training in the state—allowing policymakers to track the effect of training and education on earnings over time.
	• Maine used LMI and other analyses to really target where the jobs are and are likely to be. "One of the things that folks have really been paying attention to is, 'Where are the jobs?' Maine is a participant in the Northeast Labor Market Information consortium. We've been looking at real-time data on vacancies and seeing how it can be used to adjust our 10-year projections."

Michigan

- Many youth (21,000) were served across the state in the WIA Summer Youth Program as a result of ARRA funding. The Summer Youth Program was mounted quickly and provided much-needed income and work experience for youth enrolled in the program (at a time when there were few available Summer Youth jobs in the state). Also, the ability to use private employers under the program for the first time was a big plus, as was the ability to serve youth up to age 24 (instead of 21, as had been the case in past years).

- WIA Dislocated Worker and Adult Recovery Act funding about doubled as a result of ARRA. This added funding was particularly helpful with regard to expanding training (and especially longer-term training) opportunities for an increased number of adults, dislocated workers, and youth. A high proportion of the Recovery Act WIA funding went to training, which has helped to boost skills of the workforce and prepare them for new jobs.

- ARRA provided a total of $7.8 million in funds allocated across the state's 25 Michigan Works! agencies (MWAs) to provide expanded and intensified RES for UI claimants. MWAs across the state used funding to expand temporary staffing to provide RES orientations and case management services for UI claimants. Additionally, MWAs had considerable latitude to use RES funding to better serve and connect UI claimants to One-Stop Career Centers and other services available through the workforce system, including: providing comprehensive assessments and one-on-one case management services, development of individual service strategies, orientation to training available under Michigan's "No Worker Left Behind Initiative," and targeting white-collar UI claimants.

- ARRA funding made it possible for MWAs across the state to respond flexibly to an onslaught of unemployed and underemployed workers as a result of the deep recession. ARRA funding was used by MWAs to pay overtime and hire temporary (limited-term) staff at One-Stop Career Centers, to expand hours of operation, and to lease additional space to respond to heightened demand for services. Without ARRA funding, local workforce areas would have been seriously challenged to respond to the overwhelming demand for workforce services.

- ARRA-ES funding provided $2.2 million (allocated by formula to all MWAs within the state) to pay for costs associated with implementing National Career Readiness Certificates (NCRCs) statewide. With availability of ARRA funds, the state policy was changed to require all program participants using MWAs across the state (including those receiving services under WIA, W-P, and TAA) to complete NCRC testing. This resulted in thousands of WIA, ES, and UI claimants receiving NCRC certifications. Without ARRA funding, it would not have been possible to expand NCRC testing across the state.

(continued)

Table 10.3 (continued)

State	Major accomplishments
Montana	• ARRA funding permitted a major expansion of services without increasing the "size of the business." According to state agency officials, "We doubled the number of people served and helped a whole bunch of people." With ARRA funding, the state was able to identify efficiencies in the delivery of services (cross-training staff, strengthening use of software, developing new tools and coordinating efforts).
	• Recovery Act funding provided an opportunity to redesign and reprioritize workforce services to incorporate a one-on-one client-focused approach for all ES and UI customers.
	• At the local level, ARRA funding made additional training possible; an infusion of ES and RES funds allowed additional staffing during a time when Job Service Centers were experiencing a huge crush of the newly unemployed.
	• With ARRA funding, it was possible to mount a Summer Youth Program involving 800 youth.
Nebraska	• ARRA provided supplemental financial support to hire additional staff to serve those in need of assistance because of the recession; ARRA provided an enhanced ability to provide access to training services for Nebraskans who could benefit.
	• RES ARRA funding supported the expansion of RES as an ongoing feature of service design.
	• The state was able to expand virtual services with ARAA funding. The state was able to restructure the business services model of the workforce system to use technology and limited resources to serve more clients better and increase the capacity of individuals to engage the labor market. ARRA provided funding for technological upgrades, and improved and expanded computer labs in the career centers.
	• The state has been able to restructure the public image of the workforce system as a prime source of information, provider of job-search skills, and employment and training access.
	• With added resources, the state and local workforce areas were able to provide more focused employer outreach, stronger employer contacts, and more employer workshops.
	• ARRA provided resources to mount a successful Summer Youth Program.

Nevada

- Mounting a huge and successful Summer Youth Program on a moment's notice was a major accomplishment.
- With added ARRA resources, the state eliminated the lines and served many more people in the One-Stops.
- The state continued its very successful RES/REA programs.
- The state was able to direct Recovery Act resources into business services, which have the potential to enhance job opportunities.

New York

- ARRA funding provided resources for development and expanded use of technology tools to enable the state and LWIAs to manage workforce and UI programs and better serve customers. For example, the state's Re-Employment Operating System (REOS) helped One-Stop center staff schedule and track UI claimant involvement in reemployment services.
- Through its LMI efforts and improvements in its MIS and customer service tools (financed in part with ARRA funding), the state believes it is well-positioned to use data in real-time for planning services for UI claimants and other One-Stop participants.
- Recovery Act funds provided resources for purchase and implementation of a new software tool (SMART, developed by Burning Glass Technologies Inc.) that automatically scans résumés of job seekers for worker skills and provides instantaneous and ongoing job matches.
- NYSDOL built the Regional Business Service Teams with WIA and Wagner-Peyser Act partners to ensure that job development is conducted in a regional context instead of just for one local area. The state noted that businesses do not care where their workforce comes from; employers want to make sure they are getting workers with the appropriate skills. In the past two years, the governor has focused on regional economies. The Jobs Express site uses regions rather than local areas to help with job searches.

North Carolina

- The state was proud of its successful Summer Youth Program and its use of existing staff with experience in these programs to quickly deploy efforts.
- State officials noted the success of the regional initiatives implemented. ARRA funding was able to support its ex-offender and juvenile offender initiatives and reinforced its commitment to better serving these populations. Staff believed that many of these initiatives would last beyond ARRA in some form.

(continued)

Table 10.3 (continued)

State	Major accomplishments
North Carolina *(cont.)*	• The state agency officials credited Recovery Act funding for initiating the RES program, which has helped to engage UI claimants with the One-Stop system. The state had an RES program in the late 1990s and tapped staff that had previous RES experience to coordinate programs in local offices and train staff. The state workforce agency hired about 450 full-time employees in local offices using ARRA and state funds, many of those to support RES. The state was also able to create a new position—"job coach"—to enhance its assessment and counseling services to UI claimants in 63 local workforce offices.
North Dakota	• The state mounted a successful Summer Youth Program.
	• The state purchased TORQ software and used this software to develop STA (Skills Transferability Analysis) reports for those occupations affected by layoffs. These reports were provided to One-Stop offices to be used at rapid response events and in working with laid-off workers.
	• With ARRA funding, the state began longitudinal studies of workers affected by major layoffs.
	• The state developed an improved database to store and analyze data from its Dislocated Worker Survey and began work on special research studies on births and deaths of businesses in North Dakota, the relationship between oil and gas prices and employment in that industry, veterans employment in North Dakota, tracking of WIA participants, etc.
Ohio	• Perhaps the greatest accomplishment with ARRA funding (according to state officials) was the successful implementation of the Summer Youth Program, which served 18,000 youth. The program was made possible with ARRA funding. The TANF emergency fund allowed some local workforce areas to continue to serve large numbers of youth the following summer (after ARRA funding had been spent the first summer).
	• The state and local areas were able to substantially increase the numbers of adults, dislocated workers, and youth served and enrolled in training as a result of ARRA funding.
	• The state hired 100 intermittent Wagner-Peyser staff to help One-Stops deal with the huge surge in customers in One-Stops and expand RES orientations for UI claimants.

Ohio	• ARRA-provided funding allowed the state to systematically analyze green jobs and plan for future training of workers to fill green jobs.
	• ARRA funding (and particularly Project HIRE) enabled local workforce areas to test effectiveness of OJTs and to establish linkages with employers to sponsor OJTs. This "testing out" of OJTs and establishment of linkages with employers under ARRA has meant that the state and local areas were able to respond quickly and effectively to the new governor's workforce policy that stresses OJTs (and short-term training).
	• The Recovery Act funded 4 training initiatives that have enhanced worker skills and employability: 1) Project HIRE, 2) Recovery Conservation Corps, 3) Urban Youth Works, and 4) Constructing Futures.
Pennsylvania	• State and local representatives identified improved communication and partnership between state and local offices as a primary accomplishment. Interviewees said the increased collaboration "changed to whom anger was directed" at local and state workforce offices.
	• The availability of additional funding through ARRA enabled the state workforce system to evaluate the overarching system and determine where to introduce improvements. The system served a greater volume of customers and improved efficiencies in the service delivery infrastructure.
	• Local workforce officials indicated that the greatest achievement was serving more people through training and support services during the ARRA era. Additionally, they indicated that employer engagement and partnerships have continued to increase and solidify. In one local area, ARRA funds were employed to build a component of an integrated advanced manufacturing employment system and career opportunity partnerships.
	• The new competitive grant process refined for the Recovery Act state training grants allowed the state to issue local and regional grants using the Recovery Act funding more efficiently and fairly. Local representatives were able to use the funds to move the projects already in development to implementation and expansion. This would not have occurred in the absence of ARRA funding, as the local funding needed to focus on core activities that were demanded by an increased number of individuals.

(continued)

334

Table 10.3 (continued)

State	Major accomplishments
Rhode Island	• The state was able to quickly mount a Summer Youth Employment Program (serving 1,200 youth).
	• ARRA helped with creating a career tech program combining work readiness training and work experience in Year 1 of ARRA funding; this was expanded in Year 2 to include occupational exploration and internships for eighth-graders. Now there is a shared vision in the state regarding youth programs and moving funds quickly and strategically in partnerships with technical schools, which would not have been possible without ARRA.
	• JobsNowRI/TANF Emergency Grant served 700–900 in 3 months, which had huge impact on low-skilled workers.
	• ARRA funding enabled workforce system to serve about twice as many customers as would have been possible, expanding quality services (more one-on-one) to substantial numbers of unemployed and underemployed individuals who had not previously interacted with the workforce system. ARRA funding also substantially increased the numbers of individuals entering training.
Texas	• The state served more than 25,000 Summer Youth, about 10 percent of all youth served nationwide.
	• Recovery Act funding allowed Texas to put more money and people into training and has increased training options.
	• ARRA provided additional resources to expand the number of customers served through One-Stops. Texas opened new One-Stop centers in Dallas, Tarrant County, and Alamo (San Antonio) workforce areas with Recovery Act funds.
	• Texas Workforce Commission (TWC) staff noted ARRA-related accomplishments in working with the state's Health and Human Services Commission to draw down TANF Emergency Contingency Funds to provide subsidized employment for economically disadvantaged youth and UI claimants who previously earned less than $15/hour (the Texas Back to Work program).
	• TWC also worked with the state's Libraries and Archives agency on a broadband technology grant from the National Telecommunications Administration. The grant provided funds to train library staff and upgrade library equipment to better serve job seekers using public library resources.

Virginia
- The Summer Youth Program served 4,000 youth.
- The state implemented the Community College "On Ramp" pilot for new training and career pathways in areas of highest unemployment.
- New VEC and UI express offices opened with ARRA funding, significantly increasing access points and a return to one-on-one assessments.
- New Business and Economic Development Specialists (BEDs) were hired with ARRA funding to provide one-on-one services to employers and UI claimants.
- ARRA motivated thinking, strategies, logistics, improved coordination/collaboration, and data-sharing.

Washington
- Washington offered a Summer Youth Program for the first time in 10 years and put 5,600 youth in work experience.
- The Recovery Act funds enabled the state to increase its capacity to meet the greater volume of customers during the recession. The state invested ARRA funding in front-end processes, business services, and staff training—all of which will continue to pay dividends in the post-ARRA period. The Recovery Act also promoted collaboration within the broader workforce system.

Wisconsin
- Many youth were served (4,400) in the WIA Summer Youth Program—this program was mounted quickly and featured some "green" jobs and training. While this was described as a "godsend" for the state and local areas, it was a one-time provision of funds—and post-ARRA, little funding has been available within the state to provide subsidized summer jobs for youth.
- ARRA funding brought training and other services to many adults, dislocated workers, and youth who might otherwise not have received services. Recovery Act funding in the WIA program was particularly concentrated on training—a state requirement that at least 70 percent of Recovery Act funds be expended on training (versus 35 percent for regular DW/Adult WIA funds) helped to ensure that a high proportion of Recovery Act funds were dedicated to training and upgrading worker skills.
- ARRA funding helped to bring the Unemployment Insurance (UI) and workforce system program closer together. ARRA provided much additional funding to expand availability of RES workshops (conducted in local workforce centers) for UI claimants. This also helped to bring many more UI claimants into the local workforce centers for employment and training services.

(continued)

Table 10.3 (continued)

State	Major accomplishments
Wisconsin (*cont.*)	• ARRA funding provided additional funding to enhance IT systems, better linking ES, WIA, and TAA programs. Also, the state made a variety of enhancements to IT systems in response to reporting changes required for the TAA program by USDOL; additionally, the emphasis on "transparency" under ARRA necessitated some IT changes (particularly to reports produced and tracking of expenditures).
	• ARRA funding was critical to beef up staffing at One-Stops to meet demand for a variety of employment, training, and support services as a result of the deep recession. ARRA ES funding resulted in the ability to better meet the needs of job seekers through the call center and the ability to better staff workforce centers.

SOURCE: Table is based on site visit interviews conducted in states.

boost to WIA, Wagner-Peyser, and RES funding that helped states and local areas cope with the tide of newly unemployed and underemployed workers swamping One-Stops and other workforce programs. For example, the Recovery Act provided about twice the previous WIA funding available to local workforce agencies (largely expended during the first year that Recovery Act funding was available) and, in particular, provided a temporary source of new funding for WIA Summer Youth Programs across the country. Funding for the Summer Youth Program was largely exhausted during the first summer that Recovery Act funding was available (in line with USDOL directives), with some states able to continue the Summer Youth Program with TANF emergency funding the year following exhaustion of Recovery Act funding. Some states and local areas indicated a strong desire to continue their Summer Youth Programs once Recovery Act and TANF emergency funding had been exhausted, but generally they had to substantially cut back or eliminate Summer Youth initiatives because of a lack of alternative funding, although in some instances states and local workforce areas were able to identify sources of funding to continue Summer Youth initiatives.

Across states and local workforce areas, there was general consensus that Recovery Act funding had been particularly instrumental in providing much-needed funding to temporarily expand WIA, Wagner-Peyser, and RES staffing levels. In particular, Recovery Act funding was instrumental in expanding staffing levels at One-Stop centers across the country to meet surging demand for employment and training services. Once Recovery Act funding was exhausted, however, in most states and localities, staffing levels reverted to pre–Recovery Act levels, with temporary staff hired with Recovery Act funding either being let go or filling the vacancies of permanent staff leaving workforce agencies because of normal attrition.

Recovery Act funding also provided a temporary source of additional funding to expand training opportunities under WIA. This expansion in the numbers trained—like increases in staffing levels—was also a temporary phenomenon in most states; e.g., as discussed earlier, there was a substantial boost for several quarters in the numbers entering WIA Dislocated Workers and Adult training that can be directly attributed to the availability of Recovery Act funding, but the numbers entering training dissipated after several quarters and largely returned to pre–Recovery Act levels in most states once Recovery Act funding had been exhausted.

Additionally, in some states and local areas, Recovery Act funding helped to expand the types of training provided—for example, providing states and local workforce areas with opportunities to expand and experiment with the following: greater employer involvement in structuring the types of training offered; targeting training on specific high wage/high growth industry sectors within a locality; targeting training and employment services on specific population subgroups (such as UI claimants, long-term unemployed, older workers, and white-collar workers); and expanding use of on-the-job training and other internship-type initiatives linked closely with employers. The Recovery Act also strongly encouraged states to develop and implement innovative training programs related to green occupations and other occupations that were projected to be in high demand or offering career ladders. Many of these training initiatives started with Recovery Act funding have continued in some form after Recovery Act funding was exhausted—though generally on a smaller scale. Several states expressed concern that WIA funding could remain flat or even be cut back in the future—with particular concern for WIA Dislocated Worker funding (which can fluctuate much more year-to-year because there is no "hold-harmless" provision, as there is under the WIA Adult Program). Several states indicated hope that other funding sources might fill the gap left by the loss of Recovery Act funding—for example, added funds from an ETA competitive grant or a National Emergency Grant (NEG), though in comparison to funding made available under the Recovery Act for the WIA program, grants made under such sources are quite small and often targeted on a locality or region of a state.

A substantial number of state and local workforce agencies were also able to open additional (temporary) overflow offices and to purchase new hardware and software with Recovery Act funds to cope with the extremely high levels of customer demand. States and local areas have had to cut back or close temporary offices as Recovery Act funding has been exhausted and funding levels have reverted to pre–Recovery Act levels, though in some instances states have secured additional resources to keep facilities open. The new hardware and software acquired with Recovery Act funding has continued to be deployed in One-Stop resource rooms, helping to expand availability of self-service resources (versus mediated services) to the many unemployed and underemployed customers using resource rooms. Additionally, some states and local workforce areas used Recovery Act funding (particularly Wagner-Peyser and RES funding) to expand use of new assessment, credentialing, and social media tools (such as expanding use of the National Career Readiness Certificate and encouraging customers and staff to use social media and networking tools, such as Facebook, LinkedIn, YouTube, and Twitter). As Recovery Act funding wound down, states and local areas continued to emphasize and expand use of social media and other self-help tools, both with the intent of decreasing reliance on more costly staff-assisted services and because of the growing importance of the various social media and networking tools in mounting an effective job search.

At the time of the second visit to each state, in 12 of the 20 states visited, administrators expected that RES programs and staffing would be cut when the Recovery Act funding expired. Eight of those states indicated that cuts would likely be to pre–Recovery Act levels. Other states hoped to maintain RES programs (though perhaps on a smaller scale than during the Recovery Act) through trained staff, dedicated reemployment centers, state and local workforce agencies were asked to reflect enters, and LMI/IT investments. The investments made by states to improve LMI and IT systems and infrastructure were most often cited as a means of continuing some level of RES post-Recovery Act. For example, Maine planned to maintain its expanded RES program through staff cross-training and its LMI/IT investments. In Nevada, New York, and Pennsylvania, RES programs continue to operate post–Recovery Act, as these states provide state funds for RES. Nevada and New York have funded an RES program through employer taxes for a number of years. Pennsylvania has operated its Profile Reemployment Program (PREP) since 1995 using its regular Wagner-Peyser ES funding.

As noted in the chapter on RES, ETA's Reemployment and Eligibility Assessment (REA) initiative is similar in some respects to RES, and states interested in maintaining RES activities that provide services to UI claimants to help them gain new employment can apply for REA grants to sustain them. The program funded activities in 33 states and the District of Columbia in 2010 during the Recovery Act period.[1] In May 2012, ETA awarded $65.5 million in REA grants to 40 states, the

District of Columbia, and Puerto Rico. The funded states included 16 of the 20 states included in our study. One of our sample states, Pennsylvania, was a new REA grant recipient, and Montana did not apply for funding in this round; the other 15 states in our study had their REA grants extended with additional support; they received grants ranging up to $10.3 million in one state (New York).

CHALLENGES AND ACCOMPLISHMENTS— UI PROVISIONS

At the conclusion of each teleconference interview, UI officials in the 20 interview states were asked to identify the most important agency accomplishments and successes of the 2008–2012 period. They also were asked to identify the most significant remaining challenges associated with current UI program administration. In their summaries, the states also identified administrative problems and bottlenecks caused by specific statutory provisions of the Recovery Act and later legislation that exacerbated their administrative challenges and that should be avoided in future recessions.

Challenges

In administering payments to claimants from 2009 through 2012, nearly all states mentioned two major challenges caused by the Recovery Act and follow-up legislation that extended the EUC and EB programs. The first was problems created by changes in program end dates that were modified by legislation extending both programs to later periods. This was especially problematic during 2010, when the programs lapsed on three different occasions and then were reinitiated with reach-back provisions to allow benefit payments during the break periods. If workers did not maintain active claims during the break periods, their eligibility had to be redetermined, greatly increasing workload and causing delays in payments. The states almost always advised workers to continue claiming during the break period, but many claimants did not follow this suggestion since no payments were currently being received. While the underlying reason for the benefit extensions is understandable (continuing high unemployment), political disagreements caused legislative delays in the Congress, which exacerbated state administrative problems due to time pressures to make extension-related payments. These problems were more daunting in the majority of states because of the advanced age of their benefit payment IT systems.

The second challenge was posed by federal additional compensation (or FAC). This $25 addition to weekly benefits was paid during most of 2009 and 2010. In previous recessions, the legislation that provided federal emergency benefits (like EUC) had increased potential entitlements by extending the maximum period for benefit receipt. Because FAC increased the weekly benefit amount, this posed serious challenges for many state benefit payment systems. Some states had delays caused by bottlenecks in reprogramming the benefit payment algorithms, while most developed "work-around" programs or systems that made FAC calculations separately from the regular and extended weekly benefit payments.

Four other administrative challenges were frequently mentioned by the states:

- Starting in November 2009, the states needed to keep records of payments for the four separate tiers of EUC benefits. This included adding a fourteenth week to the second tier of EUC. Partial weeks of entitlements at the end of individual tiers had to be accurately recorded. Keeping accurate records of these payment categories was difficult, especially if there was an intervening payment of EB because of a break in EUC intake.

- The availability of new quarters of earnings data meant that records for recipients of extended benefits had to be reviewed for possible reversion to regular UI payments.

- The optional weekly benefit amount (WBA) calculations first available to claimants in legislation of July 2010 introduced a new element into WBA determinations. Many states (at least initially) relied on manual processes to identify persons who would benefit from the new calculation (because their WBA would otherwise decrease by at least $100, or by 25 percent under a new base period).

- After the passage of federal legislation extending benefit eligibility, federal guidance to the states interpreting the legislation was sometimes delayed, causing delays in informing agency staff and claimants of the implications for administrative procedures and benefit entitlements. Again, added pressures were experienced because the changes had to be implemented quickly to make timely benefit payments.

In short, the UI system exhibited a strong response to the recession, but benefit payments during 2009–2012 were made through a very complicated multi-tiered UI program. In making benefit payments, the UI administrators in the states faced and overcame a complicated set of challenges. Their administrative challenges would have been reduced if there were just a single program that paid extended benefits, no breaks in intake for extended benefit programs, no changes in the calculation of the WBA for individual recipients, and no add-on payment like the FAC payment. Most state administrators would agree that the presence of these four elements would help facilitate the timely and accurate payment of extended benefits during the next recession.

Accomplishments

The states were nearly unanimous in identifying their greatest administrative accomplishment during this difficult recessionary period. They noted with pride their success in delivering a huge volume of benefit payments to the unemployed, usually in a timely manner. Michigan officials, for example, relayed that the most important result of the incredible staff effort was the economic support provided to the community. Without the support, it was their view that entire Michigan communities would likely have been destabilized, because unemployment in some communities was so high. For nearly all states, the unprecedented growth in claims and payments after mid-2008 was not anticipated, and it occurred against a backdrop of staffing reductions caused by decreases in federal allocations for program administration. Between April–June 2008 and April–June 2009, the simple average of state-level growth rates in initial claims for regular UI benefits across the 51 state programs was 72 percent, for weeks claimed was 130 percent, for weeks compensated was 139 percent, and for benefit payments was 159 percent.

Payments of benefit extensions—both EUC and EB—started from zero prior to the downturn and grew by unprecedented amounts. During both 2010 and 2011, combined payments for EUC and EB actually exceeded payments of regular UI benefits. The states also delivered FAC payments of roughly $20 billion in 2009–2010, after establishing on very short notice procedures to supplement weekly payments for all three tiers of UI benefits by $25. Annual payments of all UI-related benefits during 2009 and 2010 (including FAC) averaged about $140 billion (nearly 1.0 percent of GDP), about 4.5 times the $32 billion total for the prerecession year 2007.

The 20 states in our interview sample participated fully in these increased payment activities. This is clearly illustrated in Table 10.4, which displays simple averages of state-level ratios for benefit-related activities between April–June 2008 and April–June 2009. The simple averages for the two groups of states are remarkably similar for all four benefits activities. The 20 states provide a good representation of state experiences for the UI system as a whole.

Table 10.4 Growth in Regular UI Benefit Payments, April–June 2008 to April–June 2009

No. of states	Initial claims	Weeks claimed	Total benefits
20 interview states	1.743	2.299	2.610
31 other states	1.698	2.300	2.560
51 states	1.716	2.299	2.585

NOTE: All entries are simple averages of state-level growth ratios: April–June 2009 divided by April–June 2008. Puerto Rico and the Virgin Islands not included.
SOURCE: ETA 5159 reports.

To accomplish these increases in payments-related activities, the state benefit payment systems implemented a host of modifications. The net effect of the changes was to greatly enlarge their capacity to service claims and make payments. Several of these changes resulted in a permanent expansion of administrative capacity, whose advantages will be noticeable in future recessions when claims increase.

The expansion of administrative capacity and services to claimants encompassed several dimensions. A detailed description of the changes was given in Chapter 8. To summarize, a listing of important adaptations follows:

- Enlarged staffing and an increase in the physical plant—adding call centers, hiring new staff, reassignment of existing staff to claims activities, rehiring retirees, increasing daily hours of office operations and adding Saturday hours, adding phone lines, using debit cards for benefit payments
- Load-leveling to reduce wait times for claimants—claims staggered by day of week, automated callback, virtual hold
- Improved routing of phone and Internet contacts—better separation of information requests from applications, improved phone IVRs for initial claims and continued claims, improved scripts for Internet claims
- Technology upgrades—these included installation of new tax or benefit systems, system add-ons or applications to streamline operations, movement to modern source languages, improved access to earnings and benefits data

Many of the changes represented permanent additions to the capacity of the agencies to make benefit payments. Many states plan further enhancements to administrative capacity through IT projects currently planned or underway. The supplemental $500 million made available to the states by the Recovery Act is making an important contribution in financing some of these enhancements, but the limited availability of other funding, and other challenges, could affect progress.

Note

1. The ETA announced REA grants to 40 states, Puerto Rico, and the District of Columbia in May 2012 (USDOL 2012d).

Appendix A

Interesting or Innovative Changes/Initiatives Fostered by ARRA Funding

Table A.1 Interesting or Innovative Changes/Initiatives Fostered by ARRA Funding (identified during visits to state or local areas)

State	Statewide or local initiative	Type of ARRA-funded initiative/innovation	Description of initiative/innovation
AZ	Statewide	Enhanced effectiveness with increased demand and broader non-traditional client base	The Arizona Workforce Connection has adapted and become more responsive to a broader client base, including incumbent workers; long-term and skilled/semiprofessional workers displaced by the recession (with little or no prior contact or knowledge of the public workforce system); and the rising tide of unemployed seeking employment assistance. For example, the Phoenix WIB with ARRA funding added a "Computer Literacy Assessment" to Dislocated Worker services and "Linked-In Training" to its job search/job readiness services. ES/RES has reworked résumé writing and job search workshops to meet the needs of long-term employed who have had little (and anticipated less) contact with the career centers.
AZ	Local	Training innovations	WIBs and partners have introduced efforts to foreshorten the duration and reduce the unit cost of training, as part of the effort to serve more clients, maximize results, and conserve resources as funding returned to regular formula levels. • Phoenix and Pima County have funded third-party contractors assigned to the postsecondary training providers to provide short-term specialized training. Phoenix (under SEPSA) linked the local Association of Energy Engineers director with Arizona State University to fast-track its "Certified Energy Manager" and "Sustainable Building Advisory" training. Pima County secured a subcontractor to add a one-week "Hybrid Training" component within the two-year auto tech curriculum at Pima Community College.

- Phoenix fast tracked LPN training to prepare professionals for long-term, home health, and hospice care, and expanded Six-Sigma Green Belt and Black Belt training (Six-Sigma is a methodology that provides individuals/businesses with the tools to improve business processes) as well as other project management and skills certifications to help career-displaced job seekers.

- Pima County, which places emphasis on education as essential to workplace success, helped to push Pima Community College towards contextualized learning curricula in its adult and developmental education offerings, a significant contribution towards preparing customers for more advanced education and training.

AZ Statewide and local Scalable staffing strategies

The state orchestrated the transition of temporary and seasonal workers initially funded by the Recovery Act to maximize retention and continuity of a skilled employment services workforce.

Local hiring and contracting strategies were similarly designed to minimize the impact on staff reductions after the expiration of funding through innovative contracting practices with community-based providers.

- The City of Phoenix contracted WIA Adult and Dislocated Worker programs to Goodwill Phoenix and Friendly House, both long-established community-based, human services and advocacy organizations.

- Pima County contracted *individual staff positions* for WIA programs with an array of local entities (Tucson Urban League, Goodwill Industries of Tucson, Catholic Community Services, SER Jobs for Progress) already providing WIA services, connecting these entities in the workforce development system.

(continued)

348

Table A.1 (continued)

State	Statewide or local initiative	Type of ARRA-funded initiative/innovation	Description of initiative/innovation
AZ	Statewide and local	Scalable staffing strategies	New hires were largely absorbed by the nonprofits, the county, or partnering entities in the local continuum. One Pima County official noted that they avoided significant RIFs by "spreading the jobs around," which also deepened the reach of the workforce system into the community and helped to link with other available resources and programs.
CO	Statewide	• Assessment	**CareerReady Colorado Certificate (CRCC).** Prior to receipt of Recovery Act funding, the state had launched a statewide initiative to emphasize use of what is referred to as the CareerReady Colorado Certificate (CRCC), which is based on the National Career Readiness Certificate (NCRC). Recovery Act funding (state discretion funds) has supported the expanded use of CRCC—over 10,000 workers have received certificates (as of May 2011). Currently, this certificate is WorkKeys-based, but it could also involve other assessment products in the future. The state is also conducting an outreach campaign to make employers more knowledgeable about CRCC and to encourage employers to use the certificate as part of the hiring process. Workforce regions may use ACT's NCRC tests (i.e., three tests), but they have the option to identify another contractor with a similar type of testing regime. There is, however, some concern and uncertainty over whether there will be sufficient funding to support CRCC in PY12 (due to the end of ARRA funding and likely cuts in 2011–2012 and 2012–2013 WIA funding).
CO	Statewide	• Special populations (TANF recipients) • OJTs and work experience	**HIRE Colorado.** In August 2009, the Colorado Department of Human Services (DHS) created a subsidized employment program with $11,200,000 in ARRA supplemental TANF Reserve Funds that would provide a safety net for individuals who had exhausted their UI benefits. The intent of the program was to help stabilize the state's TANF program by providing an alternate source of income support for eligible families. DHS entered into an interagency agreement with the

Colorado Department of Labor and Employment (CDLE) to implement HIRE Colorado, providing subsidized training and employment opportunities for UI claimants, exhaustees, and other individuals eligible for TANF Reserve initiatives. HIRE Colorado expanded upon best practices currently in use by the state's workforce centers, involving paid work experiences, supportive services, and on-the-job training. The program offered work experiences and OJTs lasting up to 6 months and providing up to 100% wage subsidies. Many participants were coenrolled in WIA and other programs to leverage funds for assessments and supportive services. Workforce Center Business Services staff recruited employers seeking to expand, but not yet ready to incur the costs of full-time workers. This yearlong program served 1,724 participants and 1,122 employers, with almost half of the participants hired permanently by the participating employers, at an average wage of $13.27/hour. Feedback from employers regarding the program was highly favorable. This program has ended, as additional TANF funding was not available to continue the program (once Recovery Act funding was exhausted).

Green Careers for Coloradans. This $3.6M, two-year grant which was initiated in January 2010 is a DOL/ETA Competitive ARRA Grant. The award is to Labor's Community Agency. The state workforce agency receives only a very small part of this grant ($25K). Key partners in this effort are the International Brotherhood of Electrical Workers, iCast, the Denver Joint Electrical Apprenticeship, the Community College of Denver, and several other organizations. This project has two goals: 1) to provide opportunities for incumbent, newly trained, and unemployed construction workers to gain industry-endorsed green certifications and 2) to increase access to registered apprenticeship programs to address worker shortages facing the targeted industries because of an aging skilled workforce. The initiative, with an enrollment goal of 1,913 participants, provides short-term training in energy efficiency and renewable energy fields, such as weatherization and retrofitting.

CO   Local (Denver)   • Sectoral initiative — construction
                        • Linkage to apprenticeship
                        • Green jobs

(continued)

Table A.1 (continued)

State	Statewide or local initiative	Type of ARRA-funded initiative/innovation	Description of initiative/innovation
CO	Local (Denver)	• Special populations —ex-offenders; high school dropouts, and minorities • Linkage to apprenticeship • Green jobs	**Pathways Out of Poverty—Denver Green Jobs Initiative.** This $3.6 M. two-year grant, funded by USDOL using ARRA funding, was awarded to the Mi Casa Resource Center (located in Denver). Partners in this effort include Charity House, iCAST, Denver Institute of Urban Studies, American Pathways University, and the Denver Office of Economic Development. The focus of this effort is on Denver's Five Points Neighborhood, with a specific focus on unemployed individuals, high school dropouts, individuals with a criminal record, and minorities. The goal is to serve 500 participants, with 400 receiving supportive services and completing education/training activities and 150 receiving a degree or certificate. There are twin efforts: 1) the initiative will offer a range of training courses from basic life skills to highly technical apprenticeship programs, and 2) the coalition of project partners will create a unique training program and supportive services package for each client. Among the types of short-term training to be offered are weatherization and retrofitting.
CO	Local (Boulder and Arapahoe)	• Special populations— dislocated workers and other unemployed individuals • Green jobs	**Energy Sector Green Jobs Training Grant**. This three-year ARRA-funded grant from USDOL to CDLE provides scholarships for training for green jobs. This project has a long list of partners (including the Boulder and Arapahoe Douglas Workforce Investment Board, the Rural Workforce Consortium, the Governor's Energy Office, and others). The Boulder and Arapahoe WIB received a portion of the state's $6 million SESP grant to fund this initiative. Key project components include: an Entrepreneurial Pilot Project; Statewide Apprenticeship Partnership; Energy Scholarships; Youth Conservation Corps: Public Awareness and Youth Outreach; Asset Map of Training; Energy Sector Research; a career information Web site (greenCareersCO.com); and Smart Grid Training. The target populations for training are unemployed individuals (including dislocated workers affected

State	Level	Focus areas	Description
			by national energy policies); incumbent workers who need skill updates related to energy efficiency in order to keep their jobs; and entry level and incumbent workers who need additional skills for career advancement.
CO	Local (Denver)	• Special populations—youth • Sectoral—construction trades • Green jobs • Linkages to apprenticeship	**Green Capacity Building.** This $100,000, ARRA-funded grant from USDOL to the Mile High Youth Corporation is aimed at 1) developing capacity-building strategies that focus on energy efficiency and renewable energy and 2) developing an energy-efficient assessment industry that will target high-growth occupations such as energy efficiency specialists and weatherization technicians. Under this initiative, multiple credential options are available to YouthBuild participants, such as Building Analyst Professional Certification, Introduction to Energy Efficiency and Green Building Techniques (a college credit course), and Pre-Apprenticeship Certification Training. This initiative is limited to Mile High Youth Build participants.
CO	Local (Douglas/Arapahoe counties)	• RES • Special populations—dislocated workers; UI claimants	**Employment by Design.** This three-day "boot camp," instituted with ARRA funding, offers a series of intensive workshops aimed at helping dislocated workers and long-term unemployed to return to work. The workshops examine the psychology of job hunt and provide instruction on intensive job search approaches. The state's profiling model is used to identify and invite about 20–25 invitees to each boot camp session. Boot camps are held at the Community College of Aurora. As of June 2011, a total of 634 claimants had attended the workshop sessions, with 212 being placed in jobs following the boot camp. The boot camps are expected to continue after the exhaustion of ARRA funding, though the number of boot camps held may have to be cut back.

(continued)

Table A.1 (continued)

State	Statewide or local initiative	Type of ARRA-funded initiative/innovation	Description of initiative/innovation
CO	Statewide	• Green jobs • Linkage to apprenticeship	**State Energy Sector Partnership (SESP).** SESP is a three-year partnership between Colorado businesses, training providers and government to give businesses the workforce they need to thrive and grow and help Colorado workers develop a future with a career in the energy-efficient or renewal energy fields. Training opportunities focus on industry-recognized certifications and degrees. This grant has several components, including: • Statewide Apprenticeship Partnership. The SESP grant has a goal of supporting over 300 registered apprenticeships in programs that include a green curriculum focused on the skills apprentices need to meet the demand of Colorado businesses. Not all energy-efficiency or renewable energy jobs require the skills learned in an apprenticeship. That is why over 500 scholarships will be awarded to Coloradans who want to earn certificates or add to their education to meet the demands of employers in renewable energy and energy-efficiency. • Energy Scholarships. With not all energy-efficiency or renewable energy jobs requiring the skills learned in an apprenticeship, SESP has a goal of awarding over 500 scholarships to Coloradans who want to earn certificates or add to their education to meet the demands of renewable and energy-efficient employers. • Public Awareness and Youth Outreach. Student ambassadors will be trained through a public awareness campaign to help students and adults increase their awareness of the benefits of energy-efficiency and renewable energy. • The Energy Sector Entrepreneurial Pilot Project. Partnering with venture capital sources, business incubators, and Colorado Small Business Development Councils, the SESP is to provide training to support 30 entrepreneurs in starting energy-efficient or renewable energy–related businesses.

- Energy 101. In order to take advantage of the career opportunities with renewable energy and energy-efficiency businesses, Coloradoans must know about the associated jobs and the training needed for them. GreenCarersCO.com was developed as an on-line resource for job seekers to learn about green industries in Colorado. Outreach workshops will also be delivered using this tool.
- Smart Grid Training. With several Colorado communities implementing smart grid technologies, SESP is partnering with these communities to provide the needed training to engineers and other occupations to support this implementation.

| FL | Statewide | Subsidized employment for TANF recipients | The state used $200M of $285M of TANF emergency funds to launch a pilot in September 2009 and then extend statewide one-time purchases of subsidized employment slots through the Florida Back-to-Work program. The subsidy continued for up to 12 months, with a commitment to hire at the end of the subsidy. The program was negotiated locally and had identified over 900 employers and projects, of which the program had placed over 800 at the time of the first site visit. ARRA allowed the state to create a huge statewide focus on subsidized employment, resulting in a very large number of employers ready to engage TANF and other low-income individuals. There is no funding in regular TANF to subsidize employers and manage such a program. |
| FL | Statewide | Summer Youth Program | The state spent $42M for its Summer Youth Program, which it had not had since the JTPA, and which employed 14,000 in 2010 and 1,882 in 2011. |

(continued)

354

Table A.1 (continued)

State	Statewide or local initiative	Type of ARRA-funded initiative/innovation	Description of initiative/innovation
FL	Statewide	Help Wanted OnLine and TORQ	The state used ARRA dollars to purchase Help Wanted OnLine, a tool that assesses real-time job openings. The system was developed by the Conference Board in New York and feeds into the TORQ, below, for career planning. Every registrant has his/her own account, and the tool scans all local ads to identify opportunities. It looks at a claimant's skills, career paths, and transferable occupations within the LMI and helps identify real job openings. It is mainly for UI claimants but available to others as well. Officials are now conducting training to demonstrate how to use the system. Since UI claims are always processed on the Web or by phone—few use phone or mail; most use the web—these improvements are particularly important. The only claims processed in the One-Stops are of those claimants who come to the resource room themselves. The state also used ARRA funds to purchase a new tool, TORQ (Transferable Occupation Relationship Quotient) to enhance real-time labor market information for frontline staff and job seekers. Help Wanted OnLine feeds into TORQ. This is an advance over using UI covered employment data, which has a time delay. Help Wanted OnLine also produces Leading Economic Indicators. It is licensed statewide and provides information on real-time occupations in demand so that training can be linked to specific jobs in demand. TORQ provides analysis of transferable skills, industries in decline, those with very good work histories, and those where jobs are chancy. After ARRA, LWIBs will have to use their own formula funding to renew licenses. They are capturing data on effectiveness.

FL	Statewide	TAA	As in some other states, officials cited the ARRA 2009 amendments as facilitators of both enrolling more individuals in prerequisite training, such as for a nursing degree, individuals with associate's degrees being able to complete a bachelor's degree, which made them more marketable, and prerequisite and remedial training generally improved under the 2009 rules, with a 15–20 percent increase in remedial training.
			Prerequisite training was an entirely new focus. Remedial training was broader—beyond just a GED, one could get a college placement test or other prep courses that were now considered remedial, which opened the door for many. LWIBs created more contracts with community colleges because of the prerequisite training based on acceptance into a skills training program, but this has now returned to restrictive remedial-only training (e.g., ESL, math, or reading, based on TABE test scores) as a pre-requisite to other training.
FL	Statewide	Other LMI improvements	LMI expansions are a major accomplishment under ARRA. Their LMI system is reportedly well respected nationally and by local WIBs. ARRA funds have been used especially to improve the TAA system, veterans programs, and the Employ Florida Marketplace (EFM, their LMI system), which is a combination MIS case management and job matching system and can be used by staff, employers, and customers. They have used ARRA funds to increase bandwidth and storage capacity with new software. The state has a contract with Geo Solutions, which developed the EFM system for basic labor exchange for WIA, W-P, and TAA, and will eventually include the new profiling system. The EFM has a link to permit claimants to use the on-line information more effectively—for example to upload their résumé and make a two-way match to jobs in the job bank. ARRA funds permitted a one-time cost for upgrading.

(continued)

Table A.1 (continued)

State	Statewide or local initiative	Type of ARRA-funded initiative/innovation	Description of initiative/innovation
FL	Statewide	Expansion of Elevate America initiative	The state is participating in a nationwide initiative, Elevate America, sponsored by Microsoft. In Florida the initiative provided training to 1.5 million individuals through the use of 35,000 free vouchers for either a Microsoft suite of tools or a certificate using Microsoft certification testing. Nationwide, the majority using the vouchers are 41–55-year-olds who use the tools but do not apply for certification. They expect the response will be different in Florida because of the state focus on career education and industry certification. Therefore, the Work Readiness Council elected to use $3M of ARRA funds to expand the Elevate America program through competitive awards to local WIBs to either build on or credit local digital access systems, such as partners' donated computers. The initiative also encourages local WIBs to partner with community colleges to develop more wraparound programs.
FL	Statewide	Employ Florida Health Care Initiative	Employ Florida Health Care Initiative was begun in January 2009 with $6M of WIA funds and $3M from ARRA, and involved working with employers to put together proprietary and publicly available assessment tools that might create better matches between customers and training and better training models to reflect current job descriptions. The models also included the development of common forms and more streamlined OJT contracts. The initiative is now operating in 14 WIBs, and four are using the new contract and applications.
FL	Local. Jacksonville	Small van mobile One-Stops	A signature accomplishment of Jacksonville's use of ARRA funds, unique to this region, was the purchase and outfitting of five small vans (the size of a small panel truck), which the office uses as mobile One-Stops to travel to sites (e.g., local military bases, homeless shelters, libraries, community centers, churches) where potential customers had less access to regular One-Stop services. The vans cost

about $25K each to purchase and about $25K to outfit, compared to the $350K large tracker-trailer-size mobile units that One-Stops in other regions have used. The small vans are operated at a fraction of the cost in part because of the dramatic differences in insurance costs and their 20 miles/gallon of fuel consumption compared to 5 miles/gallon for the larger vans. The small vans are outfitted with 25 laptops, which the drivers take into libraries, community centers, synagogues, and churches, set up in 20 minutes, and stay for 2 hours. They then move on to other communities, particularly those harboring harder-to-reach customers, such as the homeless, and military personnel or veterans confined to institutions, or they aggregate the vans at job fairs, creating 125 computer stations at one spot.

From July 1, 2010, to June 30, 2011, they served 177,000 customers. The prior year, from July 12, 2009, to June 30, 2010, they served 145,000 customers.

As the economic crisis peaked and unemployment numbers soared, a number of highly skilled individuals with extensive backgrounds in human resources, marketing, and communications (among other fields) in northern Cook County, Illinois, were unemployed and hard-pressed to find a job. Throughout the downturn, *"Stay connected to the labor force, stay engaged, and keep your skills tuned,"* was the message and mantra of the Northern Cook County WorkNet Center (the One-Stop in northern Cook County).

Walking the walk, the WorkNet Center recruited from among its clients a Volunteer Network whose members used their skills to serve other job seekers by offering support in résumé writing and interviewing techniques and running monthly Employment Empowerment Workshops. Formed in 2009, the Volunteer Network brought over 160 unemployed volunteers into its ranks, who in turn delivered workshops and support to over 4,500 of their unemployed peers. And, in part because they were able to stay active and connected, 70 percent of the volunteers themselves were re-employed within six months.

IL   Local   Volunteer network leverages expertise, leads to jobs[a]

(continued)

Table A.1 (continued)

State	Statewide or local initiative	Type of ARRA-funded initiative/innovation	Description of initiative/innovation
IL	Local	Cohort project marries class-sized training with peer group for support[a]	Largely because the bulk of its clients were dislocated workers, the Workforce Board of Northern Cook County didn't have a huge demand for bridge training, and OJTs were difficult to organize and carry out when employers weren't hiring. Instead, the board launched a highly successful *cohort project* to meet demand for IT managers. Fifty-two clients participated as a cohort in a project that was tied directly to the demand for skilled workers from a set of employers, with training designed to meet this demand and supply an industry-recognized credential. Cohort members had a heightened sense of accountability to the effort because of the job at the end, and because of their classmates. "They were accountable to each other," said one official.
LA	Statewide	Labor market information	ARRA funds were used to build a simulation model to match employer demand with worker skills and identify gaps in order to inform training strategies. This tool will be useful to consumers and policy partners (e.g., Economic Development, LWS, State Workforce Investment Council, Department of Education, and Board of Regents) and will be available on-site. ARRA funds supported the effort to build and launch the simulation and bring partners together. ARRA funds were also used to improve occupational forecasting (through Micro Matrix software). Training providers were not satisfied with two-year forecasting and hired LSU to seek input from 150 "driver firms"—those with the most economic impact and highest employment—in order to develop an annual forecasting model, with more focused and richer information.
ME	Statewide	Economic and workforce development	Just prior to the recession, the Tri-County Workforce Area (LWIA, Area 2, covering Piscataquis, Penobscot, and Hancock counties) merged with the Eastern Maine Development Corporation to maximize the potential for creating long-term growth

for their region and its workforce through the strategic alignment of economic and workforce development.

"We're putting all the requirements together for one coherent strategy for the region. . . . (We seek to) integrate and align workforce and economic development systems on the ground to work better for employers," said one official.

As the Recovery Act period wound down, together the parties requested and received permission from the Maine Department of Labor to allocate unobligated ARRA Dislocated Worker Program resources to conduct an intensive outreach campaign to businesses in the Tri-County Workforce area to assist in the matching of job seekers to available employment opportunities with local companies.

The outreach effort was targeted to industries and sectors that represent existing or emerging high-wage, high-growth employment, particularly those that employ workers with the types of skills/experience WIA customers currently possess and where training is currently offered or can be accomplished on the job. They also reached out to employers who are currently listed in EMDC's Business Services database, including employers who have hired participants from the Career Center programs over the past three years. This group formed the first tier of targets for the outreach effort. Each business was contacted by phone, by letter, or by e-mail to ascertain its current hiring needs/plans and to offer to refer job candidates to that business to fill employment vacancies.

All job leads/openings uncovered as a result of the outreach were directed to the Career Center to coordinate referrals of qualified job seekers to the employer. All businesses were also being encouraged to list job openings with the Maine Job Bank and to coordinate other recruitment and hiring efforts with the Tri-County Career Center system on an ongoing basis.

(continued)

Table A.1 (continued)

State	Statewide or local initiative	Type of ARRA-funded initiative/innovation	Description of initiative/innovation
MI	Statewide	• Assessment (ES/W-P/TAA)	**National Career Readiness Certification (NCRC).** The largest portion of ARRA Wagner-Peyser funding ($2.2 million) was allocated by formula to all Michigan Works! agencies (MWAs) within the state to pay for costs associated with implementing NCRC, including paying testing fees for Wagner-Peyser participants (averaging about $60 per participant) and administration of the NCRC. A small portion of funding ($32K) was also expended on a statewide campaign to market NCRCs to employers (so that NCRCs would be more valued and a credential employers request during the hiring process). The state policy was changed to requiring that all program participants using MWAs across the state (including those receiving services under WIA, W-P, and the TAA) take NCRC testing (though individuals can opt out if they do not wish to take the test). Though there was a shift toward using NCRC testing within the state prior to ARRA, the Recovery Act provided funding necessary for implementing this policy statewide. Although ARRA funding has been spent, the policy to provide NCRC testing continues throughout the state with other funding sources.
MI	Statewide	• Apprenticeship	**Energy Conservation Apprenticeship Readiness (ECAR) Program.** In an effort to prepare Michigan's female, minority and economically disadvantaged workforce for apprenticeship positions, weatherization projects, and other green construction jobs, Michigan launched ECAR in June 2009 with ARRA funds. ECAR was based on an earlier preapprenticeship initiative—the Road Construction Apprenticeship Readiness (RCAR) Program (an initiative providing tuition-paid, fast-track customized training in job readiness skills, applied math, computers, blueprint reading, workplace safety, and an overview of the construction trades). In addition to the 240-hour RCAR Program curriculum, the ECAR program included a 32-hour energy conservation awareness component. This component included curriculum/ training on lead, asbestos, and confined space awareness; mold remediation and safe

working practices; principals of thermal insulation, geothermal and solar energy; and principals of green construction. Similar to RCAR, ECAR offered supportive services, placement assistance, and completion certificates.

Disability program navigators (DPNs). ARRA Wagner-Peyser funding ($750,000) was used to fund DPN positions within the state for an additional year after federal funding for such positions had dried up. ARRA funding for these positions ended in July 2011, though some MWAs have continued to cover the costs of DPNs in local offices/One-Stops using regular W-P funding.

Expanded/intensified RES services for UI claimants. A total of $7.8M of ARRA-RES funding was allocated for Michigan Works! Agencies (MWAs) to provide expanded and intensified RES for UI claimants. Each MWA had to submit a plan and request a specific amount of RES funding. The state capped funding amounts for each MWA at 175 percent of the local area's W-P allocation. RES funding was to be used exclusively to serve UI claimants, including to support delivery of the following types of services: comprehensive assessment; one-on-one case management services; development of an individual service strategy; orientation to training available under Michigan's "No Worker Left Behind Initiative"; targeting white-collar UI claimants (such as holding workshops and job clubs for white-collar workers, as well as providing networking opportunities and social supports); and other activities to better connect UI claimants to workforce services. RES funding could be used to pay for technological improvements (for example, for new software to help with case management and tracking of UI claimants). Funding could be used to rent additional office space needed to handle increased numbers of UI claimants attending RES orientation sessions. Most RES funding was expended on increased staffing levels to provide RES services—especially to pay costs for hiring temporary (limited-term) staff and to pay overtime for existing staff. An objective of the added resources was to help MWA extend hours and secure temporary additional office space and temporary staff to handle increased numbers of UI claimants being served in local workforce areas.

MI   Statewide

- Disability navigators
- Special populations

MI   Statewide

RES

(continued)

362

Table A.1 (continued)

State	Statewide or local initiative	Type of ARRA-funded initiative/innovation	Description of initiative/innovation
MI	Statewide	LMI green jobs	**LMI Consortium Grant.** Under the LMI consortium grant (on which Indiana, Ohio, and Michigan collaborated), there were number of important achievements. First, LMI staff in Michigan and Ohio produced a Green Jobs Report, which assessed the types of green jobs emerging in the consortium states and the skills required of workers to fill these jobs (including transferable skills that auto workers possessed and would use to make the transition to employment within the green jobs sector). Second, the consortium staff developed a Web site (www.drivingworkforcechange.org), which disseminates information about the initiative and is a resource on green jobs for employers, job seekers, and workforce development professionals. Third, the consortium developed an Internet-based tool that provides job seekers with the ability to translate the skills they used in their former occupations to identify potential green jobs/occupations for which the job seeker would likely qualify. This tool is focused, for example, on providing assistance to autoworkers that have lost their manufacturing jobs in recent years and may not be knowledgeable about their transferable skills to emerging green jobs. Fourth, under this grant, the state Michigan workforce agency purchased a one-year subscription to the Conference Board's Help Wanted OnLine. This LMI system provides administrators and staff (including staff in One-Stop Career Centers) with real-time data on job openings, including those in high-demand and emerging occupations. The data from the Help Wanted OnLine system was found to be extremely helpful and, as a result, the state workforce agency decided to continue its subscription with the Conference Board after ARRA funding was exhausted. Fifth, under the consortium grant a green jobs conference ("Driving Workforce Change"), which was focused on the greening of the automotive industry, was held in Dearborn, Michigan, in May 2009. A total of 225 attended this conference, including representatives of MWAs, academia, employers, and economic and workforce development officials.

| MT | Local (Helena and Kalispell) | Community college collaboration | During the recession and Recovery Act, Montana's community colleges proved themselves strong and dedicated partners—joining with the public workforce system to support reskilling the state's residents. The Helena Center for Technology offered a 50 percent reduction in tuition for dislocated workers on a seat-available basis. The Educational Opportunity Center out of Northern Community College (whose focus is on supporting the first in a family to attend an institution of higher education) offered twice weekly workshops on applying for Pell Grants. In Kalispell, where unemployment reached levels twice that of the rest of the state, the Flathead Valley Community College increased both its class offerings and its class sizes. It also began a special welding track in conjunction with Stinger Welding in Libby, Montana, where an expected 250 jobs were to open up. |
| NC | Statewide | Training | **JobsNOW.** The state supported the priority to train as many individuals as possible and as quickly as possible through its JobsNOW initiative, created by the governor. JobsNOW is a statewide effort that coordinates ARRA economic development and training resources on creating new jobs, sustaining current jobs, and finding residents employment opportunities. The JobsNOW initiative also focuses on sector strategies that linked workforce and economic development. DWD and its partners saw that there was business growth or stability in some industry sectors and in certain regions of the state. For example, there is still a need for workers in manufacturing, but workers need skill upgrades to qualify for advanced manufacturing jobs. Health care, biotechnology and pharmaceuticals, and aerospace are other sectors in North Carolina that need skilled workers. While the state is interested in building the green economy and there are positive signs of its growth, it is still an evolving sector in North Carolina, and there are not enough jobs yet to dedicate significant training dollars to the sector. Part of this initiative is a program called "12 to 6," where ARRA funds are being used to develop short-term training opportunities in the state's community colleges. The intent of the program is to refer WIA-eligible individuals to obtain a certification in one of 12 high-demand occupations within six months. Begun in the fall of 2009, this initiative used $13.45 million in WIA ARRA funds and pays for tuition, fees, transportation, books, and other related instructional materials. |

(continued)

364

Table A.1 (continued)

State	Statewide or local initiative	Type of ARRA-funded initiative/innovation	Description of initiative/innovation
NC	Statewide	Special populations—ex-offenders (adult and juvenile)	**North Carolina Department of Corrections—Prisoner Reentry Initiative. The** Prisoner Reentry Initiative is a federally funded program that provides employment assistance to recently released offenders in Mecklenburg, Nash/Edgecombe, and New Hanover counties. ARRA funds were used to expand the program to more populated parts of the state and expand services beyond job placement—services such as housing, transportation, child care, on-the-job training, basic education, and occupational skills training. Employment training opportunities (i.e., OJT) were also developed for ex-offenders where employers were reimbursed up to 50 percent of wages for providing these experiences. Between January 2010 and June 2011, Job developers provided direct employment services to 4,224 recently released offenders and secured employment for 530 of these individuals. They found jobs as cooks, stock clerk order fillers, welders, dishwashers, food service preps, construction workers, housekeepers, upholsterers, laundry operators, sales representatives, landscape specialists, personal care aides, truck drivers, heating, ventilating and air conditioning (HVAC) technicians, packagers, and certified nursing assistants. Twenty-two ex-offenders also participated in employment training opportunities. Job developers also enrolled 157 into training using ITAs. **North Carolina Department of Juvenile Justice and Delinquency Prevention (DJJDP) Demonstration Project.** The DJJDP project is being funded through ARRA WIA dollars to develop OJT opportunities for youth in the department's system. Students are paid minimum wage to participate in internships in the stock/ system, warehouse, custodial, cafeteria, kennel management, horticulture, car wash, retail stocker, teacher's assistant, and clerical assistant fields. Career specialists assess youth using the WorkKeys certification program. As of April 2011, the project had worked with 274 youth, and 120 had internships. The project also worked to bring a

4-H club to youth at the different campuses. Career specialists made presentations to community leaders and youth councils on the project.

| NC | Regional—Charlotte | Special populations—dislocated workers from the financial sector | **Charlotte Area Workforce Recovery Project.** Begun in July 2009, DWD supported the development of the Charlotte Area Workforce Recovery Project, which used $800,000 in ARRA funds to help laid-off workers in the financial services industry find new employment opportunities, and to revitalize existing businesses hit by the economic downturn. Laid-off workers in this industry could take classes and earn certification as a project management professional through an accelerated three-week program. These workers could also take advantage of entrepreneurial training provided by the Small Business and Technology Development Center (SBTDC) through an initiative called FastTrac New Venture. The ProNet Career Center was also created in the Charlotte area; at this center, dislocated workers could take workshops, receive career counseling, and attend forums to help them find new employment. The center also offered a community resource guide, created a regional confidence index, and developed an "app" for iPhone and Android users. The project ended in December 2010. Forty-eight dislocated workers earned a Project Management certificate through the accelerated course, with 28 of these individuals completing the PMP Exam Preparation course and 10 opting to complete the process in order to receive the official PMP certification. Twenty of the 48 participants found new employment. All participants believed they were more marketable to employers and would recommend the training to others. For the FastTrac NewVenture program, 31 training programs were offered from July 2009–July 2010 and 26 had sufficient numbers to run the program. 453 applicants were invited to attend the program, with 390 accepting the invitation. Eighty-five percent (333) of participants completed the program, and nearly 86 percent of those who completed it said that they would continue to pursue business ownership. Business ideas were generated for retail, food, manufacturing, real estate, construction, computer services, cleaning, nonprofit, energy, and agriculture/farming industries, among others. |

(continued)

366

Table A.1 (continued)

State	Statewide or local initiative	Type of ARRA-funded initiative/innovation	Description of initiative/innovation
NC	Regional—Charlotte	Business services—layoff aversion	**BIZ BOOST (Charlotte pilot).** Beginning in June 2009, NCDOC developed the BIZ BOOST, an ARRA WIA-funded layoff aversion effort led by the Small Business and Technology Development Center (SBTDC) at the University of North Carolina. The program, a $340,000 effort, is based on the Steel Valley Authority model, and staff work directly with business to retain jobs. Staff work with vulnerable small- to mid-sized businesses to help them retain the jobs they have and grow their businesses through counseling services and leveraging partnerships. From June 2009–May 2011, BIZ BOOST helped to create 318 jobs and retain 76 jobs at a cost of $862 per job created or retained. In addition, 41 business loans (worth $28 million) and 193 government contracts (worth $33 million) were awarded. Over 6,000 hours in direct counseling were provided to 269 businesses.

NC	Statewide	• Special populations—rural workforce areas	**Rural Community Mobilization Project.** The goals of this project, which used ARRA funds, were to help 1) at least 80 rural leaders gain a better understanding of community mobilization, 2) at least 750 rural dislocated workers or other rural residents facing economic challenges receive direct services, and 3) at least 500 rural North Carolinians obtain jobs through the project or be on a viable career path. Twelve grants were awarded in rural communities across the state, and activities began in January 2010. The project achieved the following goals by the end of the grants on April 30, 2011:
			• 172 rural leaders were trained in community mobilization
			• 1,821 participants received workforce services
			  – 322 found jobs
			  – 6 started a business or expanded a current one

- 576 obtained credentials
- 159 obtained a job and a credential
- 195 received a career readiness credential

NC	Regional—Fayetteville and other areas	Youth	**BRAC Regional Task Force—i3D project.** The task force is working with 11 counties and 70-plus municipalities in the Fort Bragg and Pope Air Force Base region. Workforce development was to be a key part of the strategy for the expansion of Fort Bragg in 2011 as there will be many employment opportunities for local residents. The task force is using ARRA funds to expand its interactive three-dimensional (i3D) initiative, which uses portable learning systems installed at eight community colleges and 11 high schools around the region. By the end of the grant, the task force had trained approximately 150 high school teachers on the learning technology, with new training material developed for students throughout the project.
ND	Statewide	RES-Wagner-Peyser	Development of Resource Guide with Wagner-Peyser funds that could not be spent after September 30, 2010. See entry under RES.
ND	Statewide	Wagner-Peyser-RES	**Dashboards and Special Research Projects** • Effect of the price of oil on hiring in Bakken Oil Reserve area • WIA study • *Business Survivability in North Dakota*—research publication exploring the trends in business survivability in the state of North Dakota
ND	Statewide	RES	**Provided case management services by phone**: The RES clients are sent a letter notifying them that they have been selected to participate in the program. They are given a phone appointment time and the name of their case manager. The case manager helps them prepare their career/job search plan, offers suggestions about job search resources, assists with résumé preparation, and schedules workshops at the local JobService North Dakota office. The case manager is housed with the UI operation and does not meet with clients face to face at any point in the process.

(continued)

Table A.1 (continued)

State	Statewide or local initiative	Type of ARRA-funded initiative/innovation	Description of initiative/innovation
ND	Statewide	RES	**Automated verification of employer contact:** UI staff created an automated work-search review. A letter is generated and sent to every employer listed as a contact by a claimant. Employers are requested to reply if there they have no record of a contact or if the claimant was offered a job and declined.
			Financed a job search workshop through community college system: Included development of the *Effective Job Search Strategies* manual now being used throughout the JSND system.
ND	Statewide	Not stimulus but interesting	State officials mentioned a state-funded workforce development program. North Dakota New Jobs Training, which is designed to provide incentives to businesses and industries that are starting operations, expanding within the state, or relocating to the state. Funds to help businesses offset the cost of training new employees are generated through the capture of state income tax withholdings from the new jobs created. The program targets primary-sector businesses or businesses engaged in interstate commerce that create new employment opportunities in North Dakota. To qualify for the program, new companies or those opening new locations in North Dakota must commit to adding five new jobs. Existing employers can participate if they expand by one or more jobs within the state. There is also a state-sponsored $1.5 million dollar incumbent worker training program.
NE	Statewide	NEworks	NEworks has become the virtual foundation for workforce services in Nebraska and the state's MIS. Its development and introduction required a significant use of ARRA funds to consolidate the functionalities of the Nebraska Workforce Access System (NWAS), the Tracking and Reporting Exchange System (TREX), and the Staff Assisted Services Interface (SASi). Case management, labor exchange activities, employer services, job orders, automated job matching, UI claimant registration.

NE	Statewide	Retooled business model	and the spectrum of workforce programs at the One-Stops, as well as self-directed assessment and other services, are accessed through NEworks. While there may yet be a few development refinements needed, it is central to the approach for Nebraska's drive to provide better services to the increasingly broad swath of job seekers cost-effectively and efficiently. Since enactment of the Recovery Act, Nebraska has increased the role of self-directed and technology-driven services as part of the restructured workforce system business model. The intent is to use technology to serve more clients better and increase the capacity of individuals to engage the labor market. An initial self-directed assessment (Kuder assessments and additional on-line tools) is available at all points of the system through NEworks. The state can track the use of self-assessment tools accessed through the One-Stops and planned to introduce this as a performance measure by July 2012. As part of this effort, Nebraska has invested ARRA resources to improve and expanded computer labs in the career centers
NE	Statewide	syNErgy Partnership SESP/sustainable energy	The syNErgy Partnership is a noteworthy effort in terms of scope and scale. The Nebraska Workforce Investment Board (grant recipient) oversaw the development of an SESP charter by a blue-ribbon panel of business sector representatives. Regional teams composed of members from business, education, and the public sector, including state and local WIBs, career centers, organized labor, industry associations, community colleges and universities, as well as federal and state agencies, have guided the project's development in the three geographic areas. Each area has a specific focus: • Renewable wind energy and technologies in the 12-county western region • Renewable wind and biofuel technologies in the 30-county northeastern region • Energy-efficient building and technologies in the 7-county metro region

(continued)

370

Table A.1 (continued)

State	Statewide or local initiative	Type of ARRA-funded initiative/innovation	Description of initiative/innovation
NE	Statewide	syNErgy Partnership SESP/sustainable energy	The regional teams developed the projects. Service providers conduct outreach, recruitment, and placement; and provide training opportunities, including classroom, on-the-job, customized training, and registered apprenticeship. As part of its role in curriculum development, the University of Nebraska prepared a comprehensive inventory of relevant new and ongoing programs and courses available in the state. Providers include labor organizations (comprising the trades of plumbing, sheet metal, electrical, and construction labor), the Association of General Contractors, the National Association of Realtors, and the six community colleges. The project began enrollment in January 2011, targeting incumbent and unemployed workers, including veterans, ex-offenders, and at-risk youth. The initial enrollment goal was 950 participants: 600 from the ranks of the unemployed and 350 incumbent workers (broadly defined as anyone with a job, not limited to those in a related occupation or industry.) Already the project is escalating its enrollment performance target. The take-up among incumbent workers has far exceeded expectations; 153 enrolled in the first four months. (The target was 85 in six months.) Response has been weak among unemployed persons; only 20 have enrolled during the same four months. The project now forecasts enrolling 800 to 1,000 incumbent workers, who also can be served at significantly lower costs per training and skills upgrades. SyNErgy draws from WIA best practices and is considering coenrollment where appropriate. Unlike WIA, the project uses cohort/class-size training.

NY Statewide | General organization of state workforce system

Workforce development staff training. The Division of Employment and Workforce Solutions (DEWS) planned, implemented, monitored, and oversaw WIA ARRA funding. DWES has a Human Resource Development unit responsible for development and delivery of capacity building. Training for the One-Stop system also supports DWES professional development activities. A counselor academy was implemented to train local One-Stop career counselors, particularly new hires, on the preparation of education and training plans for customers since the state was encouraging LWIAs to use their ARRA funds to support training. NYSDOL uses a variety of mechanisms to communicate policy and reporting requirements, including ARRA requirements, to LWIAs. It conducts meetings with One-Stop operators and WIB Directors every 6–8 weeks and conducts weekly Web or telephone conferences where issues of current interest are explored and participants can call in with questions. The state's efforts to train staff have also helped to ensure that the state could respond effectively to the needs of workforce system customers. The state noted that if they did not devote time to training the frontline staff, they would not know the value of these tools developed or the policies implemented for their customers. The training also helped to build the confidence of staff in working with customers on how to use the available tools properly.

NY Statewide | Approach to ARRA funding

Case management system. State staff identified NASWA as one of their main resources in understanding and planning for the advent of ARRA funding. A new effort by NYSDOL is the development of an integrated case management system across nine other state agencies. This effort is being funded through a 2.75 million grant from the National Association of State Workforce Agencies. The new case management system started from a Medicaid infrastructure grant to integrate systems from the state offices of mental health, developmental disabilities, aging, and vocational rehabilitation. The employment and training programs will be linked to the case management system so case workers in different offices can track employment-related information. The creation of this system will allow New York to be involved in the Ticket-to-Work program.

(continued)

Table A.1 (continued)

State	Statewide or local initiative	Type of ARRA-funded initiative/innovation	Description of initiative/innovation
NY	Statewide	WIA training	**Expenditure monitoring.** NYSDOL instituted IT procedures to track spending on training for the ARRA funds. It has expanded this to its regular formula funds.
NY	Statewide	RES for UI	**UI customer needs and tracking.** The development of on-line/virtual tools for customers has been important to the success of New York's system during the recession. They used technology to figure out how to assist customers and do real-time triage of customer needs. The new efforts to link case management systems will also help with information-sharing across programs. In addition, the development of better job-search technology and assessment tools has helped counselors to better assist their customers with less. Moreover, use of technology tools enabled the state and LWIAs to manage workforce and UI programs and better serve customers. In particular, the Re-Employment Operating System (REOS)—a scheduling and appointments-tracking system for UI customers—helped One-Stop centers handle the large increase in UI claimants and manage staffing and resource needs. The SMART 2010 technology was appropriate for serving customers with Internet access at home and has had positive feedback. Finally, JobZone has been successful for career exploration by adults, especially for those whose skills are no longer viable in the workforce.
OH	Statewide	• Sectoral • Training program • Assessment	**Entry-Level Manufacturing Certification Pilot Project.** WIA Statewide ARRA funds were used to implement an Entry-Level Manufacturing Certification Pilot Project in four WIA areas. Up to $315,000 was set aside for the short-term project. This pilot program is designed to test the effectiveness of the National Career Readiness Certification (NCRS), earned as a result of the ACT WorkKeys tests, coupled with the Manufacturing Skills Standards Council (MSSC) certificate as basic certifications for entry-level manufacturing production workers. Four local areas (2, 7, 12, and 15) volunteered to participate in the pilot, based upon Ohio

Skills Bank competitive applications, which focused on the manufacturing sector. This pilot project includes an instructional program and testing of completers in both WorkKeys and the MSSC. Local WIA Areas recruit a pool of candidates who are unemployed or underemployed, hold a HS diploma, are drug-free, do not have any outstanding warrants, and are interested in manufacturing. Candidates who successfully complete the certifications are placed with a manufacturing employer who has agreed to participate in this pilot initiative. The instructional training is provided through University System of Ohio Partners. Local workforce areas receive a fixed amount of $3,000 per pilot project participant.

Curriculum content is to 1) be employer-driven (designed to meet specific employer needs); 2) be focused on measurable knowledge and skills; 3) lead to a job and a career pathway; 4) result in academic credit, if possible; 5) demonstrate application in the workplace setting; and 6) result in a "stackable" certificate. Instruction is to be in the range of 75–150 hours and to involve both classroom and hands-on experience.

OH   Statewide   LMI   **Ohio Here to Help.** The push toward the use of technology is in part a response to continuing high customer levels within One-Stops across the state. With respect to promoting ES and UI integration, the state agency has used ARRA Wagner-Peyser funds to create the Web site ohioheretohelp.com, which provides UI claimants and job seekers with a holistic overview of services available (e.g., help with housing, food, and other aspects of life as well as getting a job). This site is a compendium of state, county, and local service providers with content from each of these organizations. This Web site is intended to assist customers in removing barriers to employment by connecting them to a wide variety of available services.

(continued)

Table A.1 (continued)

State	Statewide or local initiative	Type of ARRA-funded initiative/innovation	Description of initiative/innovation
OH	Statewide	• Green jobs • Sectoral	**Building the education, career pathways, and labor exchange infrastructure within the new business paradigm of a green economy.** Ohio received a $1.0 million ARRA-funded High Growth and Emerging Sectors grant from the U.S. Department of Labor. The goal of this project is to better position Ohio to compete in the green economy by developing a statewide infrastructure to support green jobs workforce development, education, and training. A competitive advantage in the green economy will require workers with unique and specific green knowledge and skill sets. Employer demand for these unique green skills cannot be met without coordination among Ohio's training and education institutions. Coherent and centralized information about educational and training opportunities and potential employers did not exist prior to this grant for those interested in joining the green workforce. The project is aimed at helping the state workforce agency assess knowledge and skills gaps for green jobs in the state's 12 economic development regions by: evaluating current green job definitions and measures; identifying green employers for project participation; mapping the educational curricula assets; identifying curriculum gaps; developing green jobs curricula; publishing green curricula guidelines; producing an Ohio green jobs training directory; disseminating green career pathways information through One-Stops and WIA-eligible training providers; and developing new green jobs interfaces for the state labor exchange system.
OH	Statewide	• Special targeted populations—youth	**Urban Youth Works.** The Ohio Department of Job and Family Services (ODJFS) awarded $6.7 million of ARRA funding for urban youth programs as part of the Urban Youth Works competitive grant program. The grant addressed the needs of urban youth to successfully participate in education and training programs that will ultimately lead to self-sufficient wages and occupations based on the labor market

demand. Grantees included 15 organizations representing 12 nonprofit organizations, two local workforce investment areas, and one state agency. Organizations represent low-income youth in seven counties: Cuyahoga, Franklin, Hamilton, Lucas, Mahoning, Montgomery, and Stark. An estimated 1,500 youth were served from October 2009 to December 31, 2010.

OH Statewide

- Wagner-Peyser
- Special targeted populations—UI claimants/job seekers

Opening/staffing of overflow centers. ARRA funding was critical in the opening of 10 "overflow" centers throughout Ohio to perform various employment functions or reemployment functions. For the most part the overflow centers were opened in metropolitan areas across the state: Cleveland, Dayton, Akron, Cincinnati, Toledo, and Belmont-Jefferson. The centers were opened in locations found to be accessible to the community—on bus lines, for example. The state wanted to make sure that individuals that needed employment services could access these areas easily. The centers particularly serve UI claimants, providing UCRS and REA workshops, as well as résumé-building workshops. The centers have helped the ES to meet surging demand for services among UI claimants and job seekers at the local level. The focus has been on providing services that will reach and help the long-term unemployed. With ARRA funding, the first overflow center opened in August 2010, and the last site opened in February 2011. These 10 sites are still in operation (as of July 2011). The state has projected a 12–18 month opening for these centers, with all expected to close by August 2012. The state initially used ARRA dollars to fund these centers, but with the exhaustion of ARRA funding, the state is now using regular Wagner-Peyser funds to keep these overflow offices open.

(continued)

Table A.1 (continued)

State	Statewide or local initiative	Type of ARRA-funded initiative/innovation	Description of initiative/innovation
OH	Statewide	• Special targeted populations—youth, minorities, and women • Preapprenticeship • Green jobs • Sectoral	**Constructing Futures.** The governor's 15 percent discretionary ARRA funds have been in part used to fund Constructing Futures, a preapprenticeship program for youth. The goal of the Constructing Futures Initiative is to train Ohioans of historically underrepresented populations in the building trades so that they may excel in a career in union construction, ultimately leading to a family-sustaining wage and occupation. ODJFS used $3.2 million from the ARRA statewide workforce funds to award grants to provide preapprenticeship training. Funded programs are required to help trainees attain careers in construction occupations by preparing them to enroll and succeed in the full registered apprentice program in those occupations. A competitive request for proposals was released statewide to workforce investment board applicants (allowing for two or more workforce boards to apply together). Grant awards ranged from $400,000 to $1,000,000 and were given to four organizations from Cincinnati, Columbus, and Toledo, with programs running from January 2010 to June 30, 2011. Applicants were required to provide a 50% match, which could come from any or all of the partners on the application. This initiative targets low-income, nonworking and dislocated workers with a special emphasis on minority groups, women, veterans, and ex-offenders. Each local workforce investment area recruits eligible participants for awarded programs. Eligible applicants and required partners include: Workforce Investment Boards, registered apprenticeship sponsors, and University System of Ohio institutions. Optional partners in these efforts include: community nonprofits, faith-based organizations, community action agencies, local governments, and One-Stop agencies. Eligible activities for grant funds include outreach to targeted populations, supportive services (including both preapprenticeship and during apprenticeship), basic literacy and GED attainment through the University System of Ohio institutions, training stipends for preapprentices while in classroom work, and eligible tools and equipment.

PA	Statewide	Approach to ARRA funding	**Aligning state and federal goals.** By aligning the goals of Job Ready PA and the ARRA provisions, the state developed a strategy for use of the ARRA funding. The strategy specifically addresses: preserving and creating jobs and promoting economic recovery; assisting those most affected by the recession; promoting targeted industries and priority occupations, and expanding energy development and green jobs to provide long-term economic benefits. Use of data and reports generated by the Center for Workforce Information and Analysis (CWIA) has also informed the ARRA strategy.
PA	Statewide/local	Assessment and counseling	**Experimenting with assessment tools.** Prior to the ARRA, the state began working with the LWIAs to improve assessment activities. Two LWIAs began enhancing their assessment tools and were experimenting with WorkKeys, KeyTrain, and WIN. Another LWIA expanded efforts to assess the workforce needs of the economically disadvantaged. From the success of these local efforts, the state and the LWIAs recently agreed to jointly purchase WorkKeys to implement its use in assessment statewide. All staff, including WIA, RES, W-P, and TAA, is being trained by one of the local WIB staff to conduct the WorkKeys assessment and read and interpret results.
PA	Statewide	Reemployment services for UI recipients	**UI Profiling.** Relationships with workforce system partners improved. Specifically, the RES program known as Profiling Reemployment Program (PREP) and utilizing an increased number of UI entry points assisted claimants and tracked their ongoing participation. The change added follow-up information on clients entering the workforce system as well as 99ers. PREP staff is located at the PA CareerLink offices. UI claimants who are determined to be likely to exhaust their benefits through the state's worker profiling system are called into their local CareerLink. Each claimant meets one-on-one with a Career Specialist and receives an assessment using WorkKeys or another assessment tool. An individual reemployment plan is then developed for each customer. According to the state WIA plan, the ARRA funds have allowed the state "to expand its focus to emphasize service to both profiled and other UI claimants." As mentioned earlier, 50 permanent staff members were hired using UI ARRA funds to provide PREP services in PA CareerLinks. This has allowed the state to serve more UI claimants coming into the centers. *(continued)*

Table A.1 (continued)

State	Statewide or local initiative	Type of ARRA-funded initiative/innovation	Description of initiative/innovation
PA	Statewide	System-wide issues	**LMI and green jobs.** The state also was a recipient of a $1.25 million ARRA State Labor Market Information Improvement Grant in FY2009. The activities under this grant, led by the CWIA, have included listening sessions with the local WIB directors, industry partnership members, and education to define green jobs and industry and to learn what occupations and skills are needed for these jobs. To track how much investment and how many jobs are involved in Pennsylvania's green economy, a survey of 25,000 Pennsylvania employers was fielded. In addition, a job tasks analysis was conducted to examine the knowledge, skills, and abilities (KSAs) needed for the green jobs identified. This also allowed them to identify career pathways into green jobs. A report on the findings is available at: www.portal.state .pa.us (search "green jobs survey"). A second major activity of the LMI grant is to develop a green career tool. The tool will allow job seekers, employers, and educators to research careers in green industry. They can learn what KSAs are necessary to enter into the 800 green occupations in over 1,000 industries in Pennsylvania. In conjunction with the State LMI Improvement Grant, Pennsylvania was also awarded a three-year, $6 million ARRA State Energy Sector Partnership Grant. The activities for this grant are being conducted in partnership with the state WIB, which serves as the fiscal agent. The main purposes are to develop the Pennsylvania Center for Green Careers and to provide green job training throughout Pennsylvania. The state issued a solicitation for competitive grants in April 2010 to develop green job training programs, which includes the training activities, curriculum development, and supportive services. One key is that the grants have to have a regional focus. The target population for the training programs is disadvantaged individuals, including those with LEP, those below poverty, those on welfare, youth, and veterans, among others. The award decisions for two-year projects were scheduled for the summer of 2011.

RI Local (Greater Rhode Island WIB) adopted statewide SYEP

The GRI WIB created a career tech program with work experience jobs consisting of a combination of work readiness training (a minimum of 20 hours over the summer in a classroom environment) and work experience (20 hours per week on average at minimum wage, or with stipends). The career tech program included a module of occupational exploration and internships for eighth-graders, in which participants cycle through four occupations in four weeks and then spend an intensive final two weeks in one of those occupations. Vendor staff accompanies youth to the campus-based training, a unique feature of this SYEP program. A pilot career tech at five schools for middle-school-age youth at risk of dropping out would expose them to a nontraditional school environment, contextual learning, and would help connect them to vocational areas in which they could develop an interest. The career tech program covered 27 different vocational areas of focus (e.g., aquatic natural science/bay environment, cosmetology, forensic science, graphic arts, IT, and office technology).

The career tech high school would ordinarily be closed in the summer, but the state used ARRA set-aside funds for career tech schools in four career centers for an after-school program. Participants attended 4 days per week for 2 hours each day after school. The Dept. of Education runs the programs. Because the program used an ARRA set-aside, which could be used for pilot and demonstration projects but could not be transferred to the LWIBs, they did not have to follow regular WIA rules, including the issuance of RFP and contracting with other state agencies. In order to be fair in the absence of an RFP process, they invited all career centers to participate. Also, normally WIA criteria would have required connections to other state agencies to provide wraparound services. This was the first time officials had operated this sort of a program statewide in conjunction with but not within WIA, using the tech center partnered with 16 youth centers throughout the state. ARRA and the additional funding was the platform for creatively expanding the collaboration with the career centers, and the relationships have continued to grow since. There is now a shared vision with respect to youth programs in the state, and the program is an example of new money creating innovation.

(continued)

Table A.1 (continued)

State	Statewide or local initiative	Type of ARRA-funded initiative/innovation	Description of initiative/innovation
RI	Statewide and local (Providence/Cranston)	TANF Emergency Grant program	RI's Department of Labor and Training administers the TANF employment program, Rhode Island Works, for the state's Department of Human Services, and it administered the TANF Emergency Grant, JobsNowRI, for DHS as well through the local WIBs. Despite having only about 4 months to operate by the time the funds were received and distributed, there was a large response from UI claimants and potential private and nonprofit employers for job slots. Between 700 and 900 employees were placed in 3 months. In Providence/Cranston the program had a huge impact on low-skilled workers, serving over 250 in 2–3 months, with about a 50% retention rate per month by employers after the program ended.
RI	Statewide	Adult and DW training	The state has established new training programs, one of which is contextualized training for very low-skilled individuals, in which remedial and adult education are taught in the context of occupation-specific training (e.g., math taught in the context of shop-related problems). Group training was not allowable before ARRA, only the use of ITAs. The program was begun earlier as a pilot in the TAA program, and it was so successful that it is now being used in WIA programs. The RFP for contextual training was codeveloped by the state and the local WIBs, with a strong collaborative process and a planning process that involved multiple stakeholders (e.g., state agencies, CBOs, labor unions, and adult education providers). Contextualized training was already being thought of in order for very low-skilled people to get basic education and vocational training at the same time. They used WIA ARRA state set-aside funds, which they could use strategically and leverage over time, issued one RFP, and the local WIBs divvied up the contractors. The vendor list, consisting of both community colleges and private providers, has expanded greatly, and the programs are targeted to low-skilled workers and allow some funds to be used for curricula development, so nonprofit literacy providers were among the contractors.

			Now that group training is allowable using WIA formula funds; it has been given high priority—$1.5 million statewide, from state ARRA set-aside funds. The state also expects to increase OJT, because it has applied for an NEG OJT grant in response to April flooding, in which it lost at least 1,400 jobs (another official placed the number of jobs lost at 3,500) and received disaster designation.
TX	Statewide	Back-to-work initiative	Collaboration of labor and HHS ARRA funding drew down $50M to subsidize employment for economically disadvantaged youth and UI claimants who previously earned less than $15/hour. One aspect praised by TWC is that HHS allowed the state to project expenditures forward and to draw down funds for future services. Because funds were distributed by HHS/ACF, eligible individuals were primarily parents. The program was structured to target permanent jobs: the subsidy was kept at a low level (up to 4 months, up to $2,000) so that employers would also invest in the individuals hired.
TX	Local	Dislocated Worker services targeted at executive-level clients	The Capital Area Board pilot tested DW services targeted at individuals who formerly worked at the executive level. The board contracted with a local company using ARRA funds to provide counseling, job coaching, and transition services in a professional setting away from the One-Stop office.
TX	Local	Cost structure for cohort-based training model and outcomes	The Capital Area Board approached the ARRA training funds as grant dollars and used them to pilot-test new ideas. After convening groups of employers to identify hiring needs and opportunities for training investments, the board approached Austin Community College with a proposal for a class-sized training model. The board negotiated a new cost structure for class-sized training on par with the cost of an ITA, with some capacity to increase class size for further efficiency.

Surveys of students and faculty found that the class model was successful, enabling students to build peer supports leading to better retention and completion rates. The structure also provided a feedback loop, allowing them to engage with the community college on curriculum and instruction in a way that is not possible under the traditional ITA structure. |

(continued)

Table A.1 (continued)

State	Statewide or local initiative	Type of ARRA-funded initiative/innovation	Description of initiative/innovation
TX	Statewide	Leveraging investments in the state's Skills Development Fund and college training to target green jobs	Texas set aside ARRA funds to invest in green and renewable energy programs. Through a competitive SGA, TWC funded six projects. The largest award ($1.13M), for a regional collaboration of five WIBS and six IHEs on the I-35 corridor, developed content for layering green job skills into the existing curriculum of HVAC, electrical technologies, and power management systems.
VA	Statewide	Creation of business and economic development specialists (BEDS)	A new personnel category, business and economic development specialist (BEDS), was established for regional and state-level positions. BEDS personnel offer workshops and instruction to businesses and job seekers on the new Web-based LMI/Job Matching system, including offering workshops in libraries in communities without local VEC offices, One-Stop centers, or reemployment offices. The BEDS facilitate access to employers, Chambers of Commerce, local partners, and others with business relations. They help with finding applicants, listing job openings, and other functions to connect employers with potential hires. There are four statewide coordinators and about 12 regional specialists.
VA	Statewide	Increasing access and services integration	ARRA is credited with institutionalizing the integration of workforce services. Past attempts to integrate services failed because of lack of funding. ARRA allowed the state to proceed with the institutionalization of REA, RES, UI, and WIA services integration, which helped expand and expedite services. There had been prior attempts, but after ARRA officials had the staff that could do outreach, perform workshops, and invite customers. Before ARRA, services would have ended with REA and the hope that an ES person would be available to help with job search.

383

The VEC opened 6 "UI Express" offices just to handle UI claims. The eleven RES centers and the new BED positions allowed the VEC to return to one-on-one assessments for UI claimants who, as one official put it, had previously been "pushed into self-service mode." The new positions also led to more operational cooperation across programs (among reemployment services, UI processing, and TAA). ARRA funds also allowed VEC to create folders of OJT materials for ES outreach, which did not exist before.

VA   Statewide   Demonstration projects and project expansions through the community college system

VCCS used ARRA funds to implement demonstration projects and funded and expanded successful ongoing projects, including "Great Expectations" (a foster youth program), "Commonwealth Scholars" (for high school science and math students), "Career Coaches" (a manufacturing careers program), and "Middle College" (for youth 18–24 who lack basic workplace skills and a high school diploma or equivalency).

Middle College expanded from five to nine community colleges by the fall of 2011, solely due to ARRA, and serves 1,000 students a year across all community colleges. These projects have a very high success rate (more than 70% get GEDs, and 35% enroll in postsecondary career certification or a degree program). In order to increase the number of young adults, including high school dropouts, in high-performance manufacturing through mentoring, short-term training and access to other services in the workforce system, "Career Coaches" was continued and expanded under ARRA. "Commonwealth Scholars," a program to improve the number of high school students enrolled in classes identified by national councils as prerequisites for career and postsecondary success (e.g., physics, algebra II), was initially funded with a two-year U.S. Department of Education grant and continued with ARRA funds. These two programs are being discontinued, but administrators are looking to merge the programs to move from boutique programs to broader systemic applications.

(continued)

Table A.1 (continued)

State	Statewide or local initiative	Type of ARRA-funded initiative/innovation	Description of initiative/innovation
WA	Statewide	Training emphasis, especially on cohort/class-sized training	The state legislature incentivized the use of ARRA funds for training by using $7M in state general revenues to match training investments. Local workforce areas earned 75 cents for each dollar invested in contracted class/cohort training and 25 cents for each dollar invested in ITAs. The governor's office supplemented the state incentive pool with $5.2M from the state's 10% WIA set-aside. Incentive funds were targeted at training in green jobs, renewable energy, forestry, and aerospace.
WA	Statewide	Linkages to and collaborations with community colleges	The training emphasis for ARRA funds led to increased linkages between community colleges and local workforce system organizations. Lessons learned included the need to streamline policies and program implementation, opportunities to leverage other funds in support of students, and necessary improvements in referral processes between systems.
WA	Local	Broader training options with greater customization	With ARRA funding, the Seattle-King County WDC was able to broaden its training options to more providers with greater customization. ARRA funds supported shorter-term training geared to labor market credentials, and also supported cohort or class-sized training. In addition, ARRA funds were used for training in the middle (e.g., providing support for prerequisite courses needed to move from one step on a career path to another, such as moving from CNA to LPN). Cohort training offers a number of advantages over the traditional WIA ITA model. With cohort training the WDC works directly with the college to set the details of training design, curriculum, cost-effectiveness, support services integration, and other aspects. The model also enables peer supports and mentoring to increase student success. Finally, the cohort model provides a feedback loop between the WDC and college to support program improvement.

WA	Statewide	New customer flow model	ARRA funding allowed Washington to fully implement a new customer flow model in the One-Stop centers. The new model emphasizes an initial customer assessment to determine service needs. The new model also focuses on three key workforce services: up-skilling (formal training programs as well as on-line training in resource rooms); packaging (building résumés as marketing tools); and job referrals (building on job listings developed by new business services teams).
WA	Statewide	Career-broker model	The Recovery Act experience led Washington to start developing a new "career-broker" model for working with UI exhaustees and the long-term unemployed. The model is a universal case manager who will work to engage the unemployed with the workforce system on a longer-term basis.
WA	Statewide	Green jobs LMI	The ARRA grant is allowing Washington to develop tools and LED analysis focused on green jobs that One-Stop staff can easily access when working with a client.
WA	Local	Longer-term customer engagement	Olympic WDC directed its WIA contractors to use ARRA funds to support customer engagement over the long-term. Half of the long-term unemployed in this area have never been to a One-Stop center or connected with the workforce system. Staff focused on creative outreach and engagement, identifying individuals in compliance-mandated programs (UI, TANF) who were the most motivated in their job-search activities.
WI	Statewide	• Apprenticeships • Sectoral • Green jobs	**Sector Advancement for Green Economy (SAGE).** In February 2010, DWD received a USDOL ARRA discretionary grant of $6 million to implement the SAGE initiative. DWD is both the fiscal agent and provides staffing under the grant. Key objectives of SAGE are to: 1) establish enduring energy sector partnerships; 2) equip workers with green skills required to obtain and retain energy industry jobs (e.g., in energy efficiency, renewables and manufacturing, and utilities/smart grid); and 3) prepare workers for careers in energy through connection to career pathways. SAGE-funded activities and services are focused on 3 main areas: 1) energy efficiency ($2.7M), to support establishment of two

(continued)

Table A.1 (continued)

State	Statewide or local initiative	Type of ARRA-funded initiative/innovation	Description of initiative/innovation
WI	Statewide	• Apprenticeships • Sectoral • Green jobs	new apprenticeship programs to provide training in at least 3 skilled trades; 2) renewables & manufacturing ($2.5M), to establish one new apprenticeship program to providing training in at least 5 skilled trades; and 3) Utilities/Smart Grid ($600K). In the energy-efficiency area, for example, funding is being used to establish and support the following apprenticeship programs: a weatherization installer apprenticeship, an energy auditor apprenticeship, a sheet metal worker apprenticeship, a steamfitter apprenticeship, and a heat and frost apprenticeship. These apprenticeship programs will provide journey worker upgrade and apprenticeship training for an estimated 2,545 workers (510 new workers and 2,035 incumbent workers). Within the renewables and manufacturing area, SAGE grant funds are being used to create a new wastewater treatment plant operator apprenticeship program to train 150 workers (50 new and 100 incumbent workers). With the utilities/Smart Grid area, SAGE funds are being used to retool and expand electric line worker and metering tech apprenticeships and substation electrician apprenticeships, with the goal of training 116 workers. All of the apprenticeship programs provide portable, nationally recognized credentials and link workers to clear career pathways. Grant funds are also being used to establish or refine a local energy sector plan, which identifies economic and workforce needs of regional energy sector industries, increases worker skills for sector careers, establishes enduring sector strategy, and leverages existing or new WIA sector planning funds.
WI	Local (South Central Wisconsin Workforce Development Board)	• Subsidized jobs • Targeted on low-income populations/ TANF participants	**Transitional Jobs Demonstration Project (TJDP).** TJDP, a two-year initiative running through June 30, 2012, was being conducted under an agreement with the Wisconsin Department of Children and Families. The purpose of the initiative is to provide subsidized transitional jobs (TJs) and supportive services to provide immediate income, diagnose work readiness, create positive work history, and

encourage longer-term career preparation to secure and maintain unsubsidized employment. SC Wisconsin WDB TJDP grant is aimed at placing 375 low-income/TANF participants into subsidized jobs in public, private, and nonprofit entities. Employers may bring workers on and provide training and supervision for workers of between 20 and 40 hours per week for up to six months. A participating employer, which can hire between one and three workers per six-month cycle, receives full payment of worker wages and payroll taxes under this initiative, in exchange for providing training and worksite supervision of each worker. Entry-level jobs are targeted and workers receive the minimum hourly wage for each hour worked.

Substantial increase in UI claimants attending RES workshops; change in UI "Profiling Model." ARRA funding was used to greatly expand RES staffing (expanding RES staffing from 5 to 44), to greatly increase the number of RES workshops held each month, and to provide opportunities for claimants to obtain the National Career Readiness Certificate (NCRC). Whereas prior to ARRA about 50 UI claimants attended RES sessions, the numbers attending RES workshops has increased on average to 700–800 per week (statewide) with ARRA funding. An estimated 40,000 UI claimants have attended RES workshops since July 2009. RES workshops are more substantive than before ARRA, increasing in duration from about 45 minutes to 3 hours. Before the session, those scheduled to attend are required to complete a job barrier survey, register on Job Center Wisconsin, and complete an on-line résumé. During the session, each RES participant is pulled out of the class and provided with a one-on-one counseling session to help identify service needs and triage RES participants toward services needed to regain employment (i.e., job search, additional education/training). According to state staff, RES services appear to be making a difference in terms of reducing UI duration (e.g., those attending RES workshops have 12 weeks' shorter duration and obtain higher wages). With the availability of ARRA funds (and expansion in the number of RES workshops), the state altered its approach to selection of participants for RES

WI   Statewide   RES—workshops
                   UI profiling model

(continued)

Table A.1 (continued)

State	Statewide or local initiative	Type of ARRA-funded initiative/innovation	Description of initiative/innovation
WI	Statewide	RES—workshops UI profiling model	workshops. With the much-expanded numbers being selected for RES, claimants at both ends of the profiling ranking are being selected—i.e., when the profiling model is run, those most likely to exhaust their benefits are selected as well as those least likely to exhaust them. So, whereas before, RES orientations were attended exclusively by those most likely to exhaust benefits, now half of those selected to attend are from those UI claimants most likely to exhaust benefits and half are from those least likely to exhaust benefits. Finally, as part of available RES opportunities, claimants can use KeyTrain to improve skills valued by employers and take three WorkKeys tests to qualify for the National Work Readiness Certificate.
WI	Statewide	ES/TAA/RES— call center	**Toll-Free Job Service Call Center Implemented.** ARRA-ES funding was instrumental in instituting and staffing a toll-free call center. This call center serves several purposes and is particularly aimed at dealing with changes in TAA provisions and the much higher service volumes being faced by Workforce Centers as a result of the recession. State officials note that the call center, staffed by 12 ES/TAA workers, fills a niche between in-person services and information available via the department's Web site. The call center also helps to provide information and referral services for job seekers located in outlying areas and has helped in responding to heightened demand for services within the workforce system. Key features or services offered through this toll-free call center include the following: 1) the call-center serves as a general job seeker help line, answering questions and providing job leads to unemployed or underemployed individuals; 2) the call center staff includes a TAA case manager who can handle inquiries about the TAA and changes to TAA provisions; 3) the call center staff responds to customers needing to reschedule missed RES workshops (note: ARRA RES funding was used to vastly expand the number of RES workshops offered, and about one-half

			of those scheduled for these workshops are no-shows—as a result, the call center has rescheduled about 35,000 customers for RES sessions); 4) the call center has the capability to serve as an "employer call center"—employers can call in with questions or to place job orders; and 5) the call center serves as the central point for scheduling customers for the Work Keys testing, a major initiative undertaken by the state and local workforce centers in recent years to provide customers with a transferable credential.
WI	Statewide	Wagner-Peyser	**Use of Social Media.** ARRA funds have provided added resources (mainly in the form of staffing) to push state and local areas to increasingly use "social media," such as Facebook, Twitter, and LinkedIn, as a tool for better connecting with job seekers and making additional services to the customer more readily available. For example, local workforce staff can now make announcements about training and job opportunities available to job seekers instantaneously via Twitter; Facebook is being used to disseminate information on job orders and create a virtual job club environment. Workforce centers have also conducted workshops on how to use Facebook and LinkedIn as an effective job-search tool.
WI	Local (South Central Wisconsin Workforce Development Board)	Wagner-Peyser	**Added Remote Access Points for Customers.** ARRA provided funding to increase the number of access points from which job seekers could obtain information about available workforce services (e.g., employment and training opportunities) and remotely attend activities sponsored by the LWIB. The SCWDA was able to better meet the surge in customer demand and make services more readily available/ convenient for customers by establishing Internet access points at community colleges and other community locations. Customers could go to these additional remote locations to search for jobs and training opportunities, as well as attend (via computer access) group workshops offered by One-Stops serving the local area.

(continued)

Table A.1 (continued)

State	Statewide or local initiative	Type of ARRA-funded initiative/innovation	Description of initiative/innovation
WI	Local (South Central Wisconsin Workforce Development Board)	• Subsidized jobs • Targeted on low-income populations/TANF participants	**On-the-Job Training Program.** The On-the-Job Training Program, a two-year initiative running through December 2011, is aimed at putting dislocated workers back to work earning a wage while receiving training. Participating employers can be reimbursed for the costs associated with training a new, regular full-time employee. The amount of the subsidy for employers can range from as high as 90 percent of hourly wages (for small employers) to a minimum of 50 percent of hourly wages. To be eligible under this initiative, workers have to have been laid off after January 1, 2008, or have been unemployed for 26 consecutive weeks or more.

SOURCE: Table is based on information gathered during visits to states and local service providers.

Appendix B

Data from the Public Workforce System Dataset Used in the Analysis in Chapter 9

The data in Appendix B come from the U.S. Department of Labor's Public Workforce System Dataset and have been updated and analyzed by the Upjohn Institute for use in this volume.

Table B.1 Unemployment Insurance Initial Claims, First Payments, and Worker Profiling and Reemployment Services Data, 2005Q3–2011Q3

Quarter	Initial claims	First payments	Profiled UI applicants	UI applicants in profiling pool	Referred to services	Reported to services
2005Q3	3,896,287	1,840,511	1,533,816	765,454	291,567	213,643
2005Q4	4,646,805	1,868,300	1,571,287	770,607	274,238	197,640
2006Q1	4,179,806	2,267,820	1,862,104	797,663	310,614	229,846
2006Q2	3,660,448	1,507,401	1,348,479	700,827	271,636	201,260
2006Q3	3,652,877	1,677,972	1,503,237	735,763	294,368	209,796
2006Q4	4,607,343	1,795,202	1,626,433	778,532	293,508	215,685
2007Q1	4,470,950	2,366,012	1,947,272	848,502	318,172	231,114
2007Q2	3,731,587	1,560,822	1,398,941	743,796	299,509	219,600
2007Q3	3,675,574	1,687,762	1,493,469	791,625	326,161	235,002
2007Q4	4,891,813	1,936,965	1,746,797	797,567	286,177	225,294
2008Q1	4,911,905	2,621,771	2,134,902	907,105	311,675	238,649
2008Q2	4,468,052	1,900,876	1,666,923	821,297	291,861	233,208
2008Q3	4,984,845	2,196,135	1,921,441	923,519	314,404	230,495
2008Q4	7,590,779	3,228,705	2,793,507	1,293,646	350,051	235,158
2009Q1	8,484,931	4,727,331	3,913,067	1,738,041	420,916	294,191
2009Q2	7,350,657	3,335,600	2,980,088	1,483,595	455,892	351,486
2009Q3	6,426,894	3,000,100	2,651,429	1,310,645	492,981	358,324
2009Q4	7,136,948	2,973,934	2,706,914	1,367,300	535,977	396,319
2010Q1	6,429,042	3,476,037	2,805,074	1,236,123	521,065	470,314
2010Q2	5,542,633	2,348,863	2,139,366	1,050,761	531,917	490,651
2010Q3	5,331,718	2,341,463	2,213,097	1,053,632	550,299	484,665
2010Q4	6,128,674	2,438,963	2,182,738	1,037,029	456,940	413,201
2011Q1	5,606,898	2,949,480	2,424,017	1,112,735	466,541	464,774
2011Q2	5,084,985	2,083,037	1,842,565	932,742	450,419	468,914
2011Q3	4,773,695	2,159,283	1,873,608	960,012	440,259	462,947

SOURCE: Public Workforce System Dataset (PWSD), updated and analyzed by the Upjohn Institute.

Table B.2 Number of Profiled Claimants Referred to and Reporting to Various Reemployment Services, 2005Q3–2011Q3

Quarter	Orientation	Assessment	Counseling	Job placement	Job search workshop	Education and training
2005Q3	153,057	91,264	28,449	93,878	87,360	18,638
2005Q4	145,845	84,338	26,446	86,873	81,811	19,381
2006Q1	168,149	99,326	33,626	106,708	97,270	24,678
2006Q2	149,880	92,859	32,672	97,453	87,682	20,562
2006Q3	152,691	96,398	32,764	102,536	89,184	22,183
2006Q4	156,948	117,575	35,775	98,861	95,428	24,777
2007Q1	169,816	113,522	40,099	109,569	101,782	26,625
2007Q2	163,146	107,415	41,068	104,570	97,805	24,075
2007Q3	162,014	98,329	37,546	123,570	95,989	24,260
2007Q4	149,776	106,400	30,343	100,013	94,878	25,809
2008Q1	158,620	111,661	32,603	104,876	96,106	30,789
2008Q2	154,866	114,378	36,849	101,286	94,681	28,876
2008Q3	170,878	120,810	37,928	107,228	96,298	31,827
2008Q4	182,906	134,010	35,647	90,812	98,060	32,807
2009Q1	233,177	157,300	43,295	106,273	111,174	38,850
2009Q2	271,023	167,154	50,959	139,442	136,108	47,506
2009Q3	272,343	153,476	53,107	141,943	142,098	54,213
2009Q4	299,108	180,104	67,302	150,115	168,366	58,650
2010Q1	316,160	220,768	84,440	166,054	178,947	59,473
2010Q2	341,362	274,008	82,889	180,968	180,237	59,342
2010Q3	334,178	273,048	87,275	186,410	172,778	53,233
2010Q4	288,315	233,262	73,615	159,131	132,235	39,336
2011Q1	292,598	228,445	74,846	201,215	141,289	38,470
2011Q2	282,211	170,427	77,245	215,748	144,350	38,977
2011Q3	259,607	161,433	69,261	231,419	139,262	36,378

SOURCE: PWSD, updated and analyzed by the Upjohn Institute.

Table B.3 Share of Profiled Claimants Referred to and Reporting to Various Reemployment Services, 2005Q3–2011Q3

Quarter	Orientation	Assessment	Counseling	Job placement	Job search workshop	Education and training
2005Q3	0.52	0.31	0.10	0.32	0.30	0.06
2005Q4	0.53	0.31	0.10	0.32	0.30	0.07
2006Q1	0.54	0.32	0.11	0.34	0.31	0.08
2006Q2	0.55	0.34	0.12	0.36	0.32	0.08
2006Q3	0.52	0.33	0.11	0.35	0.30	0.08
2006Q4	0.53	0.40	0.12	0.34	0.33	0.08
2007Q1	0.53	0.36	0.13	0.34	0.32	0.08
2007Q2	0.54	0.36	0.14	0.35	0.33	0.08
2007Q3	0.50	0.30	0.12	0.38	0.29	0.07
2007Q4	0.52	0.37	0.11	0.35	0.33	0.09
2008Q1	0.51	0.36	0.10	0.34	0.31	0.10
2008Q2	0.53	0.39	0.13	0.35	0.32	0.10
2008Q3	0.54	0.38	0.12	0.34	0.31	0.10
2008Q4	0.52	0.38	0.10	0.26	0.28	0.09
2009Q1	0.55	0.37	0.10	0.25	0.26	0.09
2009Q2	0.59	0.37	0.11	0.31	0.30	0.10
2009Q3	0.55	0.31	0.11	0.29	0.29	0.11
2009Q4	0.56	0.34	0.13	0.28	0.31	0.11
2010Q1	0.61	0.42	0.16	0.32	0.34	0.11
2010Q2	0.64	0.52	0.16	0.34	0.34	0.11
2010Q3	0.61	0.50	0.16	0.34	0.31	0.10
2010Q4	0.63	0.51	0.16	0.35	0.29	0.09
2011Q1	0.63	0.49	0.16	0.43	0.30	0.08
2011Q2	0.63	0.38	0.17	0.48	0.32	0.09
2011Q3	0.59	0.37	0.16	0.53	0.32	0.08

SOURCE: PWSD, updated and analyzed by the Upjohn Institute.

Table B.4 Average Duration of UI Benefits and the Rate of Exhaustion of Regular UI Benefits

Quarter	Average duration	Exhaustion rate
2005Q3	15.26	0.36
2005Q4	15.26	0.36
2006Q1	15.38	0.36
2006Q2	15.28	0.35
2006Q3	15.40	0.35
2006Q4	15.20	0.35
2007Q1	15.00	0.35
2007Q2	15.04	0.35
2007Q3	15.17	0.35
2007Q4	15.15	0.35
2008Q1	15.15	0.36
2008Q2	15.23	0.37
2008Q3	15.29	0.39
2008Q4	14.83	0.41
2009Q1	14.84	0.46
2009Q2	16.14	0.51
2009Q3	17.39	0.54
2009Q4	18.76	0.55
2010Q1	20.11	0.56
2010Q2	19.99	0.55
2010Q3	19.36	0.54
2010Q4	18.91	0.53
2011Q1	18.56	0.52
2011Q2	18.00	0.51
2011Q3	17.57	0.50

SOURCE: PWSD, updated and analyzed by the Upjohn Institute.

Table B.5 Wagner-Peyser Program Participants, UI-Eligible Participants, Service Receipt, Exiters, and Entered Employment Rate

Quarter	Total participants	UI-eligible	Receive staff-assisted services	Exiters	Entered employment rate
2005Q3	3,383,963	1,143,249	2,982,878	2,847,597	0.606
2005Q4	3,304,209	1,117,141	2,882,911	2,825,303	0.613
2006Q1	3,362,428	1,228,847	2,637,007	2,859,789	0.626
2006Q2	3,259,593	1,169,492	2,555,038	2,934,357	0.620
2006Q3	3,449,174	1,196,089	2,623,389	3,012,236	0.626
2006Q4	2,962,450	1,080,670	2,256,619	2,534,014	0.618
2007Q1	3,045,005	1,059,991	2,282,869	2,561,486	0.615
2007Q2	3,124,169	1,107,798	2,332,372	2,633,507	0.604
2007Q3	3,147,341	1,132,079	2,294,392	2,565,119	0.601
2007Q4	3,196,555	1,163,925	2,285,545	2,639,560	0.617
2008Q1	3,353,222	1,234,180	2,385,520	2,690,664	0.623
2008Q2	3,471,006	1,258,230	2,434,399	2,822,989	0.635
2008Q3	3,573,811	1,297,386	2,477,680	2,842,321	0.629
2008Q4	3,762,491	1,447,585	2,636,634	2,914,266	0.622
2009Q1	4,048,405	1,641,744	2,803,110	3,072,280	0.612
2009Q2	4,273,683	1,816,112	2,954,561	3,197,900	0.590
2009Q3	4,509,072	1,999,235	3,043,114	3,365,872	0.552
2009Q4	4,706,310	2,174,296	3,120,994	3,517,226	0.514
2010Q1	4,877,374	2,335,787	3,130,664	3,625,467	0.488
2010Q2	4,942,837	2,350,989	3,094,178	3,737,587	0.469
2010Q3	4,957,405	2,291,602	3,094,190	3,809,935	0.459
2010Q4	4,976,778	2,303,554	3,058,983	3,849,023	0.463
2011Q1	4,862,646	2,199,509	3,003,712	3,726,157	0.470
2011Q2	4,931,191	2,242,989	2,961,590	3,797,746	0.480
2011Q3	4,817,840	2,189,468	2,811,021	3,748,478	0.488

SOURCE: PWSD, updated and analyzed by the Upjohn Institute.

Table B.6 Participants, Entrants, Exiters, and Average Days in the WIA Adult Program

Quarter	Participants, beginning of quarter	New entrants	Exiters	Days in the program
2005Q3	173,336	61,951	57,507	295
2005Q4	177,780	51,637	58,052	320
2006Q1	171,365	66,756	57,152	267
2006Q2	180,969	66,662	70,318	282
2006Q3	177,313	150,644	115,914	147
2006Q4	212,043	146,076	142,815	119
2007Q1	215,304	197,715	176,921	105
2007Q2	236,098	182,952	181,323	127
2007Q3	237,727	221,595	185,360	104
2007Q4	273,962	202,325	199,502	116
2008Q1	276,785	260,728	227,912	98
2008Q2	309,601	214,151	218,548	126
2008Q3	305,204	280,290	241,405	107
2008Q4	344,089	281,237	243,091	106
2009Q1	382,235	336,485	253,578	103
2009Q2	465,142	327,649	288,655	123
2009Q3	504,136	354,294	305,946	111
2009Q4	552,484	288,989	281,575	131
2010Q1	559,898	304,589	292,519	134
2010Q2	571,968	280,714	306,581	154
2010Q3	546,101	381,480	331,301	133
2010Q4	596,280	301,316	300,472	143
2011Q1	597,124	326,123	298,271	145
2011Q2	624,976	279,089	313,863	181
2011Q3	590,202	256,361		

SOURCE: PWSD, updated and analyzed by the Upjohn Institute.

Table B.7 Percentage of WIA Adult Entrants Receiving Various Services

Quarter	Staff-assisted core service	Intensive service	Training service	Supportive service
2005Q3	100.0	70.6	43.5	21.3
2005Q4	100.0	69.6	40.4	21.4
2006Q1	100.0	68.3	40.8	20.6
2006Q2	100.0	63.3	41.1	19.6
2006Q3	100.0	35.1	20.1	10.6
2006Q4	100.0	31.3	16.2	10.1
2007Q1	100.0	27.2	14.0	9.2
2007Q2	100.0	28.7	15.6	9.8
2007Q3	100.0	27.9	15.3	9.9
2007Q4	100.0	27.2	13.0	8.1
2008Q1	100.0	23.8	11.3	6.9
2008Q2	100.0	29.3	13.9	7.8
2008Q3	100.0	37.1	13.1	8.2
2008Q4	100.0	36.7	10.9	7.1
2009Q1	100.0	40.6	12.2	7.8
2009Q2	100.0	43.3	15.9	9.0
2009Q3	100.0	44.1	17.2	9.2
2009Q4	100.0	42.6	14.9	7.8
2010Q1	100.0	42.7	14.2	8.0
2010Q2	100.0	42.4	13.7	7.7
2010Q3	100.0	30.6	9.5	5.3
2010Q4	100.0	32.8	8.5	5.3
2011Q1	100.0	33.0	8.9	4.8
2011Q2	100.0	30.1	7.4	4.2
2011Q3	100.0	25.3	4.7	3.1

SOURCE: PWSD, updated and analyzed by the Upjohn Institute.

Table B.8 Entered Employment Rate and its Components of WIA Adult Program Exiters

Quarter	Exiters	In performance measure denominator	Employed	Entered employment rate
2005Q3	57,507	45,160	34,572	76.6
2005Q4	58,052	43,301	32,758	75.7
2006Q1	57,152	44,522	32,753	73.6
2006Q2	70,318	48,159	35,815	74.4
2006Q3	115,914	93,539	64,824	69.3
2006Q4	142,815	118,787	75,798	63.8
2007Q1	176,921	151,815	110,949	73.1
2007Q2	181,323	146,306	101,761	69.6
2007Q3	185,360	154,944	112,977	72.9
2007Q4	199,502	162,846	108,617	66.7
2008Q1	227,912	191,424	140,223	73.3
2008Q2	218,548	174,936	119,596	68.4
2008Q3	241,405	194,212	124,808	64.3
2008Q4	243,091	201,365	107,436	53.4
2009Q1	253,578	214,193	115,991	54.2
2009Q2	288,655	241,039	131,579	54.6
2009Q3	305,946	258,528	142,768	55.2
2009Q4	281,575	238,360	119,834	50.3
2010Q1	292,519	246,492	139,969	56.8
2010Q2	306,581	250,805	143,072	57.0
2010Q3	331,301	275,991	159,412	57.8
2010Q4	300,472	252,310	129,316	51.3
2011Q1	298,271			
2011Q2	313,863			

SOURCE: PWSD, updated and analyzed by the Upjohn Institute.

Table B.9 Participants, Entrants, Exiters, and Average Days in the WIA Dislocated Worker Program

Quarter	Participants, beginning of quarter	New entrants	Exiters	Days in the program
2005Q3	153,884	60,677	47,972	359
2005Q4	166,589	59,727	54,148	292
2006Q1	172,168	62,762	66,386	256
2006Q2	168,544	48,024	61,325	306
2006Q3	155,243	70,710	70,432	238
2006Q4	155,521	60,392	65,063	214
2007Q1	150,850	63,315	61,905	220
2007Q2	152,260	56,044	69,752	257
2007Q3	138,552	58,445	58,347	236
2007Q4	138,650	59,253	55,249	213
2008Q1	142,654	70,519	62,168	191
2008Q2	151,005	64,231	63,258	217
2008Q3	151,978	87,859	65,645	190
2008Q4	174,192	111,738	76,515	155
2009Q1	209,415	167,674	91,909	127
2009Q2	285,180	175,285	124,164	140
2009Q3	336,301	177,973	130,501	140
2009Q4	383,773	158,920	132,455	157
2010Q1	410,238	194,262	152,054	157
2010Q2	452,446	166,341	166,957	189
2010Q3	451,830	226,167	182,357	178
2010Q4	495,640	184,218	176,269	182
2011Q1	503,589	199,628	177,689	195
2011Q2	525,528	162,648	183,531	251
2011Q3	504,645	148,226		

SOURCE: PWSD, updated and analyzed by the Upjohn Institute.

Table B.10 Percentage of WIA Dislocated Worker Entrants Receiving Various Services

Quarter	Staff-assisted core service	Intensive service	Training service	Supportive service
2005Q3	100.0	72.0	27.8	22.2
2005Q4	100.0	69.7	25.1	24.6
2006Q1	100.0	63.5	33.0	19.8
2006Q2	100.0	62.8	32.6	20.7
2006Q3	100.0	48.5	26.2	14.2
2006Q4	100.0	50.4	26.9	15.9
2007Q1	100.0	52.4	28.5	15.8
2007Q2	100.0	51.1	27.0	15.8
2007Q3	100.0	54.4	29.2	16.9
2007Q4	100.0	48.5	23.0	13.5
2008Q1	100.0	48.8	22.4	12.7
2008Q2	100.0	50.8	23.4	13.0
2008Q3	100.0	52.4	24.2	14.2
2008Q4	100.0	52.7	21.4	12.0
2009Q1	100.0	58.2	24.2	13.5
2009Q2	100.0	59.2	27.6	13.8
2009Q3	100.0	63.8	31.7	14.4
2009Q4	100.0	57.7	24.4	11.5
2010Q1	100.0	52.6	20.2	9.3
2010Q2	100.0	49.7	17.0	8.6
2010Q3	100.0	34.9	12.0	5.0
2010Q4	100.0	36.6	10.5	4.4
2011Q1	100.0	37.9	10.2	4.3
2011Q2	100.0	36.3	9.1	3.6
2011Q3	100.0	31.0	6.2	2.3

SOURCE: PWSD, updated and analyzed by the Upjohn Institute.

Table B.11 **Entered Employment Rate and Its Components of WIA Dislocated Worker Program Exiters**

Quarter	Exiters	In performance measure denominator	Employed	Entered employment rate
2005Q3	47,972	44,339	34,919	78.8
2005Q4	54,148	49,631	36,326	73.2
2006Q1	66,386	60,596	43,110	71.1
2006Q2	61,325	55,830	42,344	75.8
2006Q3	70,432	64,262	47,432	73.8
2006Q4	65,063	59,767	42,595	71.3
2007Q1	61,905	57,812	42,455	73.4
2007Q2	69,752	64,385	46,794	72.7
2007Q3	58,347	54,834	41,030	74.8
2007Q4	55,249	51,490	36,417	70.7
2008Q1	62,168	58,751	40,887	69.6
2008Q2	63,258	60,050	40,355	67.2
2008Q3	65,645	62,224	39,442	63.4
2008Q4	76,515	72,867	37,968	52.1
2009Q1	91,909	88,063	45,093	51.2
2009Q2	124,164	119,294	59,333	49.7
2009Q3	130,501	125,388	66,564	53.1
2009Q4	132,455	126,499	62,930	49.7
2010Q1	152,054	143,742	83,088	57.8
2010Q2	166,957	158,493	95,381	60.2
2010Q3	182,357	172,007	106,666	62.0
2010Q4	176,269	164,527	91,735	55.8
2011Q1	177,689			
2011Q2	183,531			

SOURCE: PWSD, updated and analyzed by the Upjohn Institute.

Table B.12 Wagner-Peyser Employment Service Program Total and per Participant Expenditure, with and without ARRA Funds

Quarter	Total participants	Expenditure without ARRA funds	Expenditure with ARRA funds	ARRA funds expenditure	Expenditure per participant without ARRA funds	Expenditure per participant with ARRA funds
2005Q3	2,975,715	181,325,533	181,325,533		61	61
2005Q4	2,878,066	185,296,807	185,296,807		64	64
2006Q1	2,933,479	154,891,119	154,891,119		53	53
2006Q2	2,819,271	124,929,126	124,929,126		44	44
2006Q3	3,004,199	173,545,576	173,545,576		58	58
2006Q4	2,962,444	171,978,452	171,978,452		58	58
2007Q1	3,044,998	165,313,287	165,313,287		54	54
2007Q2	3,124,165	138,054,130	138,054,130		44	44
2007Q3	3,147,335	178,196,538	178,196,538		57	57
2007Q4	3,196,550	180,894,077	180,894,077		57	57
2008Q1	3,353,218	143,746,568	143,746,568		43	43
2008Q2	3,471,001	125,503,383	125,503,383		36	36
2008Q3	3,573,804	165,125,097	165,125,097		46	46
2008Q4	3,762,486	143,907,546	143,907,546		38	38
2009Q1	4,048,400	139,097,945	139,097,945		34	34
2009Q2	4,273,676	129,235,427	165,148,946	35,913,519	30	39
2009Q3	4,509,067	141,124,174	185,668,805	44,544,631	31	41

2009Q4	4,706,302	157,199,612	207,995,024	50,795,412	33	44
2010Q1	4,877,363	128,853,464	200,676,963	71,823,499	26	41
2010Q2	4,942,826	137,842,406	218,486,773	80,644,367	28	44
2010Q3	4,957,401	132,473,832	156,008,416	23,534,584	27	31
2010Q4	4,976,774	173,395,463	181,501,786	8,106,323	35	36
2011Q1	4,862,637	175,007,229	191,012,683	16,005,454	36	39
2011Q2	4,931,185	147,711,506	149,720,314	2,008,808	30	30
2011Q3	4,817,832	178,972,659	178,972,659		37	37

NOTE: PA and TX are missing for W-P ES participation data, so these two states are not included in calculating the average expenditure.
SOURCE: PWSD, updated and analyzed by the Upjohn Institute.

Table B.13 WIA Adult Program Total and per Participant Expenditure, with and without ARRA Funds

Quarter	Total participants	Expenditure without ARRA funds	Expenditure with ARRA funds	ARRA funds expenditure	Expenditure per participant without ARRA funds	Expenditure per participant with ARRA funds
2005Q3	234,967	166,570,650	166,570,650		709	709
2005Q4	229,296	216,114,095	216,114,095		943	943
2006Q1	237,999	219,009,230	219,009,230		920	920
2006Q2	247,522	242,400,570	242,400,570		979	979
2006Q3	327,840	178,706,602	178,706,602		545	545
2006Q4	357,952	226,193,824	226,193,824		632	632
2007Q1	412,720	218,910,848	218,910,848		530	530
2007Q2	418,749	246,716,242	246,716,242		589	589
2007Q3	459,127	197,983,449	197,983,449		431	431
2007Q4	476,139	241,268,776	241,268,776		507	507
2008Q1	537,330	198,057,614	198,057,614		369	369
2008Q2	523,527	206,848,696	206,848,696		395	395
2008Q3	585,238	179,177,200	179,177,200		306	306
2008Q4	625,060	219,123,783	219,123,783		351	351
2009Q1	718,451	268,027,959	268,027,959		373	373
2009Q2	792,499	268,027,959	299,273,968	31,246,009	338	378
2009Q3	858,029	186,124,452	272,247,776	86,123,324	217	317
2009Q4	841,044	237,549,956	336,982,979	99,433,023	282	401

2010Q1	864,077	219,429,343	309,750,820	90,321,477	254	358
2010Q2	852,256	222,047,016	314,022,311	91,975,295	261	368
2010Q3	927,170	199,805,998	247,414,129	47,608,131	216	267
2010Q4	897,253	224,396,801	254,856,765	30,459,964	250	284
2011Q1	922,962	210,767,314	262,302,999	51,535,685	228	284
2011Q2	903,813	203,128,949	227,707,008	24,578,059	225	252

SOURCE: PWSD, updated and analyzed by the Upjohn Institute.

408

Table B.14 WIA Dislocated Worker Program Total and per Participant Expenditure, with and without ARRA Funds

Quarter	Total participants	Expenditure without ARRA funds	Expenditure with ARRA funds	ARRA funds expenditure	Expenditure per participant without ARRA funds	Expenditure per participant with ARRA funds
2005Q3	214,547	210,178,545	210,178,545		980	980
2005Q4	226,304	246,486,957	246,486,957		1089	1089
2006Q1	234,922	268,076,426	268,076,426		1141	1141
2006Q2	216,563	374,683,569	374,683,569		1730	1730
2006Q3	225,938	260,419,091	260,419,091		1153	1153
2006Q4	215,840	277,905,263	277,905,263		1288	1288
2007Q1	214,022	284,547,317	284,547,317		1330	1330
2007Q2	208,163	355,051,919	355,051,919		1706	1706
2007Q3	196,871	230,162,401	230,162,401		1169	1169
2007Q4	197,822	291,161,471	291,161,471		1472	1472
2008Q1	213,119	312,736,624	312,736,624		1467	1467
2008Q2	215,177	327,767,971	327,767,971		1523	1523
2008Q3	239,762	244,949,782	244,949,782		1022	1022
2008Q4	285,840	276,955,672	276,955,672		969	969
2009Q1	377,024	245,628,145	245,628,145		651	651
2009Q2	460,350	245,628,145	290,214,351	44,586,206	534	630
2009Q3	514,083	217,627,449	346,935,533	129,308,084	423	675
2009Q4	542,513	257,380,025	409,624,644	152,244,619	474	755

2010Q1	604,322	245,031,709	418,699,419	173,667,710	405	693
2010Q2	618,605	310,267,934	508,238,204	197,970,270	502	822
2010Q3	677,821	220,355,970	337,637,273	117,281,303	325	498
2010Q4	679,707	279,534,354	402,174,520	122,640,166	411	592
2011Q1	703,051	261,319,512	377,359,475	116,039,963	372	537
2011Q2	688,033	332,619,201	452,956,934	120,337,733	483	658

SOURCE: PWSD, updated and analyzed by the Upjohn Institute.

Authors

Burt S. Barnow is the Amsterdam Professor of Public Service and of Economics at George Washington University in Washington, D.C.

Yvette Chocolaad is director of employment and training at the National Association of State Workforce Agencies in Washington, D.C.

Randall W. Eberts is president of the W.E. Upjohn Institute for Employment Research in Kalamazoo, Michigan.

Richard A. Hobbie is executive director of the National Association of State Workforce Agencies in Washington, D.C.

Joyce Kaiser is a senior research analyst for Capital Research Corporation in Washington, D.C.

Tara C. Smith is a research associate at the Ray Marshall Center for the Study of Human Resources at the University of Texas at Austin.

John Trutko is president of Capital Research Corporation in Washington, D.C.

Wayne Vroman is a Senior Fellow at the Center on Wages, Human Services, and Population at the Urban Institute in Washington, D.C.

Stephen A. Wandner is a Visiting Fellow at the Urban Institute in Washington, D.C.

Index

The italic letters *b*, *f*, *n*, and *t* following a page number indicate that the subject information of the entry heading is within a box, figure, note, or table, respectively, on that page. Double letters, e.g., *nn*, indicate more than one such feature.

About the Institute

The W.E. Upjohn Institute for Employment Research is a nonprofit research organization devoted to finding and promoting solutions to employment-related problems at the national, state, and local levels. It is an activity of the W.E. Upjohn Unemployment Trustee Corporation, which was established in 1932 to administer a fund set aside by Dr. W.E. Upjohn, founder of The Upjohn Company, to seek ways to counteract the loss of employment income during economic downturns.

The Institute is funded largely by income from the W.E. Upjohn Unemployment Trust, supplemented by outside grants, contracts, and sales of publications. Activities of the Institute comprise the following elements: 1) a research program conducted by a resident staff of professional social scientists; 2) a competitive grant program, which expands and complements the internal research program by providing financial support to researchers outside the Institute; 3) a publications program, which provides the major vehicle for disseminating the research of staff and grantees, as well as other selected works in the field; and 4) an Employment Management Services division, which manages most of the publicly funded employment and training programs in the local area.

The broad objectives of the Institute's research, grant, and publication programs are to 1) promote scholarship and experimentation on issues of public and private employment and unemployment policy, and 2) make knowledge and scholarship relevant and useful to policymakers in their pursuit of solutions to employment and unemployment problems.

Current areas of concentration for these programs include causes, consequences, and measures to alleviate unemployment; social insurance and income maintenance programs; compensation; workforce quality; work arrangements; family labor issues; labor-management relations; and regional economic development and local labor markets.

CPSIA information can be obtained at www.ICGtesting.com
Printed in the USA
BVOW03s1712131014

370610BV00007B/12/P

9 780880 994712